Jerome Bruce Crabtree

The passing of Spain and the ascendency of America

Jerome Bruce Crabtree

The passing of Spain and the ascendency of America

ISBN/EAN: 9783337228972

Printed in Europe, USA, Canada, Australia, Japan

Cover: Foto ©ninafisch / pixelio.de

More available books at **www.hansebooks.com**

THE

PASSING OF SPAIN

AND THE

ASCENDENCY OF AMERICA.

BY

J. B. CRABTREE.

"The old order changeth,
Yielding place to new."

PUBLISHED ONLY BY
THE KING-RICHARDSON PUBLISHING CO.,
SPRINGFIELD, MASS.

RICHMOND. DES MOINES. INDIANAPOLIS.
TOLEDO. SAN JOSE. DALLAS.

1898.

WEED-PARSONS PRINTING CO.,
ELECTROTYPERS, PRINTERS AND BINDERS,
Albany, N. Y.

PREFATORY NOTE.

The aim of this book is to give in a condensed but readable form the information necessary to an intelligent understanding of the present question as a whole. That the statements might be as nearly accurate as possible, constant reference has been made to the highest available authorities, often quoting verbatim and naming the author in each instance.

There is appended a condensed list of these authorities, which will be of value to the student who wishes to pursue the subject more fully, as well as of interest to the general reader.

We gratefully acknowledge the courtesy of the publishers of the "Scientific American," of Henry Holt & Co., and of others, who have generously allowed us to make use of matter covered by their copyrights.

One cannot follow the history of Spain's career without coming to believe that true freedom must ever go hand in hand with religious and intellectual liberty. It is as true now as of old that "righteousness exalteth a nation, but sin is a reproach to any people."

J. B. C.

AUTHORITIES CONSULTED.

American Law Review. Boston.
Army and Navy Journal. New York.
Baird, Henry M. The Huguenots and Henry of Navarre. New York.
Battleships, Cruisers and Torpedo Boats of the Spanish Navy. Publication of the Adjutant-General's Office. Washington.
Bernaldiaz del Castillo.
Bowen. International Law.
Brassey, Lord T. A. (ed.) Naval Annual, '92, '93, '94, '95, '96, '97, '98. London.
Bruff. Ordnance and Gunnery. New York.
Cassier's Magazine. New York.
Consular Reports. Washington.
Cortez, Hernando. Despatches to the Emperor Charles V. New York.
Creasey, Sir Edward, Fifteen Decisive Battles of the World London.
Davis, Geo. B. Outline of International Law. New York. 1887.
Draper, John W. The Intellectual Development of Europe New York.
    Conflict of Science and Religion.
Dyer, Thomas Henry. History of Modern Europe. London.
Engineer (The). London.
Engineering. London.
Engineering Magazine.
Field, David Dudley.
Fortnightly Review. London.
Green, J. R. Greater History of the English People. New York.

AUTHORITIES CONSULTED.

History Studies of Johns Hopkins University. Baltimore.
Information from Abroad. Publication of the Naval Intelligence
  Office. Washington.
Journal of United States Artillery.
Macaulay, Thomas B. Spain Under Philip II.
  Church of Rome.
Mahan, Captain A. T. Influence of Sea Power Upon History.
  Boston. 1890.
  Influence of Sea Power Upon the French Revolution and
  Empire. Boston. 1892.
Marine Engineering. New York.
Messages of the Presidents. Washington.
Motley, John L. Rise of the Dutch Republic. New York.
Parkman, Francis. Pioneers of France in the New World.
Pearce. History of Spain.
Prescott, William H. History of the Conquest of Mexico.
  Philadelphia.
Proceedings of the United States Naval Institute, Annapolis.
Radford. Hand-Book on Naval Gunnery. New York.
Scientific American. New York.
State Department Documents. Washington.
Trench, R. C. Gustavus Adolphus in Germany. London. 1872.
Twiss, Sir Travers. Belligerents' Rights on the High Seas Since
  the Declaration of Paris. London.
United Service. Magazine.
Wharton, Francis (ed.) Digest of the International Law of the
  United States. Washington. 1889.
Woolsey, Theodore D. International Law.
Yeats, John. Growth and Vicissitudes of Commerce. London.
  1872.

LIST OF ILLUSTRATIONS.

U. S. Protected Cruiser "Olympia."
Spanish Leaders,
    Blanco — Weyler — Cervera — Montijo.
Present and possible rulers of Spain,
    Queen Regent — Alfonso III — Castelar — Don Carlos.
Maj.-Gen. Jos. Wheeler, U. S. Volunteers.
U. S. 2nd Class Battleship "Maine."
Wreck of the "Maine."
Rear Admiral Dewey.
U. S. Monitor "Monterey."
Maj.-Gen. Fitzhugh Lee, U. S. Volunteers.
Cuban Leaders,
    Marti — Garcia — Gomez — Maceo — Palma.
Commodore Winfield Scott Schley.
Bird's-eye View of Santiago Harbor and Defenses.
Spanish Mercy (Shooting Insurgents).
William McKinley.
Battle Plan of Manilla Bay.
Crew of the "Maine."
Acting Rear Admiral W. T. Sampson.
Richmond Pearson Hobson.
Russell A. Alger, Secretary of War.
Military Leaders,
    Miles — Merritt — Shafter — Roosevelt — Mahan.
U. S. Coast Defense Battleship "Oregon."
U. S. Torpedo Boat "Winslow" and Ensign Worth Bagley.
Spanish Armored Cruiser "Vizcaya" (Destroyed at Santiago).
Gen. John M. Schofield (Retired).
Spain's Naval Strength at the Beginning of the War.
John D. Long, Secretary of the Navy.
Our First Prizes.
U. S. Armored Cruiser "New York," Flagship of the Atlantic Squadron.
U. S. Dynamite Cruiser "Vesuvius."
Six Inch Rapid-Fire Gun of the "New Orleans."

LIST OF ILLUSTRATIONS.

U. S. Ram "Katahdin."
Mortar Pit in Action,
Battle of Manilla (Double page colored).
Sectional View of Commerce Destroyer "Minneapolis."
Sectional View of Armored Cruiser "Brooklyn."
Sectional View of Battleship "Oregon."
Sectional View of Spanish Battleship "Pelayo."
Sectional View of Six Spanish Cruisers.
Sectional View of the Monitor's Turret.
View of Keel of U. S. Ram "Katahdin."
Thirteen-Inch Gun at the Proving Grounds.
Maxim Automatic Naval Gun.

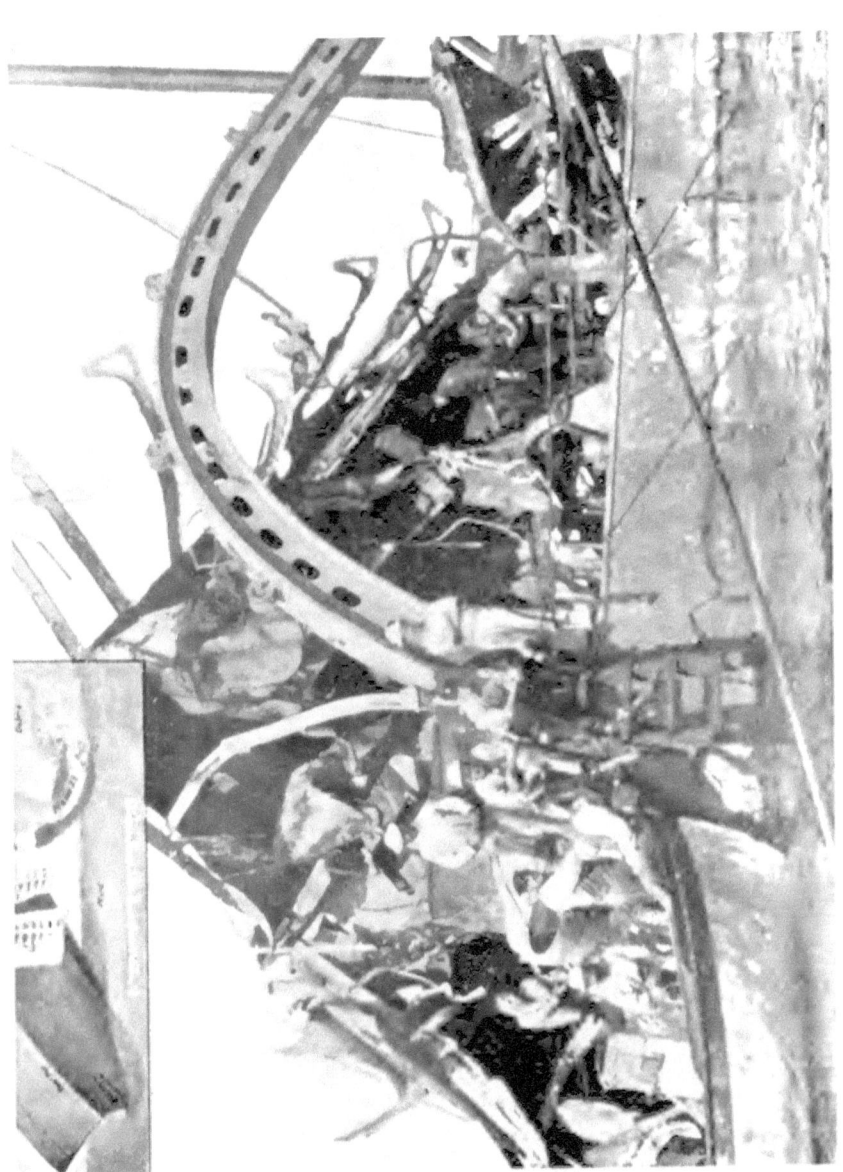

REAR-ADMIRAL GEORGE DEWEY.

U. S. PROTECTED CRUISER "OLYMPIA," FLAGSHIP OF THE PACIFIC SQUADRON.

JOSEPH WHEELER, MAJOR-GENERAL U. S. VOLUNTEERS.

SPANISH MERCY.

WILLIAM M'KINLEY.

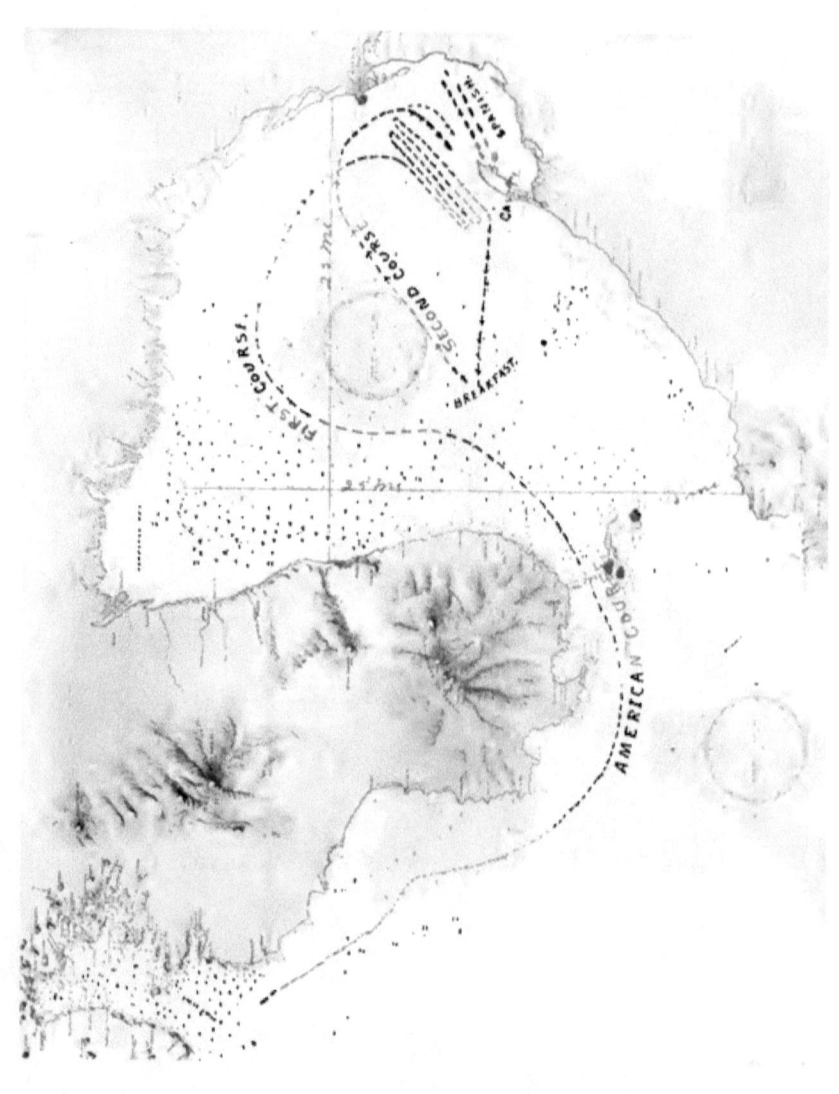

CREW OF THE "MAINE."

FITZHUGH LEE, MAJOR-GENERAL U. S. VOLUNTEERS.

COMMODORE WINFIELD SCOTT SCHLEY.

BIRDSEYE VIEW OF HARBOR OF SANTIAGO DE CUBA.

ACTING REAR-ADMIRAL WILLIAM T. SAMPSON.

RICHMOND PEARSON HOBSON.

RUSSELL A. ALGER, SECRETARY OF WAR.

U. S. COAST DEFENSE BATTLESHIP "OREGON."—THE BATTLESHIP THAT CAUGHT A SPANISH CRUISER.

U. S. TORPEDO-BOAT "WINSLOW."

ENSIGN WORTH BAGLEY

GENERAL JOHN M SCHOFIELD.

SPANISH ARMORED CRUISER "VIZCAYA." — DESTROYED AT SANTIAGO.

JOHN D. LONG, SECRETARY OF NAVY.

A CORNER OF A MORTAR-PIT IN NEW YORK HARBOR DEFENSES.

THE PASSING OF SPAIN.

CHAPTER I.

Spain.

A kingdom of Europe occupying the greater portion of the Iberian Peninsula and reaching farther south than any other country of Europe, and farther west than any other but Portugal. Its greatest length from north to south is 560 miles, from east to west 650 miles, the average width about 380. Including the Balearic and Canary Isles, its area is 195,738 square miles; its population in 1887, its last official census, was 17,673,838. It increases in population very slowly. From '77 to '87 the gain was 4.7 per cent. For the decade preceding '77, the gain was 3.5 per cent.

In 1890 the United States, exclusive of Indian Territory and Alaska, had an area of 2,939,000 square miles, with a population of over 62,000,000, a gain in population of 24.9 per cent since 1880.

Cities.

Spain's largest city, Madrid, has a population about equal to that of Boston.

The principal Mediterranean ports are: Barcelona, population 272,000; Malaga, 134,000; Cartagena, 84,000.

Atlantic ports: Cadiz, 63,000, and Ferrol, 22,000.

Biscayan ports: Bilbao, 50,000, and Santander, 31,000.

All these are fortified. Ferrol has one of the best harbors in Europe. The entrance is narrow and might be well defended. Spain has here a large arsenal and a good ship-building plant. Corunna, twelve miles southwest of Ferrol, has also a good harbor well fortified and has some government ship-yards.

Surface.

The surface of Spain is more varied than that of any other country of Europe of the same size. There are seven distinct mountain ranges, between which flow the great rivers Duro, Tagus, Guadiana and Guadalquivir. The central region, comprising about one-half the whole area, is a great plateau, having an average elevation of about 2,300 feet. The rivers are navigable only for small boats near their mouths. "Spain has 1,400 miles of coast line, which is little indented except on the northwest, where it is bold and rocky."

Climate and Soil.

The climate varies with the configuration of the country. Madrid is said to have experienced weather so severe that sentinels on duty were frozen to death. The soil is generally fertile, and eighty per cent of it is classed as productive. Wheat, rye, barley, corn, olives, grapes and oranges are the principal agricultural products. Spain is rich in minerals. Iron is abundant. In 1895 its mineral exports were valued at thirty-four millions of dollars, the chief of which were iron, copper, zinc, phosphorus, coal and salt.

Religion.

The Constitution enacts: "The nation binds itself to maintain the worship and ministers of the Roman Catholic religion." Nearly the whole population are Roman Catholic. In 1887 there were 6,654 Protestants and 400

Jews. By the Constitution of 1876 a restricted liberty of worship in private is allowed Protestants, but all public announcements of such services are forbidden.

In 1894 there were 32,435 priests, 1,684 monks, 14,592 nuns. There were 65 cathedrals, 30 religious colleges, 18,564 churches, and 11,202 other buildings of a religious character.

Education.

By the law of 1857 there was to be a primary school for every five hundred inhabitants, and compulsory education was to be rigidly enforced. The theory did not materialize. The average teacher's wages ranges from fifty to one hundred dollars per year; and of the population, 68.1 per cent can neither read nor write; 3.4 per cent can read but not write; and only 28.5 per cent can read and write. There are about two males to one female of those who can read and write. The entire sum spent for education in 1887 was less than $400,000.

Finance.

"The Bank of Spain is the great financial institution of the country. It was organized in 1874 and possesses the exclusive right to issue circulating notes. The limit of issue was originally about $150,000,000, but in 1891 this limit was doubled. Ostensibly the Bank is required to keep a reserve of one-third of its circulation, one-half of it being gold. The actual outstanding circulation in 1890 was $46,800,000, and the notes were then at a slight discount in gold, and with the continual increase in the issue of notes which has been going on the premium on gold is now fifty per cent.

"The fact is that the Bank has not for a long time paid for its notes. It professes to redeem them in silver, but the fall in the price of silver has made the gold value of the bullion in the silver coin of less value than the gold value of the bank notes of the same denomination. The stock of gold in the Bank is simply held and is of no particular service as circulation, although it may be drawn on in the emergencies of the war. The circulation has steadily increased as the Government has made demands on the Bank, until last April the limit of $300,000,000 had nearly been reached.

"The Bank makes advances to the Government on the security of bonds and treasury notes. Therefore, as the Government has now unlimited power to make loans and to lay taxes, there seems to be no limit to the extent to which the issues of the Bank of Spain may be extended in support of the war. No doubt they will continue to depreciate from the gold par and will very soon be worth less than the silver coin, but when a nation becomes thoroughly aroused and determined, paper money becomes merely a means of bringing into action all the material strength of the country. It is really a forced loan levied upon the whole property of the nation regardless of individual rights and of everything except the one object of preserving the life of the nation. The assignats of France, the paper money of the Confederate States, the Continental money of the Revolution, all served the purpose, and finally remained valueless in the hands of the last holders. The legal-tender notes of the Civil War did not depreciate to this extent, but at one time they progressed far in this direction and the losses to individuals through their fluctuations never were and never can be adjusted.

"It is well, however, not to count too much on the inability of Spain to carry on war on account of financial weakness. There may be other reasons why she may fail to make headway against this country, but it will not be wholly from lack of money."*

---

*"Bankers' Magazine," June, 1898.

THE ASCENDENCY OF AMERICA. 45

Spain's total debt in 1897 was $1,709,806,331.64, the interest on which was $67,584,525.80. About one-half her debt was held in France, and for $400,000,000 of it the revenues and monopolies of Cuba are pledged as collateral security. This will very naturally make the owners of such bonds much averse to losing their collateral. Just before the Maine disaster Spanish 4 per cent bonds sold for 62½ in London. When the American fleet appeared off Havana they had fallen to 30½. At that rate, if she wished to float a bond at par, it would be necessary for it to bear 13 per cent. interest. The United States bond bearing 4 per cent. interest is selling to-day for 121. On the receipt of the news of the American victory at Manila, gold went to a premium of 111 in Madrid; or, in other words, a dollar of her paper currency was worth about 47 cents.

The revenues of the Spanish Government are raised by direct and indirect taxes, stamp duties, income from government property and from various government monopolies.

Direct taxes are levied on real estate, certain industries, commerce, titles of nobility, mortgages and certain products of the mines.

Indirect taxes are levied on imports, specified articles of commerce, the tolls of roads, bridges, canals, etc.

Her revenue in 1897 was $212,983,527.92, and the expenditure about as much. To-day her expenditures have greatly increased, and now much exceed her income, and ruin or repudiation of her debt stares her in the face. Repudiation is nothing new to her, as she repudiated no longer ago than the '70's. The unit of value in Spanish currency is the peseta (pā-sā'-ta), divided into one hundred centesimos.

In 1895 the total exports of Spain were 686,700,802 pesetas, and the imports were 660,875,994 pesetas, France and Great Britain getting the lion's share of the trade.

A bulletin of the Department of Agriculture, just issued, shows the amount and character of our trade with Spain:

"Our trade with Spain, although subject to minor fluctuations, appears to have been gradually shrinking for about fifteen years. It attained its maximum development in 1883, when the combined imports and exports reached the value of $24,725,632, or more than $10,000,000 in excess of the present figures. The returns for 1897, with the single exception of those for 1895, which fell to $14,501,195, were the lowest recorded since 1878, twenty years ago. The average value per annum for the last five years, 1893-1897, amounted to $16,240,588, as against $18,305,404 for the five years immediately preceding.

"In our commercial intercourse with Spain the balance of trade has been very decidedly in favor of the United States.

"Of the commodities that enter into our commercial transactions with Spain about 75 per cent may be classed as products of agriculture. The preponderance of agricultural matter is particularly noticeable in our exportations to that country.

"Among the products of agriculture that are imported into the United States from Spain, fruits and nuts comprise the most important item, constituting in value considerably more than half of the total agricultural purchases. After fruit and nuts the product of greatest value is wine. These two items, fruits and nuts and wine, form about 85 per cent of the imported agricultural matter. The only other agricultural imports of any considerable importance are, in the order of their value, argol, hides and skins, vegetables, and vegetable oils.

"Raisins, oranges and lemons are the principal fruits imported from Spain. Figs, currants, and several other varieties are also imported, but in very small and irregu-

THE ASCENDENCY OF AMERICA. 47

lar quantities. Raisins are still the leading item, although they were formerly brought from Spain in much larger quantities than now.

"The total value of the several varieties of fruit imported from Spain, which amounted to $2,190,363 per annum during 1888-1892, fell to $1,289,194 per annum during 1893-1897.

"The most important classes of merchandise included in our non-agricultural imports from Spain are: Cork wood or bark and its manufactures; chemicals, drugs and dyes; iron ore; lead and lead manufactures; palm leaf manufactures, and wood and its manufactures. The several commodities mentioned constitute in value about 70 per cent of the total imports of non-agricultural merchandise.

"Cork in its crude and manufactured forms is the most valuable of these imports. Our purchases during the last five years have amounted to nearly $500,000 per annum.

"Licorice root is another article of this group that is imported quite extensively from Spain. The imports for 1897, amounting to 2,222,982 pounds, valued at $60,515, were unusually small.

"Iron ore is one of our leading non-agricultural imports from Spain. The quantity now imported, however, is much smaller than formerly, the last few years showing a marked falling off.

"Products of agriculture comprise in value fully 85 per cent of the domestic merchandise exported from the United States to Spain. Cotton and tobacco are by far the most important items. Together they form more than 90 per cent of all the agricultural produce we send to the Spanish market. The only other agricultural exports of any considerable importance are wheat, wheat flour, and corn among the breadstuffs, lard and tallow among the meat products, and sausage skins.

"Cotton is the mainstay of our export trade with Spain. Measured in value, it constitutes over 80 per cent of our agricultural exports to that country, and about 70 per cent of all the merchandise we market there. During the past twenty years the shipments have more than doubled in size, and much of this growth has occurred within a decade.

"After cotton, our most important agricultural export to Spain is leaf tobacco. The annual shipments average about 20,000,000 pounds, and their value about a million dollars.

"Our exports of breadstuffs to Spain vary greatly from year to year. The largest shipments of the decade were made in 1863, amounting in value to $1,941,206, while the smallest—those for 1895—were valued at only $4,432.

"The shipments of wheat, which is the leading item in this group, have been extremely spasmodic. In 1893 they aggregated as high as 2,443,105 bushels, while in 1895 there appear to have been no shipments whatever.

"The only other American cereal marketed to any extent in Spain is Indian corn. The shipments of this grain, like those of wheat, have been subject to great fluctuations.

"Of the various meat products shipped from the United States to Spain, lard is the only item of any considerable importance. Formerly this commodity was sent to the Spanish market in much larger quantities than now.

"Of the various non-agricultural commodities shipped from the United States to Spain, the most conspicuous are wood and its manufactures, and crude mineral oil. The sum we receive for these two items constitutes more than 85 per cent of the entire amount the Spanish pay for our non-agricultural exports. The only other items of any considerable importance among this class of exports are bituminous coal, the group of articles entitled chemicals, drugs, dyes and medicines, merchandise included under iron and steel and their manufactures, and rosin.

"Iron and steel and their manufactures were marketed in Spain to the extent of $26,261 per annum during 1888-1892, and $29,133 per annum during 1893-1897. In 1897, however, the shipments were much smaller than usual, only $15,724. Machinery is the leading item."

Government.

Spain has a written Constitution consisting of eighty-nine articles, established in 1876. It specifies that Spain shall be a constitutional monarchy, leaves the execution of the laws resting with the king, and vests the power to make laws "in the Cortes with the king."

Cortes.

The Spanish Cortes is composed of a senate and a congress, equal in power. Of the senators there are three classes:

First.—Senators by their own right. To this class belong sons of the king, if any, and of the next heir to the throne who is of age; grandees in their own right who have an annual income of $12,000; captain-generals of the army; admirals of the navy; the Patriarch of the Indies; and the archbishops; the presidents of the Council of State, of the Supreme Tribunal, and of the Supreme Council of War and of Navy, after they have held office two years.

Second.—This class comprises life senators appointed by the crown. As a safeguard the senators of the first and second classes must never exceed in number the senators of the elective class.

Third.—This class consists of 180 senators elected by corporations and the highest taxpayers. Of the elected senators one-half must be chosen every five years, and all of them whenever the monarch dissolves that part of the Cortes.

Congress.

Congress consists of 432 members elected for five years and in the proportion of about one to every 50,000 population. The right of franchise is held by all male Spaniards 25 years of age who enjoy full civil rights and have been citizens of the district for at least two years. Members of congress, unless they belong to the cabinet, cannot hold state office nor receive salaries or pensions. Congress and the senate must meet each year.

The monarch has the power of convoking, suspending or dissolving the Cortes, but if dissolved, a new Cortes must meet within three months. The monarch appoints the president and vice-president of the senate, from members of the senate. Congress chooses its own officers and has the power of impeaching ministers before the senate. The monarch cannot marry without the approval of the Cortes; nor marry anyone excluded by law from succession to the throne.

Ministry.

The Spanish ministry corresponds to the English and American cabinet. The monarch is inviolable, but his ministers are responsible for all acts that offend the people, and are frequently punished. All decrees of the king must be signed by one of the ministers.

Army and Navy.

All Spaniards over 19 years of age may be required to serve three years in the active army, three years in the first reserve, and six years in the second reserve, but may purchase exemption from service for about $300.00. Spain has thirteen military schools and colleges. Spain claims to be able to mobilize an army of more than one million in case of necessity. Spain has a fairly powerful navy, consisting of one first-class battleship, eight splendid armored cruisers, and other vessels which we shall describe in detail. The present navy is manned by about 1,000 officers, 800 machinists, 14,000 sailors and 900 marines. The recruits for the army and navy are secured by conscription. The individual courage of the men ranks high, but Spanish officers throughout their whole history have shown marvelous capacity for doing the wrong thing at the wrong time. They are wretched engineers, and depend almost wholly upon the Scotch and French to fill these positions. Their gunnery does not enjoy a high reputation for accuracy, and the poverty of their resources has prevented target practice.

War Strength. — In March, 1896, exclusive of 56 line battalions, and 10 rifle battalions then in Cuba, there were available for mobilization in the peninsula, including the garrisons of the Balearic and Canary Islands, and of North Africa:

Infantry — 56 second battalions at 1,000, 56,000 men; 56 third battalions at 1,000, 56,000 men, and ten rifle battalions at 1,200, 12,000 men.

Cavalry — 28 regiments at 596 horses and 700 men, 19,600 men.

Artillery — 14 field artillery regiments, each of 8 batteries of 6 guns, with an equal number of artillery and infantry ammunition columns, 25,606 men; 3 mountain artillery regiments and ammunition columns, 7,254 men; 9 battalions fortress artillery, partly of 6, partly of 4 companies, 8,175 men.

Engineers — 4 sapper and miner regiments at 2,000, 8,000 men; 1 pontoon regiment, 3,442 men; 1 railway regiment, 1,040 men; 1 telegraph battalion, 1,272 men; total, 198,389 men.

To these have to be added the administrative and

sanitary services, 4,845 men. The cavalry takes the field with 16,708 horses; the artillery has 816 field guns.

The following reserve troops were also available:

Infantry — 112 reserve battalions (56 regiments of 3 battalions) at 1,000 men, 112,000 men.

Cavalry — 14 reserve regiments of 4 squadrons, with 600 horses and 702 men, 9,828 men.

Artillery — 7 field artillery regiments, 1 for each army corps district, and 136 guns, 14,140.

Engineers — New formations, 6,000 men; total, 141,968 men.

Apart, therefore, from the troops in Cuba, 130,000 men in round numbers, there were in March, 1896, available on mobilization, 340,000 men, with 25,108 horses (cavalry) and 952 guns.

Military Schools.

Spain has thirteen schools for the instruction of the officers of her army and navy.

The principal primary naval school at Ferrol, on the northwest coast, has a course of from two and one-half to three years, and includes natural philosophy, mathematics, hydrography, fencing, gymnastics, drawing, and the study of one foreign language. From this school they are graduated to a higher institution at Cadiz, and complete their course in the academy of San Carlo or San Fernandino.

The school at San Carlo is for artillery only, and supplies from its graduates the officers for the guns of both the army and navy. The engineer students are educated at other schools, and the marine officers at a school where they have a special system of their own. Service in this corps is esteemed but lightly, and the cadets are made up of those who have failed in other schools, non-commissioned officers, etc.

The Spanish naval cadet comes only from the higher

classes. There are a few sons of professional men among them, but in a large majority of cases their fathers are officers, either active or retired.

Their system of education in theory is excellent, and should turn out well-equipped officers, but one weak point is that a candidate with sufficient "pull" is accepted at the higher institutions without being required to pass through the training schools, and the preliminary examination is made easy for him in proportion to the amount of influence he possesses. Such a course must, not infrequently, result in placing men in responsible positions who are totally unqualified for the office. The strict discipline and high standing which are so characteristic of the naval schools of Germany, England and America, are unknown quantities with Spain. Such a system of favoritism is not well calculated to develop the men best fitted to handle the complicated military engines of modern warfare.

Character of the People.

Perhaps not another nation can show such a mixture of blood, made up as it is of descendants from the old Iberians, Celts, Carthaginians, Romans, Vandals, Suevi, Goths and Moors.

They are generally well-formed and of a dark, clear complexion, black hair, dark eyes, sharp features, and of dignified manner. In character they are proud, courteous, patriotic, but frequently vain, intolerant and vindictive. As soldiers they have displayed marked courage, enterprise and endurance.

History.

Iberia was the name given to Spain by the ancient Greeks, and the country about the mouth of the Guadalquiver is generally understood to have been the Tarshish of Scripture. It was early colonized by the Phœnicians, but little was known of it until the first war between Rome and Carthage, 264 B. C., when Spanish troops served in the Carthaginian armies. Hamilcar, Hasdrubal and Hannibal cultivated the friendship of Spain. They encouraged marriages between their soldiers and officers and the native women, and even Hannibal married a Spanish woman. The warlike population and the great mineral wealth were by these leaders turned to good account in their warfare with Rome.

Hamilcar founded New Carthage, now Cartagena. After the destruction of Carthage by the Romans 146 B. C., Spain was conquered and became a Roman province, though insurrections were frequent.

When Alaric sacked Rome in 409 A. D. the Suevi, Alani and Vandals swept over Spain and brought it to the lowest depth of misery. About 415 the Visigoths, as Roman allies, swept out these tribes and established an independent empire which lasted until the fall of Roderick 711 A. D., the last of the Gothic kings.

"Spain under its Gothic kings may have been a fairly well governed country, but long before the end came there must have been languor and decay among its people. Anything like a vigorous national resistance seems to have been too much for the Spaniards, enervated as they were by long familiarity with Roman civilization."

Spain at this time contained many Jews who had done much in building up its trade and industry with other countries.

"In the old times under Visigothic rule these people had greatly prospered, but the leniency that had been shown to them was succeeded by atrocious persecution, when the Visigoths abandoned their Arianism and became orthodox. The most inhuman ordinances were issued against them — a law was enacted condemning them all to be slaves. It was not to be wondered at that when the Saracen invasion took place the Jews did whatever they could to promote its success. They, like the Arabs, were an Oriental people; both traced their lineage to Abraham, their common ancestor; both were believers in the unity of God. It was their defense of that doctrine that had brought upon them the hatred of their Visigothic masters."*

As early as 709 the Moors made forays into Spain and discovered its fascinating weakness.

Count Julian, one of Roderic's captains, feeling that he had been wronged by the king, sought revenge, and plotted with the Moslems for the invasion of the country and the overthrow of the Gothic power. The proposition was referred to the caliph, who gave it his approval.

"The Khalif Alwalid next authorized the invasion of Europe, the conquest of Andalusia, or the Region of the Evening. Musa, his general, found, as had so often been the case elsewhere, two effective allies, sectarianism and treason — the Archbishop of Toledo and Count Julian, the Gothic general."

"Tarik, a lieutenant of the emir, was sent across the Straits with the van of the army. He landed on the rock, called in memory of his name, Gibraltar, April, A. D. 711. In the battle that ensued, a part of Roderic's troops, together with the Archbishop of Toledo, consummated their treasonable compact and deserted to the Arabs; the rest were panic-stricken."

"With great rapidity, Tarik, the lieutenant of Musa, pushed forward from the battle-field to Toledo, and thence northward. On the arrival of Musa the reduction of the Spanish peninsula was completed, and the wreck of the Gothic army driven beyond the Pyrenees into France. Considering the conquest of Spain as only the first step in his victories, he announced his intention of forcing his way into Italy and preaching the unity of God in the Vatican. Thence he would march to Con-

---

* Draper's "Conflict of Science and Religion."

stantinople, and having put an end to the Roman Empire and Christianity, would pass into Asia and lay his victorious sword on the footstool of the khalif at Damascus.

"But this was not to be. Musa, envious of his lieutenant Tarik, had treated him with great indignity. The friends of Tarik at the court of the khalif found means of retaliation. An envoy from Damascus arrested Musa in his camp; he was carried before his sovereign, disgraced by a public whipping, and died of a broken heart.

"Under other leaders, however, the Saracen conquest of France was attempted. In a preliminary campaign the country from the mouth of the Garonne to that of the Loire was secured. Then Abderrahman, the Saracen commander, dividing his forces into two columns, with one on the east, passed the Rhone and laid siege to Arles. A Christian army, attempting the relief of the place, was defeated with heavy loss. His western column, equally successful, passed the Dordogne, defeated another Christian army, inflicting on it such dreadful loss that according to its own fugitives 'God alone could number the slain.' All Central France was now overrun; the banks of the Loire were reached; the churches and monasteries were despoiled of their treasures.

"The progress of the invaders was at length stopped by Charles Martel (A. D. 732). Between Tours and Poictiers a great battle, which lasted seven days, was fought. Abderrahman was killed, the Saracens retreated and soon afterward were compelled to re-cross the Pyrenees. The banks of the Loire, therefore, mark the boundary of the Mohammedan advance in Western Europe.*

It was not the generalship of Charles Martel which saved Europe from further invasion so much as the internal dissensions that sprang up among the Saracens themselves. During the tenth century violent civil wars

---

*Draper's Intellectual Development of Europe.

THE ASCENDENCY OF AMERICA.

occurred among them, and at one time there were three caliphs residing in as many different cities. Christian Europe found its safeguard in the quarrels of the rival potentates. After the battle of Tours the Saracens fell back to the peninsula, the greater part of which they occupied and brought into a high state of cultivation.

Cordova was the capital city of their caliph, who declared himself independent.

For many years the Spanish Moors represented the highest advance of culture and intelligence.

History has done scant justice to them, and science, especially medicine, astronomy and chemistry, owes them a large debt of gratitude.

Cordova.

"Scarcely had the Arabs become firmly settled in Spain when they commenced a brilliant career. The Emirs of Cordova distinguished themselves as patrons of learning, and set an example of refinement strongly contrasting with the condition of the native European princes. Cordova, under their administration, boasted of more than two hundred thousand houses and more than a million of inhabitants. After sunset, a man might walk through it in a straight line for ten miles by the light of the public lamps. Seven hundred years after this time there was not so much as one public lamp in London. Cordova's streets were solidly paved. In Paris, centuries subsequently, whoever stepped over his threshold on a rainy day stepped up to his ankles in mud."

"In whatever direction we may look we meet, in the various pursuits of peace and war, of letters and of science, Saracenic vestiges. Our dictionaries tell us that such is the origin of admiral, alchemy, alcohol, algebra, cotton, and hundreds of other words."

Globes in Schools.

"Almaimon, A. D. 830, had ascertained the size of the earth from the measurement of a degree on the shore of the Red Sea. While the cities of Europe were asserting the flatness of the earth, the Spanish Moors were teaching geography in their common schools from globes. They also promoted many important branches of industry, improved the manufacture of textile fabrics, earthenware, iron and steel. The Toledo sword blades were everywhere prized for their temper. They also introduced inventions of a more ominous kind — gunpowder and artillery. The cannon they used appears to have been made of wrought-iron. But perhaps they more than compensated for these by the introduction of the mariner's compass.

'I join, as doubtless all natural philosophers will do, in the pious prayer of Alhazen (1100 A. D.) that in the day of judgment the All Merciful will take pity on the soul of Abur-Raihan because he was the first of the race of men to construct a table of specific gravity, and I will ask the same for Alhazen himself since he was the first to trace the curvilinear path of the ray of light through the air.

Darwin's Theory Not New.

" He upheld the affirmation of those who said man in his progress passes through a definite succession of states; not, however, 'that he was once a bull and was then changed to an ass and afterward into a horse, and after that into an ape, and finally became a man.' This, he says, is only a misrepresentation by the 'common people' of what is really meant. The 'common people' who withstood Alhazen have representatives among us to-day."

THE ASCENDENCY OF AMERICA. 59

Jewish Trade.

"From Barcelona and other ports an immense trade with the Levant was maintained, but it was mainly in the hands of the Jews, who, from the first invasion of Spain by Musa, had ever been the firm allies of the Arabs. In the days of their prosperity they maintained a merchant marine of more than a thousand ships. With Constantinople alone they maintained a great trade. It ramified from the Black Sea and East Mediterranean into the interior of Asia to reach the ports of India and China, and extended along the African coast as far as Madagascar. As on so many other occasions, on these affairs they have left their traces. The smallest weight they used in trade was a grain of barley, four of which were equal to one sweet pea, called in Arabic, carat. We still use the grain as our unit of weight, and still speak of gold as being so many carats fine.

"In the middle of the tenth century they were using bills of exchange and writing treatises on the principles of trade and commerce."*

Pelayo.

Northern Spain, with its broken surface, offers many opportunities for strong, defensive positions, where comparatively weak forces may hold out against superior numbers. It is here, that in all ages, the defeated, or those who were too independent to yield, have fled, and to-day the land is inhabited by their descendants, the Basques, an extremely brave, hardy and liberty-loving people. It was to this broken, mountainous region that the Christians, under the leadership of Pelayo, fled from the Saracen invader, seeking refuge in the wilds of Asturias. They found in the Cave of Covadonga a safe retreat, from which they repulsed the Moors with terrible

---

* Intellectual Development of Europe.

slaughter in 717. "In Christian Spain the fame of the single battle will endure as long as time shall last; and 'La Cueva de Covadinga,' the cradle of the Monarchy, may be one of the proudest spots on the soil of the peninsula." The fame of the leader and the safe retreat attracted other Christians, and under the wise and cautious leadership of Pelayo they gradually descended into the plains and valleys and annexed the territory as fast as it was abandoned by the Moslems. From this feeble germ grew the kingdom of Leon.

Navarre.
South of the Pyrenees and bordering on the Bay of Biscay, at the beginning of the tenth century, was one of the most easily defended portions of the peninsula. The inhabitants had yielded a nominal obedience to the Goths, the Moslems or the Franks, as either party rose to power, but about the year 900 Sancho declared it independent and founded the kingdom of Navarre. Through his marriage connections, diplomacy, and skill as a general he was able to extend his boundaries, and took in a large part of what afterward became the kingdom of Aragon. The little kingdom of Navarre is famous as having furnished one of France's greatest rulers, Henry IV.

The dissensions among the Moors and the rise of Charlemagne lost them their possessions in France. Allying himself with the defeated faction of the Moslems, Charlemagne pushed his boundaries as far south into Spain as the Ebro river. One of his armies was compelled to retreat, and suffered a severe defeat (778) at Roncesvalles, where the celebrated Paladin, Roland, or Orlando, of historic myth, was killed.

By 950, in spite of disorder, factional quarrels and petty strife, the Christian kingdoms were well established in the northern half of the peninsula. Their importance was sufficiently felt by the Moslems to secure to them

THE ASCENDENCY OF AMERICA. 61

treaties and alliances. For the next five hundred years the history of Spain is a complex and monotonous recital of the little wars of little states, insurrections of ambitious leaders of factions, broken promises and petty jealousies. The Moslems and Christians, alike, were divided into numerous rival factions, and the defeated on either side was glad to ally himself, for the time being, with the prevailing power of the other religion in an attack upon his own brother in the faith.

It was by the marriage of Ferdinand and Isabella that several of the larger Christian kingdoms of Spain came to be united in purpose, and under a strong religious stimulus rallied in opposition to the Saracens.

Synopsis of Events Contemporary with this Period.

A. D.

9. The Germans under Arminius inflict an overwhelming defeat on the Romans under Varus which secures the independence of the German States. Augustus Cæsar Emperor of Rome.

43. Romans commence the conquest of Britain. Claudius was then Emperor of Rome and the inhabitants of England, Celts.

64. First persecution of the Christians at Rome under Nero.

325? Council of Nicaea adopts the Nicaean creed.

330. Constantine makes Constantinople the seat of the Roman Empire instead of Rome.

364–365. The Roman Empire is divided, Valentinian taking the Empire of the West and Valens the East.

375–395. Yielding to attacks from the Huns, the Goths are allowed to pass the Danube and settle in Roman provinces. They soon engage in war with the Romans and destroy Emperor Valens

A. D.	
	and his army. Finally subdued by Emperor Theodosius.
410.	Alaric king of the Visigoths captures the city of Rome.
414.	Spain invaded by the Visigoths. Britain abandoned by the Roman Empire of the West.
451.	Attila the king of the Huns, called "The Scourge of God," checked at the battle of Chalons, France, by the allied Goth and Roman armies.
455–582.	Anglo-Saxons invade England and found petty kingdoms.
476.	The Empire of the West crushed and extinguished by Odoacer, who becomes the first barbarian ruler of Italy.
533–568.	Justinian, Emperor of Constantinople, conquers Italy and northern Africa; issues "Code of Justinian," which formed the basis of the law of the empire for centuries, and has had great influence on the law of all nations with which the empire came in contact.
622.	Mohammed driven from Mecca. This constitutes the Hegira or "Flight," from which date Mohammedans reckon their time.
632.	Mohammed becomes supreme in Arabia.
651.	The Mohammedans complete the conquest of Persia.
709.	Mohammedans complete the conquest of northern Africa and plan the invasion of Spain.
768–814.	Reign of Charlemagne. His empire extended into Spain as far as the Ebro; into Germany as far as the Elbe; and into Austria nearly to Vienna.

"In a life restlessly active we see him reforming the coinage, establishing the legal divisions of money, gathering about him the learned of

A. D.

every country, founding schools and collecting libraries, and trying to harmonize the discordant codes of Barbarian and Roman law."

786. Accession of Haroun al-Raschid, famous Caliph of Bagdad.
787. Danes invade England.
800. Accession of Egbert, the first to call himself "King of the English."
871–900. Reign of Alfred the Great.
911. The Northman Hrolf (Duke Rollo) invades France and secures from its king the province called after them, Normandy, and the people and their desendants, Normans.
1017. Canute becomes king of England and Denmark.
1041. Edward the Confessor king of England.
1060. Battle of Hastings. William, duke of Normandy, defeats Harold, last Saxon king of England, and becomes William I of England, and first of the Norman dynasty.
1096. First Crusade. Peter the Hermit, its apostle; Godfrey de Bouillon, Defender of the Holy Sepulchre; Robert, duke of Normandy first son of William the Conqueror; Tancred; and Baldwin, brother of Godfrey de Bouillon, were the chief leaders. Jerusalem captured. "So terrible, it is said, was the carnage which followed, that the horses of the Crusaders rode up to the Mosque of Omar through a stream of blood; infants were seized by their feet and dashed against the walls or hurled over the battlements, while the Jews were all burned alive in their synagogue. In the midst of these horrors Godfrey entered the Church of the Sepulchre clothed in a robe of pure white, barefooted and bareheaded, and knelt at the tomb to offer his thanksgiving for the Divine Goodness

A. D.	
	that had granted the realization of the yearning of their hearts."
1140.	Feuds in Italy between the Guelfs and Ghibellines.
1146.	Second Crusade. St. Bernard its popular preacher as Peter the Hermit had been of the first. Crusade a failure.
1154.	Henry II, king of England, first of the Plantagenets. Thomas à Becket, Archbishop of Canterbury. First Saxon since the Conquest to hold high office.
1189–1199.	Reign of Richard I. Third Crusade; Richard and Philip take part. Saladin had captured Jerusalem 88 years after Godfrey had been proclaimed "Defender of the Holy Sepulchre." He treated the captives with marked leniency considering the custom of the times. He held Jerusalem in spite of the Third Crusade, which resulted in a truce by which the pilgrims for 3 years and 8 months might visit the Holy Sepulchre, untaxed.
1212.	Children's Crusade; 50,000 children perish or are sold into captivity.
1215.	The barons and freeholders of England compel John to sign Magna Charta. This was a formal acknowledgment by the crown of the rights which for many years had been claimed by the people.
1346.	War between France and England. Edward III gains a decided victory at Crecy. The blind king of Bohemia, fighting for France, was slain, together with the flower of the French chivalry. The Black Prince, son of Edward III, distinguished himself and adopted the crest and motto — "Ich Dien," of the Bohemian king, still worn by the Prince of Wales.
1356.	English gain battle of Poictiers and take King John of France, prisoner.

THE ASCENDENCY OF AMERICA. 65

A. D.

1399. Richard the Second deposed; Henry IV, son of John of Gaunt, first of the Lancaster line of kings, crowned.

1415. Henry V of England defeats the French at battle of Agincourt.

1420. Treaty of Troyes, by which it was agreed that Henry should succeed Charles VI of France to the French throne. The people of France refused to acknowledge the treaty.

1422. Henry V of England and Charles VI of France die and part of France acknowledge Henry VI. War ensues.

1429. Joan of Arc victorious at Orleans and the French Dauphin crowned as Charles VII of France.

1431. Joan of Arc tried before an Ecclesiastical Tribunal on the charge of witchcraft, and burned alive at the market-place at Rouen.

1452. English finally driven out of France.

1453. Mohammed II captures Constantinople and the Roman Empire of the East is destroyed.

1455. Beginning of "War of the Roses" in England, between the Houses of York and Lancaster. The House of York was descended, through a daughter, from Lionel, third son of Edward III. The House of Lancaster from John of Gaunt, fourth son of Edward III. The white rose was the badge of York, the red rose, that of Lancaster.

1461. Henry VI, last of House of Lancaster, deposed; Edward IV, first of House of York, crowned by aid of the Duke of Warwick, styled "King Maker."

1470. Warwick restores Henry VI. to the English throne.

1471. Edward wins battle of New Barnet, and Warwick is defeated and slain.

CHAPTER II.
Period of Discovery and Conquest.

The great discoveries which form such an important part of the history of this epoch were in no small measure due to the occupation of the east by the Turks, who, in their rapid rise to power had captured Constantinople in 1453, gained command of the eastern Mediterranean, and thus cut off trade with the Orient by the route that had made Venice and Genoa so rich and famous. The invention of the mariner's compass and more correct ideas of geography were also potent factors.

After the union of the numerous Christian kingdoms of the Iberian Peninsula and the conquest of the Moors, the adventurous spirit of the age found an outlet in the discovery and conquest of the new world.

Reign of Ferdinand and Isabella — 1474-1516.

In 1469 occurred the marriage of Ferdinand and Isabella, the event which, more than any other, tended to unite numerous discordant factions, reconcile opposing interests and give to the various Christian kingdoms of Spain a religious unity. At one time Spain had as many as fourteen petty kingdoms, but by the union of Ferdinand of Aragon and Isabella of Castile and Leon about all of the Christian portion of the peninsula was united, the chief exceptions being Navarre, a petty kingdom on the north, and Portugal, which was then independent. At the time of the marriage neither of the parties were reigning monarchs, they themselver were rival claimants to a little kingdom, and the possessions falling to them by inheritance were trivial and insignificant compared with those acquired later by conquest or discovery.

THE ASCENDENCY OF AMERICA. 67

Isabella was the daughter of John of Castile, and a lineal descendant of the famous English "John of Gaunt," Duke of Lancaster, from whom the Lancastrian kings of England were descended. On the death of her father, her brother, Henry IV, became king of Castile, and afterward declared her his lawful heir. Numerous candidates for her hand appeared, among whom is said to have been the Duke of Gloucester, afterward Richard III of England. She became queen of Castile and Leon upon the death of her brother Henry in 1474. It was claimed even then by Ferdinand that he should have been king of Castile, on the plea that he was the nearest male heir to Henry IV, and that under the Salic law a female could not inherit. His claim was not urged strongly, as the sovereigns were engaged in suppressing an insurrection, and had as much as they could do to make good their joint claim to the throne.

The question is interesting, and occurs later in Spanish history in the claims of the Carlists.

Having reduced the affairs within their own kingdom to order, the sovereigns turned their attention to their Moorish neighbors in Granada, and after a desultory war of ten years captured Granada and overthrew the Moorish power in Spain forever.

Under the joint sovereigns the country continued to thrive until the death of Isabella in 1504, when some trouble arose concerning the succession to Castile, but Ferdinand was successful, and when he died in 1516 had acquired possession of all Spain.

The chief events of their reign were the institution of the Inquisition, the Conquest of Granada from the Moors, the Discovery of America, the Expulsion of the Jews, the Expulsion of the Unbaptized Moors, and the adoption of the pope's line dividing the Spanish and Portuguese colonies.

The Portuguese discovered and colonized the western

coast of Africa, the islands adjacent, and doubled the Cape of Good Hope. Upon the return of Columbus in 1493 the Spanish and Portuguese claims were likely to conflict. The Pope claimed sovereignty over all heathen lands, and settled the question May, 1493, by drawing an imaginary line north and south one hundred leagues west of the Azores Islands, giving to Spain everything discovered and to be discovered west of that line. This solution was based on the supposition that the earth was flat. It worked well until the circumnavigation of Africa discredited the old theories and enhanced the value of trade with the Spice islands of the East Indies.

Isabella had a powerful mind, and it was largely due to her guiding hand that Spain suddenly took rank among the great kingdoms. Her daughter, Catherine of Aragon, was the first wife of Henry VIII. of England, and mother of Queen Mary. Another daughter, Joanna, married Philip of Austria, son of the emperor of Germany. Her character is marred, however, by two traits — intolerance and bigotry — which seem characteristic of the race.

The unbelieving Jews in Spain were a source of great grief to her. Next to them were the infidel Moors. Although Granada had surrendered under a solemn pledge of civil and religious liberty, she did not hesitate to break it, for to her devout soul heresy was the greatest of all evils. It was for the suppression of these evils that she gave her consent to the institution of a Court of Inquisition.

Inquisition.

"Under the influence of Torquemada, the confessor of Queen Isabella, that princess solicited a bull from the Pope for the establishment of the Inquisition. The method had been tried before. A bull was accordingly issued in November, 1478, for the detection and suppression of heresy. Anonymous accusations were received. The accused was not confronted by witnesses. Torture was relied upon for conviction. Llorente, the historian of the Inquisition, computes that Torquemada and his collaborators in the course of eighteen years burned at the stake 10,220 persons and otherwise punished 97,321."*

Expulsion of the Jews.

Spain at that time contained many Jews and Saracens who would not embrace the Christian religion. Accordingly, March 30, 1492, an edict for the expulsion of the Jews was issued, and all were ordered to leave the realm by the end of July of that year.

"They might sell their effects, but could not carry gold or silver away with them. Nobody would purchase what could be got for nothing after July. Whoever helped them was punished. Of the banished persons some made their way into Africa, some into Italy — the latter carrying with them into Naples ship fever, which destroyed twenty thousand in that city. Some reached Turkey; a few England. Thousands, especially the mothers, the infants, and old people, died by the way."†

This action against the Jews was soon followed by one against the Moors.

Expulsion of the Unbaptized Moors.

"An edict was issued February, 1502, ordering all unbaptized Moors in the kingdoms of Castile and Leon to leave the country by the end of April. They might sell their property, but not take away any gold or silver. They were forbidden to emigrate to the Mohammedan dominions. The penalty of disobedience was death. Their condition was worse than the Jews, who had been

---

* "Science and Religion."
† Intellectual Development of Europe.

permitted to go where they pleased. The intolerance of the Spanish doctrine is shown by its assertion that the government would be justified in taking the life of all Moors because of their infidelity. Granada had surrendered under the solemn guaranty of the full enjoyment of civil and religious liberty."*

By this action Spain had deprived herself of citizens that could have been made of inestimable value to her. By expelling the Jews they lost much needed capital and, more valuable still, the intellect and training that had made that capital available and useful to them. With the expulsion of the Saracens she was deprived of the captains of industry and her manufacturing and agricultural interests have not yet recovered from the blow. Spain at that time was supposed to have a population of more than thirty millions; to-day she has about half that. Her very discoveries sapped her vital powers. They cost her the best blood of her young men, lost by fever, shipwreck, and battle; they discouraged industry by painting larger and quicker returns for courage and daring; they brought slave labor and all the evils attendant in its train. She never, like England, made her colonies a part of herself, but pitiless in her exaction, drained their resources to the last drop and preserved her hold on them only by force and not by any sense of loyalty to her.

Synopsis of History Contemporary with This Reign.

A. D.

1483. Edward IV, first Yorkist king, dies; his son Edward V reigns a few months and is put aside by his uncle, Richard III. Luther and Raphael born; (d. Luther, 1546; Raphael, 1520.)
1484. Zwingli, great Swiss reformer, born. (d. 1531.)
1485. Battle of Bosworth Field. Death of Richard III. Accession of Henry VII, first Tudor of England.

---

* Draper's Conflict of Science and Religion.

THE ASCENDENCY OF AMERICA.

A. D.
1497. Cabot, in employ of Henry VII, discovers North America. Vasco di Gama, Portuguese navigator, passes around Cape of Good Hope to the East Indies. Melancthon born. (d. 1560.)
1500. Cabral of Portugal discovers Brazil. Charles V, son of Philip of Burgundy and Joanna of Spain, grandson of Ferdinand and Isabella, born.
1503. Gonsalo de Cordova, the great Spanish general, defeats the French at Naples and conquers it for Spain.
1505. John Knox, the Scottish religious reformer, born. (d. 1572.)
1509. Death of Henry VII. Accession of Henry VIII. Calvin born. (d. 1564.) Portugal makes good her claim to nearly all the West Indies.
1513. Battle of Flodden. Defeat of the Scotch. Death James IV of Scotland.

Charles I — 1516-1556. First of the Spanish House of Hapsburg.

Charles I of Spain — Charles V of Germany — was born at Ghent February 24, 1500, and united in his person the claims of four royal lines.

First. — Through his father, Philip of Austria.

Second. — Through his father's mother, daughter of Charles the Bold, which gave him a claim to the Netherlands.

Third. — Through his grandfather, Emperor Maximilian First, a good claim to the imperial crown of Germany at the next election.

Fourth. — Through his mother, Joanna, daughter of Ferdinand and Isabella, he became heir to Spanish possessions.

He succeeded to the Netherlands in 1506, on the

death of Ferdinand, his grandfather; to his Austrian possessions in 1519, on the death of his grandfather Maximilian, and the same year was elected to the imperial crown. Spain was only a small part of his empire, and never the choicest part. Before his death the Spanish flag floated over Florida, New Mexico, Mexico, nearly all of South America except Brazil, the Philippine Islands, and all the West Indies. Throughout his reign he was kept busy defending from ambitious rivals the frontier of his extensive dominion. At last in 1556, broken in health and weighed down by the burden of his responsibilities, he voluntarily abdicated, giving up the Netherlands, Spain and its possessions to his son, Philip II; Germany and his Austrian possessions to his brother Ferdinand. It was agreed between the brothers Charles and Ferdinand that in the event of the male line of either family becoming extinct, the other family should succeed to its territorial possessions. This was one of the claims that later made even more complex the question of "Spanish Succession."

Charles retired to a monastery, where he died September, 1558. He was by long odds the ablest and most powerful monarch of the sixteenth century, and it was in his reign that Spain reached the highest point of her material development. For him Pizarro conquered Peru, Cortez gave him Mexico, Magellan circumnavigated the globe, and the great wealth of the New World poured into his treasury.

Among his contemporaries were Henry VIII of England, Francis I of France, whom he defeated and captured at the battle of Pavia; Frederick Barbarossa of Algiers, whom he defeated and compelled to release thousands of Christian slaves; Luther, Melanchthon, Zwingli and Erasmus, leaders of the Reformation then starting, and Solyman the Magnificent, emperor of Turkey.

Two important events having a bearing on religious

matters were the founding of the Order of Jesuits and the Council of Trent.

Order of Jesuits. Loyola.

In 1521 the French attempted the invasion of Spain. They captured the fortress of Palpuma, but were quickly driven out, and the incident has no military importance. In another way, however, it has had a marked effect on the history of the world. At the capture of this fortress, Ignatius de Loyola, a gallant Spanish soldier, was severely wounded and taken prisoner. "His constitution was shattered, and he was doomed to be a cripple for life. The palm of strength, grace and skill in knightly exercises was no longer for him. A new vision then arose in his mind, which those who know how close was the relation between religion and chivalry in Spain will be at no loss to understand. He would still be a soldier; he would still be a knight-errant; but the soldier and knight-errant of the spouse of Christ. His restless spirit led him to the Syrian deserts and to the Chapel of the Holy Sepulchre. His activity and zeal bore down all opposition; and under his rule the Order of Jesuits began to exist and grow rapidly to the full measure of his gigantic powers.

The great outbreak of Protestantism in one part of Christendom had produced an equally violent outbreak of Catholic zeal in another. Two reformations were pushed on at once with equal energy and effect: a reformation of doctrine in the North, a reformation of manners and discipline in the South. In this great Catholic reaction Ignatius de Loyola bore the same part which Luther bore in the great Protestant movement."*

There had been numerous organizations within the Latin Church — like the Templars, Hospitalers and

---

*Macauley's "Church of Rome."

Knights, into which military ideas entered largely; others, like the Benedictines, Dominicans and Franciscans, were chiefly given spiritual labors and the education of the young.

The Jesuit differed from all these. The earlier associations sought to withdraw from contact with the world and its concerns, to seek spiritual perfection in a retired life of contemplation and prayer within the cloister. On the contrary, the Jesuit system was to take religious men from retirement, to bring them into active intercourse with the world, waiving all regulations of dress or rule, that their members might be free to mix in any company as agents of the Order. The general wielded almost unlimited power; the vow of obedience was taken to him; the tenure of each member depending upon his will.

Frequently in their history they have been engaged in controversy with the Powers of Rome, and that general has stood toward the pope much as one of the powerful feudal leaders of the Middle Ages might towards a weak sovereign.

"The Order was established by a bull of Paul III, 1540, the rules being that the general, chosen for life, should be obeyed as God; that they should vow poverty, chastity, obedience, and go wherever they were commanded; their obedience was to the pope, not to the Church — a most politic distinction, for thereby an unmistakable responsibility was secured. They had no regular hours of prayer; their duties were preaching, the direction of consciences, education. By the Jesuits, Rome penetrated into the remotest corners of the earth, established links of communication with her children who remained true to her in the heart of Protestant countries, and, with a far-seeing policy for the future, silently engrossed the education of the young.

"There was no guise under which the Jesuit might

not be found — a barefoot beggar clothed in rags; a learned professor, lecturing gratuitously to scientific audiences; a man of the world, living in profusion and princely extravagance; there have been Jesuits the wearers of crowns. There were no places into which they did not find their way; a visitor to one of the loyal old families of England could never be sure but that there was a Jesuit hidden in the garret or secreted behind the wainscot of the bedroom. They were the advisers of the leading men of the age, sat in the cabinets of kings, and were their confessors.

"With implicit, and unquestioning obedience to his superior, like a good soldier, it was the paramount duty of the Jesuit to obey his orders, whatever those orders might be. It was for him to go, at the summons of a moment, with his life in his hand, to the very center of pagan or of reformed and revolted countries, where his presence was death by law, and execute the mission entrusted to him. If he succeeded, it was well; if he should fall, it was also well.

"In South America they obtained a footing in Paraguay and commenced their noble attempt at the civilization of the Indians, bringing them into communities, teaching them social usages, agricultural arts and the benefits arising to themselves and the community from labor. They gave them a military organization, subdivided according to the European system, into the customary arms — infantry, cavalry, artillery; they supplied them with munitions of war."

Men found by bitter experience that within the silken glove there was an iron hand. From their general in Rome, who was absolute commander of their persons and unchallengeable administrator of their prodigious wealth, down to the humblest missionary who was wearing away his life among the Andes, or on the banks of the Hoang-ho, or in the solitary prairies of Missouri, or under the blazing sun of Abyssinia, whether he was confessing the butterfly ladies of Paris, whispering suggestions into the ear of the King of Spain, consoling the dying peasant in an Irish cabin, arguing with mandarins in the palace of the Emperor of China, extorting the admiration of learned societies by the profundity of his philosophy and the brilliancy of his scientific discoveries, whether he was to be seen in the exchanges and marts of the great capitals, supervising commercial operations on a scale which up to that time had been attempted by none but the Jews; whether he was held in an English jail as a suspected vagabond, or sitting on the throne of France; whether he appeared as a great landed proprietor, the owner of countless leagues in the remote parts of India or South America, or whether he was mixing with crowds in the streets of London and insinuating in Protestant ears the rights of subjects to oppose and even depose their monarchs, or in the villages of Castile and Leon preaching before Catholic peasants the paramount duty of a good Christian implicitly to obey the mandates of his king — wherever the Jesuit was or whatever he was doing, men universally felt that the thing he had in hand was only auxiliary to some higher, some hidden design. This power became at last so intolerable that the Jesuits were banished from France, Spain, Portugal and other Catholic countries.*

Council of Trent.

Upon the accession of Paul III in 1534 to the papal throne, energetic measures for church reform were put forth.

In 1545 he issued a bull summoning delegates for the whole Latin Church to meet in council at Trent. Twenty-five sessions in all were held, ranging, with frequent interruptions, from 1545 to 1563, and during which

---
* Draper's "Intellectual Development of Europe."

time three popes died. Most of the enactments had reference to church government, or questions of theology not especially interesting to-day. Among other things it declared that Scripture and tradition are to be received and venerated equally; that the Vulgate should be the sole, authentic and standard Latin version of the Bible, and gave it such authority as to supersede the original text. It appointed a committee to investigate and report on heretical books. The enforcement of its regulations against the Protestants was another source of bitter strife.

Battle of Pavia — 1525.

The title of Emperor of Germany was elective and not hereditary. On the death of Maximilian numerous candidates appeared, Francis I of France and Charles I of Spain being the leading ones. Henry VIII of England had promised his influence to Francis. Charles was elected and the French king believed Henry had played him false. Soon after a meeting was arranged between Henry and Charles, in which the emperor skillfully played upon Henry's dreams of enforcing his vague claims to the throne of France, and an alliance was made in 1522. The war that followed was wholly to the advantage of Spain, and Henry, convinced that he had been outwitted by his cleverer nephew, opened secret negotiations with Francis and lent him some aid. Previous to this Francis had insulted and reduced to beggary the Duke of Bourbon, Constable of France, who went over to the side of the emperor.

At the battle of Pavia, Bourbon greatly distinguished himself, won a great victory for Charles, and made prisoner his former ungrateful master. This victory, however, convinced Henry that he was again on the wrong side, and he offered to join with Charles in an invasion of France, pledging a large army at his own expense. If the war was successful Henry was to be crowned king of France and to cede to the emperor numerous provinces thereof, and in addition give him the hand of his daughter Mary. The people of England rose in opposition to a tax levied to raise the funds necessary for this invasion. Charles, with little regard for his uncle, made a treaty with Francis which the French king did not hesitate to repudiate once he was safe at home, urging that his assent was given under compulsion. The Spanish army then, under the leadership of Bourbon, attacked Rome and captured the city, 1527, with the loss of their leader. The pope was now a prisoner in the hands of Charles, and never, even from the barbarians, did Rome suffer more than at the hands of her Spanish captors.

Voyage of Magellan.

"Ferdinand Magellan had been in the service of the King of Portugal; but an application he had made for an increase of half a ducat a month in his stipend having been refused, he passed into the service of the King of Spain. Magellan persuaded the Spanish government that the Spice Islands could be reached by sailing to the west, the Portuguese having previously reached them by sailing to the east, and, if this were accomplished, Spain would have as good a title to them, under the bull of Alexander VI, as Portugal. Five ships, carrying 237 men, were accordingly equipped, and on August 10, 1519, Magellan sailed from Seville. He struck boldly for the south-west, not crossing the trough of the Atlantic, as Columbus had done, but passing down the length of it, his aim being to find some cleft or passage in the American continent through which he might sail into the Great South Sea. His perseverance and resolution were at last rewarded by the discovery of the strait named by him San Vittoria, in affectionate honor of his ship, but which, with a worthy sentiment, other sailors soon changed to 'the Strait of Magellan.'

"And now the great sailor having burst through the barrier of the American continent, steered for the northwest, attempting to regain the equator. For three months and twenty days he sailed on the Pacific, and never saw inhabited land. He was compelled by famine to strip off the pieces of skin and leather wherewith his rigging was here and there bound, to soak them in the sea and then soften them with warm water, so as to make a wretched food; to eat the sweepings of the ship and other loathesome matter; to drink water that had become putrid by keeping; and yet he resolutely held on his course, though his men were dying daily. As is quaintly observed, 'their gums grew over their teeth, and so they could not eat.' He estimated that he sailed over this unfathomable sea not less than 12,000 miles.

"In the whole history of human undertakings there is nothing that exceeds, if indeed there is anything that equals, this voyage of Magellan's. That of Columbus dwindles away in comparison. It is a display of superhuman perseverance — a display of resolution not to be diverted from its purpose by any motive or any suffering, but inflexibly persisting to its end. Well might his despairing sailors come to the conclusion that they had entered on a trackless waste of waters, endless before them, and hopeless in a return. He comforted himself when he considered that in the eclipses of the moon the shadow cast of the earth is round; and as is the shadow, such, in like manner, is the substance. It was a stout heart — a heart of triple brass — which could thus, against such authority, extract unyielding faith from a shadow.

"This unparalleled resolution met its reward at last. Magellan reached a group of islands north of the equator — the Ladrones. In a few days more he became aware that his labors had been successful; he met with adventurers from Sumatra. At an island called Zebu, or Mutan, he was killed, either, as has been variously related, in a mutiny of his men, or — as they declared — in a conflict with the savages, or insidiously by poison. Through treason and revenge it is not unlikely that he fell, for he was a stern man; no one but a very stern man could have accomplished so daring a deed. Hardly was he gone when his crew learned that they were actually in the vicinity of the Moluccas, and that the object of their voyage was accomplished. On the morning of November 8, 1521. having been at sea two years and three months, as the sun was rising they entered Tidore, the chief port of the Spice Islands. The King of Tidore swore upon the Koran alliance to the King of Spain.

"And now they prepared to bring the news of their success back to Spain. Magellan's lieutenant, Sebastian d'Elcano, directed his course for the Cape of Good Hope, again encountering the most fearful hardships. Out of his slender crew he lost twenty-one men. He doubled the Cape at last; and on September 7, 1522, in the port of St. Lucar, near Seville, under his orders, the good ship San Vittoria came safely to an anchor. She had accomplished the greatest achievement in the history of the human race. She had circumnavigated the earth.

"Magellan thus lost his life in his enterprise, and yet he made an enviable exchange. Doubly immortal, and thrice happy! for he impressed his name indelibly on the earth and sky, on the strait that connects the two great oceans, and on those clouds of starry worlds seen in the southern heavens. He also imposed a designation on the largest portion (Pacific Ocean) of the surface of the globe."*

A dispute arose at once between the Spanish and the Portuguese over their new possessions. After a time a congress was called representing the best geographers

---

* Draper's "Intellectual Development of Europe."

and scientists of the two nations. No actual agreement was reached, but it was tacitly understood that the Moluccas, or Spice Islands, and the Philippine Islands should belong to Spain, and the greater part of Brazil fell to Portugal. The congress had another and more important influence in diffusing better ideas of the geography of the world.

Abdication of Charles V.

"On the 25th day of October, 1555, the estates of the Netherlands were assembled in the great hall of the palace at Brussels. They had been summoned to be witnesses and the guarantees of the abdication which Charles V had long been resolved upon and which he was that day to execute. None knew better than he the influence of great spectacles upon the masses of mankind. Plain even to shabbiness in his own costume and usually attired in black, no one ever understood better how to arrange such exhibitions in a striking and artistic style. The closing scene of his long and energetic reign he had now arranged with profound study. The termination of his own career and the opening of his beloved Phillip's were to be dramatized in a manner worthy of the august character of the actors and the importance of the great stage where they played their parts.

At the western end a spacious platform or stage with six or seven steps had been constructed, below which was the range of benches for the deputies of the seventeen provinces. Upon the stage itself there were rows of seats covered with tapestry upon the right hand and upon the left. These were for the Knights of the Order and the guests of high distinction. In the rear were other benches for the members of the three great councils. In the center of the stage was a splendid canopy beneath which were placed three gilded arm chairs. All the seats upon the platform were vacant, but the benches below were already filled. Grave magistrates in chain and gown, executive officers in the splendid civic uniforms for which the Netherlands were celebrated already filled every seat within the space allotted. As the clock struck three the hero of the scene appeared, leaning on the shoulder of William of Orange, and immediately followed by Phillip II accompanied by a glittering throng of warriors, counselors, governors, and Knights of the Fleece. The curtain was about to fall forever upon the mightiest emperor since Charlemagne, and where the opening scene of the long and tremendous tragedy of Philip's reign was to be simultaneously enacted.

It is worth our while to examine minutely the appearance of the two principal characters. Charles V was then fifty-five years and eight months old, but he was already decrepit with premature old age. He was about middle height, had been athletic and well proportioned, broad in the shoulders, deep in the chest, thin in the flank, very muscular; he had been able to match himself with all competitors in the tourney and the ring, and he vanquished the bull with his own hand in the favorite national amusement of Spain. He had been able in the field to do the duty of captain and soldier, to endure fatigue and exposure, and every privation except fasting. Now corpulent in hands, knees and legs, he supported himself with difficulty upon a crutch with the aid of an attendant's shoulder. In face he had always been extremely ugly, and time had certainly not improved his physiognomy. His hair, once of a light color, was now white with age, close clipped and bristling. His beard was gray, coarse and shaggy. His forehead, spacious and commanding; his eye dark blue, with an expression both majestic and benignant. The lower part of his face was famous for its deformity. The under lip, a Burgundian inheritance, as faithfully transmitted as the duchy and the country, was heavy and hanging; the lower jaw protruding so far beyond the upper that it was impossible for him to bring together the few fragments of teeth which still remained, or to speak a whole sentence in an intelligible voice. So much for the father! The son, Phillip II, was a small, meager man, much below the middle height, with thin legs and narrow chest, and the shrinking, timid air of a habitual invalid. His body was but a human cage, which, however brief and narrow, held a soul at whose flight the immeasurable expanse of heaven was too contracted. In face, he was the living image of his father. Such was the personal appearance of the man who was about to receive into a single hand the destinies of the whole world, whose single will was for the future to shape the fortunes of every individual then present, of many millions more in Europe, America, and to the ends of the earth, and of countless millions yet unborn."*

Synopsis of History Contemporary with this Reign.

A. D.

1516. Las Casas made Protector of the Indians by Ximenes.
1517. Dispute between Tetzel the Peddler and Luther, concerning the sale of indulgences. Balboa condemned to death by a jealous governor. Cordova discovers Yucatan.
1519. Cortez lands in Mexico. Magellan sails. Maximilian I dies, Charles V elected Emperor of Germany.
1520. Cortez captures City of Mexico. Montezuma dies.
1521. Cortez completes the conquest of Mexico. Luther excommunicated. Turks capture Belgrade.

---

* Motley's "Rise of the Dutch Republic."

A. D.
- 1522. Turks capture Island of Rhodes from the Knights of St. John.
- 1524. Chevalier Bayard killed at battle of Rebec.
- 1525. Battle of Pavia. Francis I of France defeated and captured by Charles.
- 1526. Treaty of Madrid. Francis I released.
- 1529. League formed by Protestant princes of Germany. Turks under Solyman the Magnificent besiege Vienna. Fall of Cardinal Woolsey from power.
- 1532. Pizarro conquers Peru.
- 1533. Catherine of Aragon divorced. Henry VIII renounces papal supremacy. Marries Anne Boleyn. Queen Elizabeth born.
- 1536. Anne Boleyn executed. Henry VIII marries Jane Seymour the next day.
- 1537. Jane Seymour dies. Edward VI born.
- 1539. De Soto discovers Florida.
- 1540. Henry marries and divorces Anne of Cleves. Marries Catherine Howard. Printing press established in Mexico. The Society of Jesuits founded.
- 1541. Pizarro assassinated.
- 1542. Catherine Howard executed. De Soto dies and is buried in the Mississippi. Calvin organizes his religious states in Geneva. Mary Stuart, Queen of Scots, born. (d. 1587.)
- 1543. Henry VIII marries Catherine Parr. Copernicus, a Prussian astronomer, publishes his works proving the sun the centre of the solar system.
- 1547. Henry VIII dies, his son, Edward VI, accedes to the throne. Francis I of France dies. Henry II accedes to the throne. Ivan the Terrible rises to supreme power in Russia and is the first to be called Czar.

THE ASCENDANCY OF AMERICA. 85

A. D.

1552. Raleigh born. (d. 1618.) Spenser born. (d. 1599.)
1553. Edward VI dies. Wills the crown to Lady Jane Grey, great-granddaughter of Henry VII. Mary and Elizabeth had each been declared illegitimate by separate act of Parliament. The country supports Mary. She accedes to the throne.
1554. Mary marries Philip II of France. Lady Jane Grey executed.
1555. Rogers, Latimer and Ridley, English Bishops, burned at the stake.
1556. Cranmer burned. By abdication of Charles V, Philip II becomes King of Spain, and Ferdinand I Emperor of Germany.

PHILIP II. — 1556-1598.

Son of Charles V. and Isabella of Portugal. In 1554 he married his cousin, Mary queen of England, daughter of Henry VIII and Catherine of Aragon, and acceded to the throne in 1556 upon the abdication of his father.

Spain under his father Charles had been but one of the kingdoms of a large empire, and it saw but little of its monarch; under Philip everything was centralized in Spain. He was cold, reserved, ambitious, and intensely bigoted, possessing all the ambition of his father and but a part of his ability. The growth of Protestantism was a source of great trouble to him, and the long, bitter wars in which it involved him in his endeavors to suppress it exhausted his kingdom and left him but the form, and not the substance, of power to transmit to his son.

The great events of his reign were the wars of the Netherlands for independence, the attempted invasion of England, the conquest of Portugal, the defeat of Turks at Lepanto, wars with France and Italy, and colonization of New World.

His marriage with Mary gave him no heir, and was a bitter disappointment to him. A son would have united all the English possessions to those of Spain and made its ruler the most powerful in the world. After the death of Mary he proposed marriage to Elizabeth, which she, with characteristic shrewdness, appears to have taken under consideration until such time as she was able, with safety, to decline it.

"Philip has been accused of indolence. As far as the body was concerned, such an accusation was well founded. Even when young he had no fondness for the robust and chivalrous sports of the age. He never, like his father, conducted military expeditions in person, but it would be a great mistake to charge him with sluggishness of mind. He was content to toil for hours and long into the night at his solitary labors. No expression of weariness or of impatience was known to escape him. He received petitioners graciously and listened to all they had to say with patience, for that was his virtue; but his countenance was exceedingly grave, and there was a reserve in his deportment which made the boldest feel ill at ease in his presence. It was natural that men of even the highest rank should be overawed in the presence of a monarch who held the destinies of so many millions in his hands, and who surrounded himself with the veil of mystery which the most cunning politician could not penetrate. He kept his spies at the principal European courts, who so furnished him with intelligence that he was as well acquainted with what was passing in England and in France as if he had resided on the spot. His mind was filled with suspicions, and he waited until time had proved their truth, treating the object of them with particular favor until the hour of vengeance arrived. His own historian says, 'His dagger followed close upon his smile.' It was a defect in his administration that his love of power and his distrust of others made him desire to do everything himself. As he was slow in making up his own mind, and seldom acted without first ascertaining the opinions of his counsel, we well understand the consequences of such delay. Even when a decision did come, it often came too late to be of service, for the circumstances which led to it had wholly changed."*

"Philip II was absolute master of an empire so superior to the other states of the world in extent, in resources, and especially in military and naval forces, as to make the project of enlarging that empire into a universal monarchy seem a perfectly feasible scheme. Since the downfall of the Roman empire no such preponderating power had existed in the world. When Philip II reigned, France had become so miserably weak through her civil wars that he had nothing to dread from her. In Germany, Italy, and Poland he had zealous friends and divided enemies. Against the Turks he had gained glorious and great successes. He could look around the continent of Europe without discerning a single antagonist of whom he could stand in awe. Beside the Spanish crown Philip succeeded to the kingdom of Naples and Sicily, the Duchy of Milan, Franche-compte, and the Netherlands; in Africa he possessed Tunis, Oran, the Cape Verde and the Canary Islands; in Asia the Philippine, the Sunda, and part of the Molucca Islands. He was lord of the most splendid portion of the new world; the empires of Peru and Mexico, New Spain and Chili, with their abundant mines of the precious metals; and Hispaniola and Cuba were provinces of the sovereign of Spain. Philip had also the advantage of finding himself at the head of a large standing army in a perfect state of discipline and equipment, in an age when except some few insignificant corps, standing armies were unknown in Christendom. The renown of the Spanish troops was justly high, and

---

* Motley's "Rise of the Dutch Republic."

the infantry in particular was considered the best in the world." *

"The impetuous chivalry of France, the serried phalanx of Switzerland, were each found wanting when brought face to face with the Spanish infantry."†

Agriculture.

This, under the Moors, had reached such a high state of perfection, now rapidly declined, and suffered greatly by reason of short-sighted legislation. "A company of sheep-farmers (Mesta) contrived to obtain the rights of pasture over the whole of Spain under certain limitations. They claimed over any farm a right of way 240 feet wide at certain seasons for their flocks to and from the uplands in winter pasture. Lands once reduced to pasture could never afterward be plowed without the sanction of this powerful body and the payment of a fine fixed by themselves. The sheep consumed the Spaniards and not the Spaniards the sheep. It was computed that 200,000 acres of good, arable land had gone out of cultivation, and as much more was left in a state of nature by the Monks, who were its owners." ‡

Trade and Industry.

These suffered equally with agriculture. Spain's colonies were founded not to increase trade but to wring the last possible ounce of gold from them, no matter at what expense to native life. Charles was shrewd enough to see the advantage of an extensive commerce, but his successors were blind to an opportunity which, had it been cultivated, would have been worth more to them than all the treasure she secured. "From 1701 to 1809 her colonies on the mainland yielded her in gold and

---

* Creasey's "Fifteen Decisive Battles of the World."
† Macaulay's "Spain Under Philip II."
‡ Yeates' "Growth and Vicissitudes of Commerce."

silver alone 2,515,660,000 piasters," or about as many dollars.

"A short-sighted and slavish policy, however, led to ruin. The natives were systematically crushed. Mulattos and Mestizos sprung of Spanish parentage were excluded from posts of trust. Only those of the Spanish sent out by council could exercise authority, and these were not allowed, while in office, to settle in the country. Creoles of white parentage, but born and brought up in the country, could not administer any department of government. Spain kept all the traffic to herself and jealously excluded foreigners from her ports.

"Seville first, and afterward Cadiz, were the harbors to which the royal monoply of colonial trade was confined." *

Home manufactures were stagnant. The whirr of 10,000 looms might once have been heard in many of the Moorish cities. Now there were not so many in the whole peninsula. Merino wool was highly valued throughout Europe, but Spain imported the cloth woven from the fleece which she had supplied.

In spite of the enormous treasures from the new field pouring into the coffers of Spain the country was continually running in debt.

Revolt of the Netherlands.

Spanish soldiers were quartered in the Netherlands, under the Duke of Alva, and their presence was a constant source of irritation to the people. A rebellion arose in 1566, which was mercilessly crushed. The Inquisition was introduced, and within a few months after Alva's arrival 2,000 people had felt its power. Even the Pope besought Philip to be more lenient. The country was overawed by these stern measures, and when William of Orange came to their help with troops

---

* Yeates' "Growth and Vicissitudes of Commerce."

from Germany there were few bold enough to take sides with him.

England in an industrial way was the gainer by these troubles, as large numbers of skilled artisans fled to that country for safety, and established in England the industries for which Holland had long been famous.

Alva soon proceeded to impose taxes upon the Dutch for the support of his soldiers. This was the last straw. The seven northern provinces immediately arose in rebellion, 1572, and chose the Prince of Orange as their captain. They were secretly encouraged by Elizabeth, the King of France, and others, who were glad of an opportunity to annoy Philip. Under the leadership of the Prince of Orange substantial progress was made. Spain issued a proclamation offering a reward to anyone who would remove such an enemy of the king and church. After several attempts at assassination, one was at last successful, and closed the career of the great leader of the Netherlands, July 10, 1584.

In 1586, Elizabeth actively engaged in their assistance, sent the Duke of Leicester and Sir Philip Sidney with 5,000 soldiers. Leicester besieged Zutphen, and Sir Philip Sidney fell before its walls. Nothing came of the expedition, and in 1587 it was recalled.

In 1588 the Dutch lent material aid to England by blockading the Duke of Parma, so that he was unable to join the "Spanish Armada."

For eighty years, with but one considerable interruption, a desultory war was carried on with Spain, though their independence was recognized by England and France about 1581.

Philip had prepared an armada of 300 ships of war with which to crush the Netherlands once and forever. A pestilence seized the fleet when ready to sail, and of 15,000 troops on board more than half died in less than a month. The same fleet later as the "Spanish Armada" was no happier.

Antwerp.

"The siege of this prosperous and splendid city by the Duke of Parma was the great success of Philip's reign. The slaughter of 3,000 citizens in cold blood and the plunder to which the city was subjected for many days were his reward. He had the glory of destroying a harbor where a forest of masts was once to be seen and of causing grass to grow in the streets of the city, which had contributed to his revenues far more than any other in his wide dominion."*

Lepanto.

Turkish power in the east had assumed gigantic proportions, and their navy controlled the Mediterranean.

In 1571, a large fleet under the command of Don Juan of Spain, natural brother of Philip II, and the most skillful warrior of his time, aided by the Venetian and papal fleets, was sent against them. It fell in with the Turkish fleet off Lepanto on the coast of Greece, and gained one of the most decisive battles of the world. Even Constantinople was threatened, but Philip was jealous of his brother and the victory was not followed up.

The defeat of the Turks before Vienna in 1529 and at Lepanto occurred at the highest tide of Turkish power.

Don Juan afterwards took charge of the Spanish affairs in the Netherlands, and under his care they were rapidly improving, when he died so suddenly as to leave strong suspicions of having been poisoned.

---

*Yeates' "Growth and Vicissitudes of Commerce."

Invasion of England Planned.

Philip's ambitious plans for the marriage of Elizabeth having failed, he now determined to secure by force what he had been unable to effect by diplomacy.

"One nation only had been his active, his persevering, and his successful foe. England had encouraged his revolted subjects in Flanders and given them aid in men and money, without which they must have fallen. English ships had plundered his colonies; they had inflicted defeats on his squadrons; they had captured his cities and burned his arsenals on the very coasts of Spain; were she once subdued the Dutch must submit; France could not cope with him, the empire would not oppose him, and universal dominion seemed sure to be the result of the conquest of that malignant island."*

With the enormous resources at his hand he began to plan the invasion of England. A veteran army under the Duke of Parma was mobilized at Dunkirk, just across the channel, and only forty-five miles from Dover. He gathered the largest fleet that the world had ever seen; well equipped, with a high reputation, and a complement of over thirty thousand men.

"Escorted by an overpowering naval force, Parma and his army were to embark in their flotilla, cross the sea to England, where they were to be landed together with the troops which the Armada brought from the ports of Spain. The Armada set sail from Tagus the 29th of May, 1588, but near Corunna met with a tempest that drove it into the port with severe loss. The Armada sailed again from Corunna on the 12th of July. On the 20th of July it was discovered by the English scouting ships drawn up in the form of a crescent, which, from horn to horn, measured some seven miles.

"A match at bowls was being played, in which Drake and other high officers of the fleet were engaged. At

---
*Creasey's "Decisive Battles of the World."

this exciting information the captains began to hurry down to the water, and there was a shouting for the ship's boats, but Drake coolly checked his comrades and insisted that the match should be played out."*

Charles Kingsley, in "Westward Ho!" describes for us the men who were waiting to "singe the beard of the king of Spain:"

"See those five talking earnestly in the center of a ring, which longs to overhear, and yet is too respectful to approach close. These soft, long eyes and pointed chin we recognize already; they are Walter Raleigh's. The fair young man in the flame-colored doublet, whose arm is around Raleigh's neck, is Lord Sheffield; opposite them stands, by the side of Sir Richard Grenville, a man as stately even as he — Lord Sheffield's uncle, the Lord Charles Howard of Effingham, Lord High Admiral of England; next to him is his son-in-law, Sir Robert Southwell, Captain of the Elizabeth Jones; but who is that short, sturdy, plainly dressed man, who stands with legs a little apart and hands behind his back, looking up, with keen gray eyes, into the face of each speaker? His cap is in his hands, so you can see the bold head of crisp brown hair and the wrinkled forehead, as well as the high cheek-bones, the short square face, the broad temples, the thick lips, which are yet as firm as granite. A coarse, plebeian stamp of man; yet the whole figure and attitude are that of boundless determination, self-possession, energy; and when at last he speaks a few blunt words, all eyes are turned respectfully upon him,— for his name is Francis Drake.

"A burly, grizzled elder, in greasy, sea-stained garments, contrasting oddly with the huge gold chain about his neck, waddles up, as if he had been born and had lived ever since in a gale of wind at sea. The upper half

---

* Creasey's "Decisive Battles of the World."

of his sharp, dogged visage seems of brick-red leather, the lower of badger's fur; and he claps Drake on the back, and with broad Devon twang shouts, 'Be you a coming to drink your wine, Francis Drake, or be you not?—saving your presence, my Lord.' The Lord High Admiral only laughs, and bids Drake go and drink his wine; for John Hawkins, Admiral of the Port, is the patriarch of Plymouth seamen, if Drake be their hero, and says and does pretty much what he likes in any company on earth; not to mention that to-day's prospect of an Armageddon fight has shaken him altogether out of his usual crabbed reserve, and made him overflow with loquacious good humor, even to his rival Drake."

The Engagement.

"By nine o'clock on the thirty-first of July on the Cornish coasts the fleets had their first meeting. There were one hundred thirty-six sails of the Spaniards, of which ninety were large ships, and sixty-seven of the English. Their Captain-General (Medina Sidonia) sat on the deck of his great galleon, the St. Martin, surrounded by generals of infantry and colonels of cavaliers, who knew as little as he himself of naval matters. The English ships, on the other hand, swift and easily handled, could sail round and round those unwieldy galleons, hulks, and galleys rowed by fettered slave gangs. The superior seamanship of such experienced captains as Drake, Frobisher and Hawkins obtained the weather gauge at once, and cannonaded the enemy at intervals with considerable effect, easily escaping at will out of range of the Armada, which was incapable of bearing sail in pursuit, although provided with an armament which could sink all its enemies at close quarters. Their whole fleet did its utmost to offer general battle, but in vain. The English, following at the heels of the enemy, refused all such invitations and attacked only the rear guard.

"They (Spanish) had been out-manœuvred, out-sailed, and thoroughly maltreated by their antagonists, and unable to inflict a single blow in return.

"(Second day). Never since England was England had such a sight been seen as now revealed itself in those narrow straits between Dover and Calais. Along that low sandy shore, within the range of the Calais fortifications, one hundred thirty Spanish ships, the greater number of them the largest and most heavily armed in the world, lay face to face and scarcely out of cannon shot, with one hundred fifty English sloops and frigates, the strongest and swiftest that the island could furnish, and commanded by men whose exploits had rung through the world. Farther along the coast, invisible but known to be performing a most perilous and vital service, was a squadron of Dutch vessels of large size lining both the inner and outer edges of the sandbanks off the Flemish coast. These fleets of Holland blockaded every port, and longed to grapple with the Duke of Parma as soon as his fleets of gunboats should venture forth.

"(Last engagement). The battle lasted six hours — long, hot and fierce. The English still maintained the tactics which had proved so successful, and resolutely refused the fierce attempts of the Spaniards to lay themselves alongside. The well disciplined English mariners poured broadside after broadside against the towering ships of the Armada, which afforded so easy a mark, while the Spaniards on their part found it impossible, after wasting incredible quantities of powder and shot, to inflict any severe damage on their enemies. Throughout the action not an English ship was destroyed and not a hundred men were killed. There was scarcely a ship in the Armada that did not suffer severely. Sixteen of their best ships had been sacrificed and from four to five thousand soldiers killed. The Captain-General was a bad sailor but a brave soldier. Crippled as he was he would still have faced the enemy, but the winds and currents were fast driving him on a lee shore and the pilots, one and all, assured him it would be inevitable destruction to remain. But blackness of night seemed suddenly to descend. Damaged, leaking, without pilots, without a captain-commander the great fleet entered that fierce storm and were whirled along the iron crags of Norway and between the savage rocks of Faroe and the Hebrides. Disaster after disaster marked their perilous track; gale after gale swept them hither and thither; the coasts of Norway, Scotland and Ireland were strewn with the wrecks of that famous fleet which claimed the dominion of the sea. Thirty-nine vessels were driven upon the Irish coast, where nearly every soul on board perished, where the few who escaped to the shores were either butchered in cold blood or sent coupled, in halters, from village to village, in order to be shipped to England. Of one hundred thirty-four vessels which sailed from Corunna in July but fifty-three, great and small, made their escape to Spain, and these were so damaged as to be utterly worthless. The 'Invincible Armada' had not only been vanquished, but annihilated."*

The English Admiral, Drake, says that on their return "They were not ashamed to publish in sundry languages, in print, the great victory which they pretended to have obtained against this realm, and spread the same in a most false sort over all parts of France, Italy, and elsewhere."

Navarre.

Henry, king of Navarre, upon the assassination of Henry III of France in 1589, acceded to the French

---

* Motley's "Rise of Dutch Republic."

throne as Henry IV. France was torn asunder by civil strife, and Henry the Huguenot did not have the hearty support of the Catholic faction. Philip would not allow a Protestant king to accede to the throne of his chief rival power, and so, aided with money and men, a Catholic league formed in opposition to Henry. The forces met for the decisive contest March 14th, 1590.

"The king had fastened a great white plume to his helmet and had adorned his horse's head with another equally conspicuous. He now exclaimed to those about him, 'Comrades, God is for us; these are His enemies and ours; if you lose sight of your standards rally to my white plume; you will find it on the road to victory and to honor.' The king plunged into the thickest of the fight two horses' length ahead of his companions. That moment he forgot he was king of France and general-in-chief, both in one, and fought as if he were a private soldier. The enemies outnumbered the knights of the king's squadron more than as two to one. No wonder that some of the latter flinched and actually turned back, especially when the standard-bearer of the king, receiving a deadly wound in the face, lost control of his horse and went riding aimlessly about the field, still grasping the banner in grim despair. But the greater number emulated the courage of their leader and the white plume kept them in the road to victory and to honor. But, although fiercely contested, the conflict was not long. The troopers of Mayenne wavered and finally fled. Henry of Navarre emerged from the confusion safe and sound, covered with dust and blood not his own. The battle had been a short one. 'Between ten and eleven o'clock the first attack was made, and in less than an hour the army of the League was routed." *

---

* Baird's "Huguenots and Henry of Navarre."

This was the death-blow of the League and the turning-point in the career of Henry IV. and when he adjured Protestantism in 1593 he received a fairly cordial support of all the discordant elements of his kingdom. By the Edict of Nantes, which he issued in 1598, provision was made for the re-establishment of Catholic worship wherever it had been banished within thirty years, and religious toleration was granted to the Protestants throughout the French dominions. He was now fairly seated on the throne, and Philip experienced not only the mortification of the defeat but saw with fear the development of a rival power that was to cause his successors unmeasurable trouble. Although Philip II. transmitted to his son Philip III. an empire which was apparently intact, it was only so in form and not in substance.

Synopsis of Events Contemporary with this Period.

1558. The French recover Calais. Mary dies and Elizabeth accedes to the throne.
1559. Papal Index Expurgatorius names the books that must not be read.
1561. Francis Bacon, author of "Novum Organum" born. (d. 1626).
1562. Religious war breaks out in France; Coligny, Protestant leader. Sir John Hawkins introduces slavery into the West Indies.
1564. Shakespeare born. (d. 1616.) Galileo born. (d. 1642.)
1565. Slaughter of the French Huguenot settlement in Florida by the Spaniards, and the founding of St. Augustin. Famous defense of Malta by Knights of St. John from attacks of the Turks.
1566. The Netherlands revolt against Spanish rule.
1567. Duke Alva arrives in the Netherlands. French religious war. Mary Stuart deposed. Her son, James VI, of Scotland, accedes to the throne.

THE ASCENDENCY OF AMERICA. 99

1568. Inquisition condemns all the inhabitants of the Netherlands to death.
1571. Don John of Austria aided by Spanish, Venetian and papal squadrons, defeats the Turks in the famous naval battle of Lepanto. Kepler, German astronomer, discoverer of "Kepler's Laws," born. (d. 1630.)
1572. Massacre of Protestants in France on St. Bartholomew's Day. Marriage of Henry of Navarre and Margaret of Valois.
1577. Drake circumnavigates the globe.
1580. Philip II. of Spain conquers Portugal.
1583. Adoption of the Gregorian Calendar.
1584. Prince of Orange assassinated.
1585. Raleigh attempts to plant colonies in the new world. Richelieu born. (d. 1642.)
1587. Mary Stuart executed. Henry of Navarre meets with some success against the Catholic League.
1588. Defeat of Spanish Armada.
1589. Catherine de Medici dies. Henry III. of France last of the Valois, assassinated. Henry IV. of Navarre, first of the Bourbon kings of France, accedes to the throne.
1590. Henry IV. defeats the League in the battle of Ivry.
1594. Henry IV., having adjured Protestantism and solidified the factions of France, ends the civil war that had lasted forty years, and accedes to the throne.
1596. The Turks defeat the Bohemians and Hungarians with great slaughter on the plain of Cerestes. English and Dutch capture Cadiz. Descartes, French metaphysician, born. (d. 1650.)
1598. Navarre, by Edict of Nantes, grants religious toleration in France. Philip II. of Spain dies leaving a ruined navy and an exhausted kingdom.

CHAPTER III.

DECLINE OF SPANISH POWER.

Though Philip II. had suffered some severe defeats, his power was by no means broken, and he left his son an empire magnificent in its extent. Its territory on the American continent alone equaled in area twice that of the inhabitable part of Europe.

Philip III.—1598-1621.

Philip III., the son of Philip II. by his fourth wife Anne of Austria, was born 1578, succeeded his father to the throne of Spain in 1598, and died 1621. He inherited all the bigotry and ambition of his father with none of his ability.

The Moors had been driven into rebellion by tyrannical edicts which they could not possibly obey, and now the final expulsion of all the race was ordered. They were given three days' time in which to comply, and any remaining after that limit were to be put to death together with any Christians who afforded them relief. Agriculture and industry by this act received blows from which they never recovered in Spain. Spain has never since brought agriculture to the high state in which the Moors left it.

The Spanish Moors Persecuted into Rebellion.

"The constancy with which the Moors adhered to the faith of their fathers gave great scandal to the old Christians, especially to the clergy. A commission was appointed to examine into the matter. Among its members we find the Duke of Alva; at its head, Espinoso, the favorite minister of Philip. After due deliberation the Junta came to the decision that the only remedy for the present evil was to lay the axe at the root of it, to cut off those associations which connected the Moors with their earlier history and which were so many obstacles in the way of their present conversion. They should be interdicted from speaking or writing Arabic, and were to use only Castilian. Their family names were to be exchanged for Spanish ones. All written instruments and legal documents were void unless written in Castilian. Three years' time was allowed to change the entire language of the people. They were required to change their national dress for that of the Spaniards; the women to go abroad with their faces unveiled, a scandalous thing among Mohammedans. Their weddings were to be conducted in public after Christian forms. These several provisions were to be enforced by penalties of the sternest kind. The public crier from an elevated place read in the Arabic language the royal ordinance. Some of the weaker sort gave way to piteous and pained exclamations, wringing their hands in an agony of grief; others of sterner temper broke forth into menaces and fierce invections accompanied with the most fierce gesticulations; others listened with that dogged and determined air which showed that the mood was not less dangerous that it was silent. They had only to choose between implicit obedience and open rebellion. It was not strange that they chose the latter."

Netherlands.

It was during Philip III.'s reign that Spain lost all claim to the richest of her provinces, the seven northern states of the Netherlands, the scene of so much bloodshed and the source of such a fatal drain on her treasury. These provinces had been recognized as independent during the reign of Philip II. by all nations except Spain, and now, after about sixty years' war, Spain so far recognized them by the treaty of Antwerp as to conclude a ten years' truce.

The soil of the Netherlands is made up wholly of varying deposits from fresh and salt water as the battle between land and sea surged back and forth. Nearly all of the Netherlands to-day is too low for natural drainage, and a large part of it is from 16 to 18 feet below sea level. It is protected from the ocean by numerous embankments, called dikes, some of them 60 feet high. On the tops of the dikes run the roads and canals which empty into the rivers. Along the banks are numerous windmills, which pump the water from the ditches to the canals. Many of the canals are navigable.

The Netherlands, to which Charles V. acceded, comprised the seventeen provinces made up of the four duchies of Brabant, Limbourg, Luxemburg and Guelderland, the seven counties of Artois, Nainault, Flanders, Namur, Zutphen, Holland, Zealand, the five lordships of Friesland, Mechlin, Utrecht, Overyssel and Groningen, and the margraviate of Antwerp. The four provinces on the French border, where French was spoken, were called Walloon. They were merely a loose confederation without any supreme authority. Each province was independent, governed by its own laws and constitution.

It was during the time of Philip II. that the Seven Northern Provinces, Holland, Zealand, Utrecht, Guelderland, Overyssel, Groningen and Friesland, revolted, formed a republic, and chose William of Nassau, Prince of Orange, as their leader, with the title of stadtholder.

It was during the reign of Philip III. that the famous Thirty Years' War broke out. It began May, 1618, by the Protestant nobles of Bohemia (then a province of Germany, now a part of Austria) rebelling against Ferdinand, Archduke of Austria, who was elected Emperor of Germany 1619. The Netherlands was now the scene of a bitter quarrel between the Lutherans under John of Barneveldt and the Calvinists, under Maurice, and the ten years' truce expiring, the time seemed ripe to Philip when he could take advantage of this and regain what Spain had ever refused to acknowledge as wholly lost. The temper of his people also compelled him to take the part of Catholicism against the revolting Protestants. "The time had come for securing her road to the Netherlands, as well as for taking her old stand as the champion of Catholicism. Spinola, the Spanish general in the low countries, was ordered to march to the aid of the Emperor, and the famous Spanish battalions were soon moving up the Rhine. Their march turned the local struggle in Bohemia into a European war."*

Philip died about 1621, before the whole effect of his joining with the Emperor could be felt.

"The affairs of Spain were in a deplorable condition, with seventy per cent. of her domestic trade and ninety per cent. of her foreign trade in the hands of aliens. Philip III. was insane enough to close Spanish harbors and deliberately put an end to commerce, thus completing the ruin which his father had failed to effect.

More gold and silver had been coming into Spain in one generation than had been accumulated in all the previous ages of history, and yet the country became burdened with debt." †

Synopsis of Events Contemporary with this Period.
1599. Oliver Cromwell born. (d. 1658.)
1600. Publication of Shakespeare's "Henry IV.;"

---
* Green's "History of the English People."
† Yeates' "Commerce."

"Henry V.;" "Much Ado About Nothing;" "Merchant of Venice," and "Midsummer Night's Dream." Bruno burned at the stake for having written heretical books.

1603. Death of Elizabeth, last of the Tudors. Accession of James VI. of Scotland, James I. of England, the first of the Stuart kings. The French found colonies in Nova Scotia.

1605. Conspiracy of Catesby and Guido Fawkes to blow up the English parliament, known as "The Gunpowder Plot."

1607. The English found the first settlement at Jamestown, Virginia. Milton born. (d. 1674.)

1609. Discovery of the Hudson river by Henry Hudson, in the employ of the Dutch. Publication of the Catholic Douay Bible. Final expulsion of the Moors from Spain. Galileo invents the telescope and discovers Jupiter's moons, thus proving the Copernican theory.

1610. Henry of Navarre, king of France, assassinated by Ravaillac. Louis XIII. accedes under the regency of Marie de Medici.

1611. Montreal founded by Champlain. Charles IX. of Sweden, dies. Gustavus Adolphus succeeds to the throne. Publication of King James' Bible (Authorized version). Birth of Turenne, one of the ablest marshals of France. (d. 1675.)

1613. English destroy French colony at Port Royal in Nova Scotia. Michael Romanoff accedes to the Russian throne, the first of the reigning dynasty.

1614. The last States General (national convention) of France held prior to the Revolution. Raleigh's "History of the World" published.

1615. The first known weekly newspaper regularly published at Frankfort-on-the-Main.

1616. War begun between Sweden and Poland. Cervantes, Spanish dramatist and author of "Don Quixote" dies.

1618. The Protestants of Bohemia (then a province of Germany, now a province of Austria-Hungary), revolt and begin the Thirty Years' War. As a result, eventually, all the Protestant and Catholic powers of Europe were arrayed against each other. "This, which had been a civil war at the first, did not continue such for long, or rather, it united all the dreadfulness of a civil war and a foreign. It was not long before the hosts which trampled the German soil had in large part ceased to be German, every region of Europe sending its children, and, as it would seem, of those whom it must have been gladdest to be rid of."

"The bitterest irony of all was that this war, which claimed at the outset to be waged for the highest religious objects, for the glory of God, and for the highest interests of His church, should be signalized by a more shameless treading under foot of all laws, human and divine, disgraced by worse and wickeder outrages against God, and against man, the image of God, than probably any war which modern Christendom has seen."* Three-quarters of the population of many of the German states were killed or driven abroad, and in more than a century certain provinces had not regained their former prosperity. Gustavus Adolphus of Sweden, during his life, was the chief leader of the Protestant officers. Tilly and Wallenstein were the best leaders of the Imperial officers. Wallenstein was an able general, but utterly unscrupulous, and was plotting the overthrow of his own party when assassinated.

1619. Negro slavery introduced into Virginia.

---
* R. C. Trench. "Gustavus Adolphus in Germany."

1620. Puritans land at Plymouth. Bacon's "Novum Organum" published
1621. First Thanksgiving Day observed in New England.

Philip IV.—1621-1665.

Son of Philip III. and Margaret of Austria, born 1605 married Isabella of France 1615, succeeded to the throne on the death of his father in 1621.

The ten years' truce with the Seven Northern Provinces of the Netherlands having now expired, and the Lutherans and Calvinists being engaged in a quarrel there, Philip thought this a good opportunity to recover his lost dominion. At first he met with some success in his land operations, but the Dutch had been building up a steady trade with the East Indies and Brazil, and, since the defeat of the Spanish Armada, had risen to be the most powerful nation on the sea, and in 1628 captured his "silver fleet" with about $5,000,000 in pure silver. Under Admiral Van Tromp they won two crushing naval victories in 1639, and Spain, thoroughly exhausted, made her final peace and recognized their independence in 1648, eighty years after William of Nassau, Prince of Orange, had issued his call to the Seven Northern Provinces to take up arms in defense of their liberties. Richelieu, that great statesman of France, coming into power in 1624, brought one of the greatest intellects of any age to bear against them. The Spanish diplomatists were no match for the astute Frenchman, and the French under "The Great Conde" almost totally destroyed their army at Rocroi in 1643, and shattered the reputation of the "Terrible Spanish Infantry." The treaty of Westphalia in 1648 put an end to the Thirty Years' War, left Spain without an ally, and France free to give her undivided attention.

Mazarin, the minister of France who succeeded upon

the death of Richelieu in 1642, made peace with Cromwell, and, by agreeing to turn over Dunkirk to him, secured 5,000 "Ironsides" who were perhaps the best soldiers of Europe, and with this assistance, Turenne, the great French general, was irresistible.

Portugal revolted in 1640 and ever after maintained her independence.

The treaty of the Pyrenees was concluded between France and Spain, 1659, at the expense of considerable territory to Spain, and the daughter of the Spanish king married Louis XIV. of France.

"From that moment, indeed, Spain sank into a strange decrepitude. Robbed of the chief source of her wealth by the independence of Holland, weakened at home by the revolt of Portugal, her infantry annihilated by Condé in his victory of Rocroi, her fleet ruined by the Dutch, her best blood drained away to the Indies, the energies of her people destroyed by the suppression of all liberty, civil or religious, her intellectual life crippled by the expulsion of the Moors, by financial oppression and by the folly of her colony system, the kingdom which under Philip II. had aimed at the empire of the world lay helpless and exhausted under Philip IV."*

Synopsis of Events Contemporary with this Period.

1622. "The Weekly Newes," first newspaper in England regularly published. Moliere, author, born. (d. 1673.)

1623. "The First Folio" edition of Shakespeare's plays published.

1624. England, Holland and Denmark combine with the Protestants of Germany. George Fox, founder of Quakerism, born. (d. 1690.) Richelieu's ministry (1624–1642) begins. He crushes the power of the nobles and the Huguenots, increases

---

*Green's "History of the English People."

the power of the throne, aids the Protestant German princes in the Thirty Years' War to defeat Austria, the ancient rival of France. "Of the Cardinal there remains nothing but the memory of his power and the great services he rendered his country. He had no conception of that noblest ambition, governing a free country, but he was one of the greatest, the most effective, and the boldest, as well as the most prudent servant France ever had."

1625. James I. dies. Charles I., his son, accedes to the throne. Trouble between the king and Parliament now begins. Wallenstein and his army now employed against the Protestants. French Huguenots revolt.

1627. England assists the Huguenots in their revolt. Richelieu besieges Rochelle. Bossuet, great pulpit orator, born. (d. 1704.)

1628. Duke of Buckingham assassinated. Harvey publishes his "Discovery of the Circulation of the Blood." Bunyan, author of "Pilgrim's Progress, born. (d. 1688.)

1629. Charles I. dissolves Parliament and arrests the speaker.

1630. "Day of the Dupes," when Richelieu wins over his opponents. Wallenstein dismissed from command of Imperial forces in Thirty Years' War.

1631. Tilly captures Madgeburg and is defeated at Leipzig by Gustavus Adolphus. Dryden born. (d. 1700.) Publication of the first weekly newspaper in France.

1632. Battle of Lech. Tilly defeated and killed in battle with Gustavus Adolphus. Wallenstein recalled to command forces of the League. Battle of Lutzen. Gustavus Adolphus killed, but Protestants are victorious.

THE ASCENDENCY OF AMERICA. 109

1634. Assassination of Wallenstein. Sweden defeated at Nordenlingen by the League. Levy of "ship-money" in England. Milton's "Comus" acted.
1636. Harvard College founded. Roger Williams banished and founds Providence.
1640. Portugal regains her independence. Peruvian bark introduced into use in Europe. Dissolution of "Long Parliament."
1642. Beginning of England's Civil War (1642–1646.) Battle of Edgehill. Richelieu dies. Sir Isaac Newton born. (d. 1727.)
1643. Louis XIII. dies. Succeeded by Anne of Austria as regent for Louis XIV. Accession of the Mazarin ministry. Condé (the Great) defeats the Spanish at the battle of Rocroi.
1645. Cromwell defeats the Royalists at Naseby.
1646. Charles surrenders to the Scottish army.
1648. Cromwell wins the battle of Preston. Termination of Thirty Years' War. Peace of Westphalia. Alsace ceded to France. Separation of Switzerland from the empire. Spain acknowledges the independence of the United Provinces. Election of John Casimir, king of Poland.
1649. Charles I. executed. The Commonwealth established. French war of the Fronde ends.
1650. Charles II. invades Scotland. Defeated at battle of Dunbar by Cromwell. Publication of Baxter's "Saints' Everlasting Rest." Publication of Jeremy Taylor's "Holy Living." Marlborough born. (d. 1722.)
1651. Charles II. invades England with a Scotch army. Cromwell defeats him at battle of Worcester.
1652. Condè, the Great (born 1621, died 1681), one of France's ablest generals of any age, and victor of Rocroi, goes over to Spain. End of the war of the Fronde. Naval war between English and

Dutch. At the close of the year Van Tromp, the Dutch admiral, sails the channel with a broom at his mast-head as a signal of his triumph. Dutch make their first settlement at the Cape of Good Hope.

1653. Cromwell dissolves the "Rump Parliament," and the Protectorate established. Publication of Isaac Walton's "Complete Angler." Mazarin returns to power in France.

1655. Alliance of England and Franc against Spain. English capture Jamaica.

1658. Dunkirk captured from the Spaniards and given up by the French to England. Cromwell is succeeded by his son Richard. Seizure of the Mogul throne of India.

1659. Treaty of the Pyrenees between France and Spain. Louis XIV. marries the Spanish infanta.

1660. English army under General Monk declares for Charles II. and seats him on the English throne. War between Austria and Turkey.

1662. Persecution of the Scottish Covenanters. Charles I. sells Dunkirk to the French.

1605. The "Five Mile Act" enforced against nonconformists. London visited by the plague. War between English and the Dutch. English fleet under the Duke of York and Prince Rupert won a partial victory over the Dutch under Opdan and Van Tromp.

Charles II. — 1665-1700.

Son of Philip IV. and Maria Anna of Austria. He was but four years old at the death of his father, and the government was administered by his mother, as regent, until 1680, when he succeeded to the throne.

He was the last of the Spanish House of Hapsburg, feeble in body, and even more poorly equipped in intellect. Under him Spain suffered great loss of territory, Louis XIV. of France laying claim to part of the Spanish Netherlands in behalf of his wife and making good the claim with an army of 50,000 men under the great marshal Turenne.

The population in Spain had shrunken from 40,000,000 under the most prosperous period of the Moors until now it contained no more than 6,000,000 people, and the finances were exhausted.

Charles II. had no male heir, and the question of succession to the throne was absorbing the attention of all the ambitious rulers of Europe. The problem "balance of power," of which we hear so much nowadays, was then a prominent one, and William III. of England was its strongest advocate. The right of succession was a most complicated one. By law and tradition, on the extinction of a male line the crown should have passed to the nearest female or her heir. Charles had two sisters; the elder, Maria Theresa, was the wife of Louis XIV., but she had renounced her claim to the throne. In consideration of this it had been agreed that she should be paid a dowry, but as the dowry had never been paid her husband repudiated the renunciation. The other sister, Margaret, had made no renunciation, but she was dead, and had left only a daughter as heir, Maria, who was the wife of the elector of Bavaria. When Charles I. resigned his imperial possessions to his brother Ferdinand it was agreed in a family compact that if either line became extinct the other should accede to its territorial possessions, and the Austrian branch of that House now prepared to put forward its claims.

As the end of the wretched king drew near, plots and counterplots among the sovereigns of the powers for the partition of his territory were made. He died 1700. leaving the crown by will to Philip of Anjou, the grandson of Louis XIV. of France, on the condition that the prince should renounce all claim to the throne of France. Spanish pride, even in death, would not allow him to consider for a moment the partition of his kingdom or the contingency of its becoming but a province of a more powerful empire.

His reign had been one of almost uninterrupted disaster, and the unfortunate and once powerful kingdom was on the very verge of a great collapse. It now sank to the lowest depth of wretchedness, and from such a condition has never fully recovered, but "so vast was the extent of its empire, so enormous the resource which remained to it, that under a vigorous ruler men believed its old power would at once return. To add such a dominion as this to the dominion either of Louis or of the emperor would be to undo at a blow the work of European independence which William had wrought." *

"The news of the secret treaties of partition between France and Germany stirred the Spaniards to deep anger. They cared little whether a French or an Austrian prince sat on the throne of Charles II., but their pride revolted against the dismemberment of the monarchy by the loss of its Italian dependencies. The nobles dreaded the loss of their vast estates in Italy and of the lucrative posts they held as governors there. Even the dying king shared the anger of his subjects."† It was evident that upon the death of Charles all Europe was likely to be plunged into war.

Synopsis of Events Contemporary with this Period.

1666. The great fire in London. Two tremendous naval battles between Dutch and English. Four days' naval fight between English fleet under General Monk and Prince Rupert and Dutch fleet under De Ruyter and Van Tromp, with vic-

---

* Green's "History of the English People."
† Green.

tory for the Dutch (June). Second engagement in July, with victory for the English.

1667. The victorious Dutch fleet sails up the Thames. Publication of Milton's "Paradise Lost."

1668. Alliance of England, Holland and Sweden against France. John Casimir, king of Poland, abdicates.

1670. In consideration of receiving an annual subsidy from the French king, Charles II. makes a treaty with Louis XIV. of France, betrays his alliance and agrees to profess himself a Catholic.

1672. Alliance of England and France against the Dutch. Prince of Orange recalled to power in Holland. Peter the Great, czar of Russia, born. (d. 1725.)

1674. Peace declared between English and the Dutch in New Netherlands (New York), which is ceded to the English. John Zobieski elected king of Poland. Isaac Watts born. (d. 1748.)

1678. Popish plot in England, Titus Oakes pretended informer. Publication of Bunyan's "Pilgrim's Progress."

1682. La Salle explores the whole length of the Mississippi river. Peter the Great accedes to throne of Russia.

1683. Turks invade Hungary and Austria and besiege Vienna, which is relieved by Sobieski, king of Poland. Philadelphia founded by William Penn.

1685. Death of Charles II. Accession of his brother, James II. Rebellion of the Duke of Monmouth; defeated at Sedgemoor. The "Bloody Assizes" of Judge Jeffreys. The revocation of the Edict of Nantes by Louis XIV. of France. Streets of London first lighted.

1687. Publication of Newton's "Principia."

1688. Flight of James II. Arrival in England of Prince of Orange.

1689. Crown settled on William and Mary. James II. arrives in Ireland, and war begins there.
1690. First congress of American colonies called to unite them for mutual protection against the savages. England, Holland, Spain, Savoy and emperor of Germany allied against Louis XIV. of France. French fleet defeats combined English and Dutch fleet off Beachy Head. Battle of Boyne in Ireland, and flight of James II. Issue of Locke's "Essay Concerning Human Understanding."
1692. Salem witchcraft in Massachusetts. Massacre of Glencoe in Scotland. France defeated in naval battle of La Hogue by English and Dutch fleets, and invasion of England prevented.
1693. William and Mary College founded in Virginia.
1694. The Bank of England founded. Voltaire born. (d. 1778.)
1696. Sobieski, king of Poland, dies, and crown is sold to Frederick Augustus, elector of Saxony.
1697. Peace of Ryswick. Prince Eugene defeats the Turks at Zenta. Charles XII. (The Madman of the North) accedes to the throne of Sweden. Peter the Great studies ship-building in Holland disguised as a common workman.
1699. Peace of Carlowitz between Turkey, Russia, Poland, Venice and the emperor, and the sultan loses nearly half of his European dominions.
1700. Charles XII. of Sweden begins his campaign against the Danes and Russians.

Philip V. 1700-1746.

Philip of Anjou, second son of Louis the dauphin, son of Louis XIV. (Le Grand) of France.

The Spanish House of Hapsburg ended in 1700 with

the death of Charles II., and the wars of the Spanish Succession now took place.

With Philip V. began the line of Spanish Bourbon kings, who have held it, with two interruptions, down to the present.

On the death of Charles II., the king of France acted with his characteristic energy. "Louis well knew that a general European war would follow if he accepted for his house the crown thus bequeathed. But he had been preparing for this crisis throughout his reign. He sent his grandson into Spain as King Philip V., of that country, addressing to him on his departure the memorable words, 'There are no longer any Pyrenees.'"*

"The empire which now received the grandson of Louis as its king, comprised, besides Spain itself, the strongest part of the Netherlands, Sardinia, Sicily, Naples, the principality of Milan and other possessions in Italy, the Philippines in Asia, and in the new world, besides California and Florida, the greater part of Central and South America.

"Philip was well received in Madrid, where he was crowned as King Philip V. in the beginning of 1701. The distant portions of his empire sent him their adhesion, and the House of Bourbon, either by its French or Spanish troops, now had occupation both of the kingdom of Francis I. (of France) and of the fairest and amplest portions of the empire of the great rival of Francis, Charles V. (Charles I. of Spain).

"Loud was the wrath of Austria, whose princes were the rival claimants of the Bourbons, for the empire of Spain. Deep was the indignation of William III. of England, which, though not so loud, was far more energetic. By his exertions a league against the House of Bourbon was formed between England, Holland and the Austrian empire, which was subsequently joined by

---

* Dyer's "History of Modern Europe."

the king of Portugal and Prussia (Prussia was recognized as an independent kingdom in 1701), the duke of Savoy and by Denmark. Indeed, the alarm throughout Europe was now general and urgent. It was evident that Louis aimed at consolidating France and the Spanish dominions into one preponderating empire. Whether the formal union of the two crowns was likely to take place speedily or not, it was evident that the resources of the whole Spanish monarchy were now virtually at the French king's disposal. Great peril seemed to menace the Empire, England, Holland, and the other independent powers. 'Spain had threatened the liberties of Europe in the end of the 16th century; France had all but overthrown them in the close of the 17th. How then could they make head against both, united under such a monarch as Louis XIV.?'"*

Revolts speedily broke out in Italy, and in 1702 a combined Dutch and English force landed near Cadiz and began an attack on that town. The death of William III. (1702) deprived the League of the services of its greatest leader. Scarcely had the combined forces landed, when quarrels broke out among the leaders, as to precedence; and after a few ineffectual attempts the expedition was abandoned, but on the way home they found the Spanish treasure fleet at Vigo Bay, and captured it after a brilliant attack and a gallant defense.

Some of the Spanish officers of Charles II. were not well satisfied with the Bourbon king, and the Admiral of Castile, offended by the loss of some office, went over to Portugal and used his influence to induce that country to join the League. This they did in 1703, and their action gave the League a valuable base of operation.

All the contestants to the throne in September, 1703, united on Charles, Archduke of Austria, son of the

---
* Dyer's "History of Modern Europe."

Emperor of Germany, and proclaimed him King of Spain under the title of Charles III. In March, 1704, he landed in Portugal with an English and Dutch army, intending to invade Spain from that side, but met with no success. An English fleet made an attack on Barcelona, but were beaten off. On their return they made up for their failure by capturing Gibraltar.

Gibraltar. (Arabic, Jabel-Tarik, i. e., Rock of Tarik.)

"The importance of this fortress, the key to the Mediterranean, was not then sufficiently esteemed, and its garrison had been neglected by the Spanish government. A party of English sailors, taking advantage of a "Saint's Day," in which the eastern portion of the fortress had been left unguarded, scaled the almost inaccessible precipice, while at the same time another party stormed the South Mole Head. The capture of this important place was the work of a few hours, and Rooke (British Admiral) took possession of it in the name of the king of England."*

Gibraltar.

This celebrated fortress has remained in the hands of the British since 1704, although frequently besieged. It sustained under General Elliott a siege of three years by the combined French and Spanish forces, comprising 40,000 soldiers, 47 first-class battleships, besides numerous inferior ships and floating batteries.

It is interesting to note that some of these floating batteries had walls seven feet in thickness, the sloping sides of which were covered with iron.

The British forces consisted of about 7,000 soldiers, under the command of General Elliott. It was he who said: "If you want the keys of Gibraltar come and take them."

*Dyer's "History of Modern Europe."

On the 13th of September, 1781, the allied forces rallied for the final attack; 170 cannon opened on the works, and 40,000 soldiers stood ready to make the assault whenever the English batteries were silenced. The floating batteries were finally set on fire by an all-day's rain of red-hot cannon balls, and the allied forces compelled to withdraw, with a loss of 2,000 killed and wounded, while the loss of the garrison was only 84. A storm followed and scattered the allied fleet, and before they could resume, the plucky Lord Howe, with an English fleet, successfully landed supplies for the garrison and sailed away in safety.

The rock in its highest point is about 1,400 feet above the sea, and the part facing the north is almost perpendicular, while the eastern side is broken into numerous precipices. The western side is not so steep, and between the foot of the rock and the sea is comparatively level, and on this portion the town is built. It is connected with the mainland by a low, sandy isthmus, about one and one-half miles long and three-quarters of a mile wide, which is known as the neutral ground.

Enormous sums of money and immense labor have been expended in making this fortress impregnable. It is honeycombed by vast galleries two or three miles in length running through the solid rock, wide enough for ammunition wagons and connecting one point with another. Along the galleries, facing the neutral ground and parts most likely to be attacked, there are frequent port-holes mounting the most formidable product of modern gun-makers. The rock has also the ordinary defenses of a regularly fortified place.

Gibraltar has to depend upon the rainy season for its water supply, and the roof of each house is so constructed as to carry the water to a tank, where it is held in reserve.

Allied Invasion.

In 1706 the English sent a formidable expedition under the command of the Earl of Peterborough, which, co-operating with Archduke Charles, met with excellent success on the eastern coast of Spain. Another allied army, profiting by treachery within the Spanish lines, captured Cartegena, and with it the best arsenal and about all the ships at the command of Spain. They soon overran half of the peninsula, captured Madrid, and within that imperial city proclaimed the archduke king of Spain.

Difficulty of Conquering Spain.

"It seemed that the struggle had terminated in favor of the archduke, and that nothing remained for Philip but prompt flight into the dominion of his grandfather. So judged those who were ignorant of the character and habits of the Spanish people. There is no country in Europe which is so easy to overrun as Spain; there is no country in Europe which is so difficult to conquer. Nothing can be more contemptible than the regular military resistance which Spain offers to an invader; nothing more formidable than the energy which she puts forth when her regular military resistance has been beaten down. Her armies have long borne too much resemblance to mobs; but her mobs have had, in an unusual degree, the spirit of armies. Every peasant procured a fire-lock or a pike; the allies were masters of the ground on which they trod. No soldier could wander a hundred yards from the main body of the invading army without imminent risk of being poinarded. The country through which the conquerers had passed to Madrid, and which, as they thought, had been subdued, was all in arms behind them." *

The allies quarreled among themselves, and in the end

---
*Macaulay.

were forced to retreat with immense losses in killed and wounded and upwards of 10,000 prisoners.

The following year, 1707, they again advanced, and a fierce battle was fought at Almanza. The unsettled condition of the times is well illustrated by the commanders of the opposing forces. The allies were commanded by Ruvigni, Earl of Galway (a French refugee), and the Franco-Spanish by the Duke of Berwick, natural son of James II., former king of England. A regiment of French Huguenot, refugees under the celebrated Jean Cavalier, found themselves opposed by a regular French regiment on the side of the king of Spain, and the two corps almost annihilated each other. The battle was decided by the superiority of the cavalry, and the English, Dutch and Portuguese infantry were cut to pieces.

The allies lost about 5,000 killed and 10,000 prisoners, and this victory for the French served in a measure to wipe out the stain of their defeat at Blenheim; however, the loss of the Spanish treasure fleet, which was captured by the English, left Charles in very straitened financial circumstances.

The allies rallied and again invaded the peninsula, and took possession of Madrid, but a second time the Castilians rose in support of their king, and under skillful French generals forced them to retreat with a loss of thousands killed and wounded and as many more prisoners.

But in the meantime Louis XIV. had suffered staggering reverses in Germany and the Netherlands.

Blenheim.

A little town in the southern part of Germany, with less than a thousand population, has given its name to one of the great decisive battles of the world. It was here that in 1704 the allied forces, under Prince Eugene of Savoy and Marlborough of England, won a brilliant victory over the veteran troops of Louis XIV. under Marshal Tallard and the Bavarians under the elector of Bavaria.

"In one respect the struggle stands almost unrivaled, for the whole of the Teutonic race was represented in the strange medley of Englishmen, Dutchmen, Hanoverians, Danes, Wurtemburgers and Austrians who followed Marlborough and Eugene. The French and Bavarians, who numbered, like their opponents, something like 50,000, lay behind a little stream which ran through swampy ground to the Danube. Their position was a strong one, for its front was covered by the swamp, its right by the Danube, its left by a hill country in which the Danube rose, and Tallard had not only strongly intrenched himself but was far superior to his rivals in artillery.

"Though the allies were in motion at sunrise on the 13th of August, it was not until mid-day that Eugene, who commanded on the right, succeeded in crossing the stream. The English at once forded it on the left and attacked Blenheim, in which the bulk of the French infantry were intrenched; but after a fierce struggle the attack was repulsed, while as gallant a resistance at the other end held Eugene in check. Marlborough now chose the center, where the French believed themselves unassailable, and by making an artificial road across the morass which covered it, threw his 8,000 horsemen on the mass of the French cavalry, and two desperate charges, which the duke headed in person, decided the day."*

Of the defeated army, 12,000 were slain and 14,000 were captured. The prestige which one hundred victories had given the French soldiery was lost and passed to the allies, and "Marlborough" became a name of fear to every child in France.

---

* Green's "History of the English People."

The Treaty of Utrecht. 1713.

The contestants were exhausted, and were all willing to agree to a peace. By the death of Emperor Joseph in 1711 the Archduke Charles succeeded to the Imperial crown, and if he could have added to this the Spanish possessions it would have rendered him as dangerous to the peace of Europe as was Louis XIV. Political jealousies had arisen. Marlborough, charged with converting to his own use money intended to supply his army, was pronounced guilty by the House of Commons and the allies deprived of their ablest leader.

It was agreed by Treaty of Utrecht that Philip should have Spain and the Indies, while Naples, Sardinia, Milan and the Spanish Netherlands should go to the emperor. Sicily was given to the Duke of Savoy, and styled a kingdom. England secured Gibraltar, Minorca, Newfoundland, Hudson Bay and Nova Scotia. France was forced to recognize the right of Anne to the English crown and to expel the Pretender and his son, Charles Edward, while Philip renounced all right to succession to the throne of France.

On the death of Louis XIV., in 1715, Philip, unmindful of his solemn pledges in the Treaty of Utrecht, aspired to the French crown, and made war against France; but other nations interfered and compelled him to respect the agreement of the Quadruple Alliance.

Spain in 1733 played a minor part in the war of the succession to the Polish throne, and a little later quarreled with England over the latter's right to trade with Spanish colonies in America granted by the Treaty of Utrecht, but these affairs were not serious.

'Jenkins' Ear."

In 1739 war broke out with Spain over "Jenkins' ear." As the story goes, Captain Jenkins, of the ship Rebecca, of London, sailed from Jamaica and was hanging about the ports of Florida, with which the English were not allowed to trade. He claimed to have been boarded by the Spanish coast guard, who tried to find proof that he was smuggling. Angered by their failure, they put a noose about his neck and hung him until he was choked into insensibility, lowering him just in time to save his life, and further abusing him by cutting off one of his ears and telling him to take it to his king.

The House of Commons took up the case, and Jenkins, when asked how he felt while thus abused, said, "I recommended my soul to God and my cause to my country." The answer was made a political war cry, and touched a chord of popular sympathy. However, it is by no means certain that Jenkins lost his ear in Florida.

In 1740, when the war of the Austrian succession broke out, Spain was one of the nations who repudiated its solemn treaty recognizing the rights of Maria Theresa. England alone of all the signatories to that compact was faithful. The Spanish forces gained some successes, and for a time it looked as though they might recover their possessions in Italy, but Europe was tired of fighting, and one by one the enemies of the heroic Austrian empress made peace with her and withdrew from the struggle, Philip V. dying in 1746 of apoplexy before it was over.

In spite of the disturbed character of his reign his country showed marked improvement. He was earnestly desirous of seeing it prosperous and happy, and had called to his cabinet able men and those who had its welfare at heart.

Synopsis of Events Contemporary with this Reign.

1701. James II. of England dies in exile. Yale College founded. Philip of Anjou becomes Philip V. of Spain and first of the Bourbon kings. Act of Settlement, passed by English Parliament, secures the right of succession to the heirs, being Protestant, of **Sophia**, daughter of Elizabeth, daughter of James I.

1702. **William III.**, king of England and stadtholder of Holland, dies. Anne, daughter of James II., accedes to English throne. The War of the Spanish Succession begins. **First** daily newspaper, "The Courant," published in England.

1704. **Battle of Blenheim.** Capture of Gibraltar. First newspaper in United States, published in Boston. Charles XII. of Sweden completes conquest of Poland.

1706. **Marl**borough defeats **the** French under Villeroy at Ramilles.

1707. **The king**doms of England and Scotland are **united** under the name of Great Britain. Charles **XII. of** Sweden conquers Saxony.

1709. **Charles** XII. defeated at Pultowa by the Russians, and escapes into Turkey. **Dr.** Samuel Johnson born. (d. 1784.)

1712. Marlborough dismissed from command for embezzlement of funds. Frederick the Great born. (d. **1789.**) Rosseau born. (d. 1778.)

1713. **Peace of Utrecht** ends the War of the Spanish Succession.

1714. **Queen** Anne, last **of** the house of Stuart, dies, and **is succeeded** by George I. **of** the house of Brunswick (or Hanover).

1715. **Jacobite** rebellion in England. Louis **XIV. dies.** "Gil Blas" and Pope's "Iliad" published.

1718. **St. Petersburg made** capital of Russia. Charles **XII. killed at siege of** Fredrikshall. Pragmatic Sanction of Emperor Charles VI. names his daughter Maria Theresa as heir to his Austrian possessions.

1721. **Rise of Walpole to power in the** British Govern-

ment. Inoculation against small-pox introduced into England by Lady Montague.
1725. Death of Peter the Great. Accession of his empress, Catharine I. Birth of Clive. (d. 1774.) Spain, by treaty, guarantees rights of Maria Theresa.
1726. Russia, by treaty, guarantees rights of Maria Theresa. Swift's "Gulliver's Travels" published.
1727. Death of George I. of England. Accession of George II. Hostilities between England and Spain without declaration of war.
1728. Prussia, by treaty, guarantees the rights of Maria Theresa. Goldsmith born. (d. 1774.)
1730. Baltimore founded. Liverpool and Manchester Railroad in England opened. Edward Burke born. (d. 1797.)
1731. England and Holland, by treaty, guarantee the rights of Maria Theresa.
1732. George II. grants Georgia to General Oglethorpe. Franklin founds first subscription library in the United States at Philadelphia. Pope's "Essay on Man" published. Washington born. (d. 1799.) Haydn born. (d. 1809.)
1733. Bourbon family compact between France and Spain. War of Polish succession between France and Austria. Joseph Priestley, discoverer of oxygen, born. Savannah, Ga., founded.
1738. France, by treaty, guarantees the Pragmatic Sanction.
1739. England goes to war with Spain about Jenkins' ear.
1740. Frederick the Great becomes king of Prussia. Charles VI., emperor of Germany, dies. Treachery of all the powers but Great Britain, who by solemn treaty had agreed to respect the rights of the

Austrian succession. Frederick of Prussia begins the war.

1741. Prussia, France and Bavaria allied against Austria. Frederick makes a secret treaty with Maria Theresa and deserts his allies.

1742. Frederick treacherously repudiates his treaty with Maria Theresa and renews the war.

1743. England supports the cause of Maria Theresa and declares war. Thomas Jefferson born. (d. 1826.) Toussaint L'Ouverture, the negro liberator of Hayti and the greatest captain that race has produced, born. (d. 1803.)

1745. Last Jacobite revolt in England. New England troops capture Lewisburg. The French defeat the British and Dutch at Fontenoy, where the Irish refugees make their famous charge and win a victory for France. Death of the emperor Charles VIII. and election of Francis I., husband of Maria Theresa, to the throne. Peace between Austria and Prussia.

Ferdinand VI. 1746-1759.

Second son of Philip V. and Maria Louisa of Savoy, born September 23, 1713. His elder brother, Louis, died in 1725 and he was then proclaimed Prince of Asturias, which title corresponds to that of Prince of Wales. He succeeded to the throne on the death of his father in 1746.

His health was poor, his character not strong, and he left the government of his kingdom in the hands of his ministers and his wife.

During his reign he kept out of foreign complications as much as possible, and the affairs of his kingdom improved somewhat.

As he grew weaker he became melancholy and despondent, and died insane. He had no children, and, according to the terms of the Treaty of Aix-la-Chapelle, was succeeded by his half brother, Charles III.

Aix-la-Chapelle.

The Treaty of Aix-la-Chapelle (1748) ended the wars of the Austrian succession. By the terms of this treaty made between all the belligerents in that war, the prisoners were released without ransom, the conquests made during the war returned, France recognized the Brunswick succession to the English throne and expelled the Pretender from the French court; England was to have the right to trade with the Spanish colonies for four years; the election of the Austrian emperor was acknowledged and Austria compelled to give up Silesia and Glatz to Frederick.

The general verdict of history upholds the justice of the cause of the heroic Maria Theresa and condemns the treachery and injustice of the ambitious and unscrupulous rulers who sought to make her difficulty their opportunity. Of all the nations who by solemn treaty had agreed to the Pragmatic Sanction, England alone kept faith.

Synopsis of Events Contemporary with This Period.

1747. French invade Holland. Franklin proves that lightning is electricity.
1748. Treaty of Aix-la-Chapelle.
1749. Halifax, Nova Scotia, founded. Publication of "Tom Jones" and John Wesley's "Account of Methodists." Birth of Charles Fox, English parliamentarian. (d. 1806.) Laplace, one of the greatest astronomers and mathematicians born. (d. 1827.) Birth of Jenner, who discovered the principles of vaccination. (d. 1823.) Mirabeau born. (d. 1791.) Goethe born. (d. 1832.)
1751. Clive begins his celebrated military career in

India. Change of calendar in England from old style to new. Publication of Gray's " Elegy in a Country Churchyard."
1754. The French built Fort Duquesne; Washington's expedition against it. Founding of Columbia College (King's College) in New York.
1755. French and Indian war. Braddock's defeat. Lisbon earthquake. Hahnemann, founder of homeopathy, **born.** (d. 1843.) John Marshall, first Chief Justice of America, **born.** (d. 1835.)
1756. Death of English prisoners in the Black Hole of Calcutta.
1757. Byng (English admiral) fails to relieve Minorca, besieged by Spain. Frederick defeats Austria at Prague; is defeated at Colin. Clive wins important victories in India for England. Canova **born.** (d. 1822.) Lafayette **born.** (d. 1834.) Alexander Hamilton **born.** (Killed in duel by Burr, 1804.)
1758. Americans capture Lewisburg and Fort Duquesne. Nelson **born.** (d. 1805. Trafalgar.) Robespierre **born.** (d. 1794.)
1759. General Wolfe captures Quebec from French. British capture Niagara, Ticonderoga and Crown Point. Opening of the British Museum.

Charles III. 1759-1788.

Born 1716; died 1788; succeeded to the Spanish throne 1759 on the death of his half brother, Ferdinand VI.

He was a younger son of Philip V., and some possessions in Italy falling to him when he was fifteen years old, he was sent with an army to occupy them. Charles possessed more than average ability, and had the good sense to surround himself with faithful and competent advisers. When eighteen he conquered the two Sicilies, and the emperor of Germany recognized him as their king. When called to the Spanish throne he instituted some needed reforms, and under his care the domestic affairs of Spain were greatly improved.

Family Compact.

In 1761 he made what was known as the "Family Compact," with all the leaders of the House of Bourbon, the chief of whom was the king of France, by which the enemy of either was to be considered the enemy of both, and neither was to make a treaty of peace without the consent of the other. Though the treaty was secret, Pitt, the English statesman, suspected it and was anxious to declare war against Spain at once. The English ministry finally agreed to it and hostilities began in 1762.

As a result, Manila and Cuba were captured by the English, and when the Peace of Paris was made in 1763 Spain gave up Florida to England in exchange for them.

Charles and his ministers were engaged in a struggle with the church, which had numerous holdings of property throughout Spain, and some excellent reforms were made.

It was during his reign that the Jesuits were expelled from Spain, and sufficient pressure was brought to bear upon Pope Clement XIV. in 1773 to compel him to suppress the Order.

American Revolution.

This monarch is of interest to Americans, as he recognized their independence in the Revolutionary struggle and loaned them $174,017.13 in 1781, the third foreign loan that the colonies were able to obtain, France having furnished the other two.

The time seemed a good one to even old scores with England, and hostilities were commenced in 1779. A plan for the invasion of England by the allied forces was formed, and a powerful naval force rode unchallenged in the Channel. As usual, dissension arose among the leaders, and the opportunity was lost.

A long siege by the allied Spanish and French forces was conducted against Gibraltar, but without success. (See Gibraltar, Philip V.) In 1783, after much difficulty, the treaty of peace was signed at Versailles, by which the independence of the United States was recognized and East Florida, Honduras and Milan restored to Spain.

Charles died in 1788. Though not of commanding genius, he compares very favorably with Spanish monarchs, and under his administration the country materially improved.

Synopsis of Events Contemporary with this Period.

1760. **Death** of George II. Accession of his grandson, George III.
1762. England declares war against Spain and captures **Havana**, Cuba. Paris suppresses the Jesuits. **Empress** Elizabeth of Russia dies. Paul III. **accedes.** Is murdered. Accession of Catherine II. to the throne.
1763. **End** of the Seven Years' War. Treaty of Paris. Great Britain secures all the Canadian dominion from France.
1764. **Lous** XV. prohibits Jesuit organizations in France. Survey of Mason and Dixon's line. the boundary between Pennsylvania and Maryland, now begun.
1765. George III. of England has his first attack of insanity. **Passage** of "Stamp Act" for taxation of the American colonies. Blackstone's "Commentaries" published.
1767. **Andrew** Jackson born. (d. 1845.) J. Q. Adams born. (d. 1848.) Jesuits suppressed in Spain.
1769. **Spain,** France and Naples demand suppression of the order of the Jesuits of the Pope. Watt

patents his steam-engine. Arkwright patents his "water-frame." Publication of "Letters of Junius." Wellington born. (d. 1832.) Bonaparte born. (d. 1821.) Culver born. (d. 1832.)

1770. Hargrave patents his "spinning jenny." Publication of "Encyclopædia Britannica" and Goldsmith's "Deserted Village."

1772. Prussia, Austria and Russia agree to divide Poland among themselves. Lord Mansfield, English justice, decides that a slave cannot be held in England.

1773. Pope Clement XIV. abolishes the Order of the Jesuits. Warren Hastings appointed governor-general of India. "Boston Tea Party." Birth of Metternich. (d. 1859.)

1774. Death of Louis XV. Succeeded by his grandson, Louis XVI. American colonies call their first Continental Congress. Priestley discovers oxygen.

1775. American Revolution begins. Battles of Lexington, Concord and Bunker Hill.

1776. The British army evacuates Boston. Americans defeated at Long Island. Declaration of Independence. Washington victorious at Trenton. Publication of Paine's "Common Sense;" Gibbon's "Decline and Fall of the Roman Empire;" Adam Smith's "Wealth of Nations."

1777. Washington victorious at Princeton. Defeated at Brandywine and Germantown. Burgoyne surrenders at Saratoga. American army winters at Valley Forge.

1778. War between Austria and Prussia. France makes a treaty with the colonies. Indian and English irregulars massacre inhabitants of Wyoming and Cherry Valley.

1779. Wayne captures Stony Point. General Sullivan's successful expedition against the Indians near Elmira. Paul Jones, commanding "Bon Homme Richard," captures the British frigate "Serapis."

1780. Maria Theresa of Austria dies. **Treason of Benedict** Arnold. The natives of **Peru rebel** against Spain. Pennsylvania begins the emancipation of her slaves.

1781. Joseph II. of Austria abolishes serfdom. Spain recaptures West Florida (Texas), from British. Cornwallis surrenders at Yorktown. Abolition of slavery in Massachusetts. **The** Dutch **win naval** battle **over** English at Dogger Banks. **George Stephenson,** inventor of the locomotive, **born. (d. 1848.)**

1782. Rodney **(Engl**ish) wins in the West Indies the greatest **naval** victory of the **century over De** Grasee (French). Fall of Lord **N**orth from **power in the** English **cabinet.** Negotiations **for peace opened** between **the** U**nited** States and **Britain.** Froebel born. **(d. 1852.)** Calhoun born. **(d. 1850.)** Daniel W**ebster** born. (d. 1852.)

1783. **Peace of Paris** recognizes American independ**ence. Catherine** of Russia seizes the Crimean **Peninsula,** belonging **to** Turkey. Bolivar born. (d. 1830) Washington Irving born. (d. 1859.)

1784. **First** daily newspaper in **America** published in Philadelphia.

1786. **Galvani's** discoveries in electricity made public.

1787. **Warren** Hastings impeached **by** House of Com**mons.** Shay's rebellion in Massachusetts. **Convention** called to frame **the** " Constitution of **the United** States."

Charles IV. 1788-1808.

Son of Charles III., born 1748; died 1819.

The first four years of his reign under the ministry of Florida Blanca passed prosperously for Spain. Then intrigues for the elevation of the queen's favorite, Godoy, deposed Blanca and finally placed the favorite at the head of affairs.

France was in the throes of revolution, and the Spanish king was naturally inclined to assist his Bourbon cousin, Louis XVI. France declared war in 1793 and the Spanish forces invaded the territory adjacent to the Pyrenees, captured Toulon and met with some success. They were checked by the Republicans, however, and Toulon was afterward recovered by General Bonaparte. The invaders were followed across the Pyrenees, and the greater part of the kingdom of Navarre overrun by the French. Although defeated at sea, the French were brilliantly successful in their land operations and Spain was soon reduced to abject submission. Peace was concluded with the Republicans in 1795, and the French evacuated Spanish territory in consideration of Spain's ceding to them part of the Island of San Domingo.

Soon after this (1796), an alliance offensive and defensive was formed between Spain and France and war declared against England. It was wholly a naval war, and Spain met with continued defeat. Her fleet under Cordova was beaten off Cape St. Vincent by Sir John Jervis; Cadiz was blockaded, her foreign commerce almost destroyed and the English made themselves masters of Trinidad, which they have since retained.

In 1797 Spain lost Minorca to the English. The Peace of Amiens, 1801, restored Minorca to Spain and Louisiana to France.

Louisiana.

It may be of interest to notice briefly the many changes

of ownership of that part of the United States formerly comprised under the names of Louisiana and Florida.

The French based their claim to this region upon the explorations of La Salle, who, in 1681-82, explored the whole length of the Mississippi river.

A colonizing expedition left France September 24, 1698, and the 2d of March, 1699, reached the mouth of the Mississippi river. Curiously enough, they were able to identify the place, by finding in the hands of the Indians a letter which the Chevalier de Tonti had written La Salle thirteen years before. On the Bay of Biloxi the first colony was formed, and a fort erected to protect it. That fall an English vessel attempted to explore the region, but finding the French colonists, acknowledged their claims and retired.

In 1718 Bienville founded New Orleans. The site chosen was little better than a cypress swamp, but time has justified the wisdom of the pioneer's selection. Girls for wives of the settlers were sent from the houses of correction, and later, in 1728, a better class, each of whom was given by the company a casket containing articles of dress, etc. These were known as the "casket girls," and the later society of the province were proud to claim descent from them.

In 1755 Louisiana received many settlers from Nova Scotia, when the French were driven from that province by the English.

By the Treaty of Paris, 1763, France ceded her possessions east of the Mississippi river to England, excepting New Orleans. At this time, Spain gave up the southeastern portion of the United States, known as Florida, to England, in exchange for Cuba and Manila, which had been captured by the English. Spain was an ally of France, and to reimburse her, France ceded to Spain New Orleans and her possessions west of the Mississippi river. Spanish rule in Louisiana was not popular, and the inhabitants expelled the governor and sent messengers to the king of France, declaring that they would be a colony of France or a free commonwealth. Their appeal fell on deaf ears. In 1769 a Spanish fleet suddenly appeared in the mouth of the Mississippi; 2,600 Spanish troops with 50 pieces of artillery were landed under Don Alexandro O'Reilly (cruel O'Reilly); the leaders of the revolt were arrested and sentenced to be hung. One of them was killed in confinement, and the only mercy shown them was, that they were allowed to be shot by a file of soldiers rather than hung.

After the war of the American Revolution and as quickly as settlements came to be made in Kentucky and Tennessee, the commercial value of the mouth of the Mississippi river rapidly became apparent. Spain claimed the right to close it absolutely to commerce from the United States, or to exact taxes which were practically prohibitory. The United States claimed that owning one side of the river, by international law, they were entitled to free navigation the entire length, with the right to land goods at its mouth, and that further, by special treaty when France conveyed the land east of the Mississippi to England in 1763, it was specifically agreed that England should have free navigation rights to the Gulf. Spain refused to concede the justice of the American claims, levied duties sometimes as high as 75 per cent. of the value of the goods, which the sturdy backwoodsmen were little inclined to pay. There were numerous threats among them to organize an expedition to forcibly adjust matters and the question seemed prolific of international complications for the struggling colonies.

By a treaty made at Madrid in 1795, Spain had agreed that for three years the United States should have the right to free navigation to the mouth of the river and the privilege to land goods at New Orleans, and by inference nad agreed that at the end of the three years the privilege should be renewed or a new port named for the landing of the goods. At the expiration of the time named in the treaty she refused to continue the privileges, and relations at once became strained. Three thousand regular troops were mobilized in Ohio, the settlers volunteered and war seemed imminent. In the face of this preparation Spain gave way, good feeling revived, trade was resumed and immigration increased. But Spain had learned a lesson. As the American colonies on the Mississippi became more powerful they were sure to become more insistent and Louisiana would be lost to the king.

Spain Cedes Louisiana to France.

On the 21st of March, 1801, a secret treaty was ratified at Madrid, whereby Louisiana was transferred to Napoleon. He meant to occupy it with a strong army and a fleet to guard the coast, but in the face of his English foe he was unable to do this and he gladly listened to proposals for its sale from the United States, although he had agreed in treaty with Spain not to sell this territory to any other power. The treaty of sale was concluded and Louisiana passed into the hands of the United States upon the payment of 60,000,000 francs, about $12,000,000, the United States agreeing to pay some claims her own settlers had against the French government.

The territory purchased included 2,300 square miles of what is now Alabama, 3,600 square miles of Mississippi, all of Louisiana, Arkansas, Missouri, Iowa, Nebraska, part of Texas, which was re-ceded to Spain, and the Dakotas, Minnesota west of the Mississippi, all but the southwestern corner of Kansas, the whole of the Indian Territory, and such part of Colorado, Wyoming and Montana as lies on the eastern slope of the Rocky Mountains.

The southwestern boundary was not well defined and neither President Jefferson nor the French claimed that Louisiana bordered on the Pacific ocean.

In 1804 Spain again declared war against England, who had already seized her treasure fleet and held it as a pledge of Spanish faith. Every exertion was made to strengthen her navy to enable it to cope with England, but Nelson's crushing victory at Trafalgar settled that dream for all time.

Trafalgar.

Napoleon mobilized an army of 100,000 men at Bologne on the English channel and prepared to invade England "Though 300,000 volunteers mustered in England to meet the coming attack, such a force would have offered but a small hindrance to the veterans of the Grand Army had they once crossed the channel."

Everything depended upon his being able to keep the superior English fleet at a distance. He said, "Let us be masters of the channel for six hours and we are masters of the world."

His alliance with Spain had placed the Spanish fleet at his command, which, although much shattered from its fight off Cape Vincent earlier in the year, was still powerful, and joined to the French fleet made no mean antagonist. It was his plan to draw off the British fleet by a pretended attack elsewhere, then hasten back and be able to show in the channel for a short time a superior naval force. "Admiral Villeneuve, uniting the Spanish ships with his own squadron from Toulon, drew Nelson in pursuit to the West Indies, and then suddenly returning to Cadiz, hastened to form a junction with the French squadron at Brest and to crush the English fleet in the channel. But a headlong pursuit brought Nelson up with him ere the manœuver was complete, and the two fleets met on the 21st of October, 1805, off Cape Trafalgar. 'England,' ran Nelson's famous signal, 'expects every man to do his duty;' and, though he fell himself in the hour of victory, twenty French sail had struck their flag ere the day was done. The French and Spanish navies were, in fact, annihilated.

"From this hour the supremacy of England at sea remained unquestioned and the danger of any invasion of England rolled away like a dream."*

Spain was getting tired of her alliance with Napoleon, and his summary execution of the Bourbon Prince, Duke D'Enghien, displeased them and made them dread their powerful ally. A secret treaty was made with Portugal and England, in which they agreed to begin operations against France as soon as Russia should move, but the victory of Jena rendered Napoleon still more terrible, and they were soon in abject humiliation at his feet.

Godoy was becoming unpopular and the discontented rallied around Prince Ferdinand, heir-apparent to the throne. Factional strife was secretly fanned by French influence and soon the prince was accused of a plot to assassinate his father. He was tried by the Cortes and acquitted, and Godoy became more unpopular still and was overthrown.

Charles IV., worn out by the burdens of his throne, the disappointment of his favorite and the French plots, abdicated 1808 in favor of his son, Ferdinand VII.

Synopsis of Events Contemporary with this Period.

1789. Beginning of the **French Revolution.** Capture of the Bastile. Expulsion of the nobles. United States Government organizes under the Constitution. Washington first President. Tammany Society in New York founded.
1790. French assignats (bonds), based on lands of church

---
*Green's "History of the English People."

and nobles which the Revolutionists confiscated, are issued as currency.

1791. French king attempts to fly and is arrested. Rise of the Girondists. Adoption of the first ten amendments to the American Constitution. Servile insurrection in Hayti.

1792. War between France, Austria and Prussia. French Revolution continued. Mob massacres the Swiss Guards in the palace of the Tuileries. French Republic proclaimed. Battle of Valma between French Republicans and foreign supporters of the king. Trial of Louis XVI.

1793. Louis XVI. executed. War between France and England. Reign of Terror in France. Charlotte Corday assassinates Marat. Execution of the queen. Poland divided a second time. Eli Whitney invents the cotton gin. France emancipates the slaves of Hayti and joins with them under Toussaint L'Ouverture against the Spanish and English.

1794. Death of Danton and Robespierre, leaders of the French Revolution. Whiskey rebellion in Pennsylvania. General Wayne defeats the Indians on the Maumee.

1795. "The little Corsican officer" and the "whiff of grape-shot" suppresses an insurrection in Paris. Poland divided for the third time.

1796. Bonaparte invades Italy. Death of Catherine II. of Russia. Washington's farewell address delivered.

1797. Bonaparte invades Austria. Hostilities on the sea begin between America and France. British win naval victory at Cape Vincent over Spain; at Camperdown over Holland.

1798. Bonaparte goes to Egypt; captures Malta. Lord Nelson destroys French fleet at the battle of the

Nile and recaptures Malta. Jenner publishes his discovery of vaccination. Count Rumford announces "Heat is a mode of motion."

1799. Bonaparte victorious at Aboukir (Battle of the Pyramids). Austrian and Russian armies advance on France. Bonaparte returns from Egypt; overthrows Directory; is made consul. New York begins the emancipation of her slaves.

1800. England, Scotland, Ireland and Wales unite under title of United Kingdom of Great Britain. Moreau (French) wins the battle of Hohenlinden. Spain gives Louisiana back to France.

1801. Paul, Czar of Russia, assassinated. Accession of Alexander I. Louisiana ceded to France by Spain. John Marshall made Chief Justice. Toussaint L'Ouverture declares Hayti free. Farragut born. (d. 1870.)

1802. West Point Military Academy established. France subjugates Switzerland. Kossuth born. (d. 1885.) Victor Hugo born. (d. 1885.) Peace between England and France. Napoleon made First Consul for life.

1803. War between England and France renewed. France sells Louisiana to the United States. Sheep farming introduced into Australia. Ericsson born. (d. 1889).

1804. Napoleon declared Emperor for life; completes Code of Napoleon, the civil law of France. Lewis and Clark explore the Northwest territory. Decatur captures and burns the "Philadelphia" under the guns of Tripolitan fort.

1805. Duel of Hamilton and Burr. Napoleon secures the crown of Italy; plans the invasion of England; occupies Vienna; wins the battle of Austerlitz. Naval battle of Trafalgar, and the death of Nelson.

End of Tripolitan war with United States, and the payment of tribute.

1806. Issue of British Order in Council (May) declaring that all the coasts, ports and rivers from the Elbe to Brest should be considered blockaded. Issue of Napoleon's Berlin decree (November) charging England with violation of the national law, and ordering:

First. That the British Islands should be in a state of blockade.

Second. All commerce and correspondence with them prohibited.

Third. British subjects in a country occupied by French troops, or by troops of their allies, should be prisoners of war.

Fourth. All property belonging to British subjects should be deemed a good prize.

Fifth. No vessel direct from England or her colonies might enter any port subject to French authority.

Holy Roman Empire broken up. Francis II., the emperor, henceforth known as Emperor of Austria. Napoleon defeats Prussia at Jena; makes Louis Bonaparte King of Holland. England secures Cape of Good Hope from the Dutch.

1807. Jerome Bonaparte made King of Westphalia. Nelson destroys fleet in Copenhagen harbor. Trial of Aaron Burr for treason. British fire upon and capture United States frigate "Chesapeake."

Second British Order in Council prohibits any vessel from trading with an enemy's port shut against English vessels; orders English war ships to warn neutrals against such action, and to capture and declare them prizes in the event of their continuing such trade after warning.

Napoleon's Warsaw decree ordered the confiscation of all English merchandise found in certain German towns.

Third English Order in Council (November) declares that all countries where the English flag is excluded, even though not at war with Britain, are placed under the same restrictions for commerce as if they were blockaded.

Napoleon's Milan decree (December) declares that any vessel, of whatever nation, submitting to England's November order, will be considered British property and condemned as a prize. By these decrees the neutral commerce of the world suffered great damage.

1808. Napoleon seats Joseph on the throne of Spain. Spain revolts. Siege of Saragossa.

CHAPTER IV.

Ferdinand VII. — 1808-1833.

Ferdinand was the oldest son of Charles IV. and Maria Louisa of Parma; born October 14, 1784; died September 29, 1833. Upon the abdication of his father he acceded to the throne March 19th. This was no part in Napoleon's plan, and within a few days Madrid was occupied by the French troops under Murat. Napoleon compelled Charles and Ferdinand to renounce their rights to the throne, and proclaimed Joseph Bonaparte king of Spain.

"A general cry of indignation arose in Spain. The people everywhere flew to arms, except where prevented by the presence of the French troops. They proposed not to meet the enemy in pitched battles in the open field, but, to harass, wear out, and overcome him by guerilla or discursive and incessant attacks of separate small bands.

General Dupont advanced as far as Cordova, but was defeated at Baylen July 20th and compelled to surrender. On this occasion, the commencement of the French reverses in Spain, 18,000 French soldiers laid down their arms. Such was the exasperation of the people against their invaders that numbers of the French were massacred on their road to Cadiz for embarkation, and the remainder were treated with barbarous inhumanity. These cruelties had, however, been provoked by the atrocities of the French at the capture and sack of Cordova." *

England proclaimed a peace with the Spanish government about as soon as the insurrection broke out, and the latter part of July Wellington, with about 10,000 troops, landed on the peninsula. Sir John Moore, at the head of another division of about 11,000, also arrived and was

---

* Dyer's "History of Modern Europe."

directed to unite with the Spanish army and expel the French. He was unable to find the army. Napoleon had appeared in person, taken command of the French and scattered the Spanish forces. Moore conducted a most masterly retreat to Corunna and fell mortally wounded while his troops were re-embarking.

Spain was now the scene of a terrible struggle until Napoleon's abdication in 1814, though by this time the French had practically been driven out by the English under Wellington, who had not lost a battle.

Ferdinand, who had been in retirement on a pension from Napoleon, now appeared, was acknowledged king and began to quarrel with his people. Spain could not readily lay aside the habits that the long guerrilla war had induced, and the people were broken up into numerous little parties, mostly represented by leaders who were intent only upon their own personal advancement. The French intervened in 1820. Some sort of order, by the help of the French army, was preserved until they left in 1827, but then another insurrection broke out. Spain was experiencing troublous times and nearly all her American provinces seized the opportunity to declare their independence.

"The conduct of Ferdinand was in every way humiliating and caused the Spaniards in general to consider that their best blood had been spilled in vain and that, however humiliating the rule of Bonaparte, they might under him, enjoy their constitutional freedom which their restored sovereign denied them; for it was evident enough that the king had determined to be content with nothing short of despotic authority.

Ferdinand, backed by the French troops, was unpopular with the church or conservative party, who favored his brother Don Carlos. His third wife died in May, 1829, leaving him without an heir, and Don Carlos was expected to succeed to the throne. When, in December of the same year, Ferdinand married Maria Christina of Naples, the Carlists were sorely disappointed and, when, in March, 1830, he issued a decree abrogating the Salic law, which had been in force in Spain since 1713, their anger knew no bounds. By the Salic law of Spain the succession to the throne was restricted to the nearest male heir. By its repeal females were eligible. The Carlists warmly protested. In October, 1830, a daughter (Isabella II.) was born to him, and in June, 1833, he solemnly declared her his successor, nominated Christina as regent, and ordered Don Carlos and his numerous sympathizers to leave the kingdom. Ferdinand did not long survive this act, but he had lived long enough to see the loss of his American colonies, whose aggregate area was greater than that of all Europe.

Florida.

The Spanish claim to Florida dates from its discovery by Ponce de Leon in 1512.

The first settlement, however, was made by French Huguenots. In 1568 three ships were fitted out by the famous French Protestant leader Coligny and placed under the command of Laudonniere, who was instructed to found a colony in Florida for the Huguenots. They reached the shore of Florida near the St. John's river, and built a fort called Carolina. They were not desirable colonists and mutinies were frequent. A party of them manned a vessel and began a career of piracy against the Spaniards. The vessel was taken and most of the men captured and sold as prisoners or slaves. A few escaped and returned to the colony. Supplies from France reached them in 1565 and it seemed as though the followers of John Calvin were about to found a permanent colony in the New World. Spain had never relinquished her claim to this territory and the same year sent a party under Melendez to colonize Florida. It is claimed that through the treachery of Coligny's enemies at the French court the Spaniards were informed of the struggling Huguenot colony and instructions given Melendez to destroy it. He fell upon them in an unguarded moment and captured the fort. Another party having surrendered under promise of safety were treacherously stabbed to death in cold blood. All but the women and children under fifteen years of age were killed and in the first attack even some of these were not spared.

"The long dispatch in which Melendez (Menendez) reported his fiendish work to the Spanish king has been brought to light in the archives at Seville, and there is this endorsement on it in the handwriting of Philip II., 'Say to him that as to those he has killed he has done well; and as to those he has saved they shall be sent to the galley.'"* They were avenged.

A young Frenchman, de Gourgues, sold all his property and bought three small ships, which he manned with 80 sailors and 100 soldiers. He took out a commission to engage in the slave trade on the coast of Guinea and in 1567 set sail. When he reached the West Indies he disclosed his plan to his followers, who enthusiastically supported him. On arriving at the Florida coast he found that the natives, having received characteristic treatment at the hands of the Spaniards, were hostile and ready to ally themselves with him in an attack upon the colony.

The Spaniards were intrenched in three forts and greatly outnumbered their opponents. The first fort was captured by surprise and a panic fell upon the colonists. The French lost hardly a man and according to the custom of the times, de Gourgues imitated the performance of Melendez.

Melendez founded a new settlement the next year and a few others were made but when according to the Treaty

---

* Parkman's "Pioneers of France in the New World."

of Paris, 1763, East Florida passed into the possession of the English, the whole number of inhabitants did not exceed 3,000.

During the American Revolution the Spanish governor in New Orleans made an attack upon the English forts in Florida and succeeded in capturing them.

By the treaty of 1783 between Great Britain on one side, the allies, France, Spain and the United States, on the other, England restored Florida to Spain, but the boundary was not exactly defined, and a dispute between Spain and the United States at once arose. Spain claimed from the mouth of the Yazoo river running east to the Chattahoochee and everything south of it. This would give to her about half of Mississippi and Alabama and nearly all of Georgia. The United States disputed this, but Spain had possession of the territory and strengthened it by forts at Baton Rouge, Natchez, Vicksburg, and even built one at New Madrid in Missouri, just south of the mouth of the Ohio. This she made a port of entry and compelled boats from the Ohio to land there and declare their cargoes.

She also disputed the validity of the title to the territory between Mississippi and the Allegheny mountains, which the United States had received from England. When, in addition to this, she came to deny the right of free navigation of the mouth of the Mississippi, it is easy to see that excellent grounds for a quarrel existed.

Before the days of railroads the navigation of the Mississippi was indispensable to the settlers of the Ohio valley. Spanish possession of this territory was a constant source of irritation and numerous conflicts took place between the Indians and escaped negroes from the Georgia plantations on the one hand and the settlers on the other. Probably the Americans were seeking a quarrel, and a ready excuse was found in the numerous conflicts between the whites and the Indians along the frontiers.

In December of 1817 General Jackson was ordered to take command of the military forces in Georgia. He wrote President Monroe, "Let it be signified to me through any channel that the possession of the Floridas would be desirable to the United States and in sixty days it will be accomplished." Monroe was ill and did not see the letter for a year. Calhoun, as secretary of war, issued the orders to Jackson, who probably supposed he had the tacit permission of his government to capture Florida. With characteristic energy he marched through Georgia and reached the fort at St. Mark in March, 1818, which he reduced and hanged two alleged English agents on the charge of having incited the Indians to hostility. He turned aside and captured Pensacola May 24th, 1818, deposed the Spanish government and set up a new one and left a garrison there. He then came home. The affair created great excitement.

The United States gave up Pensacola and St. Mark, but defended Jackson on the plea that he pursued his enemies (the Indians) to their refuge in Spanish territory, and that Spain was incompetent or unwilling to perform the duties that devolved upon her.

Jackson's campaign seems to have had some effect upon the Spanish government, for while the matter was being discussed in Congress the Spanish minister received instructions from home to sign a treaty by which Florida was ceded to the United States in consideration of the United States assuming and satisfying various claims against the Spanish government to the amount of $5,000,000. In addition the United States further ceded and relinquished to Spain all claim to the western portion of Louisiana lying south of the Red River and west of the Sabine, and now forming a part of Texas.

Isabella II. 1833-1868.

Isabella II. is the daughter of Ferdinand VII. by his fourth wife, Maria Christina, and was born October 30, 1830.

On the death of Ferdinand, September 29, 1833, Maria Christina was declared queen regent, and at once allied herself with the liberal party in opposition to the church, or conservative party, who supported the pretensions of the late king's brother, Don Carlos. Civil war at once broke out and raged with great violence for seven years. War in Spain has never been divested to any great extent of its horrors, and when there is added to the natural temperament of the people, the bitterness of a civil strife, the picture can scarcely be overdrawn. The Basques recognized Don Carlos as Charles V., and for a time they made some headway, but France and England allowed recruiting within their own lines for the loyalist army, and under the leadership of Espartero the rebellion was crushed and Don Carlos and his followers exiled by a decree of the Cortes.

Neither her private life nor her political conduct had endeared Maria Christina to the people, and a premier-president was appointed, 1840, who administered the government as regent until Isabella II. was declared of age, 1843. Her reign was no happier than that of the queen regent. In 1860 a short-lived Carlist rebellion occurred, but it was unsuccessful, and the leader and his brother were compelled to formally renounce all claim to the throne of Spain. In 1866 republican insurrections broke out, which were temporarily suppressed, but in 1868 another burst forth at Cadiz, which rapidly spread over the whole country, and Isabella was forced to fly across the border to France. After Isabella's flight there was a provisional government for two years, and then in 1870, Amadeus, the second son of the King of Italy, was invited to become King. He accepted and reigned for two years, but never received the support of the Carlists nor of the monarchists, who were adherents of Alphonso, son of Isabella. The republicans, under Castelar, objected to any king on general principles. Seeing that he could never hope to reconcile such strong and diverse opposition, he resigned February, 1873. A republic was then declared by the Cortes and Castelar made president, but even his famous eloquence was of no avail, and he at last consented to receive the son of Isabella, Alphonso XII., who was proclaimed King in 1874. Alphonso made Canovas (recently assassinated) his chief adviser, and under his wise administration the domestic affairs of Spain made considerable improvement.

Basque Provinces.

These provinces had formerly been allowed certain "privileges," among which were exemption from contributing directly to the war expenses of all Spain and from furnishing recruits for the Spanish army. These privileges were vestiges of the right enjoyed when they were governed by their own laws as Kingdom of Navarre. Under cover of their privileges they had raised money and recruits for the Carlists. By the abrogation of these local customs national unity was established in Spain, but the provinces resented their loss and are to-day restless, uneasy, and liable at any time to declare for Don Carlos if opportunity offers.

Carlists.

Don Carlos, Count of Molina, second son of Charles IV.; born 1788; died 1855. He had expected to succeed his brother Ferdinand II., whose only heir was an infant daughter, Isabella II., as under the Salic law in force in Spain since 1713, a female could not succeed to the throne. Ferdinand abrogated the law, 1830, and

THE ASCENDENCY OF AMERICA. 151

Don Carlos at once signified his intention to contest the matter. At once, on the death of Ferdinand, he began a rebellion which lasted seven years.

In 1845 he renounced his claims in favor of his son of the same name, and withdrew to Trieste, where he died.

Don Carlos, Count de Montemolin, son of the preceding, born 1818; died 1861. Raised a revolt against Isabella in 1860, but without success. On his death the claim passed to his brother, Don Juan, who, in October, 1868, resigned in favor of his own son, Don Carlos, the third of the name.

Don Carlos, Duke of Madrid, born March 30, 1848, son of Don Juan and grandson of Don Carlos first. His followers rose in revolt in 1868, 1870, 1872, and in 1873 Don Carlos himself entered Spain to inspirit his men and oppose Alphonso XII. He soon mastered Navarre, Biscay and Asturias, and the revolt assumed serious proportions, but when the rebels killed a German citizen Bismarck sent forces to aid in restoring order.

The Duke is too indolent and has led too gay a life to render him a dangerous personage to the present government, and he will probably leave his affairs in the hands of his son Don Jayme, or Jainie, Prince of Asturias, who is about twenty-eight years of age.

During Alfonso XII.'s administration a new constitution was adopted (1876), the same under which they are now governed, and some progress toward much-needed reforms made, when he suddenly died, November, 1885, leaving his wife, Maria Christina, Archduchess of Austria, queen regent for their posthumous son, Alphonso XIII.

Birth of Alphonso XIII.

The death of Alphonso had been awaited as a signal for a civil struggle, and the Carlists saw their hopes dashed to the ground when the new heir to the Bourbon throne was born at Madrid, May 17, 1886, in the presence of the Ministers of State, his cabinet officers and members of the Regency and Privy Council. This rather extraordinary proceeding was the result of a report which had circulated that a bogus heir to the throne was to be palmed off on the Spanish people, so that when the unhappy child first opened his eyes he found himself in the midst of a cabinet council. Each Spanish queen had theoretically been subjected to this ordeal, but never, at least in modern times, had this been strictly enforced. The Spaniards rallied around the queen regent and the baby king, doing everything in their power for the continuance of the Bourbon régime.

The boy king knows that his situation is a pathetic and precarious one. He has had no happiness in his short life, and he knows there is no one in the peninsula whom he can count upon except his mother, a helpless woman and a stranger to Spain. From the time he left his cradle the little fellow has been surrounded by the stiff ceremonials of the Spanish. He can have no playmates, because in the kingdom he has no peer. He knows that politics is a game that is more cruel than war, and that Spaniards are past masters in the arts of diplomacy and duplicity.

According to the law in Spain the king attains his majority at the age of fifteen years; so, but for the Cuban trouble, he might have ascended the throne with some prospect of a fairly peaceable reign. As it is the country is bankrupt, the war in Cuba and the insurrection in the Philippine Islands are rapidly draining its vital forces, and the present outlook is gloomy in the extreme.

The Carlists hope that Alphonso may never live to wear his father's crown. Should the king die, no woman with Bourbon blood in her veins will be allowed to ascend the throne, as the disastrous reigns of Queen Christina and Queen Isabella II. are fresh in the memories of all. If Alphonso should die his eldest sister would probably marry Don Jainie, the son of Don Carlos, the Carlist Pretender. This would satisfy both monarchical parties and free Spain from the possibility of civil war. The outcome of the present struggle is difficult to foresee, and Spain may emerge a republic.

By the exercise of great courage, shrewdness and diplomacy Spain acquired princely possessions in the new world, but in the administration of these colonies she has ever displayed stupidity, bigotry and oppression. As a mother country she has shown her utter incapacity to hold the love and respect of her children, and it now seems as though she will not long be able to maintain even the nominal supremacy she claims over the few that are left to her.

Once all Europe stood in awe of her, and the Spanish infantry was the terror of the military world. Able soldiers and sailors of other nations flocked to her standard and their achievements alone would have immortalized any nation. What reward had they who gave a continent to her?

Ximenes, whose statesmanship saved Spain for Charles I., was treated with great ingratitude and died in his old age without being even granted an audience with the king whose crown he had saved.

Balboa's discoveries brought him the enmity of his jealous governor and cost him his life on a manufactured charge of treason.

Cortez, who conquered Mexico, was recalled and died in poverty and disgrace.

Pizarro, who secured with Peru the enormous treasures of the Inca, was assassinated by his own soldiers.

Ponce de Leon was not successful in his search for the fountain of youth and died in his old age, shattered in mind and body by the exposures of the expedition.

Magellan was probably killed by his sailors and Columbus died a broken-hearted old man.

The achievements of these men constitute the brightest period in Spain's history. Is their fate prophetic of her sovereignty?

Synopsis of Events Contemporary with this Period.

1809. Wellington takes command of the English forces in the Peninsula.

1810. Napoleon divorces Josephine and marries Maria Louisa of Austria. George III. of England has his final attack of insanity.

1812. Napoleon quarrels with the Czar and invades Russia. Moscow burned and the French begin their disastrous retreat. War between United States and Great Britain.

1813. Holland regains her independence from France. Perry's victory on Lake Erie. Buffalo burned by the British.

1814. Napoleon abdicates and is sent to Elba. Louis XVIII. becomes King of France. McDonough wins his victory on Lake Champlain. Stephenson builds the "Rocket," the first locomotive. British burn public buildings in Washington.

1815. Napoleon escapes from Elba and reigns "One Hundred Days." Louis XVIII. flies. Battle of Waterloo; Napoleon surrenders; the British send him to St. Helena. Marshal Ney executed. Jackson wins his victory at New Orleans.

1818. Chili becomes independent. Jackson invades Florida and hangs two British agents.

1819. Voyage of the "Savannah," the first steamship to cross the Atlantic. Venezuela becomes independent.

1820. George III. dies and his son George IV. accedes to the throne. The "Missouri Compromise" adopted, excluding slavery in the territories north of 36° 30′. The Holy Alliance meets at Laybach.

1821. Mexico becomes independent. Peru becomes independent by aid of the Chileans. Spain cedes Florida to the United States.

1822. Brazil declared independent of Portugal and Dom Pedro made Emperor.

1823. Monroe doctrine set forth in the President's annual message.

1824. Louis XVIII. of France dies, succeeded by his brother Charles X.

1825. Formal opening of the Erie canal. England carries first passengers by steam over the Stockton and Darlington Railway.

1828. Construction of the Baltimore and Ohio Railroad begun.

1829. Slavery abolished in Mexico.

1830. George IV. dies; his brother William IV. accedes. Revolution of Paris. Charles X. flies. Louis Philippe made king. Joseph Smith issues his "Book of Mormon."

1832. Nullification movement in South Carolina.

1833. England begins the emancipation of slaves in the West Indies.

1836. Texans defeat Mexicans at San Jacinto and establish their independence.

1837. William IV. of England dies. Queen Victoria accedes. Financial panic in the United States. "Patriot" rebellion in Canada.

1839. Daguerre makes his discoveries in photography.

1840. Queen Victoria married to Prince Albert of Saxe-Coburg. Mormons settle in Nauvoo, Ill.

1841. Afghanistan revolts against British rule, and the disastrous retreat of the English begins. The "Brook Farm" association formed.

1842. Ashburton treaty settles the northeastern boundary question. Dorr rebels in Rhode Island.
1844. Morse completes telegraph line between Washington and Baltimore. A Nauvoo mob murders Joe Smith, founder of Mormonism, and expels the Mormons.
1845. Texas annexed to the United States, after nine years of independence.
1846. Famine in Ireland. Repeal of the British "Corn Laws." War between United States and Mexico. Mormons go from Nauvoo to Great Salt Lake. Oregon boundary dispute settled by adoption of the 49th parallel instead of "54° 40' or fight."
1848. The revolution in France deposes Louis Phillippe. The second republic organized with Louis Napoleon Bonaparte as President. Gold discovered in California.
1849. Kossuth declares Hungary independent. Austria crushes rebellion by aid of Russia.
1850. The "Fugitive Slave Law" passed. Clayton-Bulwer treaty ratified.
1851. Louis Napoleon becomes Dictator. Gold discovered in Australia.
1853. Commodore Perry opens Japanese ports.
1854. Repeal of the "Missouri Compromise." Birth of Republican party. Crimean war; England, France, Sardinia and Turkey against Russia. Siege of Sebastopol begins. Battle of Balaclava and charge of the "Six Hundred."
1856. Crimean war ended. "Declaration of Paris" agreed upon.
1858. Atlantic cable first laid; not a success.
1859. John Brown seizes Harper's Ferry; is captured, tried and executed.
1860. Abraham Lincoln elected President. South Carolina secedes.

1861. American Civil War begins. Unionists defeated at Bull Run. Captain Wilkes stops the English steamer "Trent," and takes off Mason and Slidell, which threatened to involve war with England.
1862. Stonewall Jackson's campaign in the Shenandoah Valley. Grant captures Fort Donaldson and wins the battle of Shiloh. Battle between the Merrimac and Monitor. Battles of Fair Oaks and Malvern Hill and McClellan's advance and retreat by way of the peninsula. The cruiser Alabama begins her career. Napoleon makes Maximilian of Austria Emperor of Mexico; protest of the United States.
1863. Lincoln issues the "Emancipation Proclamation." Vicksburg captured. Hooker defeated at Chancellorsville and death of Jackson. Battle of Gettysburg. Chinese Gordon appointed to command in China.
1864. The Kearsarge sinks the Alabama. Sherman's march to the sea. Sheridan's campaign in the Shenandoah Valley. Farragut passes the forts at Mobile. Gordon suppresses Taiping rebellion in China.
1865. Lee surrenders at Appomattox Court House. Lincoln assassinated. Johnson surrenders.
1866. Atlantic cable successfully laid. Fenians in the United States invade Canada.
1867. France withdraws from Mexico. Maximilian executed.
1868. Burlingame treaty made between China and the United States.
1869. Suez canal opened. "Black Friday" in New York.
1870. War between France and Germany; France utterly defeated in less than six months.
1871. France cedes Alsace and part of Lorraine to Germany and pays $1,000,000,000 indemnity. The German states unite to form an empire and

King William of Prussia becomes the German Emperor. Chicago fire. Stanley finds Dr. Livingston in Africa.

1872. Geneva tribunal decides "Alabama Claims" in favor of the United States and England pays $15,500,000 for her failure "to use due diligence in performance of neutral obligations."

1876. Centennial exhibition in Philadelphia. Telephone exhibited.

1877. Election of Pope Leo XIII.

1879. War between Chile and Peru, in which Peru is defeated and loses territory.

1881. The French occupy Tunis. The Mahdi begins his disturbance in the Soudan. Czar Alexander II. assassinated; his son, Alexander III., accedes. Garfield assassinated. War between Great Britain and the Boers. The English defeated at Majuba Hill.

1882. De Lesseps begins work on the Panama canal. The British bombard Alexandria.

1883. The Mahdi wipes out an English army in the Soudan.

1884. French war in Tonquin, China.

1888. William I., Emperor of Germany, dies; succeeded by Frederick III., who dies in a short time and is succeeded by William II., the present Emperor.

1889. Dom Pedro deposed and Brazil becomes a republic.

1890. William II. dismisses Bismarck. Russia expels the Jews.

1891. The Chilean Congress deposes President Balmaceda. Free schools established in England.

1893. World's Fair at Chicago.

1894. War between China and Japan. Czar Alexander III. dies; Nicholas II. accedes.

1897. Celebration of the Queen's jubilee, the sixtieth anniversary of her accession to the throne. War between Greece and Turkey.

CHAPTER V.

Growth and Loss of Spain's American Colonies.

Argentine Republic.

The pope having divided the new world between Spain and Portugal, the former country proceeded vigorously to explore and conquer, and soon what now comprises the Argentine Republic came within the sphere of her influence.

The Rio de La Plata River was discovered by the Spanish explorer De Solis in 1515, and possession was taken for the crown of Spain. Sebastian Cabot explored the river for a long distance in 1528, and planned to colonize the country for Spain, but the project was not well received.

The city of Buenos Ayres was founded by Mendoza in 1535, who had taken up the scheme after it was abandoned by Cabot. The country was extremely fertile. There were no mines, and the natives were treated much better than those of Peru and Mexico. Comparatively few Spanish women came to Argentine, and the wives of the soldiers were from the native stock.

The usual wars with the natives took place, and the country passed under the almost undisputed rule of the Jesuits until their downfall in 1767. There was some trouble with their neighbors, the Portuguese, just across the river at Montevideo, but in general the colony prospered, and in 1777 Uruguay was ceded to Spain by Portugal, and under the title of Colonies of La Plata, Argentine, Paraguay, Uruguay and Bolivia were governed by one viceroy. The British attacked them in 1797, 1803 and 1806, but were never able to secure a permanent hold, and were driven out in 1807.

When Spain passed under the control of Napoleon the colonies were dissatisfied, and began (1810), under cover of opposition to Napoleon, their struggle for independence, and a confederation was formed. The spirit soon spread throughout all the American colonies. Anarchy and civil war ensued, but Spain was weak, and the confederation gained their last and decisive victory in 1821. Independence assured, they set up separate governments. The Spaniards were never able to regain control of these colonies, but the states have been nearly wrecked by their numerous quarrels among themselves. They are now in better condition, and Chile and Argentine Republic promise to become strong nations. Unfortunately, between these two there is a disputed boundary question pending, and Chile is trying to force an immediate settlement under threat of war.

Chile.

The early inhabitants of Chile, called Araucanians, were brave and warlike About 1450 Peru, which enjoyed a comparatively high degree of civilization, invaded and conquered Chile, and at the time of the Spanish conquest of Peru, Chile was a Peruvian dependency.

In 1540 Pizarro sent a few Spanish soldiers and a large body of Peruvians into Chile, who subdued the country and established Santiago in 1541. The original inhabitants were never thoroughly conquered by the Spaniards, although an incessant and costly war was kept up until 1724, when a treaty was made which acknowledged the freedom of the Araucanians and defined the boundaries of their territory.

When Joseph Napoleon was made king of Spain, the Chileans, under cover of support to the dethroned monarch, revolted, formed with the La Plata provinces a confederation, and began the struggle for independence. The Chileans were overpowered by Spanish forces from Peru, and in 1814 the Provinces of La Plata sent an army to their assistance under the command of San Martin, styled, for his success, "The Liberator." Chile was speedily freed of the Spanish forces, and in their gratitude they would have made San Martin president, but he declined in favor of General O'Higgins, who was appointed Director.

O'Higgins was a brave, able officer, of Irish descent, under whose leadership the Chileans were able to hold their own, and in 1818, with their other allies, they carried the war against the Spanish into Peru.

In 1833 a substantial constitution was framed, which has rendered them excellent service, being next to that of the United States, the oldest written constitution in the world.

In marked contrast to the usual Spanish colony on gaining its independence, Chile has had but one insurrection, that from 1885 to 1891, when the president, declaring himself dictator, was overthrown, strange as it may seem, by the moderate and conservative parties.

Mr. Egan, the American minister at Santiago, extended refuge to eighty Balmacedists after their overthrow, and by this action incurred the enmity of the congressional party and caused the attack of the Chilean mob upon the crew of the "Baltimore" October 16, 1891, by which two of the crew were killed and eighteen wounded. The United States demanded satisfaction, and the Chileans replied in an insulting manner. Secretary Blaine pressed the matter vigorously, and January 23, 1892, they made a complete and ample apology, though with rather bad grace, and are not particularly cordial toward us yet.

Peru.

Francisco Pizarro sailed from Panama December 28, 1531, with 183 men, 37 horses and three small vessels. After a voyage of about a fortnight he landed off the coast of Peru, disembarked and sent his ships back for reinforcements. They returned with 30 men and 26 more horses. With this party he undertook the conquest of a country as large as that part of the United States east of the Mississippi River, and so thickly populated that the good Las Casas, bishop of Chiapa, and the best contemporary historian, says, "In the province of Peru alone the Spaniards killed above 40,000,000 people," while it was a colony of Spain.

A volume would not suffice to tell of the wonderful civilization Pizarro found.

"Through the entire length of the empire two great military roads were built, one on the plateau, the other on the shore. The former, for nearly 2,000 miles, crossed sierras covered with snow, was thrown over ravines, or went through tunnels in the rocks; it scaled the more difficult precipices by means of stairways. Where it was possible, it was carried over the mountain clefts by filling them with masonry, or, where that could not be done, suspension bridges were used, the cables being made of osiers of maguey fibres. Some of these cables are said to have been as thick as a man and 200 feet long. Where such bridges could not be thrown across, and a stream flowed in the bottom of the mountain valley, the passage was made by ferry-boats or rafts. As to the road itself, it was about 20 feet in width, faced with flags covered with bitumen, and had mile-stones. Our admiration at this splendid engineering is enhanced when we remember that it was accomplished without iron and gunpowder. The shore road was built on an embankment, with a clay parapet on each side, and shade trees. Where circumstances called for it, piles were used. Every five miles there was a post-house. The public couriers, as in Mexico, could make, if necessary, 200 miles a day. Of these roads Humboldt says that they were among the most useful and most stupendous executed by the hand of man. The reader need scarcely be told that there were no such triumphs of skill in Spain.

"In Cuzco, the metropolis, was the imperial residence of the Inca and the Temple of the Sun. It contained edifices which excited the amazement of the Spanish adventurers themselves — streets, squares, bridges, fortresses surrounded by turreted walls, subterranean galleries by which the garrison could reach important parts of the town. Indeed, the great roads we have spoken of might be regarded as portions of an immense system of military works spread all over the country, and having their centre at Cuzco.

"The imperial dignity was hereditary, descending from father to son. His (the Inca) diadem consisted of a scarlet tasseled fringe round his brow, adorned with two feathers. He wore earrings of great weight. His dress of lama-wool was dyed scarlet, inwoven with gold and studded with gems. Whoever approached him bore a light burden on the shoulder as a badge of servitude, and was barefoot. The Inca was not only the representative of the temporal, but also of the spiritual power. He was more than supreme pontiff, for he was a descendant of the Sun, the God of the nation. He made laws, imposed taxes, raised armies, appointed or removed judges at his pleasure. He traveled in a sedan ornamented with gold and emeralds; the roads were swept before him, strewn with flowers and perfumed. His palace at Yucay was described by the Spaniards as a fairy scene. It was filled with works of Indian art; images of animals and plants decorated the niches of its walls; it had an endless labyrinth of gorgeous chambers, and here and there shady crypts for quiet retirement. Its baths were great golden bowls. It was embosomed in artificial flowers.

"The Peruvian religion ostensibly consisted of a worship of the Sun, but the higher classes had already become emancipated from such a material association, and recognized the existence of one almighty, invisible God. They expected the resurrection of the body and the continuance of the soul in a future life. It was their belief that in the world to come our occupations will resemble those we have followed here.

"An annual survey of the country, its farming and mineral products, was made, the inventory being transmitted to the government. A register was kept of births and deaths; periodically a general census was taken. The Inca, at once emperor and pope, was enabled, in that double capacity, to exert a rigorous patriarchal rule over his people, who were treated like mere children — not suffered to be oppressed, but compelled to be occupied; for, with a wordly wisdom which no other nation presents, labor was here acknowledged not only as a means, but also as an end. In Peru a man could not improve his social state; by these refinements of legislation he was brought into an absolutely stationary condition. He could become neither richer nor poorer; but it was the boast of the system that every one lived exempt from social suffering,— that all enjoyed competence.

"They terraced the mountain sides, filling the terraces with rich earth. They excavated pits in the sand, surrounded them with adobe walls, and filled them with manured soil. On the low level they cultivated bananas and cassava; on the terraces above, maize and quinoa; still higher, tobacco; and above that, the potato. The whole civilized world has followed them in the cultivation of the potato. The Peruvian bark is one of the most invaluable remedies. Large tracts of North America would be almost uninhabitable without the use of its active alkaloid quinine, which actually, in no insignificant manner, reduces the percentage of mortality throughout the United States.

"Indispensably necessary to their agricultural system were their great water works. In Spain there was nothing worthy of being compared with them. The aqueduct of Condesuya was nearly 500 miles long. Its engineers had overcome difficulties in a manner that might well strike modern times with admiration. Its water was distributed as prescribed by law; there were officers to see to its proper use. From these great water works and from their roads it may be judged that the architectural skill of the Peruvians was far from insignificant."*

Upon the arrival of Pizarro at the capital of the Inca he was cordially received. He found well built houses of masonry and regulur streets, and proceeded to dispose his forces so as to occupy the best strategic positions. Without any suspicion of treachery, Inca Atahualpa prepared to make him a visit. Upon a given signal the Inca was suddenly attacked, made prisoner, and his people slaughtered.

The Inca's Ransom.

Upon his release he offered as a ransom gold enough to fill a room twenty-two feet long, seventeen feet wide, and as high as a man could reach. This enormous treasure was collected in about two months, and after the fifth belonging to the crown had been deducted there yet remained about $18,000,000 to be divided among the conquerors. The treasure secured, Pizarro at once treacherously put the Inca to death. It is gratifying to know that De Soto and a few other followers, with Pizarro, expressed their condemnation in the warmest terms.

The Royal Fifth.

Such were the wonderful resources of the country that the treasure sent Charles V. in 1595 from Peru and Mexico amounted to $35,000,000. The country was subjugated, but no sooner done than Pizarro quarreled

---

*Draper's "Intellectual Development of Europe."

with his lieutenant, Almagro, whom he condemned and put to death, only himself to fall by the weapons of assassins a little later.

Peru was for a long time the richest province of Spain in South America, and the one on which she had the strongest hold. A revolt occurred in 1780, led by the native chief, Tupac Amaru, a descendent of the Incas. It all but succeeded, and so frightened were the tyrants that the most horrible cruelty was practiced after it was suppressed. Spain had too strong a hold on Peru for her to throw off the yoke when the other South American colonies revolted, but in 1820 assistance arrived from Chile under the command of General San Martin, and the greater part of Peru fell into the hands of the patriots. Independence was formally proclaimed July 28, 1821, and San Martin assumed the title of "Protector of Peru." As soon as a congress was assembled San Martin resigned and returned to Chile. In 1823 the Spanish forces were reinforced and gained some successes. Simon Bolivar of Venezuela came to the assistance of the Peruvians, was received with great rejoicing, and made dictator. A decisive battle took place December 9, 1824, at Ayacucho, the greatest ever fought for liberty in South America, and the Spanish power received its death blow.

Peru has had a stormy career since then, and has several times been engaged in war with her sister republics, the last, especially disastrous for her, with Chile, 1879 to 1884, from which the country has not yet fully recovered.

Colombian States.

For the sake of convenience we shall treat the history of Colombia, Venezuela and Ecuador under the title of the Colombian States, as their experiences with Spain were so similar. Colombia was visited by the Spanish about 1535 and in 1538 the city of Bogota was founded.

Numerous Spanish colonies at once sprang up and the native population was speedily subjugated.

Peru was the richest of the Spanish possessions and there the Viceroy made his headquarters, from which he governed the Colombian States as dependencies of Peru. Numerous rivalries between the different viceroys and their subordinates frequently arose and the condition of the colonies was not a particularl happy one. The Colombian States were the first to set up the struggle for independence, perhaps because they were nearer to Europe and in closer communication, or because the inhabitants were better informed and had made more progress. The native population, always restless and uneasy under Spanish rule, had been mercilessly taxed to support the wars between Spain and England, and the French revolution following had a distinct influence in increasing their restlessness. In 1797 the British captured Trinidad, and keenly alive to the advantages of cutting off Spain's revenues from her American colonies that enabled her to carry on her wars with England, began quietly to incite the states to revolution. The seed fell on fertile soil, for some of the colonists had taken part in the American revolution, noticeably, Francis Miranda who, holding a commission from France, went to America in the expedition France sent to help her ally. Of course such men would come back with ideas concerning rights and liberty well calculated to create a disturbance in colonies governed as were those of Spain.

Miranda was suspected of plotting to free his own country and for his personal safety thought it advisable to go to France. Later, an alliance between Spain and France rendered that refuge untenable and he passed over to England. While there he probably became the agent of the British government, who saw an opportunity to strike a good blow at Spain by severing the allegiance of her American colonies. He went to Trinidad in 1806, where he was joined by some Americans who sympathized with the struggle of the Spanish colonies for freedom, and at the head of about 500 volunteers, largely made up of English and American sympathizers, he landed in Venezuela. The time was not ripe and he was forced to return, but the seed was sown and in due time brought forth fruit.

The abdication of the Spanish king in 1808 and the likelihood of Napoleon's ambitious plans being realized, did much to dissipate their feeling of loyalty to the mother country, and in 1810 the Colombian States revolted and began their struggle for independence. The insurgent leaders were unable to combine heartily, dissensions arose, treachery penetrated everywhere, and the attempt was unsuccessful. So great a part did personal advantage play and at so low an ebb was patriotism, that Colonel Bolivar, afterward called "The Liberator," was accused of treachery and at least surrendered his forces to the royalists without any great provocation. The soldiers deserted Miranda and he was forced to surrender. In utter disregard for the pledge the Spanish had made him he was sent to Europe and died in prison.

One province, New Granada, still maintained its independence and thither Bolivar took his way, while the rest of the country was experiencing the usual terror of a Spanish re-conquest. The severity the conquerors used in suppressing the revolt increased rather than crushed the spirit of independence. Bolivar entered the service of New Granada, created for himself a new character, and when the time was ripe, reappeared in his native province at the head of an army. A terrible war, merciless in its practice was waged, but Bolivar's generalship succeeded and in 1813 he entered Caracas and was proclaimed "Liberator" of Venezuela and later, in 1814, "Supreme Dictator." The royalists rallied, a frightful civil war ensued and the tide swept back and forth with varying fortunes. At last in 1818 Bolivar, by the aid of French and British auxiliaries, gained several important victories and freed the states from the crown of Spain.

Bolivar, of course, became president, and the republic needed him, for the Spanish still held several fortified posts, and no one could tell at what moment the influence of the "Holy Alliance" might turn from sympathy to active support. However, in 1823, the Columbian States were in such condition that he felt free to turn his attention to the Peruvians in their struggle for freedom, and entered that province with an army in co-operation with General San Martin, the "Liberator" of Chile. As a reward for his success he was made the popular idol of Peru and then "Dictator."

Bolivar deserves his reputation as a successful general. In the struggle with Spain he proved himself brave, able and patriotic. If, as a statesman, his head became turned, it is well to remember that he was treated like a a demi-god and exposed to temptations well calculated to try the fibre of the staunchest patriot. He certainly freed the colonies from the dominion of Spain, whatever his ultimate ambitions may have been. He died December 17, 1830, having outlived his popularity, a bitter, disappointed man. In a letter to a friend he says: "I have been in power for nearly twenty years, from which I have gathered only a few definite results.

"1. America is for us ungovernable.

"2. He who dedicates his services to a revolution, plows the sea.

"3. The only thing that can be done in America is to emigrate.

"4. This country will inevitably fall into the hands of the unbridled rabble, and little by little become a prey to petty tyrants of all color and races."

For many years the affairs of the states were in a

deplorable condition, and they showed themselves but little fitted for self-government. The confederation formed in a common cause against Spain was broken up soon after their object was accomplished, and the states set up independent governments. "The Spanish misgovernment left a legacy of bitterness and anarchy that has been the cause of much misery. Political passion ran high, and its history for generations has been a continual struggle, always more or less warlike."

An insurrection is now in progress in Venezuela.

Mexico.

For many centuries prior to the discovery of Mexico by the Spanish, the country had been inhabited by different tribes of Indians, some of whom possessed a high degree of civilization. Of the earlier tribes, the Toltecs, whose period ranges from the sixth to the eleventh centuries, were the furthest advanced. They built temples and cities; they had a year of 365 days to which they added twelve and one-half days at the end of every fifty-two years, thus bringing it within a small fraction of the actual length of the solar year. Their religion was mild, their laws simple and just. The Aztecs, the succeeding dominant race, were better warriors, more forceful and sanguinary. They believed in one invisible supreme God, with numerous inferior divinities. They built imposing temples to their local divinity (Mexican Mars) and offered human sacrifices before his altar. According to their traditions, one of their divinities had retired from earth, but was expected to return. It was this superstition that rendered their conquest by the Spanish much easier; for the first appearance of the white men on the Mexican coast had filled the Montezuma with terror, because the people were expecting the return of their God, and his oracles had told him that his overthrow was at hand.

It was by accident, not by intention, that the Spaniards first beheld the shores of Mexico. Cordova, sailing from Cuba to the neighboring isles on a slaving expedition (1517) encountered severe storms, and was driven westward until he sighted the coast of Yucatan. Reporting his discovery to the Governor of Cuba, a party under Grijalva was sent out the succeeding year, who made extensive explorations along the coast of Mexico on the Carribean side, and the stories told by the sailors on his return fired the imagination of Spanish adventurers. The Cuban governor, Valasquez, selected one of his boldest adventurers, Hernando Cortez, and placed him at the head of an expedition for the conquest and occupation of the new country. Before the final preparations were made he became suspicious of Cortez's ambitions, and seemed so much inclined to deprive him of his command, that Cortez hastily departed without waiting to complete his preparations. He landed in 1519 and founded Vera Cruz, established a government for the colony sufficiently to technically comply with the requirements of the Spanish law, threw off the authority of the Cuban governor, and receiving a commission from the hands of the government he had established, scuttled his ships, and with a force consisting of about 450 Spaniards, six or seven cannon and fifteen horses, set out to conquer the powerful inland monarch of whom he had heard so much.

Bernal Diaz Del Castillo, a contemporary historian, says of Cortez:

"He was of good stature and strongly built, of a rather plain complexion and serious countenance, an excellent horseman and dexterous in the use of arms; he was something of a poet and a very good rhetorician. and, as I have been told, a Bachelor of Laws. He was very patient under insults or injuries. Some of the soldiers were at times very rude and abusive to him, but he never resented their conduct, although he had often great reason to do so. Where we had to erect a fortress, Cortez was the hardest laborer in the trenches; when we were going into battle, he was as forward as any; he was very determined and headstrong in all business of war, not attending to any remonstrances on account of danger."

Montezuma, the Aztec Emperor of the city of Mexico, held sway over but a portion of the territory which now comprises that country, but he levied tribute of numerous other petty kings or caciques, and Cortez found them ripe for revolt. With great skill and diplomacy he attached them to his own cause, and continued his march upon the capital. The rude weapons of the natives could not contend with the armor, artillery and horses of the Spaniards, and the latter especially filled them with terror. However, in his skirmishes two horses were killed, all of them hurt and many Spaniards wounded before he reached the capital of the Montezumas, which we will allow him to describe in his own words.

"This great city (Mexico) is situated in this salt lake, and from the main land to the denser parts of it, by whichever route one chooses to enter, the distance is two leagues. There are four avenues or entrances to the city, all of which are formed by artificial causeways, two spears' length in width. The city is as large as Seville or Cordova; its streets, I speak of the principal ones, are very wide and straight; some of these, and all the inferior ones, are half land and half water, and are navigated by canoes. All the streets at intervals have openings, through which the water flows, crossing from one street to another, and at these openings, some of which are very wide, there are also very wide bridges composed of large pieces of timber of great strength and well put together; on many of these bridges ten horses can go abreast. This city has many public squares, in which are situated the markets and other places for buying and selling. There is one square twice as large as that of the city of Salamanca, surrounded by porticoes, where are daily assembled more than 60,000 souls engaged in buying and selling, and where are found all kinds of merchandise that the world affords, embracing the necessaries of life, as for instance, articles of food, as well as jewels of gold and silver, lead, brass, copper, tin, precious stones, bones, shells, snails and feathers. Every kind of merchandise is sold in a particular street or quarter assigned to it exclusively, and thus the best order is preserved. They sell everything by number or measure, at least so far we have not observed them to sell anything by weight. There is a building in the great square that is used as an audience house, where ten or twelve persons who are magistrates, sit and decide all controversies that arise in the market, and order delinquents to be punished.

"This great city contains a large number of temples, or houses for their idols, very handsome edifices, which are situated in the different districts and the suburbs. Among these temples there is one which far surpasses all the rest, whose grandeur of architectural details no human tongue is able to describe; for within its precincts, surrounded by a lofty wall, there is room enough for a town of 500 families. Around the interior of this enclosure there are handsome edifices containing large halls and corridors, in which the religious persons attached to the temple reside. There are full forty towers, which are lofty and well built, the largest of which has fifty steps leading to its main body, and is higher than the tower of the principal church at Seville. The stone and wood of which they are constructed are so well wrought in every part that nothing could be better done."*

---

* Cortes "Dispatches."

On reaching the city, with characteristic daring, Cortez disposed his force in such a manner as to make Montezuma practically a prisoner, and thus a hostage for the good behavior of his Mexican subjects. The supernatural awe in which the Mexicans held the Spaniards, added to the fear of their cannon and horses, terrorized the natives so that they made no effort to release their monarch. Thus Cortez took possession and governed in the name of the king whom he held captive.

He remained here for some months, when news reached him that a force sent by the Cuban governor to arrest him had reached the coast. Leaving a part of his force in Mexico under Alvarado, he proceeded by forced marches to the coast, surprised the party sent to arrest him, wounded and captured the leader, and by his brilliant personal magnetism, induced the men to renounce their allegiance to the Cuban governor and follow him in the daring conquest he painted to their eager imaginations.

Now with over 1,000 soldiers at his command he returned to the relief of the garrison he had left, to find it closely besieged by the Mexicans, who had risen in revolt. Montezuma showed himself before his subjects in an endeavor to pacify them, was struck by stones and arrows and mortally wounded. A series of most desperate battles took place. Castillo says, "I have read of the destruction of Jerusalem, but I cannot conceive that the mortality there exceeded this of Mexico. The streets, the squares, the houses and the courts were covered with dead bodies. We could not step without treading on them. The lake and the canals were filled with them, and the stench was intolerable. Cortez himself was for some time ill from the effects of it." Whichever way the Spaniards looked the place seemed to be filled with a multitude of people, content to lose thousands of Mexicans if one Spanish life might thereby be destroyed. To retreat was dangerous; to remain was certain destruction.

"The Melancholy Night."

"At all events it was decided to abandon the city that very night. Many of the common soldiers had converted their share of the prize into gold chains, collars and other ornaments which they easily carried about their persons. Much of the rich booty of the principal cavaliers had been converted into bars and wedges of solid gold. Cortez delivered the share belonging to the crown to the royal officers, assigning one of the strongest horses and a guard of soldiers. Much of the treasure was necessarily abandoned. The metal lay scattered in shining heaps along the floor, exciting the cupidity of the soldiers. 'Take what you will,' said Cortez, 'better you should have it than these Mexican hounds. Be careful not to overload yourselves; he travels safest in the dark night who travels lightest.' His own followers took heed of his counsel, but the troops of Navarez, pining for riches of which they had heard so much and hitherto seen so little, showed no such discretion, and, rushing on the treacherous spoil, they loaded themselves with as much of it as they could accommodate about their persons. A portable bridge had been constructed to be laid over the open canals in the causeway. At midnight the gates were thrown open and the Spaniards for the last time sallied forth from the walls of the ancient fortress. A drizzling rain which fell without intermission, added to the obscurity; steadily and noiselessly as possible the Spaniards trailed their way along the great street which so lately had resounded with the tumult of battle. But as they drew near the causeway and prepared to lay the portable bridge Indian sentinels sounded the alarm and the huge drum in the deserted temple of the War-God sent forth those solemn tones which, heard only in the seasons of calamity, vibrated through every corner of the capital. Arrows and stones fell every moment faster and more furious till they thickened into a terrible tempest. As the last of the army crossed they endeavored to raise the portable bridge, but it stuck fast in the sides of the dike. The weight of the men and horses had lodged it so firmly in the stones and earth that it was beyond their power to dislodge it. The tidings soon spread from man to man; a cry of despair arose which for a moment drowned all noise of conflict; all means of retreat were cut off; order and subordination were at an end; intense danger produced intense selfishness; each thought only of his own life; pressing forward they trampled down the weak and the wounded, heedless whether it were friend or foe; the leading files, urged on by the rear, were crowded on the brink of the gulf and dashed into the water; some succeeded in swimming their horses across; others failed; some who reached the opposite bank were overturned in the ascent and rolled headlong with their steeds back into the lake. Above the combatants arose a wild and discordant clamor in which shouts of vengeance were mingled with groans of agony, with invocation of the saints and the Blessed Virgin, and with the screams of the women, for there were several women, both native and Spaniards, who had accompanied the Christian camp. Those fared best, as the General had predicted, who traveled lightest, and many were the unfortunate wretches who, weighted down with the fatal gold they loved so well, were buried with it in the salt floods of the lake. Cortez with his gallant comrades, Olid, Morla, Sandoval, and a few others, kept in advance. The first gray of the morning was now coming over the waters. It showed the hideous confusion of the scene which had been shrouded in the obscurity of night. Cortez and his companions were compelled to plunge again into the lake, though all did not escape. Alvarado, unhorsed, stood on the brink for a moment hesitating what to do. He had but a second for thought, but despair gave him unusual energy; he was a man of powerful frame, and setting his long lance firmly on the rocks which strewed the bottom of the lake, he sprang forward with all his might and cleared the wide gap at a leap. To this day the name 'Alvarado's leap,' given to the spot, still commemorates an exploit which rivaled those of the demi-gods of fable. Cortez and his companions now rode forward. A few of the enemy hung on their rear or annoyed them by occasional flights of arrows from the lake. What a spectacle did they present! Their shattered mail, their tattered garments, dripping with the salted ooze, showing through their rents many a bruise and ghastly wound, their bright arms soiled, their proud crests and banners gone; the baggage, artillery, spoil — all, in short, that constitutes the pride and panoply of glorious war — forever lost.

Cortez looked wistfully at their thin and disordered ranks, sought in vain for many a familiar face, and missed more than one dear companion who had stood side by side with him through all the perils of the conquest. The sight was too much for him. He covered his face with his hands and the tears which trickled down revealed too plainly the anguish of his soul."*

In a nearly famished condition Cortez reached the principal city of one of his allies. Reinforcements reaching him from Vera Cruz, he made another attack upon the city, which, after a most obstinate defense and terrible slaughter, was captured. The least of the estimates places the Aztec loss at 120,000. The spirit of the people was now broken, and Cortez became governor in 1522.

Spanish intrigue played its usual part, and after a time Cortez was recalled, treated with marked coldness by Charles V., and died in obscurity and disgrace. (1547.)

---

* Prescott's "Conquest of Mexico."

The country was subsequently ruled by the able Mendoza as viceroy until 1550. Under his administration colleges were founded, money coined and the first printing press in the new world introduced, from which the first book printed in America was issued. (1536.) Upon the accession of Philip II. to the Spanish throne, viceroys of less merit were appointed, and the condition of all the colonies sensibly declined. Notwithstanding the usual Spanish incapacity for colonial administration, the natural resources of Mexico were so great as to make it second only to Peru.

When Napoleon, in 1808, forced the Spanish monarch to abdicate and appointed Joseph Bonaparte king of Spain, the chain of loyalty binding Mexico to Spain was perceptibly weakened, and under the leadership of a few daring spirits, they began, in 1810, the struggle for freedom. After an unsuccessful struggle for ten years, the leaders were either killed, captured or driven from the country, and in 1820 the Spanish authority appeared fully re-established. Curiously enough, one of the Royalist officers, Iturbide, to whose soldierly qualities the defeat of the rebels had been in a large measure due, was destined to become first ruler of the independent state.

The Spanish government having refused to recognize the treaty with the insurgents with which peace was secured, Iturbide placed himself at the head of the revolutionists and May, 1822, was declared emperor. His administration lasted less than a year, and he was overthrown by the republican element under the leadership of Santa Anna, later famous as president of Mexico during its war with the United States. A constitution modeled somewhat after our own was adopted, General Victoria made first president of the republic and the independence of the new nation recognized by the United States in 1829.

About this time the presidential election resulted in a civil war, and Santa Anna became the controlling spirit of the nation. The history of Mexico for the next dozen years is but a recital of insurrections fomented by different ambitious leaders.

Texas, then a Mexican State, had about 23,000 population, 20,000 of whom were made up of colonists from other nations and of the colonists, 13,000 belonged to settlements founded by Moses Austin and his son, General Stephen F. Austin. When the republic of Mexico, by the decree of September 15, 1829, began the emancipation of all the slaves within its boundaries, the American settlers refused to obey the decree. The national authorities were not in a position to enforce it, and the Texans gained one point. Foreseeing danger, Mexico prohibited the further emigration of Americans; but this was "locking the stable after the horse was stolen," for the colony had as a leader General Sam Houston, who came there for the express purpose of separating it from Mexico and with whose plans it is supposed Jackson, then President, was familiar. In 1835 Santa Anna attempted to reduce his rebellious State to order, and collisions of armed forces took place, in which the Americans usually had the advantage. On March 2, 1836, a committee of sixty Texans, two of whom were of Mexican nationality, signed a formal declaration of independence, and under the leadership of Houston won their decisive victory at San Jacinto, April 21, 1836, made a prisoner of Santa Anna himself, who, under compulsion, acknowledged their independence and promised that the Mexican Congress should ratify it; but this Congress refused to do.

The Texans elected General Houston their first president and the United States recognized their independence in 1837, which Texas maintained until 1845, when it was annexed to the United States.

The boundaries between Texas and Mexico had never

been definitely settled, and the United States espousing the Texan claims it necessarily brought on war with Mexico. The war closed in 1848, the United States gaining thereby all the territory from California to Texas inclusive, though it is needless to say that Spain, France and England looked upon the transaction with ill-concealed displeasure.

Another period of history made up by a recital of insurrections, brings us to 1861 and the administration of Juarez, who was now President as the result of a revolution, during the progress of which Mexican debts to foreign nations had been repudiated. Spain, France and England seized this opportunity, while the United States were engaged with domestic trouble, to put forth their claims for losses sustained by their subjects in Mexico. Spain landed troops in October of '61 and France and England in January of '62. The Spanish and British claims were not serious and were settled by negotiation; their forces were then withdrawn. The French army remained and tacitly formed an alliance with the disaffected party of Mexico. They refused to treat with President Juarez and war was declared in 1862. After varying struggles Juarez was forced to flee and the French established a regency. A convention was held under French auspices, which by a vote of 250 to 20 decided upon a monarchy under a Roman Catholic Emperor. The crown was tendered Maximilian, Archduke of Austria, who accepted it and arrived in Mexico June 12, 1864. The United States had protested against the action of the French, but was herself engaged in civil war. Juarez, with a few adherents, fled to the Rio Grande. After the establishment of peace at home, Sheridan was sent to Texas with a large army, and under implied pressure from the United States the French soldiers were withdrawn. They were the support of Maximilian, who was soon defeated, captured and shot June 19, 1867. Juarez was made President and re-elected in '71, the first instance in Mexican history of a President serving his full term.

Under President Diaz, Mexico has reached a fair degree of prosperity.

The Philippine Islands.

The northern division of the Malay peninsula, lying between 5° and 19° N. latitude and next to Cuba, the most valuable colonial possession of Spain.

Authorities do not agree as to the number of them, and they are variously estimated at from 1,000 to 1,400. The total area is estimated at 116,000 square miles, and the population somewhere from seven to eight millions. Between four and five hundred of the islands are inhabited.

The largest of the islands are Luzon, area 40,000 square miles, and Mindanao, 12,600 square miles.

This group is of volcanic origin, and has a range of highlands running through from north to south, the highest of which is about 6,000 feet, and some of the peaks are still active volcanoes.

The coast line is much broken and indented by the mouths of several deep, navigable rivers, affording good harbors. Earthquakes are frequent and preclude tall, substantial buildings. The islands are also swept by fierce tropical storms and are within the belt of the monsoons.

The wild animals indigenous to the islands are the antelope, fox, wild cat, monkey, and in the rivers is found the cayman, a species of alligator.

The islands are rich in natural resources, and among the minerals are gold, copper, iron, lead, mercury, sulphur and coal.

The early policy of Spain allowed no trade with foreigners, and the Spanish colonies of America were allowed to send but one ship a year.

History.

"The islands were discovered by Magellan, in 1521, and Manila, the capital, was founded by Legaspi in 1571, and since that time they have been under the dominion of Spain. Their conquest and retention was in marked contrast to the usual Spanish methods of dealing with conquered people, methods of which Cortez and Pizarro are the chief exponents. Legaspi, with six Augustinians and a handful of soldiers, accomplished the wonderful work of conquest. Without greed for gold and without any exhibition of cruelty or persecution, these devoted men labored among the docile people until they won their confidence, so that the islands were seized with little bloodshed and no massacre or depopulation. The name "Islas Filipas" was given by Legaspi in 1567. Contests with frontier rebellious tribes, attacks by pirates, earthquakes and typhoons serve to break up the monotony of an otherwise uneventful history.

"Manila was captured by the English under Draper and Cornish in 1762, and ransomed for $5,000,000, but was restored in 1764. The present insurrection in the islands was put down with an iron hand, and many atrocities were committed, so that it is little wonder that many of the inhabitants look upon the arrival of the Americans as a deliverance.

"The Philippine Islands are peculiar in having three seasons — a cold, a hot and a wet. The first extends from November to February or March. The winds are northerly, and woolen clothing and a fire are desirable, the sky is clear and the air bracing, and Europeans in this strange clime consider it the pleasantest time of the year. The hot season lasts from March to June, and the heat becomes oppressive and thunder storms of terrific violence are frequent. During July, August, September and October, the rain comes down in torrents, and large tracts of the lower country are flooded.

THE ASCENDENCY OF AMERICA. 183

"The population of the Philippines is 7,670,000; the capital, Manila, having 54,062 inhabitants. There is a small Spanish resident population and about 100,000 Chinese, in whose hands are the principal industries. The native inhabitants are mostly of the Malay race. The government is administered by a governor-general and a captain-general and the forty-three provinces are ruled by governors, alcades or commandants, according to their importance or position.

"The estimated revenue of the islands in 1894-95 was $13,500,000 and the expenditure $13,200,000. There is an export duty on tobacco and nearly every article imported is taxed. The chief products are sugar, hemp, coffee and indigo, and there are large coal fields which are now being opened, so that it is expected that 5,000 tons of coal per month may be mined. The imports in 1896 were about $12,000,000 and the exports $20,500,000. There are 70 miles of railway on the islands and 720 miles of telegraph.

"Manila lies on the western side of the island of Luzon and is about 600 miles from Hong-Kong. It has one of the most spacious and beautiful harbors in the world. The shores are low and inland can be seen the outline of mountains. The city of Manila resembles a dilapidated fortress surrounded by stone walls 300 years old. There is also a wide, shallow moat. The gates are never closed and it is doubtful if the city could make any defense. There is also an old fort. Several creeks branch off from the landlocked bay and afford a means of communication with the suburbs. These creeks are crossed by innumerable bridges, and canoes thread their way through these narrow water-ways, which somewhat resemble a tropical Venice. Around the walls and the edge of the bay is a fashionable drive lined with almond trees. It is here that the well-to-do inhabitants walk, drive and meet their friends. Of nearly 300,000 people in the province there are not more than 5,000 Spaniards. One of the most curious sights to the traveler who comes from China are the large two-wheel drays drawn by so-called water buffaloes. They are guided by a ring through their nose to which is attached a cord leading back to the driver, who either mounts on his back or rides on the shafts. The weight of the load is borne on the neck by means of a yoke. The beasts are docile and their chief delight seems to be to wallow in the mud and to submerge themselves so that only the nose is out of the water. The water buffalo is particularly valuable to the inhabitants as a beast of burden, as it can drag a plow and can walk while knee deep in the mud. The milk of the female is very generally used instead of cow's milk, but its meat is unfit for food.

"In the two best streets of Manila there are excellent stores in which goods of all kinds can be purchased at moderate prices, many of the merchants being Chinese. The churches must have been imposing buildings years ago before they were shaken and in some cases wrecked by earthquakes. They contain no works of art of any value. The inhabitants are very faithful to their church and the archbishop possesses almost unlimited influence with the inhabitants. It has often been said, if the priests were taken away, the natives would be ungovernable.

"The dwelling houses in Manila are constructed with a view of shutting out the intense heat of the summer. The houses are rarely more than two stories in height, owing to the ravages of earthquakes. Glass is of course unknown, as the earthquakes would shiver every pane. There is coal in abundance in the Philippine Islands, as already stated, and the streets of Manila would undoubtedly be lighted with coal gas if it were not for the fact that gas pipes would be destroyed in the unstable soil. Of course, accidents are of frequent occurrence with kerosene, but as the natives' houses are very inexpensive, their loss by fire is easily made good.

"Strange to say, life in the old city does not present many points of interest to the traveler, for the streets are narrow and the houses solid and gloomy. It is a marked contrast to the business-like cities of South America. The Spaniards born in the Iberian Peninsula look down upon those born in the islands, so that class distinctions are very closely drawn. This has resulted in the failure to make political combinations. Hatred and jealousy of the foreigner are carried to the extreme limits, the Chinese coming in for a large share of their disfavor. The theatres are poor, concerts are rare and there is no library, and their amusements are mostly limited to hearing the band play, attending balls on Sundays and cockfights. The cockpits are licensed by the government, and though the betting is limited by law, the citizens will not hold to it. The revenues of the islands are furnished by direct taxes on every Indian, half-breed and Chinese, and the export and import duties that have already been referred to.

"The dress of the natives is exceedingly picturesque and is never adopted by the Spanish. Cigar makers in and around the city of Manila number 22,000 and they are all girls and women with the exception of 1,500 men. They present a picturesque appearance with their native costumes and huge hats intended to protect them from the rays of the sun. They make their cigars squatting on their heels or sitting on bamboo stools two inches high. They frequently come from considerable distances, going back and forth in boats. Tobacco always has been and probably will continue to be the most important product of the Philippines; and according to the old laws, the Indians were compelled to raise tobacco in certain regions which were not adapted to growing it, even to the exclusion of other crops, but in 1883 the laws were repealed, and the result was the securing of finer tobacco and better cigars, for they are now made at a higher rate.

"The wants of the natives are few and are easily supplied. They live along the banks of the rivers in huts made of bamboo and cane thatched with palm leaves. Some of the views in the suburbs of Manilla are enchanting."*

"The Philippine Islands have never had the advantage of a good government. Imports are heavily taxed and Spain has derived an enormous income from the islands. Insurrections have been frequent, but owing to the poverty of equipment of the natives who engaged in them, usually ended in quick failure. In 1896 the present insurrection was inaugurated. The military resources of the Spanish were insufficient to suppress the revolt, and not until the government promised greatly needed reforms and amnesty for the insurgents was any progress made. "The Spanish governor-general announced that the islands had been 'pacified'; and thereupon spat upon his own promises and began a system of persecution against the 'rebels' which, in cruelty and torture, outdid anything mankind has ever heard of, barring only the Spanish inquisition. The prisoners were put on the rack, had their limbs lacerated, and in some instances had their eyes put out, their tongues torn out and their ears cut off. Friars, of which the islands are full, clothed in the garb of religion, but disowned by the regular priests of the church, sanctioned these horrible punishments and confiscated the pitiful belongings of the victims for the benefit of their monasteries.

"That such unspeakable actions and breach of faith were resented by the people is not strange. One uprising followed another, and finally the people instituted a provisional revolutionary government, under the leadership of Gen. Emilio Aguinaldo, a patriotic, able and self-

---

* Scientific American, May 7, 1898.

sacrificing native Malay of the highest type. Aguinaldo was twice betrayed by the Spaniards with promises of reform which were never kept. He saw his brothers butchered and his country robbed into poverty. Last December Don Primo de Rivera, the Spanish governor of the islands, made peace with the rebel chieftain and then sought to deprive him of liberty and life. Aguinaldo managed to escape, however, and traveled in disguise from Singapore to Hong Kong, being assisted in his efforts to reach a neutral port by Spencer Pratt, the American consul-general at Singapore. In Hong Kong he placed himself at the disposal of Commodore Dewey and returned to the Philippines with him."

Porto Rico.

Porto Rico lies about 1,000 miles from Havana, and is the fourth in size of the West India islands. Its greatest length from east to west is 108 miles and from north to south 37 miles, with an area of 3,550 square miles. A range of mountains reaching nearly 4,000 feet at the highest point runs the entire length of the island. The rain-carrying winds for Porto Rico come chiefly from the north, and when they strike the high range of hills, or mountains, in the interior, the greater part of their moisture is condensed and falls upon the northern slope, so that water-shed has numerous small rivers. The greater part of the island is north of the range, and well watered, but south of the range irrigation is necessary. The general surface is made up of rolling hills with rich intervening valleys. It furnishes excellent pasturage for large numbers of horses and cattle, and these constitute a large part of the wealth of the inhabitants. Nature apparently set out to make Porto Rico one of the finest places on earth, and but for the interference of Spanish rule seemed in a fair way to succeed. The island presents a beautiful appearance, and has an excellent tropical climate, said to be the most healthful of the Antilles. The climate may be divided into two seasons, the wet and the dry. The dry months are from November to April; the wet are from May to November; and from July to October it is visited by frequent and severe tropical hurricanes.

Sugar was formerly the chief agricultural product, but as the sugar industry became depressed the planters turned to the raising of bananas and the production of coffee. There are many coffee plantations on the islands, and the soil and climate seem particularly well adapted to that plant.

The rivers are small, and only navigable for vessels of moderate tonnage for five or six miles near their mouths. The north coast is subject to a particularly heavy and disagreeable ground swell, capable of considerable violence. There are not many safe harbors. Guancia and Hovas on the south coast and San Juan on the north are the best.

The harbor of San Juan is one of the finest in the West Indies, and is nearly as good as that of Havana. It is large and deep, but the coral formation makes it shallow near the shore, and suitable wharves for the largest vessels have not yet been built. In 1895 over one thousand vessels entered San Juan harbor.

The chief cities are San Juan, the capital, with a population of 28,000 (English Statesman's Year Book says 23,414 in 1887), Ponce, 37,575; San German, 30,146.

By their last official census, Porto Rico contained 8,113,937 people, over 300,000 of whom were negroes.

In 1895 its exports amounted to $15,799,000, of which coffee and sugar furnished about two-fifths its value, and its imports to $17,446,000. The total revenues for the same year were $5,454,958, and the expenditures $3,905,667.

It is fairly well represented in mineral products, gold,

copper, iron, lead and coal being found; but little attention, however, has been given to its mining resources, and its industries are almost wholly agricultural, the chief of which are sugar, coffee, molasses, rum, tobacco, live-stock and timber.

History.

Porto Rico was discovered by Columbus in 1493. The Spaniards took possession of it in 1509, and in a few years their characteristic method of colonization had exterminated the entire native population, estimated to have numbered 700,000.

The English, under Drake, captured and sacked the capital in 1595, and three years later it was visited with like results by the Duke of Cumberland. Since then it has successfully withstood the Dutch in 1615 and the English in 1678 and 1797. In 1820 an unsuccessful attempt was made to throw off the Spanish yoke. Discontent exists there to-day, but as Spain has there at present an army of 40,000 men, the would-be insurgents are completely overawed.

Porto Rico was made a province of Spain in 1870, and given its premier and House of Representatives, but these are controlled by a native Spanish " ring," and are in no degree representative of the people.

San Juan is surrounded by a wall of solid masonry from 50 to 100 feet high. It has also, like Havana, a Morro Castle (round Moorish tower) situated at a considerable elevation above the harbor, from which a plunging fire on an attacking fleet could be delivered. Until a few months ago the greater part of the artillery in the fortifications about the harbor pointed toward the land as the garrison were apprehensive of an uprising. Quite a good many Krupp guns were sent them some time ago from Spain, but it is doubtful if they are all well mounted yet. The old forts of masonry suffered severely in the attack of Admiral Sampson, and nearly all the heavy guns were dismounted, but if manned by an energetic garrison a greater part of the damages could probably be easily repaired.

San Juan under present circumstances is not a healthful town, for it has nothing approaching modern drainage, and if it were not located on a hillside would be even more sickly than it is.

Why Spain Lost Her Colonies.

Spain once had a well-recognized claim to possessions in America whose aggregate area was nearly twice that of all Europe. If she had shown the wisdom in colonial administration that England has displayed for the past hundred years, she might easily have dictated terms to all the world.

Three words explain the secret of her loss and consequent downfall: BIGOTRY! **GREED!** CRUELTY!

With a fatal short-sightedness she drove from her dominions the Moors and Jews, who were her bankers, physicians, scholars, artisans and agriculturists. The Netherlands, the only colony that could have supplied their loss for her, was brought to the verge of ruin by eighty years of the most horrible war that history records.

Ignores Commerce.

Apparently wholly blind to the advantage of building up a trade with the new world that would have been worth to her many times more than the mines of gold and silver, inexhaustible though they seemed, she paid almost no attention to their natural resources other than gold and silver, and to the mining of these bent all her energies, and sacrificed the lives of the natives of every land she conquered.

Cruelty to Natives.

It is estimated that the population of Cuba at the time of its discovery ranged from one to three millions. Under Spanish administration, in forty years the entire native population had practically disappeared, and their places were taken by negroes. Las Casas says, "The Indians of Havana, seeing there was no remedy left, began to take refuge in the deserts and mountains, to secure themselves if possible from death. Some strangled themselves in despair; parents hung themselves together with their children to put the speedier end to their misery by death. I saw with my own eyes about six thousand children die in the space of three or four months, their parents being forced to abandon them, being condemned to the mines." And Cuba was not the exception, but rather the rule; 120,000 Mexicans are said to have perished in the capture of the City of Mexico alone, and more than half a million, directly or indirectly, in the conquest of Cortes. Her treatment of the natives in the lands she discovered was horrible in the extreme. "By millions upon millions whole races of nations were remorselessly cut off. The Bishop of Chiapa affirms that more than fifteen millions were exterminated in his time. From Mexico and Peru a civilization that might have instructed Europe was crushed out. Is it for nothing that Spain has been made a hideous skeleton among living nations, a warning spectacle to the world? Had not her punishment overtaken her, men would surely have said, 'There is no retribution; there is no God.'" *

Colonial Administration.

Her method of dealing with her colonies set a premium on theft, intrigue and treachery, and the dagger of the disappointed assassin was a constant menace to the ambitious and successful leader. The natives were

---

* Draper, "Intellectual Development of Europe."

studiously debarred from any part in the administration of their affairs. The offices were awarded to those who could pay the biggest bribes, which they in turn must wring by extortionate tax of fiendish cruelty from the people over whom they were placed. Allowed no part in self-government, what could be expected of such colonies when the despotic yoke was once thrown off?

"Wherever a popular government succeeded in establishing itself for a few weeks, the first act of the legislature was invariably to vote to its own members enormous salaries. Atrocities at which humanity shudders were committed by either side which happened to obtain a momentary ascendancy; thousands were butchered, not in the excitement of battle, but after fighting had ceased. The capture of a town was usually followed by an indiscriminate slaughter of the inhabitants. The republican governments, as they were called, set up by the liberators, were in reality military despotisms, which, instead of devoting themselves to the establishment of something like permanent institutions, quarreled with their neighboring peoples in the same condition as themselves, and commenced unprincipled wars of aggression before they had themselves fairly escaped from the throes of revolution. Peru and Buenos Ayres both commenced a series of such wars in the first moments of their political existence. Colombia was the scene of a dozen revolutions and counter-revolutions, none of which resulted in keeping their officers in power beyond a few months at a time, and at last split up into three independent republics, which carried on a furious internecine struggle amongst themselves. Chile, within four years, underwent two revolutions, which were succeeded by a prolonged civil war. In Central America a Republic was declared, but a civil war broke out within a few months of its establishment, in which one-half of the population gave no quarter to the other half. Every part of the vast district which was once under the domain of Spain was in the early part of the present century the theatre of endless and meaningless petty wars, got up usually by some adventurer who, having scraped together a few pistols for the purpose of bribing a handful of mutinous and half-starved soldiers to revolt, rallied around him a few of the lowest rabble and set forth on his own account to burn, devastate and destroy the unhappy land. It would be useless to give any detailed account of these frightful scenes. Each revolution originated in Spanish oppression and wickedness, but when the yoke was thrown off the emancipated people found that they had miscalculated their powers, that long misgovernment had banished public spirit, bravery, constancy, out of the land, and had left them fit only to remain in slavery. Nothing but such a government could have formed such a population, nothing but such a population would have tolerated such a government." *

"History Studies," John Hopkins University.

CHAPTER VI.

CUBA.

Cuba lies almost at our door. The cities of Havana and Matanzas in the northwestern portion are less than one hundred miles from the Florida Keys, and the island in its nearest part approaches within eighty-six miles of Key West.

The extreme length of the Island is about 760 miles, its width varies from 120 miles in its widest part in the east to about thirty miles at its narrowest part, from Havana south. In shape Cuba is somewhat like a fish, with Santiago de Cuba for its right eye and its tail curved around in the form of a crescent from the Florida Keys. Cuba lies south of Pennsylvania and extends a little farther east and west than that state and is almost as large, its area, together with its numerous small islands adjacent, being approximately 45,000 square miles, or about one-fourth that of all Spain. It is separated on the north from Florida proper by Florida Strait, 130 miles wide, on the east from Haiti by the Windward Passage, forty-eight miles wide, and on the south from Jamaica by a portion of the Caribbean Sea, ninety miles wide, and on the west from Yucatan, Mexico, by Yucatan Channel, 130 miles wide. Nearly all of Cuba is north of the twentieth parallel of north latitude, and Santiago de Cuba is nearly due south of Philadelphia, and Havana south of Cleveland.

Surface.

A chain of mountains extends throughout the whole length of Cuba. These are highest in the east, reaching a height of about 8,320 feet in the celebrated "Blue Peak," some fifty miles west of Santiago de Cuba. In the eastern portion of the island there are numerous smaller chains branching off from the central range and farther west are isolated peaks and groups. The mountains of the province of Santiago seem to have a submarine connection with the highlands of Jamaica and Haiti, as is evidenced by the simultaneous occurrence of earthquake phenomena. The lowland practically surrounds the island, being in many places a flat soft marsh, rising gradually towards the interior where the great sugar plantations are to be found, a little higher succeeded by the tobacco belt; on the slopes of the mountains the grazing and farming lands are found, and above these the forests. Tons of salt are produced annually in the salt marshes by the natural evaporation of the water. The same fossil animals are found that exist in the corresponding formation in the United States, and the rock formation is of the same character and degree of inclination.

Rivers and Lakes.

With the long watershed it is impossibe for Cuba to have large rivers. Though not long, they discharge a considerable amount of water, as the rainfall is heavy.

Cuba has few lakes, and some of them instead of being drained by rivers, have several rivers flowing into them with no apparent outlet. On the northern coast of Puerto Principe is a little bay, Sabinal, into which the river Maximo empties. This spot is of historical interest because it is supposed that here, October 27, 1492, Columbus landed.

Climate.

The seasons of Cuba are divided into two, wet and dry. The months of May, June, July, August and September, comprise the first season. The annual rainfall is about 40 inches, the rain occurring usually in the afternoon. There are 104 rainy days in the year, but it is said that there are less than twenty days a year on the average when it rains both in the forenoon and afternoon. The annual average temperature of Havana is about $78°$; for the hottest month, August, the average is about $82°$. If it were not for the high humidity, oftentimes reaching 85% the heat would not seem oppressive. Hurricanes are frequent and sometimes disastrous, although in this respect Cuba is better off than most of the West India Islands.

The climate during the dry season is delightful. A remarkable feature of the atmosphere of Cuba is its extreme clearness. Objects can be seen at a long distance; the stars are especially distinct; sunsets are brilliant, but of very brief duration. Except in the forests, the stars usually furnish sufficient light to enable one to travel by night. A tropical climate is found along the low coast line, while back from the coast, as it rises in elevation, the temperature more nearly resembles that of the Southern States. Havana is said to be an excellent place for those suffering from bronchial or pulmonary troubles, as the extremes of temperature are not great. Frosts are sometimes felt in the highlands of the interior.

The coast line belt in general is but little raised above the sea, wet throughout the greater part of the year and liable to the numerous floods and inundations characteristic of the tropics. It is here, in connection with bad sanitary measures, that their terrible fevers find a prolific culture bed. The interior is higher and better, but only about one-third of the soil is cultivated, and one-half of the island is still covered with extensive forests. The tropical heat, the heavy rainfall and the great amount of decaying vegetable matter give rise to dangerous fevers, which make a campaign in these jungles greatly to be dreaded by soldiers not acclimated. Spain's losses in this respect have been frightful.

Soil.

The soil of Cuba, is in general, extremely fertile, although highly productive tracts may be succeeded by barren ones. As frosts are unknown in Cuba except in the highlands, two crops of rice and corn can be grown in one year. The famous "red earth," a soil rich in iron, especially well fitted for the cultivation of sugar cane and coffee, is pretty generally distributed.

Mineral Products.

Cuba has some excellent copper mines, the richest about twelve miles from Santiago, where several grades of the ore are found. Gold also appears in some portions of the island, and iron ore, from which an excellent quality of steel can be made, is mined in the province of Santiago de Cuba. Many varieties of marble are found in the island, and the marble of the "Isle of Pines" is especially remarkable for its fine quality. Bituminous coal of an excellent quality also appears in many parts of the island. Near the coast it is "exceedingly soft" and in a viscous state. There are 138 iron mines; two mines near Santiago are operated by American companies.

Agricultural Products.

The condition of Cuba has not been such as to bring foreign capital to aid in the development of its mining resources and its agricultural products, the chief of which is sugar, far exceed in value those of its mines. Sugar cane was early introduced into the island, at least before 1600. In addition to the losses due to insurrections the sugar planters have had to compete with beet sugar. In 1879 Cuba and Porto Rico sent to Great Britain sugar to the amount of more than $6,000,000. In 1892, the production had fallen in value to $46,000. Consul-general Williams said that for the quarter ending March

1896, the United States secured 96⅓% of the sugar shipped from Cuba. Tobacco of a world-famous quality is indigenous in Cuba, the tobacco plantations of Pinar del Rio being especially famous. Coffee is also one of the valuable productions. It was formerly chiefly grown in the West Indies in the island of Santo Domingo, but when the revolution occurred there, it gave a great stimulus to the coffee plantations of Cuba, large numbers of the inhabitants of Santo Domingo fleeing to Cuba for safety and establishing magnificent coffee plantations there. The ravages of war and the exactions of taxes have almost wiped out the coffee industry in Cuba.

All the usual tropical fruits are produced in large quantities in Cuba, the pineapple, plantain, banana, orange and fig grow abundantly and the lowlands along the coast produce an excellent quality of sea island cotton. The dense forests covering the highlands of the interior are in themselves mines of wealth, cedar, granadillo, ebony and mahogany growing in abundance. These woods are so lightly esteemed that it is said mahogany is often used as ties for the railroad.

With a stable government that would warrant the induction of foreign capital, the natural resources of the island are sure to be enormously developed and the Cuba of the future is likely to excite our admiration.

Coasts.

The coast of Cuba is difficult and dangerous of navigation, fringed as it is by coral reefs, islands and shoals. More than half of the circumference of the island is protected in this way. Add to the dangers of this formation the tropical hurricanes peculiar to this region and the difficulties of a blockading fleet are at once apparent. At different places along the coast these obstructions become well-marked breakwaters extending for miles, one, the "Red Banks," on the coast of Pinar del Rio, another from Cardenas west of Matanzas to Nuevitas, the seaport of Puerto Principe, and on the southern coast one from Manzanillo to Trinidad, and yet another from Cienfuegos to almost the western extremity of the island.

At the mouths of some of the rivers are treacherous, shifting bars. Two hundred years ago a Spanish fleet was caught within such a harbor, a violent storm arose, the bar shifted before the fleet could escape and the vessels were abandoned.

Between these fringes and the coast proper are numerous channels navigable for light-draft vessels when directed by skilled pilots. It is an ideal locality for filibustering and blockade running ventures. In general, the coast fronted by these natural breakwaters is low and marshy, not much above the level of the sea, and the scene of constant conflict between the ocean and the land. In time these marshes will be reclaimed and become a part of the most productive region of the island.

Where the shore is not fringed with these obstructions to navigation, the coast is bold, rugged, and affords numerous fine harbors. The entrance to these harbors is usually high, narrow and easily defended. The best ones on the northern coast, beginning at the western end, are Bahia Honda, Cabanas, Mariel, Havana, Matanzas, Gibara, Nipe and Baracoa. On the south are Cienfuegos, Trinidad, Santiago de Cuba and Guantanamo.

Isle of Pines.

The largest island adjacent to the Cuban coast, almost directly south of Havana, with an area of about 800 square miles and a population of 2,000. It was originally used as a penal colony. The island has some rich mineral resources; beautiful marble in numerous varieties is produced there and the forests contain a wealth of mahogany, cedar, pine and other woods. Among its minerals are iron, silver and mercury.

The village of Santa Fe, in the interior of the island, might easily become a famous health resort on account of its wonderful hot springs. Its principal town, Nueva Gerona, has about 1,000 inhabitants and is some seventy miles from Bacabano on the southern coast of Cuba, the latter communicating by rail with Havana, and for a time blockade runners transacted a brisk business between these ports.

Provinces.

Cuba is divided into six provinces, each with a capital city of the same name as the province.

Pinar del Rio (pee'-nar-del-ree-o.)

Pinar del Rio is in the westernmost end of the island and extends to within 15 or 20 miles of the city of Havana. Its total population is about 231,000, and its capital city is Pinar del Rio, with a population of 5,500. It is connected with Havana by railroad. Pinar del Rio is divided into four districts, Guanjay, population about 60,000; Guane, population about 56,000; Pinar del Rio, about 70,000; and San Cristobal, about 45,000. Its northern coast is broken and mountainous and watered by numerous small rivers. In the south the slope is more gradual and the soil fertile until it approaches the marshy portion along the coast. It is on the southern slope that the tobacco fields are situated that have made this province famous. The crop is so highly esteemed that it is bought up in advance by speculators and always commands fancy prices. This province also produces sugar, coffee, rice, corn, cotton and tropical fruits, although these are not so important as its tobacco crop. Some copper is also mined here.

Havana (Ha-ba'-na.)

Havana, the second province, is about 65 miles in extreme length and 30 in its narrowest part. Its total population is about 375,443, and its capital city is Havana with a population of 200,000. Havana is divided into six districts, Bejucal, population 43,709; Guanabacoa, 32,344; Guines, 45,577; Havana, 213,500; Marianao, 7,352; San Antonio de los Barros, 32,961. It is the chief manufacturing province of the island, is rich in the usual agricultural products of tropical regions, and some bituminous coal is mined here.

Matanzas.

Matanzas, the third province, is about 90 miles in its extreme length and 65 miles in width. Its total population is about 253,408, and the capital city is Matanzas with a population of about 50,000. Matanzas is divided into four districts, Alphonso XII., population 33,887; Cardenas, 53,882; Colon, 79,390; and Matanzas, 86,249. No province is better worked or more thoroughly developed. It is the center of the sugar production and the other agricultural products are important; an excellent quality of peat is produced and mines of copper and coal are worked.

Santa Clara (San-ta Klara.)

Santa Clara was once called Las Cinco Vilas (Five Towns), because Diego Velazquez, the lieutenant of Columbus, laid the foundation of five towns within its boundaries. It is about 200 miles in extreme length and 80 miles in width. Its total population is about 166,671, and the capital city is Santa Clara with a population of 34,635. Santa Clara is divided into three districts, Cienfuegos, population 72,187; Juan de los Remedios, 15,358; Sagua la Granda, 79,126. It was one of the first settled parts of the island and is probably the richest. It produces all the products of the tropical regions, and in addition, some of the temperate zone grown on the sides of the gradual rising slopes of its mountains. Its mineral wealth is not to be despised, producing as it does, gold, silver, copper and asphalt.

Puerto Principe (pwer-to Pren'-se-pay.)

Puerto Principe, the fifth province, is about 150 miles in extreme length and 75 miles wide. Its total population is 124,077, and the capital city is Puerto Principe with a population of 40,679. This province is divided into two districts, Moron, population 57,620; Puerto Principe, 66,467. Puerto Principe is the wildest and least cultivated part of the island. The greater part of it is still covered by dense forests, affording with its broken surface excellent hiding places for those engaged in guerrilla warfare, and it has been the scene of numerous incipient insurrections. It is within this province that the insurgents fixed their provisional capital.

Santiago de Cuba (San-te-a-go day Koo-ba.)

Santiago de Cuba, the sixth province, is nearly 250 miles in extreme length from Cape Maysi to Cape Cruz, and from Cape Cruz to the northernmost part of the province about 120 miles. Its total population is about 195,336 and the capital city is Santiago de Cuba, with a population of 45,000. This province is divided into five districts, Baracoa, 18,057; Guantanamo, 30,044; Holguin, 58,900; Manzanillo, 25,735; Santiago de Cuba, 62,600. The Cauto (Kow-to) river, of the province of Santiago, is ninety miles in length and the longest river in Cuba. Santiago de Cuba is the oldest settled province of the island and is one of the richest. It produces everything in the way of agricultural products that the others produce and is much richer in its mineral wealth, numbering among its mining products, gold, the best copper mines of the island, iron, manganese, mercury, zinc, marble, alabaster, asphalt.

The Principal Cities and Towns of Cuba.

Alfonso XII., a town of Matanzas, thirteen miles south of that city at the juncture of the railroads. Population, about 3,000.

Alquizar, a town of Havana, about thirty-five miles from that town on the line of railroad to Pinar del Rio. Population, about 2,700.

Alto Songo, a town of Santiago de Cuba, twenty-five miles north of that city on the railroad to the mines. Population, about 400.

Bahia Honda, a town of Pinar del Rio, about sixty miles west or Havana. Population, 1,900. Has one of the best harbors on the coast, and it was here that the Virginius was surrendered to the American navy.

Baracoa, a town of the province of Santiago de Cuba, situated in the eastern part and the oldest town in Cuba (1512). Population, 5,200. It was once the capital city of the island, but is now the chief shipping port for the fruit trade. It has no railroad communications.

Batabano, forty-five miles south of the city of Havana, and connected with the capital by railroad. Population, about 1,900. It was the scene of active blockade running while Havana was blockaded by the American fleet.

Bayamo, a town of Santiago de Cuba province, about ninety-four miles northwest from that city, and between it and Manzanillo. It is the terminus of one of the short lines of railroad running out of Santiago. Population, about 3,634.

Bejucal, a town of Havana province, twenty-one miles south of that city on the railroad to Batabano. Population, 6,239.

Cabanas, fortified port on the north coast of Pinar del Rio about fifty miles west of Havana. It has a fine bay with a narrow entrance, defended by an old fort. Population, about 1,500.

Caibarien, a port town with a good harbor on the northeast coast of Santa Clara province, east of the capital and connected by railroad with some of the inland towns. Population 5,300.

Camerones, a town of 546 inhabitants, north of Cienfuegos, situated near the railroad.

Canasi, a town of Matanzas, 17 miles from that city. Population 700.

Candelaria, a town of Pinar del Rio, near San Cristobal. Population 1,200. A health resort famous for its mineral springs and excellent coffee.

Cardenas, a town of Matanzas, 30 miles from that city. Population 23,680. It is sometimes called the American city. It has an excellent harbor and was once a famous resort for wreckers and pirates. It is the shipping point of a large sugar growing district and has numerous good wharves. It was in the engagement at the battle of Cardenas that Ensign Worth Bagley, the first American officer to be killed in the present war, lost his life.

Cienfuegos, a city of Santa Clara ; one of the principal cities of Cuba. Population 27,430. It, like Cardenas, had a number of American merchants. It is connected by railroad with Santa Clara, the capital of the province, and the towns to the west. It is one of the finest, richest and most beautiful cities of Cuba.

Colon, a town in the eastern part of Matanzas and 84 miles from that city. It is the center of the sugar-producing region. Population 6,500. It is on the railroad.

Gibara, on the northern coast of Santiago. It has a fine harbor for vessels of light draft, not over 16 feet, and an extensive trade in sugar, coffee, tobacco, fruits and lumber. It has no railroad communications.

Guantanamo, a town of Santiago on the southern coast, less than 50 miles from Santiago de Cuba. Has a fine harbor. It was here that 600 marines were landed from the troop ship "Panther" to begin the invasion of Cuba and secure a base of operation for the American fleet.

Guines, a town of Havana province, 30 miles from that city by road, 45 by railroad. It is the center of a rich sugar district. Population 7,000.

Havana, the largest city of Cuba and the capital of the island. Population about 200,000. It is the center of the manufacturing, commercial, and political life of the island. The city itself lies on the western side of the bay, the finest in the West Indies, and affording ample anchorage for 1,000 large vessels. The distance from New York to Havana is 1,413 miles; from New Orleans to Havana, 475 miles; from Key West to Havana, 93 miles.

The city contains many fine residences of the wealthy, the cultured and the Spanish officials. It is said to have one of the finest opera houses in the world and its public squares are famous for their size and beauty. In normal times it is the scene of considerable commercial life. More than 3,000 ships annually touch at its port. It is well fortified both at the entrance and on either side and the city is inclosed by walls. The name of nearly every institution is either of a religious or patriotic order. Its famous fortification El Morro (the Round Tower) was first built in 1589. The twelve guns which defend it each bear the name of an apostle.

The principal defenses in the order of their importance are Principe, Cabana, San Diego, Morro, Punta, Ataras, Reina, and Santa Clara. Other batteries have lately been added of which we have no knowledge.

General Grant said he thought Havana would not be hard to take if the port was blockaded and an army landed out of range of the fortifications of the city, but surrounding it on the land side. With a strict blockade, hunger would become a powerful ally of the attacking force.

Holguin, a city of Santiago, south of the port of Gibara, and with a population of 34,767.

Juan de los Remedios, a town of Santa Clara province, 295 miles from Havana. Population 7,230. It was founded in 1545. It is four miles from its port Caibarien.

Manzanillo, a town of Santiago, 160 miles from that city. Population 9,000. It has a fine harbor and the country immediately surrounding it produces large quantities of sugar, while on the higher slopes are rich timber lands.

Mariel, a town of Pinar del Rio, 34 miles from Havana. It has a good harbor. Population 1,637.

Matanzas is the capital of the province of that name and the second richest city of the island. Connected with Havana by railroad 74 miles, by direct road 54 miles. Population 36,102. The harbor is deep, broad, and defended by fortifications. At its mouth a reef and ledge of rocks extend across, leaving only a narrow channel on each side. It has good public buildings and the finest theatre on the island.

Pinar del Rio capital of the province of the same name, 155 miles from Havana, with which it is connected by railroad. This is the center of the famous tobacco district. Population 5,500.

Puerto Principe, capital of the province of the same name. A town without hotels or sidewalks, and even when compared with other Cuban cities, is 100 years behind the times. It is connected with its port, Nuevitas, by rail. Population 46,641.

Sagua la Grande, a town of Santa Clara, 260 miles from Havana. Havana, Santa Clara and Cienfuegos are connected with it by railroad. It has a population of 14,000 and is one of the important cities of the island.

Sancti Spiriti, a town of Santa Clara, situated in the southeastern corner of that province, 55 miles from the capital, and connected by a short railroad with Tunas, at the mouth of the river Sasa. Population 32,608.

San Cristobal, a town of Pinar del Rio, 70 miles from Havana. Population 3,522.

San Fernando Nuevitas, 45 miles from Puerto Principe, with which it is connected by rail. It is a modern town in appearance, founded in 1819. Population 7,000.

Santa Clara, capital of the province of the name, 248 miles from Havana. Population 35,000. It is the center of a rich mineral district and is famous for the fine quality of asphalt which is the particular trade of its port. Gold, plumbago, and copper are among the minerals produced. It is connected by rail with Cienfuegos, Colon, Cardenas, Matanzas and Havana.

Santiago de Cuba (usually called Cuba, in the island), one of the oldest towns in Cuba and for a time the capital, was founded by Diego Valasquez on his first voyage, 1515. It was the headquarters of Hernando De Soto when he was commander of the island. It was captured by the French in 1553 and at various times was almost wiped out by the buccaneers. It has been a frequent and severe sufferer from earthquakes. In 1608 the cathedral was ruined by one and in 1776 many people were killed and buildings destroyed by another. It is the second town in commercial importance in the island. The city is situated on a bay four miles in length, the entrance to which is high, narrow and well defended by the batteries Morro, Aquadores, Estrella and Cabanas. It is a famous old town with streets regularly laid out and the houses generally of stone and well built. It would be capable of making a stubborn defense were its inhabitants as spirited as those of Saragossa. The Virginius was taken into Santiago de Cuba and here 53 of her passengers were shot, November, 1873. Shut in by the highlands, the city is low, unhealthful and a frequent abode of the dreaded yellow fever. Population 71,307.

The distance from Santiago to Kingston, Jamaica, is 200 miles; from Santiago to Greytown (entrance to Nicaragua canal), 700 miles.

Railroads.

There are ten railroad companies in Cuba and the total mileage under their control is about 1,000 miles. The most of this is in the western part of the island and communicating with Havana. Cienfuegos and Santa Clara are the farthest eastern towns with which Havana has railroad communications. A short railroad connects Puerto Principe with a seaport town of the province, Nuevitas. There are short roads of a few miles only, running from Santiago de Cuba and Guantanamo, but these two towns, although rather less than fifty miles apart in a direct line, are not connected by rail. All the larger sugar plantations have private roads connecting them with the main line.

Wagon Roads.

The wagon roads of Cuba are not any too good at the best and during the wet season are almost impassable. General Stone, Director of the Road Inquiry Bureau of the Department of Agriculture, goes to Cuba with the invading army equipped with a complete outfit of road making machinery, the first time we think in the history of military affairs when an invading army has been fitted out in this way. During our late civil war there were numerous instances where armies were compelled to wait for the mud to dry, when with good roads, decided progress could have been made. The ancient military roads of the Romans show how thoroughly they understood the advantage of good communications between military positions. The roads constructed by General Stone are likely to be not only of immense benefit to the invading army, but will remain and become of permanent value to the people of Cuba when quiet is restored.

THE ASCENDENCY OF AMERICA. 209

There are four submarine cable companies connecting with Cuba.

(1). The International Ocean Telegraph Company, with a line reaching from Havana to Florida, co-operating with the Western Union.

(2). Cuban Submarine Telegraph Company, connecting Havana, Cienfuegos and Santiago.

(3). West India and Panama Company, connecting Havana, Santiago, Jamaica, Porto Rico, the Lesser Antilles and Panama.

(4). French Cable Company, connecting Havana, Santiago, Jamaica, Haiti, Santo Domingo, Venezuela and Brazil.

There are only three towns in Cuba that have cable communications, namely, Havana, Cienfuegos and Santiago.*

Population.

We have seen that Cuba contains about 45,000 miles, inclusive of all the adjacent islands, but no small part of this is made up of marshy lowlands, barren keys and the rugged and broken mountainous districts. Probably not more than four-fifths of it will ever be thickly populated. Considering the really desirable area, Cuba in 1895 was was about as thickly populated as Virginia.

The inhabitants of Cuba are usually divided into five classes:

1. The natives of Spain, who are called "Peninsulars."
2. Those of Spanish descent born in Cuba, called "Insulars."
3. Foreign white population.
4. Africans and their descendants.
5. Asiatics.

In 1850 it was estimated that the negroes, including in this class the full bloods, mulattoes and quadroons,

---
* British consul-general's report, 1896.

numbered about 500,000, and constituted rather more than 50 per cent of the population. In 1887, their last official census, the same class numbered 485,187, and constituted a fraction over 30 per cent of the entire population, showing both an actual and relative decline in numbers compared to the white population.

Slavery became extinct in Cuba in 1887. The first law for gradual emancipation passed in 1870, and the institution entirely prohibited in 1886.

At the breaking out of the Cuban insurrection the the population of the island was estimated at rather more than a million and a half, of whom less than 500,000 belonged to the class returned in the census reports as negroes.

The third class, the foreign whites, constitute but a small part of the population of Cuba, probably not more than 11,000.

Of the Asiatics, or "coolies," imported by Spain from the Philippines, only a guess can be made. Their numbers are variously estimated at from 25,000 to 50,000. The coolie is bound to work for his master for a certain length of time at very small pay. When his period of service has expired he is almost helpless. He must either starve, leave the island or make a new contract at any terms his employer may see fit to offer.

The Insulars are estimated at about 1,000,000.

Government.

Cuba is governed by a Captain-General, assisted by a Council of Administration. Members of the Council are nominated by the Crown.

In the interval from the "Ten Years' War" up to the present one, Cuba was entitled to representation in the Spanish Cortes. The province of Havana sent three and each of the other provinces two senators to the Cortes at Madrid. The archbishopric of Santiago and two corporations sent one each. Thirty deputies were sent to the House of Deputies. The Peninsulars held all the electoral machinery in their hands and the result may be easily guessed. Even if the Cuban representatives had represented the people in fact, they would have been but a hopeless minority in the Spanish Cortes in support of any measure opposed to the wishes of the mother country.

Of the measure of autonomy recently offered them by the Sagasta Ministry, General Fitzhugh Lee has recently said: "The Spaniards could easily control one of the legislative chambers, and behind any joint action on the part of both was the veto of the Governor-General, whose appointment was made from the throne at Madrid. Blanco's Autonomistic Government was doomed to failure from its inception. The Spanish soldiers and officers scorned it, because they did not desire Cuban rule, which such autonomy, if genuine, would insure. The Spanish merchants and citizens were opposed to it, because they, too, were hostile to the Cubans having control of the island, and if the question could be narrowed down to Cuban control or annexation to the United States, they were all annexationists, believing that they could get a better government, and one that would protect, in a greater measure, life and property under the United States flag than under the Cuban banner. The Cubans in arms would not touch it, because they were fighting for free Cuba.

Electoral Franchise.

One of the qualifications in voting for representatives to the Cortes was the payment of a direct tax of twenty-five dollars, equivalent to the tax on a net income of about $1,250. It is easy to see that many Cubans would be debarred. In fact, it is said that in Spain twenty-two per cent of the population are voters and in Cuba only four per cent. The franchise in Cuba was extended to the numerous army of clerks, inspectors and government employees of all sorts, which easily enabled the "Peninsulars" to control the elections.

Compulsory Education.

Compulsory education was established in 1880. In 1892 there were 843 schools and one university.

In May, 1897, Cuban notes were at forty per cent. discount, although made legal tender for their face value throughout the island.

History.

On the 17th of April, 1492, in the city of Santa Fe, province of Granada, one of the most momentous documents in Spanish history was signed. It was the agreement between Columbus and the rulers of Spain, as to the reward he should receive if successful on his proposed voyage of discovery, and is of so much interest that we append the chief points.

1. Columbus should have for himself during his life, and his heirs and successors forever, the office of Admiral in all the lands and continents which he might discover or acquire in the ocean, with the same honors and prerogatives then enjoyed by the High Admiral of Castile, the highest office in the Spanish navy.

2. He should be viceroy and governor-general over all the said lands and continents, with the privilege of nominating three candidates for the government of each island or province, one of whom should be selected by the crown.

3. After the costs were deducted he should receive for himself one-tenth of all the gold and silver, precious stones, spices and all other articles and merchandise whatsoever found, bought, bartered or gained within his admiralty.

4. He, or his lieutenant, should be the sole judge in all causes and disputes arising out of trade between these countries and Spain, provided the High Admiral of Castile had the same jurisdiction in the home district.

5. He might then, and at all other times, contribute one-eighth toward fitting out vessels to sail to these countries, and should receive one-eighth part of the profits. *

Isabella had offered to pledge her jewels to raise the amount necessary for this enterprise, but that sacrifice was uncalled for. Both Ferdinand and Isabella signed the commissions, but all the crown's expenses were paid by Castile, Isabella's separate kingdom, and during her life few but Castilians had much to do with the new lands. Through his friends, the Pinzons, Columbus furnished his share of the expense of the enterprise, and on Friday, August 3, 1492, with ninety men and three little ships, he sailed from Palos, Spain, and began one of the most remarkable voyages in history. After a voyage full of hopes and disappointments, land was at last discovered. The signal came at two o'clock Friday morning, October 12th, from Pinzon's ship the Pinta, and a sailor named Rodrigo de Tiana was the first to behold the new world. Columbus named the island San Salvador; to the navigators of to-day it is known as Cat Island. He continued his cruise in the West Indies, and on October 28, 1492, discovered Cuba, touching the coast on the north near what is now called Nuevitas. He thought it part of a large continent, though the Indians described it to him as an island, and he accepted their opinion for a time, but later returned to his former belief, and in his official report called it a continent. After leaving the island of Cuba, Columbus steered to the eastward, and on the 6th of December, 1492, the beautiful island of Haiti appeared before him. It was here that one of his vessels was

---

* Irving's "Life of Columbus," page 77.

driven on a reef and lost. Pieces of the wreck were carried ashore and a fortress erected from them, defended by guns taken from the vessel. Thirty-nine of the crew were left behind, and in this fort, La Navidad, under command of Diego de Arana, the first colony in the new world was founded.

On his second voyage he determined to make sure that Cuba was a continent, and sailed around the eastern point of Cape Maysi, skirted the southern shore, passed the Isle of Pines, and came almost within sight of the western extremity, Cape San Antonio. A few hours' farther sail would have shown him his mistake, but he was only confirmed in his first belief, and each man and boy on board the ship took oath and signed a remarkable document, saying he believed it to be a continent. Washington Irving states he saw this document in his day.

Very little gold was found in Cuba and that little consisted of a few barbaric ornaments worn by the simple natives, which they gladly traded for the most insignificant toys offered them by the Spaniards. Nothing but the precious metals or jewels could satisfy the rapacious greed of the explorers and no attention was paid to the fertile soil and natural resources of Cuba. At Haiti more gold was found, not only in the ornaments worn by the natives, but in the sands of the rivers and rocks of the mountains, and so that island came to be the first colonized by the Spaniards in the new world.

Columbus' lot was not a happy one. He was a foreigner with little influence and surrounded by jealous and ambitious enemies, who poisoned the minds of the Spanish court. He was even accused of planning to throw off Spanish allegiance and declare himself sovereign of the lands he had discovered. The suspicion and jealousy of Ferdinand were easily aroused and a royal officer, Bobadilla, sent to Haiti to investigate. Contrary to the express provisions of the contract between Columbus and the

Crown, he was deprived of his command, arrested with his brothers, placed in irons and sent to Spain. Upon his arrival there in this condition a general wave of indignation swept over the country. The queen, convinced that Columbus had been wronged, Ferdinand was compelled to yield to her and popular opinion. He was received at court and treated with honors, but his office was not restored to him, neither was he returned to Haiti. He was now about sixty-five years of age, broken in health, and but for the support rendered by his able and vigorous brother, Bartholomew, and the affection displayed by his younger son, Fernando, would have fallen an easy prey to his jealous enemies.

Although he besieged the Crown for weary months and was put off with numerous promises, his dignities were never restored to him.

The fourth expedition for discovery was fitted out and he placed in command. He touched at San Domingo, although he had been ordered not to do so, but was refused admittance to the port. He skirted the coast of Honduras and touched the northern shore of South America. Here he was wrecked, his health suffered from privation, his men mutinied, and he returned broken in spirit. His good friend, Queen Isabella, died. Ferdinand remained cold and suspicious and deprived him of his just titles and dignity. He died May 20, 1506, about 70 years of age, a poor, disappointed, broken-hearted, old man. He had kept the chains he wore home from Haiti and at his request they were buried with him. Ferdinand's recognition of his services consisted in writing his epitaph, "To Castile and Leon, Columbus gave a new world." He made a will in which he named his son Diego as his heir.

His remains were deposited in the Convent of San Francisco at Valladolid in 1506; they were removed in 1513 to the Convent of Las Cuevas at Seville, only to be transferred again in 1536 to San Domingo and from there borne in 1795 to Cuba, where they found, together with all that is mortal of his son Diego, a final resting place in the great cathedral at Havana.

Having speedily exhausted the mining resources of Haiti and worn out the natives, Cuba was now invaded by Diego Valesquez, the lieutenant appoined by Columbus' son, who succeeded to his titles. The landing was effected 1511, and the Indians quickly subdued. The Spanish made their appearance in the isle with the customary bigotry and cruelty. One chief who had fled from Spanish oppression in Haiti offered some resistance, but was captured, and according to a very pleasant Spanish custom, burned at the stake. When urged by the priests to repent, that he might go to heaven, he replied that he did not wish to go if there were any Spaniards there.

The first settlements in Cuba were made in the following order: Baracoa (1512), Bayamo, Trinidad (1514), Sancti Spiriti (1514), Puerto Principe (1514), Santiago de Cuba (1515), Havana (1515). It was from Havana that De Soto (1538) set out in search of Eldorado and discovered only a great river in which he found a watery grave.

Santiago de Cuba was made the capital of the island, then colonization began in earnest. Sugar cane was now introduced, the natives completely subdued and portioned out as slaves among the planters, or compelled to labor in the mines. The treatment they received was severe in the extreme, and under their harsh task-masters they were worn out to satisfy Spanish greed, or destroyed themselves in their despair. In 1553, less than half a century of Spanish rule, the whole native population, estimated at 3,000,000 souls, had been ruthlessly swept away and negroes were imported in their stead. Can a nation constantly practice such inhuman cruelty and prosper?

The Spaniards did not escape unscathed. Ignorant and neglectful of proper sanitary measures they were swept off in great numbers by dreadful fevers. The mild, peaceful natives found by the Spaniards were soon worn out by work to which they were not used, and the planters were compelled to drop the cultivation of sugar cane and take up the raising of cattle, which required less help. After a time negro slaves were introduced to take the place of the native Cubans and the cultivation of sugar cane, and with it tobacco, was taken up and these have ever since been Cuba's staple products.

The tobacco trade was made a monopoly by the government, and in 1717 a revolt broke out occasioned by its obnoxious regulations. The insurrection was quickly subdued only to burst forth again in 1723, occasioned by an oppressive government's exactions. This rebellion was stamped out with much severity and the leaders hanged. From 1700 to 1750 shipbuilding was the leading industry in Havana, but the ship builders of Spain having offered a protest, such exactions were put upon the business that it was impossible for it to continue for any length of time, and it is doubtful if half a dozen ships have been built in Cuba during the present century.

The inhabitants lived in constant terror of the English, French and Dutch privateers, but a more terrible foe yet was found in the buccaneers, a combination of sailor, hunter, privateersman and adventurer. Along the coast of Santo Domingo were a few isolated settlements, whose inhabitants were by law permitted to trade only with Spain and in whose markets they were compelled to pay an exorbitant price. They welcomed the hardy smugglers, who, excited by their great gains, touched at their coasts and carried on an illicit trade, and from these the buccaneers were descended.

The island produced numerous cattle; their flesh, dried and preserved by fire and smoke, was termed "boucan." From this the name buccaneer came. Soon the island of Hispaniola (Haiti) became the recognized haunt of these adventurers. Everything Spanish excited their animosity. They were fierce fighters, utterly fearless, and were tacitly encouraged by the other nations who were covetous of Spain's territorial possessions. The most famous of these was Henry Morgan, a Welsh buccaneer, who afterward returned to England and was knighted by King Charles of England and made Deputy-Governor of Jamaica. They differed from pirates in that they did not prey upon mankind in general, but almost exclusively upon the Spaniards. Their success brought other adventurous spirits to their aid and they increased in numbers until they constituted a strong, mercenary navy at the service of any nation which had a grievance against Spain. Afterward they fell because of their vices and dissensions among themselves.

Much as Cuba suffered at the hand of the buccaneers, Spain's many wars were scarcely less disastrous to her. Havana was burned by a French privateer in 1538, and to prevent a repetition of this De Soto erected the Castillo de la Fuerza, a portion of which remains to this day. These defenses were not sufficient, and in 1554 Havana was again captured by the French. After this two other famous fortresses were added, the Punta and the Morro, the latter of which, standing to-day, is more than 300 years old. In spite of all drawbacks, the city gradually became of some importance, and all ships sailing from Mexico were by law compelled to stop at Havana and report to the Captain-General. The other colonies, being richer in gold and silver, were in a way a drain upon Cuba, whose fertile soil and wealth of forest were not yet appreciated. Harsh laws further handicapped its growth. One imposed the death penalty on all who left the island;

another prohibited anyone who was not a native of Castile from trading with or settling in Cuba.

British Capture Havana, 1762.

Toward the close of the "Seven Years' War," (see history of Spain) a British fleet under Admiral Pocock and a land force under Lord Albemarle were sent to attack Havana. This is of especial interest to Americans because in Lord Albemarle's force were New York and Connecticut troops under the command of General Phineas Lyman and Colonel Israel Putnam. The attacking forces appeared off Havana, June 7th, 1762, and a landing in small boats was made a little east of the city, near the town of Guanabacoa. The advance guard pressed forward vigorously, and soon encountered some light earthworks that had been hastily thrown up to protect the Spanish outposts. The outposts poured in a spirited fire, but, characteristic of the Spanish even to-day, were unable to hit anybody, and were soon scurrying toward Morro Castle as fast as their legs could carry them. The advance continued and soon encountered some stronger earthworks at Cojima, which brought them to a halt. The British ship "Dragon" then moved up and opened fire on the fort, and in less than an hour silenced its guns, and sent its garrison flying toward Morro Castle. Without stopping for rest the British forces continued their advance, and that night camped two miles west of Morro Castle itself, which distance rendered them safe from the artillery used at that time. To-day the Krupp guns of Morro could toss some embarrassing visitors into a camp three times as far away. The following day the town of Guanabacoa was captured and Cabanas Heights, which are now well fortified but were then destitute of defense, were occupied and the engineers began their regular approaches toward the Spanish position. The workmen suffered great annoyance from mounted guerrillas, who were continually making dashes upon them from out the country south, and necessitated a close watch and powerful skirmish line to protect the engineers.

The investment had progressed so well, that about a week after the siege had begun Colonel Carleton under a flag of truce carried a letter from Lord Albemarle to the governor demanding his surrender and naming British terms. The Spanish governor was too proud to allow Colonel Carleton to present the letter to him in person, and the English officer would not send it by any other man, so took it back to camp with him. He delivered it in person the following day, but no answer was returned.

The besiegers were handicapped greatly by continued heavy rains, only to be followed by dry days with intense, scorching, tropical heat. Suitable drinking water could only be obtained from the fleet, and the men broke down rapidly under the hardships in such climatic conditions, the death rate running very high. Nowadays, pure water would be distilled by the engines of our battleships and one fruitful source of the dreaded fever cut off.

In two weeks the engineers had completed some of their mortar batteries, and began to open an effective fire on Morro Castle. The Spanish ships in the harbor coming to the assistance of the forts were given a warm reception and compelled to return to their original anchorage. The besiegers pressed their work vigorously, and by July 1st a continual rain of shells was falling on Morro,

The position becoming too warm for them, the Spaniards sent out a forlorn hope of 600 men to attack the batteries, but the pickets and workmen, without other assistance, killed, wounded and captured a third of the attacking party and drove off the rest. It was found impossible to silence Morro by bombardment alone, and as the siege progressed the Spanish marksmanship improved so much that the British ships were driven from their position and many of the crew killed and wounded. The engineers were again called into requisition, and a mine planned to be exploded under Morro's walls. The Spaniards now sent out a larger forlorn hope, but were once more unsuccessful, and the attacking party surrendered. When some of the British went forward to secure their prisoners, they were given a sample of "Punic faith," the Spaniards rushing upon them with knives and muskets with the rage of wild beasts.

The Mine.

The last of July the engineers reported their mine completed. It was carefully filled, and exploded with great success. As an observer says, "the air appearing to be full of Spaniards." The commander-in-chief of the British force had an attacking party in readiness, and they pushed forward vigorously to the breach. The Spaniards appeared paralyzed by the shock, and little opposition was offered, though some of the officers lost their lives in a brave but fruitless endeavor to repulse the attacking party. One, Captain Velasquez, or Velosco, the worthy owner of an illustrious name, deserted by his cowardly soldiers, fell mortally wounded, and breathing his last requested to be sent into the city that he might die in Havana. It was granted him.

Morro Captured.

The British were now in possession of Morro Castle and the surrender of the town soon followed. The Spanish loss during the siege was estimated at 6,000. The British force had not suffered so heavily in killed and wounded, but their loss from disease was something frightful. The army alone lost 4,708 men by disease. The Spaniards surrendered 11 large warships, 25 merchantmen and about $3,000,000 in gold and silver.

British Influence.

The English kept possession of the island until July 6th, 1763. They imported negro labor, began the cultivation of large tracts of wild land, shipped quantities of European merchandise to the island, and gave a strong impetus to trade. They made Havana a free port and opened it to the commerce of the world, and the Spaniards upon their return to power found it impolitic to try to enforce all their former obnoxious restrictions in the way of trade with other nations.

For a century after this, Cuba enjoyed a marked period of prosperity. To be sure, there were little insurrections, but none of them attained serious proportions. Havana once did a thriving business in the way of building guard ships for the treasure fleets. More than 100 such vessels were launched from her yards, but toward the close of the 18th century they were compelled to give this up, because of the demands of the Spanish workmen that such ships should be built at home. Hardly a dozen ships have since been built in Cuba.

Sugar.

During this period she had little to sell but tobacco and animal products, but about this time sugar came into general use in the world; its production increased in Cuba and soon took front rank as the most valuable product of the island. Its price of over forty cents a pound, equal to twice that amount to-day, shows that it was not universally used. It is interesting to note that Great Britain uses more than seventy times as much sugar as she did a century ago, and that its growth seems to have kept pace with the increased use of tea and coffee.

Las Casas.

For a time after the restoration of Cuba to the Spaniards the island enjoyed the ministration of able and oftentimes just governors. Las Casas became Captain-General in 1790, and is to-day esteemed as one of the best and wisest the island ever had. He founded the "Patriotic Society," which has now become so powerful that it is allowed to send a delegate to the Spanish Cortez. He improved the roads, fortifications, hospitals, and founded a lunatic asylum, a remarkable advance in any country at that time. In June, 1791, the island was devastated by one of the most terrible hurricanes in its history, and the prompt relief that he afforded speaks highly of his executive ability.

San Domingo.

The French Revolution occurring about this time gave an impulse to the feverish unrest in the neighboring Island of San Domingo, and the terrible servile war broke forth. Thanks to Las Casas' ability, the Island of Cuba was preserved from any trouble of the kind, and he gave a safe harbor to many of the refugees who were forced to flee from San Domingo. It was during his time that the remains of Columbus were transferred from San Domingo to the cathedral at Havana.

Cuba's Title.

When Napoleon placed his brother on the throne of Spain in 1808 Cuba refused to recognize Joseph as king, and by its loyalty won for itself the title of "The Ever-Faithful Isle." The colonial government declared war against Napoleon and proclaimed Ferdinand VII. king. For a time the island was reduced to such straits that they seriously considered throwing open the ports to all nations to admit supplies, and inviting the French to take possession. A disturbance at once arose and considerable property was destroyed, but quiet was restored with the loss of a few lives.

Negro Plot.

A negro conspiracy was begun in 1812 and excited profound alarm for a time, but it was put down with unsparing severity, and the leader, Aponte, and his confederates summarily executed.

In 1810 another terrible hurricane visited the island, did great damage to the City of Havana, and destroyed no less than sixty merchant vessels at anchor in this harbor.

Influence of Spanish-American Colonies.

The success of the Spanish-American colonies on the continent in obtaining their independence naturally aroused considerable feeling in Cuba. Secret societies were formed, all having for their object the overthrow of Spanish power, or at least the securing of a more liberal form of government. From this time the lines were sharply drawn between the Spaniards or "Peninsulars" and the Cubans or "Insulars."

Bolivar.

Numerous uprisings on the part of the Cubans took place from 1820 to 1830, but petty jealousies, rivalries and imperfect organization rendered their success impossible, although at one time it was planned to invade the island by Cuban refugees and their sympathizers from Colombia and Mexico under the leadership of General Simon Bolivar. The plan was abandoned, and the island passed under the undisputed control of Spain.

Black Eagle.

In 1827 a secret society called the "Black Eagle" was organized among the Cuban refugees with headquarters in Mexico, and recruiting agencies established in Colombia and the United States. This scheme was a failure from the first, as it encountered the opposition of the slave-holding element of all the countries concerned. The conspiracy was discovered and the leaders condemned to death, but the Captain-General refrained from inflicting the extreme penalty.

Period of Conspiracies.

In 1834 began what is known as the "Period of Conspiracies," and from that time forward the history of Cuba becomes a monotonous recital of unsuccessful insurrections. In the revolt of 1844, thirteen hundred and forty-six persons were convicted. Upon seventy-eight the extreme penalty was inflicted. Of all the convicted persons only fourteen were white.

In 1847, Narciso Lopez, a native of Venezuela, who had served with the rank of major-general in the Spanish army, headed a revolutionary movement, but was unsuccessful and compelled to flee to New York.

U. S. Offers to Buy.

In 1848, President Polk tried to open negotiations with the Spanish government for the sale of Cuba to the United States for the sum of $100,000,000.

American Filibusters.

In 1849, Lopez, having organized a filibustering expedition, landed at Cardenas with about 600 men. He found the conditions for an uprising were not favorable, and hastily re-embarked and sailed for Key West. He organized another expedition, and, sailing from New Orleans, landed near Bahia Honda August 12, 1851. With him was Col. Crittenden from Kentucky, the second in command, at the head of the American sympathizers. Lopez, with the main body, pushed rapidly forward into the interior. Crittenden was left with about 50 men to cover the landing and bring up supplies. While the forces were thus divided they were attacked by the Spaniards, and all of the rear guard killed in action or afterwards shot. Lopez' division was equally unsuccessful. He was captured and garroted. The United States government soon after suppressed another expedition.

"Black Warrior."

In 1850 the United States was brought to the verge of war with Spain over the " Black Warrior " case. The " Black Warrior " was owned in New York, and made regular voyages between that city and Mobile. She was one of the largest steamers engaged in the coasting trade, capable of carrying from 200 to 300 passengers, and making the round trip in about a month. In going and returning she put into Havana to discharge and receive mail and passengers, but no freight was taken or discharged, nor was her cargo in any way disturbed. According to the exacting custom regulations of the port, she should at each time have exhibited a manifest of her cargo, but as none was to be moved she was entered and cleared as "in ballast," and had practiced this, without question, for years. There was nothing secret or mysterious about this, and it was with the full knowledge and consent of the revenue officers, and, in fact, permitted by a written order issued by the Cuban authorities dated February 27, 1847. But in 1850 considerable feeling existed between Spain and the United States. On the 28th of February the steamer was seized by the revenue authorities upon the charge of having on board an undeclared cargo. The cargo was confiscated and a fine of twice its value levied against the vessel. Captain Bullock refused to pay the fine, and protested vigorously against the whole proceedings as both unlawful and in bad faith. The revenue officers had tried to trick him into a technical violation of the customs laws by opening the hatches of the ship and getting ready the usual machinery for hoisting cargo. The captain declared this a forcible seizure, took his flag and such of his papers as he could secure, and with his passengers left the ship. The owners at once appealed to the government of the United States, demanded protection, and made a claim for damages. An indemnity of $300,000 was paid them after five years of wrangling.

The Quitman Expedition.

In 1854 another filibustering expedition under the command of General Quitman, of Mississippi, was planned, and preparations again made to invade Cuba. Before the expedition sailed, however, the Cuban leaders were discovered, imprisoned, and some of them summarily executed.

Spain's Irritating Course.

Following the "Black Warrior" case were others less serious, but still very annoying. Exorbitant fines were levied on American vessels in Cuban ports for the most trivial and purely technical offenses. American ships were stopped on the high seas and searched by Spanish cruisers, and American citizens in Cuba arrested on various charges. In addition, slave-holders felt a feeling of insecurity over the probable abolition of slavery in Cuba. The Spanish colonies of America, on declaring their independence, had abolished slavery, and it seemed likely that the existence of that institution in Cuba was doomed.

Europe Concerned.

The strained relations between Spain and the United States, and the very evident intention of the dominant political party of the latter country to either buy or seize Cuba, excited the apprehension of Europe. England and France united in a diplomatic representation to the United States, asking the latter country to join with them in an agreement by which neither of the signatory powers should ever acquire Cuba or permit any other power to do so. After due consideration the United States declined to be a party to this, urging for their action three reasons:

First. The traditional reluctance of America to become a party to "entangling alliances."

Second. That such action did not provide for future contingencies that might arise, and was perhaps unconstitutional.

Third. That each of the other parties were asking greater concessions on our part than they were giving, as by reason of its geographical position there would be strategetical advantages for the United States in the possession of Cuba, not so valuable to England or to France.

Ostend Manifesto.

The anxiety of the South to secure Cuba before it should become a dangerous asylum for runaway slaves, the evident desire of Europe not to see such a transaction consummated, the strained relations with Spain impelled President Pierce to direct Mr. Marcy, secretary of state, to instruct Messrs. Buchanan, Mason and Soule, United States ministers at the courts of London, Paris and Madrid, to meet in some European city and discuss the question of the acquisition of Cuba by the United States. The ministers met at Ostend, Belgium, and issued their famous manifesto in which they declared that it was the manifest duty of the United States to acquire Cuba; that the Union could never enjoy repose and security "as long as Cuba is not embraced within its boundaries" for fear it might "be Africanized and become a second San Domingo, seriously endangering the Union;" that Spain would find it highly advantageous to her to sell it; recommended the purchase of the island for

$120,000,000; emphatically stated that in no event should any European government be allowed to become the owner of the island. They further declared that if freedom were given to the slaves in Cuba it would so endanger the United States as to justify them in taking forcible possession. This remarkable paper excited the amazement of all Europe, and greatly intensified Spain's resentment against the United States. It was taken very seriously at home, and indorsed by President Pierce and his administration. In fact, the Democratic national conventions of 1856 and 1860 each expressed themselves emphatically "in favor of the acquisition of Cuba."

Ten Years' War.

During the Civil War of the United States, Cuba was under the administration of able and liberal governors, who successfully preserved the tranquillity of the island in spite of the disturbing influences so near at hand. The close of that war and the emancipation of the slaves, seems to have encouraged the leaders of freedom in Cuba. They took advantage of a Spanish cabinet in power at the time, seemingly more liberal than usual, and asked that a commission be appointed to examine into Cuban affairs, correct abuses and consider such vital questions and give the Cubans a constitution in place of the Captain-General, granting them the right of petition, making native Cubans eligible to public office, granting relief from the exactions of some of the industrial monopolies held by the crown, allowing representation for the island in the Spanish Cortes and providing for the "freedom of the press."

A commission was appointed, but these important subjects received little if any consideration. Only a few minor changes were made, and an additional tax of ten per cent was added to the already over-burdened colony.

The revolution in Spain that expelled Isabella II,

brought greater freedom to the Spaniards, but no relief to the suffering Cubans.

Hostilities Begin.

Plans for an insurrection had been considered for some time, and were not matured. Under the leadership of a few brave and daring men at various points in the different provinces, the discontented rallied and prepared to take up arms. On October 10, 1868, Carlos N. de Cespedes, a lawyer of Bayamo, at the head of one hundred and twenty eight poorly armed men issued the famous Declaration of Independence of Yara. "Spain has many times promised us Cubans to respect our rights, without further having fulfilled her promises; she continues to tax us heavily, and by so doing is likely to destroy our wealth; as we are in danger of losing our property, our lives, and we want no further Spanish domination, etc."

Within a short time Cespedes was at the head of from 10,000 to 15,000 men, not more than half of whom were well armed, but their enthusiasm and energy went far toward making up for their poor equipment. They repulsed the Spanish troops sent against them, and proceeded vigorously against the important towns of the interior that fell into their hands one after another, as the result of a guerrilla campaign, in which Manuel Quesada greatly distinguished himself.

Cuban Successes.

Had it not been for the Spanish fleet the Cubans would have captured even the seaport towns. Dulce was sent from Spain and made Captain-General. He offered to consider the Cuban grievances and grant a general amnesty, but his offers were indignantly refused by the Cubans, while their proffer irritated the "volunteers" and rendered him unpopular with his own party.

Cuban Provisional Government.

Cuban delegates met in convention April, 1869, elected Cespedes President, Manuel Quesada General-in-Chief, and framed a constitution. There were volunteers enough, brave and enthusiastic, but then, as now, the lack of Cuba was small arms, ammunition, provisions and medical supplies. They received some relief in this direction by the successful landing of filibustering expeditions from the United States, one under Raphael Quesada and another under Colonel Thomas Jordan, who had formerly served with honor in the Confederate army.

The unpopularity of the Captain-General, the high death rate in the unacclimated Spanish army incident to a rainy season, had deterred the Spaniards from making an active campaign against the insurgents. However, in the fall of 1870, at the close of the yellow fever season, which had been so fatal to the new troops sent out from Spain, active operations were resumed. The Cubans had made the most of the delay; their forces were in much better condition and some considerable advantages were gained by them.

Havana "Volunteers."

Then, as now, in Havana and vicinity, a large part of the military force of Spain was made up of volunteers composed of the "Peninsulars" holding office under the crown. These men were never amenable to strict discipline, and were a prolific source of trouble to any officer who excited their resentment. They resembled, in this respect, the Prætorian Guards of the early Roman Empire, paralyzing the efforts of any commander who was unpopular with them, and, perhaps, to-morrow disgracing the favorite of to-day. In June, 1870, they went so far as to seize Captain-General Dulce and send him back to Spain, and depose General Pinto, Military Governor of Matanzas. They terrorized the whole country wherever they were located, and were so powerful that they compelled the Spanish authorities to wink at their irregularities. The Cubans had no more unrelenting enemy than these "gentlemen" soldiers.

Summary.

For the first two years the Cubans made considerable headway, and had they been able to reserve an open port and command a few vessels capable of landing supplies, they might have been successful, but by the aid of her navy Spain rendered it exceedingly difficult and dangerous to import the necessary war material, and the military resources of the mother country were much superior to those of the revolting colonies.

Cubans Recognized.

At the height of their success the Cubans were recognized as belligerents by Chile, Bolivia, Guatemala, Colombia and the Republic of Mexico. Their independence was formally recognized by Peru June 15, 1869.

Not content with their natural difficulties the Cubans, in 1873, deposed their president, Cespedes, quarreled vigorously among themselves as to his successor, alienated their friends, and by this action threw away their chance of success.

Had Spain been in a position to push affairs vigorously just at that time, it would seem as though the rebellion could have been speedily suppressed, but at this period she was occupied at home with her Carlist troubles. The Cubans, without a navy, were unable to obtain the needed arms and ammunition, and the Spaniards, by the aid of their fleet, kept command of the coast towns. The terrible struggle thus dragged on, marked by heavy losses and slight gains on either side, the Cubans slowly losing ground.

Peace of Zanjon.

In 1876, General Martinez de Campos, a distinguished soldier, arrived in Cuba as commander-general, bringing with him 25,000 veterans of the Carlist wars, and prepared to push matters vigorously. The Cubans avoided battle in force, trusted to guerrilla warfare, and relied upon the yellow fever to do its terrible work upon the new Spanish troops; but Campos was an abler leader than they had yet opposed; even his enemies confided in his honor, and the numerous dissensions among themselves had weakened the Cubans until many of them listened attentively to propositions for peace. In 1878 an armistice was agreed upon, and the Cuban leaders met at Camaguey to consider the propositions for peace offered by General Campos. General Garcia, who had succeeded to the presidency of the Cuban Republic, was appointed with nine others, and commissioned to confer with the Spanish commander. The meeting was held near Zanjon, in the district of Canagua, and what is known as the "Peace of Zanjon" was proclaimed February 10, 1878. By its terms the Cubans laid down their arms, and Spain agreed to grant in substance the reforms demanded by the Cuban commission of inquiry eleven years before.

Its Reception at Madrid.

Having ended hostilities and pacified Cuba, Campos returned to Madrid and placed the treaty before his government for ratification. Canovas, since assassinated, was at the head of the cabinet and resigned his ministry rather than lay before that body the terms to which Campos had agreed for carrying out the reforms he promised to Cuba in the name of Spain. The Cubans had laid down their arms in obedience to the most solemn pledges of Campos that these reforms should be granted, and upon the resignation of Canovas in March, 1879, Campos dissolved the Cortes, secured a majority in the ensuing election and organized a new cabinet.

Promises Ignored.

However, his plans met only with a lukewarm support from his colleagues and lack of harmony prevailed in the new cabinet, Campos resigning and Canovas again returning to the ministry, while the promises so solemnly made at Zanjon to the struggling Cubans, were ignored. The most marked result of the Ten Years' War was the abolition of slavery in 1886, the institution becoming extinct in 1887.

The Good Offices of the United States.

During the progress of the insurrection the good offices of the United States government were repeatedly offered for the re-establishment of peace in the island. President Grant in his messages of 1869 and 1875 indicates this, and in 1876 he proposed a joint intervention of the United States and the European powers. Nothing came of this project. The question of recognizing the belligerency of the Cuban Republic was several times before the United States Congress, and, as we have seen, several of the South American Republics accorded them belligerent rights, and one of them, Peru, recognized their independence.

Cost of the Ten Years' War.

Spain's loss in life, as shown by the official reports in the archives at Madrid, were for her regular army alone, 81,098. More died from disease than from wounds received in battle. In 1877, with an army supposed to number 90,000 men, more than 15,000 were in the hospital. The losses of the Cubans can never be definitely settled, but it is probable that from 30,000 to 50,000 died of wounds and disease. Spain actually paid out in money, $300,000,000 and fully as much more was lost by reason of destruction of property in Cuba.

Bitterness of the Strife.

During this contest the most intense bitterness prevailed on both sides. No quarter was given, no prisoners exchanged; they were all slaughtered. The defeated of either party frequently committed suicide rather than fall alive into the hands of their enemies. The awful horrors of the "Ten Years' War" have no parallel in modern history.

Perils to the United States.

Then as now, the United States suffered great annoyance and was compelled to incur considerable expense in the enforcement of the neutrality laws. The people of the United States without doubt sympathized with the Cubans in their struggle for freedom and it was impossible for the government to prevent the successful operation of some filibustering expeditions. The most famous of these filibusters, nearly occasioning war between Spain and the United States, was the "Virginius."

The Virginius Case.

" The evidence is the facts which are detailed, as found in the custom-house papers, relative to the registry of the steamer and her clearance in New York in 1870.; the testimony of the two Venezuelan prisoners taken at Havana in November, 1871, by a Spanish magistrate in the presence of the American and Venezuelan consuls; the *ex parte* affidavits of Captain Francis E. Shepperd and of two seamen and certain depositions made in New York in November and December, 1873, before a United States commissioner. This latter inquiry was by arrangement conducted by a consul representing the Spanish Minister and by the United States district attorney, representing the State Department, the cross-examination being careful and searching.

A Blockade Runner.

"The 'Virginius' was originally an English blockade runner, captured during the war, and was the property of the United States. In 1870 she was lying at Washington. She was there sold and conveyed to John F. Patterson. There can be no doubt, however, that the purchase and conveyance were in the outset made on behalf of the Cuban Junta and in pursuance of a prearranged agreement. In September, 1870, Captain Shepperd was employed as commander. . . . Roberts told Captain Shepperd that he had bought the vessel on account of certain Cubans and that these Cubans had furnished the money to pay the purchase price. The captain naturally desired to communicate directly with the principals and an arrangement was made for his immediate introduction to them.

Cuban Agents.

"That evening, at the house of Mora, an interview took place, Roberts, Patterson, Mora, Quesada, Varona, and a number of other Cubans being present. Mora and Quesada declared that they were the owners of the 'Virginius.' . . . She was to proceed directly to Curacao, but her ultimate object was to be the transporting of arms, munitions of war, and soldiers to the island of Cuba in aid of the insurgents thereon. The vessel was registered in the name of John F. Patterson as owner, he making the necessary oaths as to his sole interest. October, 1870, the steamer cleared for New York and the necessary official documents were executed by the master showing that she was bound for Curacao. The cargo, as shown by the manifest, consisted of 170 barrels of bread, valued at $680; two boxes of saddlery, valued at $400; four boxes of clothing, at $350.

Takes Military Stores Aboard.

"The same afternoon a few miles below Sandy Hook she met a steam tug and took on board about twenty Cubans, among whom were General Quesada, and also a few boxes containing arms, ammunition, and military accoutrements. Captain Shepperd testified that during the entire voyage he acted under the directions of General Quesada.

Cuban Flag.

"At one time before reaching their destination, a merchant ship being in sight, Quesada proposed to the captain to raise the Cuban flag and capture the vessel if she should turn out to be Spanish. The worthy captain declined doing this himself, but with a true thrift suggested that it would be a very easy matter for them to overpower him, tie him in his cabin, and then make the capture on their own responsibility. This ingenious scheme was frustrated by the discovery that the vessel in sight was British. The 'Virginius' reached Curacao on the fifteenth of October. On the next Tuesday the 'Billie Butts' arrived from New York and on the same afternoon set out to sea again. The same night the 'Virginius' followed, overtook the schooner and towed her to Buen Ayre, an island about thirty miles distant. The cargo of the 'Billie Butts' was immediately transferred to the steamer. This cargo consisted of several hundred cases of shot, shell, and ammunition; more than one hundred cases of arms, boxes of leather and other goods, and hardware; six gun carriages and four brass cannons or howitzers. The crew demanded an explanation of this transaction and refused to work further. General Quesada promised them an advance in their wages and a considerable bonus in case they made a successful landing in Cuba, and they thereupon returned to their duties."

In Venezuelan Service.

The steamer now visited Venezuela, where severe war was raging. Quesada sided with one of the partisans, in return for which help was promised him in Cuba. Some small Venezuelan gunboats belonging to the opposing faction were captured while the "Virginius" was present and flying the Cuban flag. When the Venezuelan contest closed General Quesada with some Venezuelans and Cubans started for Cuba.

Successful Landing.

"On the 21st of June, 1871, she made a successful landing on the southern coast of Cuba. She at once discharged the troops and her cargo, which consisted of carbines, rifles, large quantities of ammunition, military equipments and clothing."

Prior to this, Captain Shepperd, not getting his pay promptly and objecting to the Venezuelan incident, left and returned to New York.

A New Captain.

"About the 1st of April, 1872, we find her loaded up at Aspinwall, where Francis Bowen, an experienced shipmaster, was employed by General Quesada to act as her captain. Quesada informed him that the steamer was to land an expedition on the coast of Cuba and offered $300 per month salary and a bonus of $5,000 if the attempt was successful. The new captain finding no American flag on board, purchased one. No concealment was attempted by Quesada or Captain Bowen in reference to the character or destination of the vessel. About the first of May she sailed with sealed orders issued by Quesada.

Protected by the "Kansas."

"By the direction of the American consul the United States gunboat 'Kansas' escorted her out to sea in order to protect her from an apprehended attack by the Spanish man-of-war 'Pizarro,' which was lying at Aspinwall."

She made a successful landing as before. Captain Bowen resigned and went to New York.

True Ownership Shown.

"The 'Virginius' was largely indebted to Aspinwall for repairs, supplies and other necessaries. A bottomry bond was given to Mahle Bros., merchants at that place, who had acted as her agents and also as agents for the Cuban Junta. This bond was executed by Quesada without any communication or attempt to communicate with Patterson in New York, who stood as owner in the registry. This one fact alone is conclusive. After leaving New York no communication whatever was had with Patterson, the owner in the registry. No advice was ever asked, no direction ever sought, but he was utterly ignored by masters, officers, and crew of the steamer and by the American consuls and local authorities in the ports which she visited. Quesada declared that the vessel belonged entirely to the Cubans, that Patterson had no interest in her, that his name was used as a cover because it was necessary that an American should appear in the registry as owner, and that she would never return to the United States. Repeated declarations of Patterson to the same effect were also proved.

Her Character Well Known.

"American consuls in the various ports which the 'Virginius' used were fully aware of her true character. Yet most of them not only shut their ears to Spanish complaints but openly, actively, and zealously assisted the Cuban insurgents in carrying out their projects and in consummating their fraud upon the United States sovereignty. A man at Maracaibo warned Captain Smith in the following friendly manner: 'Why don't you get rid of that damned pirate? She is nothing but a pirate and you will get caught by and by and they will hang you. I want to see you whole, anyhow, though I don't care for any of the rest.'"

British Flag Refused.

At one port it was proposed to sell her to an Englishman and take out English papers, but the English consul called on Captain Smith, asked him if he intended to hoist the British flag and said, "I have a telegraph from the British minister at Caracas to seize her as a pirate if she hoists the British flag." The flag was not raised.

The Fatal Expedition.

She went to Kingston, Jamaica, and made preparations for the third expedition. "Captain Joseph Fry, a United States citizen, who had served in the Confederate navy, arrived in July and took command.' The cargo of arms, ammunition and other war-like materials which had been accumulating was placed on board. A considerable number of persons intending to join the insurgents also embarked, a few of whom were American citizens or British subjects. All these proceedings were open, notorious, without an attempt at concealment. On the 23d of October, 1873, she cleared as a United States vessel for Port Simon, Costa Rica; proceeded to the coast of Cuba with the design of effecting a landing; she was intercepted by the Spanish gunboat, "Tornado;" a chase of eighty miles long ensued and ended by her capture on the thirty-first of October, at a point about eighteen miles distant from the east end of Jamaica. During this chase, and at the moment of capture, she was flying the United States flag.*

---

*"American Law Review, Boston

When captured, little if any contraband of war was found on board the "Virginius," but among her passengers were relatives of the Cuban leaders and officers of the Cuban army. There were in all 155 persons on board, crew 52; passengers 103 International law requires that a prize shall be taken to the nearest port, but this would have been one in Jamaica, subject to English influence, and no such indiscriminate slaughter would have been permitted there as followed at Santiago, whither the "Tornado" proceeded with her prize. The character of the "Virginius" was well known, and a great deal of resentment was quite naturally felt toward her. Four passengers, three Cubans and one claiming British citizenship, were tried by drumhead court-martial and were shot November 4th, thirty-seven of the crew, including Captain Fry, November 7th, and twelve more passengers November 8th. Of those massacred, sixteen were British subjects and eight Americans. This summary trial without the benefit of counsel before military authorities was in opposition to all treaty rights. Further, the worst that could be said of the "Virginius" was that she was a smuggler. It is said that the Spanish authorities intended to shoot the survivors, one hundred two in number, and would have done so but for the interference of Captain Lorrain of the British man-of-war "Niobe," who arrived at Santiago on the 8th. It was commonly reported that Captain Lorrain had threatened to bombard the town unless the executions were postponed, although we have been unable to find in the official documents any reference to such threat on his part.

Diplomatic Action.

At once upon the news of the capture reaching the United States, General Daniel E. Sickles, our representative at the Madrid court, was cabled to make strong representations to the Spanish government and see that all treaty rights were respected. Castelar, then president of Spain, stated to General Sickles that he had already anticipated such request and had cabled the colonial authorities to delay executions until a regular investigation could be made. The colonial authorities insisted that the cables were not in working order and that no messages were received until the 8th, after fifty-three had been massacred. It is certain that the messages of the American vice-consul at Santiago, E. G. Schmidt, to the American consul at Jamaica and to the consul-general at Havana, were detained by order of the Spanish general.

General Sickles, at Madrid, acting upon instructions from Hamilton Fish, Secretary of State, presented an ultimatum to the Spanish authorities demanding the release of the prisoners, the surrender of the vessel, the payment of an indemnity, that the American flag be saluted, and the officers responsible for the executions punished, and insisting upon a favorable reply within twelve days.

Our diplomatic representatives, both in Madrid and in Cuba, were treated with discourtesy, and while Spain was presenting one face to them she, through her ambassador at Washington, was acting in quite a different manner. Some friction developed between the State Department and General Sickles, who thought the former taking the affair out of his hands, and he tendered his resignation, but was prevailed upon to occupy his position until the question was settled. He then resigned and asked that all correspondence should be published.*

In addition to surrendering the ship and disclaiming any thought of indignity to the flag, the Spanish government paid $80,000 to the families of the American citizens who had been massacred.

The affair very nearly involved the United States in

---

*For further details the reader is refered to the Executive Documents for the year 1873, where the whole correspondence can be found.

war with Spain, and probably President Grant's vigorous preparations and cool head saved us. His special message of 1873, which follows, shows how serious he considered the danger.

"The embargoing of American estates in Cuba; cruelty to American citizens detected in no act of hostility to the Spanish government; the murdering of prisoners taken with arms in their hands, and, finally, the capture upon high seas of a vessel sailing under the United States registry, have culminated in an outburst of indignation that has seemed for a time to threaten war. Pending negotiations between the United States and the government of Spain on the subject of this capture, I have authorized the Secretary of the Navy to put our navy on a war footing, to the extent, at least, of the entire annual appropriation for that branch of the service, trusting to Congress and the public opinion of the American people to justify my action.

"On the 26th day of September, 1870, the 'Virginius' was registered in the custom house at New York as the property of a citizen of the United States, he having first made oath, as required by law, that he was the true and only owner of the said vessel, and that there was no subject or citizen of any foreign prince or state directly or indirectly, by way of trust, confidence, or otherwise, interested therein.

"Having complied with the requisites of the statute in that behalf, she cleared in the usual way for the port of Curacoa, and on or about the 4th day of October, 1870, sailed for that port. It is not disputed that she made the voyage according to her clearance, nor that, from that day to this, she has not returned within the territorial jurisdiction of the United States. It is also understood that she preserved her American papers, and that when within foreign ports she made the practice of putting forth a claim to American nationality, which was recognized by the authorities at such ports.

"When, therefore, she left the port of Kingston, under the flag of the United States, she would appear to have had, as against all powers except the United States, the right to fly that flag, and to claim its protection, as enjoyed by all regularly documented vessels registered as part of our commercial marine.

"No state of war existed, conferring upon a maritime power the right to molest and detain upon the high seas a documented vessel; and it cannot be pretended that the 'Virginius' had placed herself without the pale of all law by acts of piracy against the human race.

"If her papers were irregular or fraudulent, the offense was one against the laws of the United States, justifiable only in their tribunals.

"It is a well-established principle, asserted by the United States from the beginning of their national independence, recognized by Great Britain and other maritime powers, and stated by the Senate in a resolution passed unanimously on the 16th of June, 1858, that—

"'American vessels on the high seas in time of peace, bearing the American flag, remain under the jurisdiction of the country to which they belong, and therefore any visitation, molestation, or detention of such vessel by force, or by the exhibition of force, on the part of a foreign power, is in derogation of the sovereignty of the United States.'

"When, therefore, it became known that the Virginius had been captured on the high seas by a Spanish man-of-war; that the American flag had been hauled down by the captors; that the vessel had been carried to a Spanish port; and that Spanish tribunals were taking jurisdiction over the persons of those found on her, and exercising that jurisdiction upon American citizens, not only in violation of the rules of international law, but in contravention of the provisions of the treaty of 1795, I directed a demand to be made upon Spain for the restoration of the vessel, and for the return of the survivors to the protection of the United States, for a salute to the flag, and for the punishment of the offending parties.

"The principles upon which these demands rested could not be seriously questioned, but it was suggested by the Spanish government that there were grave doubts whether the 'Virginius' was entitled to the character given her by her papers; and that therefore it might be proper for the United States, after the surrender of the vessel and the survivors, to dispense with the salute to the flag, should that fact be established to their satisfaction.

"This seemed reasonable and just. I therefore assented to it, on the assurance that Spain would then declare that no insult to the flag of the United States had been intended.

"I also authorized an agreement to be made that, should it be shown to the satisfaction of this government that the 'Virginius' was improperly bearing the flag, proceedings should be instituted in our courts for the punishment of the offense committed against the United States. On her part Spain undertook to proceed against those who had offended the sovereignty of the United States, or who had violated their treaty rights.

"The surrender of the vessel and the survivors to the jurisdiction of the tribunals of the United States was an admission of the principles upon which our demands had been founded. I therefore had no hesitation in agreeing to the arrangement finally made between the two governments — an arrangement which was moderate and just, and calculated to cement the good relations which have so long existed between Spain and the United States.

"Under this agreement the 'Virginius,' with the American flag flying, was delivered to the Navy of the United States at Bahia Honda, in the island of Cuba, on the 16th ultimo. She was in an unseaworthy condition. In the passage to New York she encountered one of the most tempestuous of our winter storms. At the risk of their lives the officers and crew placed in charge of her attempted to keep her afloat. Their efforts were unavailing and she sank off Cape Fear. The prisoners who survived the massacres were surrendered at Santiago de Cuba on the 18th ultimo, and reached the port of New York in safety.

"The evidence submitted on the part of Spain to establish the fact that the 'Virginius' at the time of her capture was improperly bearing the flag of the United States is transmitted herewith, together with the opinion of the Attorney-General thereon, and a copy of the note of the Spanish minister, expressing, on behalf of his government, a disclaimer of an intent of indignity to the flag of the United States.*

Massacre of Havana Students.

Two years previous to the shooting of the "Virginius" prisoners, an event had occurred in Havana that shocked the civilized world. A member of the Cuban "Volunteers" died, and the body was placed in a public tomb in Havana. Later, the tomb is said to have been defaced by writing thereon things not complimentary to the volunteers. Students of the university were suspected of being implicated in the affair, and on the complaint of the volunteer corps forty-three of these were arrested, charged with having defaced the tomb, and brought to trial. The proceedings were marked by much bitter feeling. However, a brave and honorable officer of the regular army of Spain appeared before the

---

*Executive Documents, 1873.

court-martial and defended them with such ability that they were acquitted. The volunteers, used to having their own way in everything, appealed to the Governor-General, and prevailed upon him to order a new trial before a second court-martial, which they "packed" until two-thirds of that body was made up of volunteers. The result was a foregone conclusion, for the volunteers now appeared as accuser, judge and executioner. All of the students were found guilty. Eight were sentenced to be shot, and the others to long terms of imprisonment at hard labor. The sentence was carried out the next morning, November 27, 1871, 15,000 of Havana's "gentlemen soldiers" turning out in force to massacre eight school boys.

The affair excited the greatest indignation throughout the United States. The punishment was so obviously inconsistent that the Spanish Cortes was compelled to notice it by public censure. No other attempt to punish the perpetrators of the deed was made.

The students of Havana now observe "November 27th" with appropriate ceremonies, although great care is taken that it may not furnish occasion for a conflict with the authorities.

Why the Cubans Rebelled.

The Cuban debt began in 1864 by the issue of bonds to the amount of $3,000,000, for expense incurred by Spain in the wars of Santo Domingo, Peru and Mexico. There is no good reason why this should not have been paid by the peninsula, but it was saddled upon Cuba. To this has been added the expense of every insurrection in Cuba and the salary of a horde of Spanish officials, and indirectly, through unparalleled corruption, as much more has been bled from the island by thievish officials.

In 1884 the island paid for pensions of Spanish officers, $468,000; pay of Spanish officers (retired), $918,000; pay of Spanish officers (active), $10,115,420; salary of governor-general, $50,000; for the maintenance of church and clergy (all Spaniards), $379,757; pay of Spanish soldiers doing police duty, $2,537,119. Measured by American standpoints, the pay of the Spanish officials is wholly out of proportion. The governor-general receives $50,000, as much as the president of the United States; the governors of each of the provinces receive $12,000, while the governor of the State of New York, who represents four times as many people and fifty times as much wealth as the whole island, receives $10,000. Cuba pays two archbishops $18,000 each. In addition to the enormous salaries paid all these officers appointed by the Spanish crown, Cuba has stolen from her revenues each year perhaps as much as the revenue regularly raised.

General Pando, now commanding a body of Spanish troops in Cuba, stated in a public speech made in 1890, that he held the statistics of a series of embezzlements reaching more than $40,000,000.

A member of the Spanish Cortes in 1891 declared that there were 350 persons employed in Cuba as representatives of the crown, against whom proceedings had been taken for fraud, and not one of whom had ever been punished.

In June, 1895, the public debt of Cuba had nearly reached the enormous sum of $300,000,000, an average for each person of $187.00. The public debt of the United States averages for each person about $14.00.

Cuba is almost wholly an agricultural country. It produces but a small portion of the necessities for home consumption and pays for the rest with but two products, tobacco and sugar. The sugar-cane industries of Cuba have had to encounter keen competition from the sugar-beet industries of Europe. The tobacco industry has been handicapped by heavy export duties, which have

THE ASCENDENCY OF AMERICA. 249

enhanced the price of the raw material to the manufacturer until he has been driven to use inferior grades and the tobacco-growing industries of other nations have been further stimulated by Spain's exactions upon her own colonies.

The unjust laws and exorbitant taxes have driven large numbers of citizens from Cuba that the island needs, and it is estimated that there are now in the United States alone 40,000 Cubans.

Staggering under a burden of debt, deprived of privileges that Americans deem the inherent rights of man, with no hope that the future might hold alleviation for their miseries, what wonder that the inhabitants again take up arms in behalf of their independence.

Insurrection Planned.

The present insurrection was organized about the close of 1894 by Jose Marti (the father of the revolution), who was then in New York. He chartered three vessels, loaded them with arms and ammunition, intending to make a landing in Cuba, but the expedition was stopped at Fernandina, Florida, by the United States authorities. February 24th, 1895, had been fixed upon as the day for striking the first blow. Marti left New York in January, 1895, for Santo Domingo, where he joined Maximo Gomez and other Cuban leaders. Although these leaders apparently did not reach the island until May, when the eventful 24th day of February arrived, twenty-four daring spirits at Ybarra, in the province of Matanzas, defied the authorities and declared Cuba free. In spite of their lack of leaders the insurgents made rapid headway from the first. Several encounters took place in March and April, usually with advantage to the insurgents. April 1st General Maceo landed from Costa Rica and joined the Cuban army. Ten days later Jose Marti, the head of the revolution; General Maximo Gomez, the general-in-chief, and some others landed in the province of Santiago, and the news of their presence wonderfully increased the insurgents' forces. Spain soon recognized the gravity of affairs and made preparations to send Martinez Campos, the leader of Spanish forces in the "Ten Years' War," to take charge of matters in Cuba.

The "Allianca" Affair.

The colonial authorities were much exercised over reported filibustering expeditions fitted out in the United States, and were suspicious of every strange vessel. March 8, 1895, an American steamer, the "Allianca," running between New York and Colon, Panama, was fired upon when near the coast of Cuba and in the regular channel for coast vessels, the Spanish man-of-war suspecting that the "Allianca" was carrying contraband of war for the Cuban insurgents. Captain Crossman of the American ship refused to stop, and putting on full speed was soon able to leave the Spaniard behind. A complaint was made to the State Department, who in turn protested vigorously to the Spanish government against interference with American steamers. "Forcible interference with them cannot be claimed as a belligerent act whether they pass within three miles of the Cuban coast or not and can under no circumstances be tolerated when no state of war exists."*

The Spanish government made an apology, disavowed the act and relieved the Spanish officer of his command.

April 16th General Campos arrived in Cuba with reinforcements and unlimited power, and it was expected that he would make short work with the insurrection which was at that time confined to the eastern provinces.

Campos, upon his arrival, prepared to confine the insurgents to the eastern provinces and built across the island a line of forts called trocha (trenches), a system of

---

*State Department.

defenses he had successfully used in the previous "Ten Years' War." The first trocha was no barrier to the insurgents under Gomez and Maceo. The second one proved no more effectual. Campos, retreating toward Havana, drew a third, shorter and stronger one, from Matanzas across the island south. On the railroad running from Havana to Batabana he placed numerous freight cars plated with boiler iron and pierced with loopholes for rifles. These cars were kept moving almost constantly, but in spite of all his elaborate preparation Maceo passed the line and reached the rich tobacco district of Pinar del Rio, having marched the whole length of the island. Campos' failure to subdue the revolution and his retreat upon Havana aggravated the "Peninsulars" so much that they demanded his recall and he was succeeded on the 10th of February, 1896, by General Weyler.

Weyler.

Weyler constructed a fourth trocha across the island, about twenty-five miles west of Havana, which has become famous enough to warrant a description. It consists of a ditch nine feet wide and filled with water on the levels. On each side is a barbed wire fence and east of the ditch is a fairly good road which was constantly patrolled by cavalry and flying artillery. On the west bank at intervals were block houses and earthworks constantly garrisoned and connected with each other by telephone. This was supposed to be impassable, but Gomez and Maceo have shown it slight courtesy.

Marti soon fell in battle at Don Rios, May 19, 1895, but not until he had kindled a conflagration that all Spain's forces could not subdue. Upon landing in Cuba he had issued a call for representatives to a constitutional convention. It met in September, after his death. Forty representatives met, twenty from the army and twenty from the provinces, every province being represented except Pinar del Rio. On the 16th of September they adopted a constitution, and two days later elected a President, Vice-President, Secretary of State, Secretary of War, Secretary of the Treasury, General-in-Chief and Lieutenant-General. The convention passed laws establishing the political boundaries of states and districts, establishing post-offices, providing for the collection of taxes and regulating marriages. The whole appears fairly well on paper, but it is doubtful if it exists as a full-fledged institution elsewhere. At present, Bartolome Masso is President, Domingo Mendoz Capote, Vice-President, and Maximo Gomez General-in-Chief.

Cuban Capital.

Their capital, called Cubitas, is situated on top of a mountain, twenty-five miles east of Puerto Principe. The sides of the mountain are exceedingly steep. The top is reached only by narrow paths, and a few desperate and daring men could easily defend it against a large force. Neither could it well be reduced by starvation, for the top is nearly level, contains about a square mile of fertile land, easily worked, where corn, sweet potatoes and other products common to the island are grown. The insurgents have erected here some wooden buildings, a dynamite factory, etc.

The surface of Cuba is particularly well adapted to guerrilla warfare, and one needs but to look at the history of Jamaica to see how prolonged such a struggle might be. When the British took possession of that island and sought to subdue the native inhabitants, part of them, called Maroons, broke away, seized strong positions in the interior, and for more than seventy years kept up an armed resistance to the British power. The mountains of Chile to-day contain remnants of the wild race, the Araucuns, who have never been thoroughly subdued.

Death of Maceo.

December 4, 1896, General Antonio Maceo crossed the trocha west of Havana with a few men and appeared within that province. He began to rapidly collect his forces who were coming in small parties and soon had several hundred men under his command. The Spaniards at once sent a division in pursuit of him. They came upon the Cubans intrenched behind a stone fence in the San Pedro plantation and were warmly received. Upon the first repulse of the Spaniads, Maceo, believing it an opportune time for a charge, put himself at the head of his men and dashed at the enemy machete in hand. He fell within fifty paces of the Spanish line pierced by two balls. The Spaniards not recognizing the corpse as that of their dreaded opponent left it upon their retreat and it was recovered by the Cubans and buried in a secret place, those present taking oath not to reveal the spot and renewing their vows not to lay down their arms until Cuba should be free.

The "Competitor" Incident.

The American schooner "Competitor" left Key West with about forty men under Colonel Monzon of the Cuban army with arms and ammunition. A landing was made on the north coast of Pinar del Rio. The men and all the stores were put ashore, when a Spanish gunboat appeared in the offing. The "Competitor" hoisted an American flag and tried to escape, but was boarded and captured and the following taken prisoners: Alfredo Laborde, Teodoro de la Maza, Dr. Elias Bedia, John Milton of Kansas and William Gildear, an Englishman. They were taken to Havana April 30th. On the 8th of May they were tried by a naval court-martial, apparently organized expressly to convict them, for the only testimony taken was that of the Spanish commander who had captured them. Four declared themselves Americans, and the 10th of May they were sentenced to death, Weyler approving the sentence. They would have been executed on the 12th but for the energetic demands of General Lee.

"I earnestly and vigorously protested against the arrest of these American citizens, telling General Weyler that it was in violation of the treaty and protocol between Spain and the United States, which, in my opinion, limited the confinement 'in communicado' to seventy-two hours. 'In communicado' is a Spanish term, meaning literally without communication. And these Americans, without any charges against them that I could ascertain, and without warning, and without the knowledge of their friends and relatives, were arrested and thrown into these little 'in communicado' cells, about eight by ten feet, stone floors and dark, and kept in these horrid little holes for days and days without being allowed to see and talk with anyone. I told Weyler that in our country the law presumed every man innocent until he was proved guilty; but by the Spanish process every man was guilty and they did not even give him an opportunity to prove his innocence. But he replied that he had published a proclamation establishing martial law, and that the terms of that proclamation superseded the stipulations of the treaty. To which I answered that the terms of treaties between two countries at peace could not be set aside, changed or altered, except by the action of one or both of the contracting parties, and that his proclamation was therefore inoperative where its stipulations came in conflict with the treaty mandates.

Murder of Dr. Ruiz.

"The situation, however, remained unchanged until finally Dr. Ruiz, an American dentist who was practicing his profession in a town called Guanabacoa, some four miles from Havana, was arrested. A railroad train between Havana and this town had been captured by the insurgents and the next day the Spanish authorities arrested a large number of persons in Guanabacoa charging them with giving information which enabled the troops, under their enterprising young leader, Aranguren, to make the capture; and among these persons arrested was this American. He was a strongly built, athletic man, who confined himself strictly to the practice of his profession and let politics severely alone. He had nothing to do with the train being captured, but that night was visiting a neighbor opposite, until nine or ten o'clock, when he returned to his house and went to bed. He was arrested by the police the next morning; thrown into an 'incommunicado' cell; kept there some three hundred and fifty or sixty hours, and was finally (when half-crazed by this terrible imprisonment and calling for his wife and children) struck over the head with a 'billy' in the hands of a brutal jailor and died from its effects. Ruiz went into that cell an unusually healthy and vigorous man and came out a corpse.

"After this tragedy I determined no longer to submit to more violations of the treaty rights of American citizens and therefore, after viewing this dead body, went to my office, and finding that there was an American named Scott who had been arrested and was already 'incommunicado' a much longer time than the prescribed limit of seventy-two hours, I demanded that he be released from 'in communicado,' and at the end of three days he was released, and since the hour I made the issue no American citizens have been thrown into 'incommunicado' cells, and all Americans who were arrested afterwards for supposed offenses or captured in the insurgent ranks were invariably turned over to me, and I sent them to the United States."*

---

*Gen. Fitzhugh Lee, in "The Fortnightly Review," June, 1898.

How Cuba's War Has Been Conducted.

Of the methods of conducting the war both by the Cubans and Spaniards, the less said the better. If Weyler by his "reconcentrado order" has ruined the country, Gomez has no less certainly ruined the towns that he has been able to capture. If Weyler ordered within the "zone of cultivation" or "zone of starvation" all the "pacificos," Gomez showed hardly less severity in pressing into the service every able-bodied Cuban whom he found.

The Reconcentrado Order.

The style of guerrilla warfare practiced by the insurgents could be maintained for years, because the wonderfully fertile soil tilled by farmers who were in sympathy with the insurrection would produce sufficient food to feed the rebel army. General Weyler saw he would be unable to reduce the rebels to terms so long as they had such supplies to fall back upon. It was then he issued his famous "reconcentrado order," by whose terms he compelled "the old men, women and children to leave their homes and come within the nearest Spanish fortified lines, pains being taken after they were driven from their little farms to burn their houses, tear up their plant beds, and drive off and confiscate the few cattle, hogs and chickens that they were obliged to leave."

"The United States was naturally shocked at the brutality of this order, and saw with great indignation, some 400,000 of these poor innocent war victims forced away from where they could subsist themselves, to the Spanish lines where they could obtain nothing and within which nothing was tendered. As a consequence, over 200,000 (principally women and children and non-combatants) died from starvation, and starvation alone. History presents nowhere such an appalling record; nor do the military annals anywhere furnish such a horrible spectacle, the result of a military order, based upon a supposed military necessity.

"General Weyler, if anything, is a soldier, trained to no other career, and one who believes that everything is fair in war, and every means justifiable which will ultimately write success upon his standards. He did not propose to make war with velvet paws, but to achieve his purpose of putting down the insurrection if he had to wade through, up to the visor of his helmet, the blood of every Cuban — man, woman and child — on the island. And yet, I found him — in official intercourse — affable, pleasant and agreeable. He was always polite and courteous to me, and told me more than once that he wished I would remain in my position there as Consul-General as long as he did as Governor and Captain-General. He was small in stature, with a long face and square chin, and wearing side-whiskers and a moustache; quick, nervous in his manner and gait; decided in his opinions, he was loved by some and hated and feared by others."*

The farmer was compelled to grow such crops as would supply the insurgents with food and forbidden under severe penalties from growing anything that would supply the Spaniards with revenue. If one dared to travel without a passport from an insurgent general, he was likely to be captured and impressed into the army.

"The losses of the insurgent forces in their skirmishes with the Spaniards had also to be made good by these same peaceful inhabitants who were unceremoniously pressed into the rebel army, and horribly tortured to death if they refused to enlist, or deserted. And even when they obeyed all these orders with alacrity, as was generally the case, they were not by any means sure that their goods, their daughters or their lives, were safe from the avarice, the lust, or the vengeance of the colored man. Farm houses, manufactories, huts, were frequently burned

---

*Gen. Fitzhugh Lee, in "The Fortnightly Review," June, 1898.

down by the rebels, not only because the occupants were supposed to be unfriendly, or even because they were suspected of being lukewarm in the service, but in many cases the dwellings were reduced to ashes solely because they were too near a Spanish fort or too far from a Cuban prefecture.

"The following extract from the instructions officially given to the insurgent prefects and sub-prefects by the Provisional Government will enable the reader to understand the determination of the rebels to force every inhabitant of the island to join in the revolt against Spain:

'Circular A. 1. Republic of Cuba. Governmental Council. Delegation. For the purpose of improving the service of the prefecture and sub-prefectures, and in order to introduce better order into the services of the Revolution, I hereby give you the following instructions: You will make clear to all inhabitants residing in your zone the obligation imposed upon them of working for the Revolution, calling their attention to the fact that once they live under the protection of the Republic, *they are considered to be soldiers of the liberating army.* * * * At all times you are invested with the right of utilizing the individuals of your zone in everything connected with the service of the prefecture or sub-prefecture, whereas no excuse whatever on their part is admissable. Sluggishness will not be allowed under any pretext, and all those inhabitants who, in your judgment are not desirable in this place, will have to leave in seventy-two hours, for which purpose you will give them notice in advance. * * * When the prefects or sub-prefects deem it opportune, they will form companies of inhabitants for the purpose of 'lighting the candles' (burning down farm houses and villages) destroying houses, granaries, railways, telegraphs, telephones, of lifting cattle, and of doing anything else that may seem serviceable for the Revolution.'

" The means by which the pacificos or peaceful farmers of the interior were forced to become rebels are fairly well known and at the same time reveal one of the abundant sources of the stream of reconcentrados whose number and sufferings had been laid to General Weyler's charge."*

There are but few records of exchanges of prisoners among them. This alone is significant, for each side must have taken some prisoners. We should not expect much mercy to be shown rebels by Spaniards, neither should we logically expect much to be shown by those of Spanish blood or mixed Spanish and negro blood who have been forced into rebellion by Spanish exactions.

The Spanish forces have always been better armed, and numerically much stronger than their opponents, and it was plainly for their interest to come to pitched battle. It is just as evidently to the interest of the other side to break up into small armed bands and avoid pitched battles. The broken surface and dense tropical growth of Cuba affords ideal grounds for guerrilla warfare. The Cubans have not expected to win their independence by fighting heavy battles. Their war was not against Spanish flesh, but against Spanish credit. Hence they left nothing undone that would permit them to embarrass the Spaniards in this respect. They forbade the planters to grind sugar cane. It was equally for the interest of the Spaniards that the crops should be harvested. De Lome said of General Campos, " He knew perfectly well that if the sugar crop could be gathered the back of the insurrection would be broken." Because of this the Cubans burned the sugar plantations.

This was not simply a mad destruction of property but a deliberate and desperate policy. If the resources of the country were destroyed, Spain could collect no taxes; if the planters had nothing to sell, it would be impos-

---
*Dr. E. J. Dillon in " Contemporary Review," June, 1898.

sible for them to buy and Spain could collect no import duties. The vulnerable point for the Spaniards to attack was the Cuban army; the vulnerable point of attack for the Cuban army was Spanish credit.

Such conditions and such a war were sure to inflict suffering upon the innocent. The desolation caused has been simply horrible; 200,000 people have been starved to death, millions of dollars of property have been destroyed, railroad trains have been blown up with dynamite without any consideration for innocent passengers thereon.

Before the intervention of the United States, we were told that all the Cuban needed to win his freedom was recognition of belligerency. It seems now that we were misinformed.

The Cubans are excellent guerrilla fighters, but since the death of Maceo have been good for little else. Under Garcia they proved themselves of little value to General Shafter in the capture of Santiago. Gomez's army was not strong enough to effect a juction with the United States forces when several attempts to land supplies for him from the steamship "Gussie" were made.

There is no doubt but the Spaniards have been guilty of deeds of horrible cruelty, and it is not safe to say that the Cubans' conduct has always been in strict keeping with the rules of civilized warfare. It is stated upon what seems to be good authority that Captain Evans of the "Iowa" and Lieutenant Wainwright of the "Gloucester" threatened to turn their guns on the Cubans who were picking off the prisoners from Cervera's fleet as they struggled through the water from the burning vessels.

The record of the Spanish-American colonies now independent, seems to prove conclusively that people suddenly freed from Spanish rule are not for a long time capable of self-government. Spanish misrule certainly explains and may in some degree excuse, but it cannot justify such warfare as this. The wisdom of President McKinley in refusing recognition to the so-called Cuban Republic of the insurgents is daily becoming more apparent.

The Cuba of the future.

Given a government that will guarantee capital against the impositions it has suffered in the past hundred years in that island, make the laborer sure that he will not be taxed to death or have his throat cut, and we shall expect to see the magnificent resources of the island develop with marvelous rapidity. There is no soil more fertile than the best parts of Cuba. Its vast forests, at present covering a large portion of the surface of the island, contain timber valuable for ship-building and commerce. Even in the recent unsettled condition of the island, two American companies thought it worth while to develop and begin the operation of iron mines there.

A fine quality of marble is found in the Isle of Pines, and the extreme eastern and western portions of the island produce a fair quality of copper.

The chief wealth of the island will always remain in its extremely fertile soil. Owing to the absence of frost, two crops of grains, like rice or Indian corn, can be raised in one year.

We believe that under a stable government American capital will flow in and the island soon prove its just claim to the title "The Pearl of the Antilles."

CHAPTER VII.

International Law.

"A collection of rules by which nations and their members, respectively, are supposed to be governed in their relations with each other. In its exact sense law is a rule of propriety and of conduct described by sovereign power. Strictly speaking, therefore, as nations have no common superior they cannot be said to be subject to human law; but there is, nevertheless, a body of rules more or less generally recognized by which nations profess to regulate their own conduct toward each other and the conduct of their citizens, respectively. Being rules of propriety and of conduct, though not prescribed by a superior, they are somewhat loosely designated as laws, and taken together they form what is called 'International Law,' and as such are enforced by each nation separately upon persons and things within its jurisdiction. This body of rules is derived from custom or treaty. From the earliest times there must have been some sort of rule, tacit or expressed, for the intercourse, however small, which must have existed between nations and must have begun with the beginnings of nations. We find, accordingly, in the oldest historical records, mention of messengers or embassies sent by nation or king to another nation or king and of compacts between them. As now existing, International Law is a science of which the major part is generally understood and accepted.

"There is no penalty except the inevitable distrust engendered which injures the standing of the nation breaking faith in the negotiations. Yet they are direct and serious blows to that good faith which is the basis of all human intercourse and progress. This is a weakness inherent to International Law destitute as it is of a recognized means of enforcement. In spite of this, however, states do fulfill their contracts as a rule, or by their laborious excuses, in case of violation, prove their desire to be thought faith-keeping." *

How It Grew.

International Law, as we know it to-day, is a modern product. The first glimpses we catch of it in history show it in a very rudimentary form. The Orient was not likely to be a fruitful field for it, as the Asiatic had but little regard for individual rights; the Greeks and Romans made good laws for themselves but were too powerful and contemptuous of their neighbors to devise an elaborate code for the guidance of their international affairs. Only after the destruction of the great ancient powers and the rise of several nations of nearly equal strength would the intercourse of nations be between equals; then we should expect to find, and do find it guided by established principles commending themselves to reason and conscience. International Law is not unchangeable, but keeps pace with human progress, and like any other law, serves to mark the advance of civilization. Prisoners of war are no longer put to death, enslaved, or held for ransom.

Holy Alliance.

"During the occupation of Paris consequent on the Battle of Waterloo, the three rulers of Russia, Austria and Prussia, joined afterwards by the French king, formed September 26, 1815, the 'Holy Alliance,' which has been regarded as a league of absolution against the rights and the freedom of the nations. This famous league, however, at its inception, appears to have had no definite object in view. It was a measure into which the other sovereigns entered in order to gratify the emperor Alexander, whose romantic mind, then under

---

* David Dudley Field.

the influence of Madame Krudener, contemplated a golden age in which the intercourse of nations should be controlled by Christian principles. The parties to the 'Holy Alliance' bound themselves, appealing to the Holy Trinity, to exercise their power according to the principles of religion, justice and humanity; to offer one another to one another on all occasions, aid and help; to treat their subjects and soldiers with paternal feeling, and to regard their people as members of a great Christian family whose guidance was entrusted to them by God.

"'The sovereigns each regarded,' they said, 'as a fundamental basis, their invariable resolution never to depart, either among themselves or in their relations with other states, from the strict observance of the law of nations, principles which in their application to any state of permanent place are alone able to give an effectual guaranty of the independence of each government and the stability of their general association.' The unmeaning nature of such declarations was shown not long afterwards by acts of interference."

In 1820 and 1821 revolutions broke out in rapid succession in Spain, Naples and Sardinia. The alarm excited by the revolutionary spirit was the occasion of convoking a congress at Troppan in Silesia in October, 1820, which was removed near the end of the same year to Laybach. Against the proposed intervention in the affairs of Italy the British government protested in strong terms, although the existing ministry were not averse to the suppression of revolutionary liberalism; while on the other hand the French government approved openly of the intervention in order to gratify the ultra-royalist party at home, but secretly dreaded the Austrian influence which such a measure would increase. Austria, thus supported, sent an army into the Peninsula, overthrew the revolution almost without a blow in the spring of 1821, and brought back the old absolutism in all its rigor.

Soon after this, in the middle of 1821, a royalist insurrection occurred in northern Spain, to which France so far extended aid as to allow the insurgents to gather along the borders; to retreat in case of need across the line, and to make the preparation of gathering arms and money on French soil.

A congress had been arranged to meet at Verona when that of Laybach broke up. The principal measure here agitated was armed interference in the affairs of Spain, which, if undertaken, would naturally be the work of France. The British envoy, the Duke of Wellington, declared the refusal of his government to participate in any such proceeding, and also that England would not even attempt to persuade Spain to conform to the views of the congress. The French envoys, Montmorency and Chateaubriand, against the express instructions of their court, urged forward the intervention, which was supported by the other powers and energetically by Russia. A French army occupied Spain, overthrowing the constitution of Cadiz, to which the king had given assent, and left him "free," but the country enslaved.

"No stretch of interference had gone so far as this, for Spain would have been a settled, constitutional government and probably settled peaceably unless the agitators had looked for aid to foreign powers."*

The real source of action of the "Holy Alliance" was not in the treaty drawn by Czar Alexander, but emanated from congresses which were called at different times as occasion arose and seemed to demand them. Metternich, the able diplomat of Austria, made the alliance an instrument for some of his cleverest work.

---

*Theodore D. Woolsey's "International Law."

Origin of the Monroe Doctrine.

It is one of the ironies of fate that Monroe, a man of less force of character than any of his predecessors, and who did less than they to formulate certain principles of American policy, should, by mere force of circumstances, be associated with the principles, which have ever since borne his name.

George Canning, minister of foreign affairs of England in 1822, was anxious to secure the assistance of the United States to counteract the power wielded by the "Holy Alliance." Because of this, and not through any motives of disinterested philanthropy, he dropped a few diplomatic hints to the American minister at the English court. These bore fruit in the next annual message of President Monroe.

Already in 1791, 1801 and 1804, the principles had been forshadowed by the utterance of our state department, and before venturing to take any decided action in the matter, Monroe not only laid it before his own cabinet, made up of eminent men, but corresponded with ex-Presidents Jefferson and Madison. Thus it may be said that the "Holy Alliance" is directly responsible for the enunciation of the doctrine that bears Monroe's name.

Monroe Asks Advice.

Mr. Canning, in his correspondence with Mr. Rush, our minister in England in 1823, having suggested that the United States should take decided ground against the interference of the "Holy Alliance" in South America, Mr. Monroe sent the paper to Mr. Jefferson asking his advice. To this request Mr. Jefferson answered as follows:

Jefferson's View.

MONTICELLO, *October* 24, 1823.

DEAR SIR. — The question presented by the letter you have sent me is the most momentous which has ever been offered to my contemplation since that of Independence; that made us a nation; this sets our compass and points the course which we are to steer through the ocean of time opening on us. And never could we embark upon it under circumstances more auspicious. Our first and fundamental maxim should be, never to entangle ourselves in the broils of Europe ; our second, never to suffer Europe to intermeddle with cis-Atlantic affairs. America, North and South, has a set of interests distinct from those of Europe and peculiarly her own. She should therefore have a system of her own, separate and apart from that of Europe. While the last is laboring to become a domicile of despotism, our endeavor should surely be to make our hemisphere that of freedom.

One nation most of all could disturb us in this pursuit ; she now offers to lend aid and accompany us in it. By acceding to her proposition we detach her from the bands, bring her mighty weight into the scale of free government and emancipate a continent at one stroke, which might otherwise linger long in doubt and difficulty. Great Britain is the nation which can do us the most harm of any one on all the earth, and with her on our side we need not fear the whole world. With her then, we should most seduously cherish a cordial friendship, and nothing would tend more to knit our affections than to be fighting once more side by side in the same cause. Not that I would purchase even her amity at the price of taking part in her wars." — *Jefferson to Monroe.*

Mr. Madison being consulted at the same time, through Mr. Jefferson, answered as follows:

Madison's Opinion.

October 30, 1823.

DEAR SIR. — I have just received from Mr. Jefferson your letter to him, with the correspondence between Mr. Canning and Mr. Rush, sent for his and my perusal and our opinions on the subject of it.

From the disclosures of Mr. Canning, it appears, as was otherwise to be inferred, that the success of France against Spain would be followed by an attempt of the Holy Alliance to reduce the revolutionized colonies of the latter to their former dependence. The professions we have made to these neighbors, our sympathies with their liberties and independence, the deep interest we have in the most friendly relations with them, and the consequences threatened by a command of their resources by the great powers, confederated against the rights and reforms of which we have given so conspicuous and persuasive an example, all unite in calling for our efforts to defeat the meditated crusade. It is particularly fortunate that the policy of Great Britain, though guided by calculations different from ours, has presented a co-operation the same as ours. With that co-operation we have nothing to fear from the rest of Europe, and with it the best assurance of success to our laudable views. There ought not, therefore to be any backwardness I think, in meeting her in the way she has proposed, keeping in view, of course, the spirit and forms of the Constitution in every step taken in the road to war, which must be the last step if those short of war should be without avail. — *Madison to Monroe.*

The "Doctrine" Enunciated.

" From the seventh annual message of President Monroe, delivered December 22, 1823, the doctrine called by his name was thus expressed:

' In the wars of the European powers, in matters relating

to themselves, we have never taken any part, nor does it comport with our policy to do so. It is only when our rights are invaded or seriously menaced that we resent injuries or make preparation for our defense.

'With the movements in this hemisphere we are of necessity more immediately connected, and by causes which must be obvious to all enlightened and impartial observers. The political system of the allied powers is essentially different in this respect from that of America. This difference proceeds from that which exists in their respective governments; and to the defense of our own, which has been achieved by the loss of so much blood and treasure, and matured by the wisdom of their most enlightened citizens, and under which we have enjoyed unexampled felicity, this whole nation is devoted. We owe it, therefore, to candor and to the amicable relations existing between the United States and those powers, to declare that *we should consider any attempt on their part to extend their system to any portion of this hemisphere, as dangerous to our peace and safety.* With the existing colonies or dependencies of any European power *we have not interfered, and shall not interfere.* But with the governments who have declared their independence and maintained it, and whose independence we have, on great consideration and on just principles acknowledged, we could not view any interposition for the purpose of oppressing them, or controlling in any other manner their destiny, by any European power, in any other light than as the manifestation of an unfriendly disposition toward the United States. In the war between these new governments and Spain, we have adhered and shall continue to adhere to this policy, provided no change shall occur which, in the judgment of the competent authorities of this government, shall make a corresponding change on the part of the United States indispensable to their security.'"

A Policy, Not a Law.

"It is to be borne in mind that the declarations known as the 'Monroe Doctrine' have never received the sanction of an act or resolution of Congress, nor have they any of that authority which European governments attach to a royal ordinance. They are, in fact, only the declarations of an existing administration of what its own policy would be, and what it thinks should ever be the policy of the country, on a subject of paramount and permanent interest. Thus, at the same session in which the message was delived, Mr. Clay introduced the following resolution: 'That the people of these States would not see, without serious inquietude, any forcible interposition by the allied powers of Europe in behalf of Spain, to reduce to their former subjection those parts of the continent of America which have proclaimed and established for themselves, respectively, independent governments, and which have been solemnly recognized by the United States.' But this resolution was never brought up for action or discussion. It is seen also, by the debates on the Panama mission and the Yucatan intervention, that Congress has never been willing to commit the nation to any compact or pledge on this subject, or to any specific declaration of purpose or methods, beyond the general language of the message."

Not Hostile to Monarchies.

"It has sometimes been assumed that the 'Monroe Doctrine' contained some declaration against any other than democratic-republican institutions on this continent, however arising or introduced. The message will be searched in vain for anything of the kind. We were the first to recognize the imperial authority of Dom Pedro in Brazil, and of Iturbide in Mexico; and more than half of the northern continent was under the scepters of Great Britain and Russia; and these dependencies would certainly be free to adopt what institutions they pleased, in case of successful rebellion, or of peaceful separation from their parent States."

Its Principles.

"As a summary of this subject, it would seem that the following position may be safely taken:

I. The declaration upon which Mr. Monroe consulted Mr. Jefferson and his Cabinet related to the interposition of European powers in the affairs of American States.

II. The kind of interposition declared against was that which may be made for the purpose of controlling other political affairs, or of extending to this hemisphere the system in operation upon the continent of Europe, by which the great powers exercise a control over the affairs of other European States.

III. The declarations do not intimate any course of conduct to be pursued in case of such interposition, but merely say that they would be 'considered as dangerous to our peace and safety,' and as 'the manifestation of an unfriendly disposition towards the United States,' which it would be impossible for us to 'behold with indifference;' thus leaving the nation to act at all times as its opinion of its policy or duty might require.

IV. The declarations are only the opinion of the administration of 1823, and have acquired no legal force or sanction.

V. The United States has never made any alliance with, or pledge to, any other American State on the subject covered by the declaration.

VI. The declaration respecting non-colonization was on a subject distinct from European intervention with American States, and related to the acquisition of sovereign title by any European power, by new and original occupation or colonization thereafter. Whatever were the political motives for resisting such colonization, the principle of public law upon which it was placed was, that the continent must be considered as already within the occupation and jurisdiction of independent civilized nations."*

Animus of the Doctrine.

"The Monroe Doctrine," however, was leveled not only against the "Holy Alliance," but also against Russia, for claiming the title to the territory on the northwestern coast of the American continent, from Behring Straits down to the fifty-first parallel of north latitude.

Excuses no Nation.

"This doctrine is simply a presidential declaration of national policy; but as such, it has a strong hold on the mind and heart of the American people and has always seemed to our sister American republics as a great if not their greatest bulwark against European interference with their liberty and independence. Not a word, however, does it contain that justifies the belief that it was intended to relieve any American nation of its duty to meet all its obligations to European powers, or to prevent such powers from obtaining due satisfaction for any wrong they may suffer or any injury they may sustain in their intercourse with the American people.

Doctrine vs. Intervention.

"What it does contain is two plain statements, the first one being to the effect that the European nations *must not attempt to acquire* sovereignty or to extend their monarchical system over any American territory in addition to that which they already possess; and the second one being practically a promise that the United States *will not interfere with the existing American colonies* or dependencies of any European power.

---

* Wharton's "International Law."

"As the second is as clear a part of the Monroe Doctrine as the first, it would seem as if Congress has exercised much wisdom and foresight in refusing to make it law, for occasions might easily arise when it would be the duty of the United States to interfere in the American colonies of European powers; moreover, the right to interfere in proper cases in the affairs of adjacent nations is always too important to forego or surrender.*

"In the United States and in the other American nations, the Monroe Doctrine is generally understood to be confined to the principles laid down in the first statement and directed against the European powers. That principle, however, is not an article of International Law, nor is it even, as has been stated, to be found in the municipal law of the United States. Its only practical value, therefore, is that it serves as a notice to European powers of the specific grounds on which the United States, will exercise the right of interfering to prevent them from acquiring or controlling any American territory that does not already belong to them. As a warning, consequently, it is timely and useful, and it has the special and admirable merit of being at once courteous and frank; but it does not give to the United States any right to interfere, and it cannot be doubted that the general right of intervention would alone be sufficient."†

Intervention.

The measures which one State takes to prevent injury to itself, arising from the political measures of another State, or growing, for some good reason, out of the other sovereign's conduct. Since all States are independent, the presumption is against the right of intervention. The principal legitimate causes of intervention are:

(1) For the purpose of preserving the balance of power;

---

* Written before intervention in Cuba.
† Bowen's " International Law."

that is, to prevent a State from gaining by political means or force an accession of power which would be dangerous to its neighbors.

(2) To prevent changes in a form of government that would react upon the powers interfering. For example, a republican form of government in Austria would be distasteful to the adjacent monarchies. The action of the Holy Alliance in the application of this principle brought out the Monroe Doctrine.

(3) To promote the rights of humanity. In 1827 Great Britain and France interfered to prevent Turkey from utterly crushing Greece. In 1877 Russia made war upon Turkey, urging as a reason the atrocities of the Turks in Bulgaria. In 1895, Russia, France and Germany intervened in a protest to Japan to prevent the latter country acquiring territory in China where she would be a constant menace to Pekin. In 1897, Great Britain, Austria, France, Italy, Russia and Germany intervened to prevent Turkey from sending reinforcements to the island of Crete in which an insurrection was raging and landed marines to preserve order while they peacefully blockaded the harbor of Canea to prevent Greek sympathizers from entering the harbor with supplies for the insurgents. Later, at the end of the Turko-Grecian war that followed, they intervened to preserve to Greece the territory captured from it by the Turks and to abate the Turkish demand for money indemnity. A still later example is our interference in Cuban affairs.

War Growing Less Barbarous.

The Crimean war was conducted on principles which were a marked advance over previous methods. It was closed by the "Declaration of Paris," to the principles of which all the nations of importance except the United States, Spain and Mexico have since agreed. The United

States has often accepted all of it but the clause relating to privateering, and her objection to that was not that she wished to send out privateers, but that she was willing to go even farther and exempt private property on the high seas wholly from capture. The United States has not sent out a privateer in sixty years, and with the Columbia, Minneapolis, St. Louis, St. Paul, Yale, Harvard and other fleet cruisers that could be made commerce destroyers, there is not much inducement for her to do so. Further, commerce destroying would never put an end to any war. It serves only to annoy and irritate the enemy without crushing his military power.

Declaration of Paris, 1856.

"Considering that maritime law in time of war has long been the subject of deplorable disputes; that the uncertainity of the law and of the duties in such a matter gives rise to differences of opinion between neutrals and belligerents which may occasion serious difficulties, and even conflicts; that it is, consequently, advantageous to establish a uniform doctrine on so important a point; and that the plenipotentiaries assembled in Congress at Paris cannot better respond to the intentions by which their governments are animated, than by seeking to introduce into international relations fixed principles in this respect — the above-mentioned plenipotentiaries, being duly authorized, have adopted the following solemn declaration:

1. Privateering is and remains abolished.
2. The neutral flag covers enemy's goods with the exception of contraband of war.
3. Neutral goods, with the exception of contraband of war, are not liable to capture under an enemy's flag.
4. Blockades, in order to be binding, must be effective — that is to say, maintained by a force sufficient really to prevent access to the coast.

Privateering. — A vessel owned by a citizen of the United States and not by the Government itself, armed and acting under a commission called "Letters of Marque" empowering it to capture Spanish vessels, would be a privateer. Private citizens could thus embark in war simply as a speculation. In 1812, American privateers inflicted great damage upon English commerce; but the practice is coming into disrepute and is now thought to be little better than legalized piracy.

Neutral Flag. — Goods belonging to a citizen of Spain, shipped in a vesssel belonging to a neutral nation, would not be liable to capture by the United States unless the goods themselves were contraband.

Neutral Goods. — Goods belonging to the citizens of a neutral nation, shipped in a Spanish vessel, would not be liable to capture by the United States if not contraband..

Contraband. — Articles "contraband of war" are, in general, those which relate directly to the carrying on of war. To make them liable to capture two facts must be proved: first, their contraband character; second, their hostile destination. As to what articles are in themselves contrabrand there is as yet no general agreement, belligerents striving to stretch their war rights and neutrals desiring to extend their trade rights. The neutral State is not bound to protect its subjects from trading in contraband articles; that burden lies on the shoulders of the belligerent."*

Blockade Defined.

"The act of shutting out all trade by sea with certain specified ports or coasts of one belligerent by another."

"A neutral has a right to demand that these three essentials be observed:

1. Due notification must be given.
2. The blockade must be effective.

---
*Woolsey's "International Law."

3. There must be an actual attempt to evade it or break through."

"*Notification.*"— This may be given in different ways; by diplomatic announcement to all neutral powers; by a warning to the blockade runner inscribed upon the register of the ship trying to enter.

"*Effective.*"— The amount of force necessary to make a blockade legal and effective is somewhat indefinite. It does not mean that occasional evasions of the blockade will vitiate it. It is enough that there is great risk of capture so as to make blockade running dangerous.

"*Breach of Blockade.*— There must actually appear an attempt to break the blockade after it has been announced and made effective. The penalty of breach of blockade is confiscation of the ship, first, and then of the cargo, unless it can be shown that the cargo was not concerned in the act of the ship. No punishment can be visited upon the crews of the blockade runners."*

Secretary Seward's Position.

Secretary Seward said, in answer to questions concerning the blockade of the Southern ports:

"1. That the blockade will be strictly enforced upon the principles recognized by the law of nations.

2. That armed vessels of neutral States will have the right to enter and depart from interdicted ports.

3. That merchant vessels in port at the time when the blockade took effect will be allowed a reasonable time for their departure.

4. The Government cannot consent that emigrant vessels shall enter the interdicted ports."

"Temporary fortuitous absence of a blockading force, by which occasional blockade runners slip in, does not itself break up the blockade."

---

* Woolsey's "International Law."

American Practice.

The following extracts from Wharton's "International Law Digest" show what is the practice of the United States:

"The carrying of letters or passengers to blockaded ports by neutral war vessels, entering by courtesy therein, is an infraction of neutrality. A vessel sailing ignorantly for a blockaded port is not liable to condemnation under the law of nations. No neutral can, after knowledge of the blockade, lawfully enter or attempt to enter the blockaded port; and to do so would be a violation of neutral character which, according to established usages, would subject the party engaged therein to the penalty of confiscation.

"The approach of a vessel to the mouth of a blockaded port for inquiry, the blockading having been generally known, is itself a breach of the blockade and subjects both vessel and cargo to condemnation.

"The liability of a vessel to capture and condemnation for breach of blockade ceases at the end of her return voyage.

"Thus it has ever been maintained by the United States that a proclamation of ideal blockade of an extensive coast, not supported by the actual presence of a naval power competent to enforce its simultaneous, constant and effective operations on every point of such coasts, is illegal throughout its whole extent, even for the ports which may be in actual blockade; otherwise every capture made under a notified blockade would be legal because the capture itself would be proof of the blockading force. This is, in general terms, one of the fundamental rules of the law of blockade as professed and practiced by the government of the United States."— *Marshall, Secretary of State, 1800.*

A Recognized Right.

"The right to blockade an enemy's port with a competent force is a right secured to every belligerent by the law of nations. A belligerent may blockade the port of his enemy, but this blockade does not, according to modern usage, extend to a neutral vessel found in port nor prevent her from coming out with a cargo which was on board when the blockade was instituted.

"To justify the exercise of the right of blockade and legalize the capture of a neutral vessel for violating it, a state of actual war must exist and the neutrals must have knowledge or notice that it is the intention of one belligerent to blockade the ports of the other."

"In numerous treaties negotiated by the United States it is provided that notwithstanding a diplomatic general notice of blockade, a neutral vessel cannot be condemned for blockade running unless she has notice en route that the place in question is blockaded."

A Declaration of Blockade.

A Proclamation.

"Whereas, by a joint resolution passed by the Congress and approved April 20, 1898, and communicated to the government of Spain, it was demanded that said government at once relinquish its authority and government in the island of Cuba and withdraw its land and naval forces from Cuba and Cuban waters, and the President of the United States was directed and empowered to use the entire land and naval forces of the United States and to call into the actual service of the United States the militia of the several States to such extent as might be necessary to carry said resolution into effect;

Whereas, in carrying into effect said resolution, the President of the United States deems it necessary to set on foot and maintain a blockade of the north coast of

Cuba, including all the ports on said coast between Cardenas and Bahia Honda, and the port of Cienfuegos on the south coast of Cuba;

Now, therefore, I, William McKinley, President of the United States, in order to enforce the said resolution, do hereby declare and proclaim that the United States of America have instituted and will maintain a blockade of the north coast of Cuba, including ports on said coast between Cardenas and Bahia Honda and the port of Cienfuegos, on the south coast of Cuba aforesaid, in pursuance of the laws of the United States and the law of nations applicable in such cases. An efficient force will be posted, so as to prevent the entrance and exit of vessels from the ports aforesaid. Any neutral vessel approaching any of said ports or attempting to leave the same without notice or knowledge of the establishment of such blockade will be duly warned by the commander of the blockading forces, who will indorse on her register the fact and the date of such warning and where such indorsement was made; and if the same vessel shall again attempt to enter any blockaded port, she will be captured and sent to the nearest convenient port for such proceedings against her and her cargo as may be deemed advisable.

Neutral vessels lying in any of said ports at the time of the establishment of such blockade, will be allowed thirty days to issue therefrom.

In witness whereof I have hereunto set my hand and caused the seal of the United States to be affixed. Done at the city of Washington this 22nd day of April, A. D. 1898, and of the independence of the United States, the one-hundred and twenty-second.

By the President: WILLIAM MCKINLEY.
JOHN SHERMAN, Secretary of State."

Pacific Blockades.

"Since the beginning of the present century, what is called pacific blockades have been not infrequently used as a means of constraint short of war. The first instance occurred in 1827, when the coasts of Greece were blockaded by the English, French and Russian squadrons, while the three powers still professed to be at peace with Turkey. Other light blockades followed in rapid succession during the next few years. The Tagus was blockaded by France in 1831, New Granada by England in 1836, Mexico by France in 1838, and La Plata from 1838 to 1840 by France, and from 1845 to 1848 by France and England; the Greek ports were blockaded by England in 1850, and Rio de Janeiro by the same power in 1862. Since the last mentioned year no other instance occurred until 1884, when France blockaded a portion of the coast of Formosa. Finally, in 1886, Greece was blockaded by the fleets of Great Britain, Austria, Germany, Italy and Russia. Grecian forces in the Island of Crete were blockaded by the powers prior to the Turko-Grecian war.

"The manner in which these blockades have been carried out has varied greatly. During the blockade of Mexico by France in 1838, not only were Mexican ships held liable to capture, but vessels belonging to third powers were seized and brought in for condemnation. In the other early instances of pacific blockades the vessels both of the States operated against and of other powers were sequestrated, and were restored at the termination of the blockade, no compensation being given to foreign ships for loss of time and expenses."*

INSTRUCTIONS FOR THE GOVERNMENT OF ARMIES OF THE UNITED STATES IN THE FIELD.

Martial Law.

Martial Law in a hostile country consists in the suspension by the occupying military authority of the criminal and civil law, and of the domestic administration and

---

* "International Law," by W. E. Hall, page 386.

government of the place or territory, and in the substitution of military rule and force for the same as well as in the dictation of general laws as far as military necessity requires this suspension, substitution or dictation. The commander of the force may proclaim that the administration of all civil and penal law shall continue both wholly or in part, as in times of peace, unless otherwise ordered by the military authority.

All civil and penal law shall continue to take its usual course in the enemy's places and territories under Martial Law, unless interrupted or stopped by order of the occupying military power; but all functions of the hostile government — legislative, executive and administrative — whether of a general, provisional or local character, cease under Martial Law or continue only with the sanction, or if deemed necessary, the participation of the occupier or invader.

The functions of ambassadors, ministers or other diplomatic agents accredited a neutral power to the hostile government, cease so far as regards the displaced government; but the conquering or occupying power usually recognizes them as temporarily accredited to itself.

Martial Law affects chiefly the police and collection of public revenue, as taxes chiefly imposed on the expelled government or on the individual, and refers mainly to the support and efficiency of the army, its safety and the safety of its operations.

Law of War.

The law of war not only disclaims all cruelty and bad faith concerning engagements concluded with the enemy during the war, but also the breaking of stipulations solemnly contracted by the belligerents in time of peace and avowedly intended to remain in force in case of war between the contracting powers.

It disclaims all extortions and other transactions for

individual gain, all acts of private revenge or connivance at such acts. Offenses to the contrary shall be severely punished, and especially so if committed by officers.

Whenever feasible, Martial Law is carried out in case of individual offences by Military Courts; but sentence of death will be executed only with the approval of the chief executive (president), provided the urgency of the case does not require a speedier execution, and then only with the approval of the chief-commander.

Things Forbidden.

Military necessity does not admit of cruelty; that is, the infliction of suffering for the sake of suffering or for revenge, nor of maiming or wounding except in fight nor of torture to extort confessions. It does not admit of the use of poison in any way nor of the wanton devastation of a district. It admits of deception, but disclaims acts of perfidy, and the general military necessity does not include any acts of hostility which makes the return of peace unnecessarily difficult. The use of poison in any manner, be it to poison wells, food or arms, is wholly excluded from modern warfare. He that uses it puts himself out of the pale of the law and usages of war.

Returning Non-combatants.

When the commander of a besieged place expels the non-combatants in order to lessen the number of those who consume his stock of provisions, it is lawful, *though an extreme measure*, to drive them back so as to hasten the surrender.

Notice of Bombardment.

Commanders, wherever admissible, inform the enemy of their intention to bombard a place, so that the non-combatants, and especially the women and children, may be removed before the bombardment commences. But it is no infraction of the common law of war to omit thus to inform the enemy. Surprise may be a necessity.

The more vigorously wars are pursued the better it is for humanity. Sharp wars are brief.

Spoils of War.

A victorious army appropriates all public money, seizes all public moveable property until further directed by its government, and sequesters for its own benefit or that of its government all the revenues of real property belonging to the hostile government or nation. The title of such real property remains in abeyance during military occupation and until the conquest is made complete.

It is no longer considered lawful — on the contrary it is held to be a serious breach of the law of war — to force a subject of the enemy into the service of the victorious government, except the latter should proclaim, after a fair and complete conquest of the hostile country or district, that it is resolved to keep the country, district or place permanently as its own and make it a portion of its own country.

Preservation of Order.

The United States acknowledge and protect in hostile countries occupied by them, religion and morality; strictly private property; the persons of the inhabitants, especially those of women; and the sacredness of domestic relations. Offenses to the contrary shall be rigorously punished.

This rule does not interfere with the right of the victorious individual to tax the people or their property, to levy taxed loans, to billet soldiers or to appropriate property, especially houses, land, boats or ships, and churches for temporary and military uses.

Private Property.

Private property, unless forfeited by crimes or by offenses of the owner, can be seized only by way of military necessity for the support or other benefit of the army of the United States. If the owner has not fled, the commanding officer will cause receipts to be given which may serve the spoliated owner to obtain indemnity.

Native Civil Officers.

The salaries of civil officers of the hostile government who remain in the invaded territory and continue the work of their offices, and can continue it according to the circumstances arising out of the war — such as judges, administrative and police officers, officers of city or communal government — are paid from the public revenue in the invaded territory, until the military government has reason wholly or partially to discontinue it. Salaries or incomes connected with purely honorary titles are always stopped.

Violence Punished.

All wanton violence committed against persons in the invaded country, all destruction of property not commanded by the authorized officers, all robbery, all pillage or sacking, even after taking a place by main force, all rape, wounding, maiming or killing of such inhabitants are prohibited under the penalty of death or such other severe punishment as may seem adequate for the gravity of the offense.

Any soldier, officer or private, in the act of committing such violence and disobeying a superior ordering him to abstain from it, may be lawfully killed on the spot by such superior. Whoever intentionally inflicts additional wounds on an enemy already wholly disabled, or kills such an enemy, or who orders or encourages soldiers to do so, shall suffer death if duly convicted, whether he belongs to the army of the United States or is an enemy captured after having committed his misdeed.

Private Property of Prisoners.

Money and other valuables on the person of a prisoner, such as watches and jewelry, as well as extra clothing, are regarded by the American army as the private property of the prisoner, and the appropriation of such valuables or money is considered dishonorable and is prohibited.

Nevertheless, if *large* sums are found upon the persons of prisoners, or in their possession, they shall be taken from them and the surplus, after providing for their own support, appropriated for the use of the army under the direction of the commander, unless otherwise ordered by the government. Nor can prisoners claim as private property large sums found and captured in their train, although they have been placed in the private luggage of the prisoner.

Private Gain.

Neither officers nor soldiers are allowed to make use of their position or power in the hostile country for private gain, not even for commercial transactions otherwise legitimate. Offenses to the contrary committed by commissioned officers will be punished by cashiering and such other punishment as the nature of the offense may require; if by soldiers, they shall be punished according to the nature of the offense.

Crime.

Crime, punishable by all penal codes, such as arson, murder, maiming, assault, highway robbery, theft, burglary, fraud, forging, and rape, if committed by an American soldier in a hostile country against its inhabitants, is not only punishable as at home, but in all cases in which death is not inflicted the severer punishment shall be preferred.

Deserters.

Deserters from the American army having entered the service of the enemy, suffer death if they fall again into the hands of the United States, whether by capture or being delivered up to the American army; and if a deserter from the enemy, having taken service in the army of the United States, is captured by the enemy and punished by them with death or otherwise, it is not a breach against the law and usages of war requiring redress or retaliation.

Hospital Corps.

The enemy's chaplains, officers of the medical staff, apothecaries, hospital nurses and servants, if they fall into the hands of the American army, are not prisoners of war unless the commander has reasons to retain them. In this latter case, or if at their own desire they are allowed to remain with their captured companions, they are treated as prisoners of war, and may be exchanged if the commander sees fit.

Giving of Quarter.

All troops of the enemy known or discovered to give no quarter in general or to any portion of the army, receive none.

Troops who fight in the uniform of their enemy without a plain, striking and uniform mark of distinction of their own, can expect no quarter.

The use of the enemy's national standard, flag or other emblem of nationality, for the purpose of deceiving the enemy in battle, is an act of perfidy by which they lose all claim to the protection of the laws of war.

Outposts, sentinels and pickets are not to be fired upon

except to drive them in or when a positive order, special or general, has been issued to that effect.

Prisoners.

All officers when captured must surrender their sidearms to the captor. They may be restored to the prisoner in marked cases by the commander to signalize admiration of his distinguished bravery or approbation of his humane treatment of prisoners before his capture. The captured officer to whom they may be restored cannot wear them during captivity.

Exchanges of prisoners take place — number for number, rank for rank, wounded for wounded, with added condition for added condition — such, for instance, as not to serve for a certain period.

A prisoner of war is in honor bound truly to state to the captor his rank; and he is not to assume a lower rank than belongs to him in order to cause a more advantageous exchange, nor a higher rank for the purpose of obtaining better treatment.

A prisoner of war who escapes may be shot or otherwise killed in his flight, but neither death nor any other punishment shall be inflicted upon him simply for his attempt to escape, which the law of war does not consider a crime. Stricter means of security shall be used after an unsuccessful attempt at escape.

If, however, a conspiracy is discovered, the purpose of which is a united and general escape, the conspirators may be rigorously punished, even with death. A capital punishment may also be inflicted upon prisoners of war discovered to have plotted rebellion against the authorities of the captors, whether in union with fellow-prisoners or other persons.

If prisoners of war, having given no pledge nor made any promise on their honor, forcibly or otherwise escape and are captured again in battle after having rejoined their own army, they shall not be punished for their escape, but shall be treated as simple prisoners of war, although they will be subject to stricter confinement.

Bushwhacking.

Men, or squads of men, who commit hostilities, whether by fighting or inroads for destruction or plunder, or by raids of any kind, without commission, without being part and portion of the organized hostile army and without sharing continuously in the war, but who do so with intermitting returns to their homes and avocations, or with the occasional assumption of the semblance of peaceful pursuits, divesting themselves of the character and appearance of soldiers — such men, or squads of men, are not public enemies, and therefore if captured are not entitled to the privileges of prisoners of war, but shall be treated summarily as highway robbers or pirates.

Armed prowlers, by whatever names they may be called, or persons of the enemy's territory, who steal within the lines of the hostile army, for the purpose of robbing, killing, or of destroying bridges, roads, or canals, or of robbing or destroying the mail, or of cutting telegraph wires, are not entitled to the privileges of the prisoner of war.

Scouts and Spies.

Scouts or single soldiers, if disguised in the dress of the country or in the uniform of the army hostile to their own, employed in obtaining information, if found within or lurking about the lines of the captors, are treated as spies and suffer death.

A spy is a person who secretly, in disguise or under false pretense, seeks information with the intention of communicating it to the enemy.

The spy is punishable with death by hanging by the neck, whether or not he succeeds in obtaining the information or in conveying it to the enemy.

A messenger carrying written dispatches or verbal messages from one portion of the army, or from a besieged place, to another portion of the same army, or its government, if armed, and in the uniform of his army, and if captured while doing so, in the territory occupied by the enemy, is treated by the captor as a prisoner of war. If not in uniform, nor a soldier, the circumstances connected with his capture must determine the disposition that shall be made of him.

A successful spy or war-traitor, safely returned to his own army, and afterwards captured as an enemy, is not subject to punishment for his acts as a spy or war-traitor, but he may be held in closer custody as a person individually dangerous.

Acts of Citizens.

If a citizen of the United States obtains information in a legitimate manner, and betrays it to the enemy, be he a military or civil officer, or a private citizen, he shall suffer death.

No person having been forced by the enemy to serve as guide is punishable for having done so.

All unauthorized or secret communication with the enemy is considered treasonable by the law of war.

Foreign residents in an invaded or occupied territory, or foreign visitors in the same, can claim no immunity from this law. They may communicate with foreign parts, or with the inhabitants of the hostile country, so far as the military authority permits, but no further. Instant expulsion from the occupied territory would be the very least punishment for the infraction of this rule.

Guides.

If a citizen of a hostile and invaded district voluntarily serves as a guide to the enemy, or offers to do so, he is deemed a war-traitor, and shall suffer death.

A citizen serving voluntarily as a guide against his

own country commits treason, and will be dealt with according to the law of his country.

Guides, when it is clearly proved that they have misled intentionally, may be put to death.

War-Rebels and War-Traitors.

War-rebels are persons within an occupied territory who rise in arms against the occupying or conquering army, or against the authorities established by the same. If captured, they may suffer death, whether they rise singly, in small or large bands, and whether called upon to do so by their own, but expelled, government or not. They are not prisoners of war; nor are they, if discovered and secured before their conspiracy has matured to an actual rising, or to armed violence.

The war-traitor is always severely punished. If his offense consists in betraying to the enemy anything concerning the condition, safety, operations or plans of the troops holding or occupying the place or district, his punishment is death.

If the citizen or subject of a country or place invaded or conquered gives information to his own government, from which he is separated by the hostile army, or to the army of his government, he is a war-traitor, and death is the penalty of his offense.

Traitor.

A traitor under the law of war, or a war-traitor, is a person in a place or district under martial law who, unauthorized by military commander, gives information of any kind to the enemy, or holds intercourse with him.

Flag of Truce.

The bearer of a flag of truce cannot insist upon being admitted. He must always be admitted with great caution. Unnecessary frequency is carefully to be avoided.

If the bearer of a flag of truce offer himself during an

engagement, he can be admitted as a very rare exception only. It is no breach of good faith to retain such a flag of truce, if admitted during the engagement. Firing is not required to cease on the appearance of a flag of truce in battle.

If the bearer of a flag of truce, presenting himself during an engagement, is killed or wounded, it furnishes no ground of complaint whatever.

Hospital Flag.

It is customary to designate by certain flags (usually yellow) the hospitals in places which are shelled, so that the besieging enemy may avoid firing on them. The same has been done in battles, when hospitals are situated within the field of the engagement.

It is justly considered an act of bad faith, of infamy or fiendishness, to deceive the enemy by flags of protection. Such an act of bad faith may be good cause for refusing to respect such flags.

The besieging belligerent has sometimes requested the besieged to designate the buildings containing collections of works of art, scientific museums, astronomical observatories, or precious libraries, so that their destruction may be avoided as much as possible.

"In the case of a collection of Italian paintings and prints captured by a British vessel during the war of 1812, in their passage from Italy to the United States, the learned judge (Sir Alexander Croke), vice-admiralty court at Halifax, directed them to be restored to the Academy of Arts in Philadelphia, on the ground that the arts and sciences are admitted, amongst all civilized nations, to form an exception to the several rights of war, and are entitled to favor and protection. They are considered not as the *peculium* of this or that nation, but as the property of mankind at large and as belonging to the common interest of the whole species; and that the restitution of such property to the claimants would be in conformity with the law of nations as practiced by all civilized countries."*

Parole.

Breaking the parole is punished with death when the person breaking the parole is captured again.

Accurate lists, therefore, of the paroled persons must be kept by the belligerents.

Commissioned officers only are allowed to give their parole, and they give it only with the permission of their superior, as long as a superior in rank is within reach.

No non-commissioned officer or private can give his parole except through an officer. Individual paroles not given through an officer are not only void, but subject the individual giving them to the punishment of death as deserters. The only admissible exception is where individuals, properly separated from their commands, have suffered long confinement without the possibility of being paroled through an officer.

No paroling on the battle-field, no paroling of entire bodies of troops after a battle, and no dismissal of large numbers of prisoners, with a general declaration that they are paroled, is permitted, or of any value.

In capitulations for the surrender of strong places or fortified camps, the commanding officer, in cases of urgent necessity, may agree that the troops under his command shall not fight again during the war, unless exchanged.

The commander of an occupying army may require of the civil officers of the enemy, and of its citizens, any pledge he may consider necessary for the safety or security of his army, and upon their failure to give it, he may arrest, confine, or detain them.

"Generally, a belligerent contents himself with a pledge that his prisoner, unless exchanged, will not serve during

---

* Wharton's "International Law Digest," page 350.

the existing war against the captor or his allies engaged in the same war. This pledge is understood to refer only to active service in the field, and does not, therefore, debar prisoners from performing military duties of any kind at places not within the seat of actual hostilities, notwithstanding that the services thus rendered may have a direct effect in increasing the power of the country for resistance or aggression. Thus, paroled prisoners may raise and drill recruits, they may fortify places not yet within the scope of military operations, and they may be employed in the administrative departments of the army away from the seat of war. As the right of a belligerent over his prisoners is limited to the bare power of keeping them in safe custody for the duration of the war, he cannot in paroling them make stipulations which are inconsistent with their duties as subjects, or which shall continue to operate after the conclusion of peace. Thus if prisoners are liberated on condition of not serving during a specified period, before the end of which peace is concluded and hostilities again break out, they enter upon the fresh war discharged from obligation to the enemy.

The prisoner who violates the conditions upon which he has been paroled is punishable with death if he falls into the hands of the enemy before the termination of the war."*

Armistice.

An armistice is the cessation of active hostilities for a period agreed upon between the belligerents. It must be agreed upon in writing, and duly ratified by the highest authorities of the contending parties.

An armistice is binding upon the belligerent from the day of the agreed commencement; but the officers of the armies are responsible from the day only when they receive official information of its existence.

---

* "International Law," W. E. Hall, London, (p. 426).

An armistice is not a partial or a temporary peace; it is only the suspension of military operations to the extent agreed upon by the parties.

When an armistice is concluded between a fortified place and the army besieging it, it is agreed by all the authorities on this subject that the besieger must cease all extension, perfection, or advance of his attacking work, as much so as from attacks by main force.

But as there is a difference of opinion among martial jurists, whether the besieged have the right to repair breaches or to erect new works of defense within the place during an armistice, this point should be determined by express agreement between the parties.

Capitulation.

The term *parole* designates the pledge of individual good faith and honor to do, or to omit doing, certain acts after he who gives his parole shall have been dismissed, wholly or partially, from the power of the captor.

So soon as a capitulation is signed, the capitulator has no right to demolish, destroy, or injure the works, arms, stores, or ammunition, in his possession, during the time which elapses between the signing and execution of the capitulation, unless otherwise stipulated in the same.

Treating of Rebels.

Treating captured rebels as prisoners of war, exchanging them, concluding of cartels, capitulations or other warlike agreements with them; addressing officers of a rebel army by the rank they may have in the same; accepting flags of truce; or, on the other hand, proclaiming martial law in their territory, or levying war taxes or forced loans, or doing any other act sanctioned or demanded by the law and usages of public war between sovereign belligerents, neither proves nor establishes an acknowledgment of the rebellious people, or of the government which they may have erected, as a public or sovereign power. Nor does the adoption of the rules of war toward rebels imply an engagement with them extending beyond the limits of these rules. It is victory in the field that ends the strife, and settles the future relations between the contending parties.

Treating, in the field, the rebellious enemy according to the law and usages of war, has never prevented the legitimate government from trying the leaders of the rebellion or chief rebels for high treason, and from treating them accordingly, unless they are included in a general amnesty.*

Conference at Brussels, 1874.

Delegates were present from all the countries of Europe. They drew up the following rules and regulations in regard to conduct of war, but did not formally agree to them in such a manner as to render them binding upon the countries they represented. The most of the rules, however, may be considered as good international law. They are further of interest as showing what Europe will expect our conduct to be when we occupy conquered territory.

1. A territory is considered as occupied when it is actually placed under the authority of the hostile army. The occupation only extends to those territories where this authority is established and can be exercised.

2. The authority of the legal power being suspended, and having actually passed into the hands of the occupier, he shall take every step in his power to re-establish and secure, as far as possible, public safety and social order.

3. With this object he will maintain the laws which were in force in the country in time of peace, and will only modify, suspend or replace them by others if necessity obliges him to do so.

---
* Snow's "Cases on International Law."

4. The functionaries and officials of every class who at the instance of the occupier consent to continue to perform their duties, shall be under his protection. They shall not be dismissed or be liable to summary punishment unless they fail in fulfilling the obligations they have undertaken, and shall be handed over to justice, only if they violate those obligations by unfaithfulness.

5. The army of occupation shall only levy such taxes, dues, tolls, as are already established for the benefit of the State, or their equivalent, if it be impossible to collect them, and this shall be done as far as possible in the form of, and according to, existing practice. It shall devote them to defraying the expenses of the administration of the country to the same extent as was obligatory on the legal government.

6. The army occupying a territory shall take possession only of the specie, the funds, and marketable securities, etc., which are the property of the State in its own right, the depots of arms, means of transport, magazines, and supplies, and in general, all the personal property of the State, which is of a nature to aid in carrying on the war. Railway plant, land telegraphs, steam and other vessels, not included in cases regulated by maritime law, although belonging to companies or to private individuals, are to be considered equally as means of nature to aid in carrying on a war, which cannot be left by the army of occupation at the disposal of the enemy. Railway plant, land telegraphs as well as the steam and other vessels above mentioned, shall be restored, and indemnities be regulated on the conclusion of peace.

7. The occupying State shall only consider itself in the light of an administration usufructuary of the public buildings, real property, forests, and agricultural works belonging to the hostile State, and situated in the occupied territory. It is bound to protect these proper-

ties, and to administer them according to the laws of usufruct.

8. The property of parishes, of establishments devoted to religion, charity, education, arts, and sciences, although belonging to the State, shall be treated as private property. Every seizure, destruction of, or wilful damage to such establishments, historical monuments, or works of art or of science, should be prosecuted by the competent authorities.

War.

War does not extinguish debts due from the citizens of one belligerent to those of another; it merely suspends the remedy for their recovery.

After a declaration of war all intercourse is forbidden; an American citizen cannot lawfully send a vessel to an enemy's country to bring away his property.

Trading with an enemy does not *ipso facto*, forfeit the property so obtained by a citizen, but only subjects it to condemnation when regularly captured.

The citizens of one belligerent state are incapable of contracting with the citizens of another belligerent state. The effect of war is to dissolve the partnerships between citizens of hostile nations.

A sale by a belligerent of a warship in a neutral port is invalid, by the law of nations, as construed both in England and America.

Where private property is impressed into public use during an emergency, such as war, a contract is implied on the part of the Government to make compensation to the owner.

Declaration of War.

During the Middle Ages and down into the 16th century, notice of war was almost always given to the enemy either by letter or by sending heralds. The practice gradually became less general until within the past 100 years a large majority of the wars which have occurred began without any formal notice whatever.

Civil wars by their very nature begin without such notice. With the present means of communication between nations there is less necessity for a formal declaration of war. Its chief purpose is to fix a definite time from which to date the beginning of hostilities and determine the legality of the capture of prizes or other acts of war and give general notice to neutral nations.

Spanish Declaration of War.

"Diplomatic relations are broken off between Spain and the United States, and, the state of war being begun between the two countries numerous questions of international law arise, which must be precisely defined, chiefly because the injustice and provocation come from our adversaries, and it is they who, by their detestable conduct, have caused this grave conflict.

"We have observed with the strictest fidelity the principles of international law and have shown the most scrupulous respect for morality and the right of government. There is an opinion that the fact that we have not adhered to the Declaration of Paris does not exempt us from the duty of respecting the principles therein enunciated. The principle Spain unquestionably refused to admit then was the abolition of privateering. The government now considers it most indispensable to make absolute reserve on this point, in order to maintain our liberty of action and uncontested right to have recourse to privateering when we consider it expedient, first by organizing immediately a force of cruisers, auxiliary to the navy, which will be composed of vessels of our mercantile marine and with equal distinction in the work of our navy.

"Clause 1. The state of war existing between Spain and the United States annuls the treaty of peace and comity of October 27, 1795, and the protocol of January 12, 1877, and all other agreements, treaties or conventions in force between the two countries.

"Clause 2. From the publication of these presents thirty days are granted to all ships of the United States anchored in our harbors to take their departure free of hindrance.

"Clause 3. Notwithstanding that Spain has not adhered to the Declaration of Paris, the government, respecting the principles of the law of nations, proposes to observe, and hereby orders to be observed, the following regulations of maritime law:

"1. Neutral flags cover the enemy's merchandise, except contraband of war.

"2. Neutral merchandise, except contraband of war, is not seizable under the enemy's flag.

"3. A blockade, to be obligatory, must be effective — viz., it must be maintained with sufficient force to prevent access to the enemy's coast.

"4. The Spanish government, upholding its right to grant letters of marque, will at present confine itself to organizing, with the vessels of the mercantile marine, a force of auxiliary cruisers, which will co-operate with the navy, according to the needs of the campaign, and will be under naval control.

"5. In order to capture the enemy's ships and confiscate the enemy's merchandise and contraband of war under whatever form, the auxiliary cruisers will exercise the right of search on the high seas and in the waters under the enemy's jurisdiction, in accordance with international law and the regulations which will be published.

"6. Defines what is included in contraband of war, naming weapons, ammunition, equipments, engines and 'in general, all the appliances used in war.'

"7. To be regarded and judged as pirates, with all the rigor of the law, are captains, masters, officers and two-thirds of the crew of vessels which, not being American, shall commit acts of war against Spain, even if provided with letters of marque issued by the United States."

Duties of Neutrals.

The latest laws of England defining her duties as a neutral, represent pretty well the general requirements of International Law. By these laws a citizen of Her Majesty's dominions is forbidden to do the following things:

1. Build or agree to build, or cause to be built, any ship with the intent or knowledge, or having reasonable cause to believe, that the same shall or will be employed in the military or naval service of any foreign state at war with any friendly state.

2. Equip any ship with the intent or knowledge, or having reasonable cause to believe, that the same shall or will be employed in the naval or military service of any foreign state at war with any friendly state.

3. Dispatch or cause or allow to be dispatched, any ship with the intent or knowledge, or having reasonable cause to believe, that the same shall or will be employed in the naval or military service of any foreign state at war with any friendly state.

The burden of proving that a ship built for and paid for by a foreign State and employed by it in naval or military operations does not come within the statutes, is thrown on the builder.

Changing Armament.

To provide for a difficulty which arose in 1861-3, a penalty is attached to adding guns or equipments of war.

No person shall, by adding to the number of guns, or by changing those on board for other guns, or by the addition of an equipment for war, increase the warlike force of any ship which at the time of her being within the dominion of Her Majesty was a ship in the military or naval service of any foreign state at war with any friendly state.

Rights of a Neutral.

A neutral's chief right is that its neutrality shall be respected. If it sustains unlawful injuries, satisfaction for them should be given. For example, the stopping of the English steamer "Trent" by the United States forces was unlawful; the prisoners were surrendered and the act disavowed.

Fighting must not take place within a neutral's boundaries and if a vessel is captured in neutral waters, the neutral power may seize it and restore it to the owner, or if it has been taken to the prize court of the captor, demand that the captor return it to the owner.

Its diplomatic corps and consular officers shall not be molested and it may claim all the rights and privileges of neutrals on land and sea and make good its rights by force if necessary.

Indemnity.

"No principle is better established than that a nation at war has the right of shifting the burden off itself and imposing it on the enemy by exacting military contributions. The right to levy these contributions is essential to the successful prosecution of a war in the enemy's country and the practice of the nations has been in accordance with this principle. It is as clearly necessary as the right to fight battles and its exercise is often essential to the subsistence of the army."[*]

The expense of modern warfare has greatly increased the amount of indemnity or military contributions levied by the conqueror upon the unsuccessful power. The reasons usually urged for these are, that the conqueror has a right to levy contributions on the territory con-

---

[*] Wharton's "International Law Digest." Section 339.

quered to support his army and so this implies the right to repay himself for all the expenses of the war.

Further, by crippling the resources of the conquered nation, it is rendered more difficult for them to renew the war, and is a better guarantee of peace than a treaty would be.

An indemnity is a modern illustration of the proverb, "Might makes right."

There have been numerous examples of these exactions in history. Napoleon carried it further than any other leader of modern times; did not even respect works of art, which are usually considered exempt from such exactions, and his money tax aggregated many millions of dollars. France has suffered greatly from the reaction, as she paid 700,000,000 of francs in 1815 and 5,000,000,000 of francs in 1871 to Germany, besides losing her two provinces, Alsace and Lorraine.

In 1877 occurred the war between Russia and Turkey, and as a result the conquerors obtained a large accession of territory in Asia and a money damage enough to cripple the resources of Turkey for many years. Much of it is yet unpaid, and Russia recently used with effect the threat of enforcing the payments due. The indemnity proper was 802,500,000 francs, with an additional amount of 26,750,000 francs for injuries sustained by Russian subjects.

In the Japanese war, by the treaty of 1895, China was to pay Japan 200,000,000 taels,* some territory, munitions of war, etc., with other considerations. Russia, France and Germany presented a joint note of protest to the Japanese government and would not allow her to take possession of the territory ceded by China, and 30,000,000 taels was accepted by Japan in lieu of the territory.

The war of 1897 between Greece and Turkey was settled by adjusting the boundary so as to give Turkey

---

* A tael is equal to about $1.40 in our money.

THE ASCENDENCY OF AMERICA.

some strategic advantage, and Greece agreed to pay an indemnity or fine of £400,000.

The Red Cross Society.

Under this name is banded the benevolent societies of twenty-five different countries for the purpose of relieving the suffering in warfare of those enlisted either in the army or the navy.

To Monsieur Henri Dunant is due the credit of the initial movement in this direction. He was a Swiss physician, who published a striking account of the appalling suffering he had seen in two military hospitals on the battle-field of Solferino. He was ably seconded by Monsieur Gustave Moynier, chairman of the Geneva Society of Public Utility, and Dr. Louis Appia, of Geneva. Their first movement was to "neutralize the sick wagons"—that is, have the ambulances containing the wounded exempt from attack by an opposing force. They urged these views upon the different governments until an international conference was called at Geneva, Switzerland, in 1863, which formulated rules they considered proper for carrying on modern warfare. Since that time twenty-five or more nations have joined it, including all the nations of Europe, and even Persia, and one of our Western States has ceded the society a small tract of land, which by international agreement would be neutral ground if this country were invaded. The society, as a whole, is international, but it is made up of different relief societies, each of which is strictly national and governed by its own laws, rules and necessities.

The red cross was chosen as its emblem out of compliment to the Swiss Republic, in whose territory the first conference was held. The Swiss colors being a red field with a white cross, the badge chosen reversed the colors and gave it a red cross on a white field.

" There are no 'members of the Red Cross' but only

members of societies whose sign it is. There is no
'Order of the Red Cross.' The relief societies use, each
according to its convenience, whatever methods seem
best suited to prepare in times of peace, for the necessities and sanitary service in times of war. They gather
and store gifts of money and supplies, arrange hospitals,
ambulances, methods of transportation of wounded men,
bureaus of information, correspondence, etc. All that
the most ingenious philanthropy could devise and execute has been attempted in this direction." They have
abundantly proven their efficiency by their conduct
during the Franco-German and Turko-Greek wars, while
nearer our home their prompt action in the Johnstown
flood, the relief of the reconcentrados and the wounded
in the Spanish-American war, shows that the American
branch is not behind its sister organizations in efficiency.
Miss Clara Barton at the head of the society in this
country is frequently called the "Florence Nightingale
of America."

Articles of Geneva Convention.

Article I. Ambulances and military hospitals shall be
acknowledged to be neutral, and as such shall be protected and respected by belligerents so long as any sick
or wounded men be therein. Such neutrality shall cease
if the ambulances or hospitals should be held by any
military force.

Article II. Persons employed by hospitals and ambulances comprising the staff for superintendence, medical
service, administration, transport of wounded, as well as
chaplains, shall participate in the benefit of neutrality
while so employed and so long as there remain any
wounded to bring in or to succor.

Article III. The persons designated in the preceding
articles, may even after occupation by the enemy continue to fulfill their duties in the hospitals and ambu-

lances which they serve, or may withdraw in order to join the corps to which they belong.

Under such circumstances, when these persons shall cease from their functions they will be delivered by the occupying army to the outposts of the enemy.

Article IV. As the equipment of military hospitals remains subject to the laws of war, persons attached to such hospitals cannot, in withdrawing, carry away any articles but such as are their private property.

Under the same circumstances, an ambulance shall, on the contrary, retain their equipment.

Article V. Inhabitants of the country who may bring help to the wounded shall be respected and shall remain free. The generals of the belligerent powers shall make it their care to inform the inhabitants of the appeal addressed to their humanity and neutrality which will be the consequence of it. A wounded man entertained and taken care of in a house shall be considered a protection thereto. Any inhabitant who shall have entertained wounded men in his house shall be exempted from the quartering of troops as well as from a part of the contributions of war which may be imposed.

Article VI. Wounded or sick soldiers shall be entertained and taken care of, to whatever nationality they may belong. Commanders-in-chief shall have the power to deliver to the outposts of the enemy, soldiers who have been wounded in an engagement when circumstances permit this to be so, and with the consent of both parties.

Article VII. A distinctive and uniform flag shall be adopted for hospitals, ambulances and evacuations. It must on every occasion be accompanied by the nation's flag. An arm badge (brassard) shall also be allowed for individuals neutralized, but the delivery thereof shall be left to military authority.

The flag and arm badge shall bear a red cross on a white ground.[*]

---

[*] Snow's "Cases on International Law," page 531.

CHAPTER VIII.

Evolution of the Modern Navy.

Development of the Ironclad.

The idea of armor for ships is an old one. The galleys of the early Greeks and Romans were frequently strengthened by bands of iron which sometimes met at the prow and formed a ram. The Norse "Sea Kings" hung the shields of their soldiers along the sides of their galleys. Coming down to modern times, the floating batteries used by the Spanish when besieging Gibraltar in 1783, were protected by thick walls of timber strengthened by thicknesses of hide and bars of iron.

Fulton.

In our own country, Robert Fulton, in the war of 1812, proposed to build an impregnable floating battery, propelled by steam, that would relieve the blockade at the mouth of the Delaware. Congress authorized him to begin the work, and he began the construction of a peculiar one with two hulls, between which the paddle-wheel worked. The walls were made of wood, but of great thickness. The boat was not completed in time to take part in the military operations. Something like it was afterwards rebuilt and it is said to have been covered with thin plates of iron.

After the war of 1812 the development of home industries and internal improvements offered such a wide and profitable field to American ingenuity and industry that not much attention was paid to naval affairs. The United States seemed to be content with the building of wooden frigates similar to those that had distinguished themselves in single combat with vessels of a corresponding class of the British navy.

THE ASCENDENCY OF AMERICA. 307

Stevens Family of Inventors.

Fulton had as rivals, " foemen worthy of his steel," in the famous Stevens family, who were distinguished American engineers. In 1804, Colonel John Stevens fitted out a steamboat with a double screw. His propeller was a crude four-bladed one and the engines were not powerful enough to make it a success, but beyond the shadow of a doubt the modern screw propeller is its lineal descendent. In 1812, Colonel Stevens planned a fort for the defense of New York, which was to be plated with iron and revolved by machinery, and the same year submitted a plan for a boat closely resembling the Monitor type, also to be armor clad. It is said that this was the first plan for a fully armored ship. About this time, Edwin A. Stevens, a son of Colonel John Stevens, was making experiments with a 6-pound cannon to determine the resisting power of iron plates.

First Ironclad.

In 1841, the Stevens family submitted plans for a ship to be protected by 4 1-2 inches of iron, which their experiments had proven would resist the cannon of that day, and in 1842 Congress voted an appropriation of $250,000 for the building of such a vessel by the Stevens Brothers. It was to be 410 feet long, 45 feet inside the armor, of light draft, 2 feet of freeboard and with a square, immovable turret. Through the fault of Congress it was never completed.

Ericsson improved over the Stevens' idea by combining the Stevens boat of light draft, low freeboard and armored sides, with the Timby revolving turret.

Forced Draft.

The air-tight fire room devised by Edwin A. Stevens and patented April, 1842, marks another step in advance for our battleship, as it made possible " forced draft," by which air is forced into the furnaces by a powerful fan, blowing the fires like a blacksmith's bellows.

Revolving Turret.

This period seems to have been a prolific one for military ideas and we find Theodore R. Timby, of Dutchess county, New York, presenting in 1841 a model of a metallic revolving tower. He filed his caveat with the patent office January 18, 1843, and the same year completed and exhibited an iron model, and a little later presented a model to the Emperor of China through the American representative, Caleb Cushing. In 1848 a commission of Congress made a favorable report to the Secretary of War upon Timby's proposed system, and when the Civil War broke out he had patents for "a revolving metallic tower" and for a "floating battery to be propelled by steam." His claim was so good a one that when Ericsson began the construction of the "Monitor," a United States court granted Timby an injunction, restraining Ericsson from proceeding until he should have paid Timby a royalty for the use of his invention. Timby settled with Ericsson and his financial backers, Bushnell and Delamater, for $100,000. In 1862, Timby devised the method now used for firing heavy guns by electricity.

In 1843 John Ericsson made the "Princeton" for the United States. She was the first warship to be moved by the screw propeller, and her engines were below the water line. With the engines where they were not liable to injury by the artillery of the day, and a screw propeller out of harm's way beneath the water substituted for the fragile side paddle-wheel, the modern warship made quite an advance.

Armored Ships.

In 1854 the French constructed three floating batteries with the speed of 4 knots an hour, armed with 68-

pound guns and protected by iron plates. They were very successful in the Crimean war. In the same war the annihilation of the Turkish fleet in one hour by shells fired from Russian guns, demonstrated the absolute necessity of some protection. The Crimean war over, France at once proceeded to construct an iron-plated frigate. She took the "Gloire," a wooden two-decker, removed the upper deck and used the weight thus gained to carry 4½ inch armor from end to end. She had no ram, but the iron plates made her bow strong. This ship was fitted with sail and steam power, and could make 13 knots an hour. Her appearance alarmed the English; they at once set to work, and in 1859 produced the "Warrior," made of iron and especially designed to carry armor. She was 420 feet long, and had a great patch of plate 218 feet long, 4½ inches thick over her battery and water line amidships. The same year the French laid down two more ironclad ships, the "Magenta" and the "Solferino," and fitted these with rams.

First English Turret Ship.

In 1860 Captain Coles, of the English navy, submitted a plan for a ship to carry nine conical turrets, each to contain a pair of guns. The first English turret ship was the "Royal Sovereign," a three-decker cut down to Captain Coles' plan, plated on the water line and above with 4½-inch iron, with 4 turrets, 10 inches thick in the exposed positions and 5 inches thick elsewhere. She was tried July, 1864, and accepted soon afterward.

American Ironclads.

In 1861, Captain Eads, of St. Louis, made some Mississippi gunboats with curved decks and plated with thin iron. These were the first ironclads the United States used in warfare, and in the curved deck of Captain

Eads we have the prototype of the protective deck of to-day.

Monitor.

In 1862 appeared Ericsson's "Monitor," especially designed as a light-draft boat, fitted to navigate shallow harbors and rivers and to be impregnable to the fire of forts. Her length was 173 feet, beam 42 feet and 6 inches, side armor 5 inches, turret, 8 iron plates each 1 inch thick. The turret inside was 20 feet in diameter and 9 feet in height, and carried two 11-inch guns, firing with 15 pounds of powder a projectile weighing 166 pounds. The service charge was afterward increased to 45 pounds. Had such a charge been used in her memorable battle at Hampton Roads, it is doubtful if the casemates of the "Virginia" would have withstood her attack.

How Warships are Classed.

The boy who asked his father the difference between a battle-ship and a cruiser, and was answered that the battle-ship was one named after a State and the cruiser one named after a city, may have been satisfied for the moment, but his confidence in his father's infallibility will sometime receive a rude shock.

One may take up a newspaper and read that Congress has authorized the building of a ship of a definite *displacement* to carry as thick armor and as heavy guns as are practicable. The *displacement* alone, unless the cost be attached, is the only definite quantity named.

Displacement.

Displacement is the weight of the ship complete, and is measured by the weight of water she displaces when afloat. It is not to be confused with tonnage, which means how much she can carry.

Usually the basis for the designer is the displacement, which may be likened to a bank account, in exchange for which he may have certain things whose total weight must not exceed his proposed displacement. These are the hull, engines, fittings, provisions, coal, stores, ammunition, armor, guns, etc. Their total weight, as we have seen, is limited, but in what proportion shall he dispose of them? That will depend upon the requirements of the kind of ship he is to build.

Class Requirements.

If a cruiser to catch unarmed merchantmen, speed is the prime requisite. If a cruiser capable of overcoming other cruisers she is likely to meet, more allowance will be made for armor and guns. If a battleship, armor and guns will receive the first consideration. If a torpedo boat, to make its way unseen in a foggy night, the maximum speed and minimum size will be required. All these types make fairly distinct classes. Let us see what will be required of the cruiser.

Cruiser's Duties.

1. To destroy commerce by capturing unarmed or lightly armed merchantmen and also by creating such terror that merchantmen will not dare put to sea when the cruiser is known to be abroad.

2. To protect commerce by "convoying" or accompanying as a guard, merchant fleets through the dangerous parts of the route or from port to port.

3. To protect commerce by clearing the route from hostile cruisers.

4. To attack unprotected coasts or those but poorly fortified, and by their theatening presence compel the enemy to retain ships and men for defense that he would otherwise use in an attack elsewhere.

5. To carry on small wars at a distance where a powerful fleet is not needed, and to make reprisals.

6. To act as scouts, to be the "eyes of the fleet." It is important that they have great speed to do this, as

after an enemy is sighted every hour of time or fraction thereof that may be given the opposing commander for preparation is valuable.

7. To keep up communication between a squadron and the base of supplies.

8. To form the front, rear, and wings of a fleet when in motion, and to be the first to discover the enemy.

9. To make blockades effective by being able to catch the fastest merchantmen. To be sure the monitor "Terror" did capture a prize off Havana, but it was because the prize was within range of the monitor's guns when discovered. A hunter doesn't take a bull dog to capture a fox.

Commerce Destroyer.

Suppose we want a cruiser to act as a commerce destroyer; she must have speed enough to catch the fastest merchantmen afloat, and sufficient gun-power to overcome them when caught. That she may have speed, the most powerful engines must be given her, and that she may keep at sea for a long time, large supplies of coal must be carried, while enough protection must be given to the "vital parts" of the cruiser to defend them from any guns the merchantman may carry.

Vitals.

The parts that *must* be defended are the engines, the magazines and the steering gear; only less urgent is defense for the guns. How is it given? The "vitals" of the ship will be placed below the water-line because few projectiles except plunging-shot at close range will penetrate much below the water. The "vitals" will further be covered overhead by a "protective deck."

Protective Deck.

This protective deck extending the whole length of the ship and from side to side much resembles a huge inverted platter. On the sides and ends it is below the waterline, but it slopes or curves upward from the sides, until over the middle part of the ship it is as high, or a little higher, than the water, and presents a flat, or nearly flat, surface, like the bottom of the platter. This deck is made of excellent steel, ranging in different ships from one to six inches in thickness. The slopes are thickest and are intended to present an inclined surface, from which shot and shell will glance without penetrating. Along the middle part of the ship, between the slopes and the outer wall, bunkers (coal bins) are arranged. These also assist in protection, for a foot of coal is equal to about one inch of wrought-iron, or half an inch of steel in this respect.

Next, the guns will need attention.

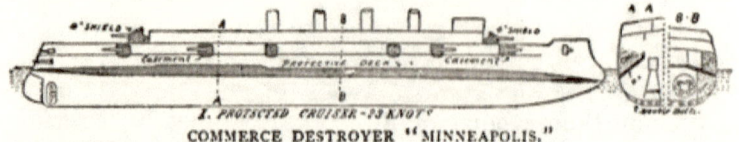

COMMERCE DESTROYER "MINNEAPOLIS."

Gun Shields.

The cruiser of this class will not mount many heavy guns. If 4-inch or 6-inch guns, they will be placed on the highest deck and protected by circular gun shields of steel armor attached to the gun carriage and revolving with it. The shield will probably be face-hardened steel about four inches in thickness, and will successfully resist common shell. If larger than 6-inch guns they will probably be placed within a turret.

Turret.

The turret is a circular steel tower, with openings through which guns project, and is made to turn by machinery in any desired direction. Only the heavy guns of the ship will be placed within turrets.

Along the sides of the ship (broadside) and projecting through portholes will be other guns, and the space in front of these will be protected by light armor.

Double Bottom.

Having provided for defense against shot and shell, let us see what next will be required. The warship must stand attacks from three weapons, the gun, the ram and the torpedo. In cruising an unknown coast she may encounter reefs and shoals not down on her chart, or in the darkness of night may come in collision with another vessel. She will be protected in this respect by giving her a double bottom. The inner and the outer walls will be from one to three feet apart, and the space intervening divided into numerous little water-tight chambers. From the protective deck up as high as the water will reach she will probably have a cofferdam of cellulose, made from corn pith, which has the peculiar property of swelling rapidly when exposed to water, so any break in the wall, if not too large, would be speedily closed by the cellulose. Beneath the protective deck there will be several partitions running across the ship (transverse bulkheads) and probably one or more partitions running the whole length of the ship (longitudinal bulkheads). These will divide the ship into numerous compartments, which can be closed by water-tight doors, and the ship might keep afloat indefinitely with two or perhaps more of the compartments flooded, if no damage were done to her engines. Her engines will be such as to give the greatest power with the least possible weight, the economy of fuel not counting for so much as in a ship used for purely commercial purposes. So powerful are the engines of the cruiser that they would drive the machinery to furnish the electric light for five cities of 50,000 inhabitants each. Her enormous coal bunkers will hold hundreds of tons of coal that she may make long voyages without being compelled to put into port.

To recapitulate, then, our cruiser is protected against the ram and torpedo by her double bottom and belt of corn pith; her vitals covered by the protective deck and her broadside guns by armored casements; her guns on deck by gun shields and light-weight turrets. Any of this armor could be penetrated by the heaviest guns, and the commerce destroyer must be able to show a clean pair of heels to anything she cannot whip.

Armored Cruiser.

The armored cruiser must be able to brush away hostile commerce destroyers and leave the route clear for merchantmen. She will be a pretty formidable fighting machine, and might occupy a position in the reserve of a fleet next the fighting line. We shall expect to find in her, high speed, greater displacement, heavier guns and thicker armor than in the protected cruiser. The protective deck will be thicker; the armor on the gun positions heavier. In addition, she will have about her

ARMORED CRUISER "BROOKLYN."

waterline a belt of armor, probably seven feet or seven and a half feet wide and from two to twelve inches thick. This may extend completely around her or along her side far enough to cover the most vital parts of the ship. About three feet of belt will be above the waterline. It is this belt that gives her the name "armored cruiser." The ammunition hoists (elevators), passing from the magazines beneath the protective deck up to the turrets containing the guns, will be protected by an armored tube from three to ten inches in thickness. The great quantity of coal that her powerful engines require, and other considerations, will usually forbid her protecting the space between the turret and protective deck by armor, but the coal will be arranged along her sides so as to give some protection in itself. The cofferdam of cellulose, made from corn pith, or some similar substance, will be thicker, the hull heavier and stronger, with double bottom like the cruiser of the other class. The "Brooklyn," a fine armored cruiser, is divided below the deck by twelve transverse and two longitudinal bulkheads, and above the deck by ten tranverse bulkheads, which are again subdivided into 140 compartments. None of the bulkheads on our cruisers are armored. The cofferdam along the side above the armored deck is filled with cellulose up to the level of the gun deck.

Sponsons.

Our armored cruiser will mount some pretty heavy guns. In the United States navy for vessels of this class they are 8 inches; in the Spanish 11.2 inches. Some of her broadside guns will be placed in an armored projection resembling a bay window, called a "sponson," which will enable them to be pointed directly ahead or astern, and thus increase materially their area of fire.

Recessed Ports.

Guns in the bow of the ship may look out of ports which have been notched, depressed, or cut in to allow the gun to be trained directly ahead. An arrangement somewhat similar is sometimes made along the side to give greater freedom of motion to the gun, and ports of this character are said to be "recessed."

Our armored cruiser will have speed sufficient to catch anything but the very fleetest commerce destroyers, and coal endurance sufficient to make long voyages from home. Cruisers have a high freeboard, that is, they stand well out of the water, mounting their guns twenty feet or more above the waterline, which enables them to be used in rough weather. In this respect they possess a marked advantage over a monitor and the coast defense battleship, whose guns might sometimes be almost under water, or their muzzles so far depressed that if fired their projectiles would strike the tops of the waves between them and their target.

Conning Tower.

Back of the forward turret, and high enough above the deck to give a good view, will be the "conning tower," an armored steel tower pierced by narrow slits through which the commanding officer will watch the progress of the battle and direct the movements of his vessel. This tower will be connected by electric bells, speaking tubes and telephones with every portion of the ship with which the captain will need to communicate. The conning tower should be strong enough to resist the ordinary fire to which it is likely to be subjected, and the electric wires communicating with it usually run through an armored tube until they pass beneath the protective deck. Above the conning tower will usually be found a rather frail structure, not built to resist shot and shell, called the "chart house," from which the ship will be navigated except in battle.

Military Masts and Fighting Tops.

Cruisers of this class usually carry what are known as "military masts." These are not intended for the use of sails, but are hollow, tapering, steel structures, about which are built one or more platforms or balconies, where riflemen and machine guns will be placed. The fire from these will be expected to sweep off the men from the exposed positions of the hostile ships. Our cruiser will also be furnished with powerful electric searchlights, perhaps of 100,000 candle power, which may be turned so as to throw their rays in any direction. The electric light and the small rapid-firing gun are the warship's defense against her small but terrible enemy, the torpedo boat.

The armored cruiser will not be expected to engage

the battleship unless the conditions are such as to give her some advantage to make up for her lighter guns and thinner armor. If the battleship had been injured so that she could not fire all her guns, or if water had entered some of her compartments and thrown her off an even keel, so that but few of her guns could be pointed in some particular direction, the cruiser might take this position, and by means of her superior speed remain where, without great damage to herself, she could pour in a destructive fire upon the disabled battleship. In general, however, she will trust to her speed to protect her from anything she cannot whip.

Battleships.

Admiral Colomb of England says: "The battleship is a representative of the force waiting to be attacked and daring attack. If there is ever to come anything which is stronger, offensive and defensive, than the battleship, she must disappear, for the theory on which she rests is that there is nothing but another battleship which is capable of offering her any fair match. She has always to secure herself against special attack. The other day it was the unarmored gun vessel which threatened her; she met it by adding her medium battery; later she was to be swept off the seas by a swarm of torpedo boats; she met it by adding the machine gun battery; at the present moment it is suggested that rams, pure and simple, small and swift, will be too much for her; she looks calmly down and would like to see them try. All such threats annoy her, but she sees clearly that whatever beats her must take her place. No special rams, no special torpedo boats can take up and hold her defensive position. If they cause her to disappear they must follow, because it is only her existence which justifies theirs. I believe firmly that the battleship, as a battleship, will hold her own to the end of time."

Requirements.

Since the battleship is built to fight and not to run, we shall expect to find in her the most powerful guns and the strongest armor consistent with her displacement and seagoing requirements. The United States is building two distinct types of battleships; one, of the Indiana class, with the low freeboard, called a coast defense battleship; the other, like the Iowa, with a higher freeboard, called the seagoing battleship. She will be given displacement somewhat larger than the armored cruiser, the hull will be stronger, perhaps with a triple bottom reaching up to and forming a shelf on which her armor belt rests, and divided into numerous water-tight chambers. She will have a heavy protective deck, an armor belt

BATTLESHIP "OREGON."

from seven feet to eight feet in width and from eight inches to eighteen inches in thickness. Above the protective deck transverse armored bulkheads will be built fore and aft to stop the enemy's shells which come in at the stern and bow. Along the sides, above the armor belt connecting the bulkheads, armor will be placed suficient to keep out medium gun fire, that is, common shells and projectiles from guns six inches and smaller. The latest five and six-inch guns have shown on the proving ground their ability to pierce armor thicker than that usually carried to protect the secondary battery of our battleships, but in actual battle, with the gun and target each in motion and the armor inclined at an angle to the projectile, normal hits are likely to be few. Then the armor piercing shell, because of its thick wall, cannot carry so large a bursting charge as the common shell, so its effect within the ship would not be so terrible as that of the other.

Redoubt.

Since this armor must be so heavy (perhaps one-third of the entire displacement of the ship is given to it), it will be impossible to completely cover the ship with it, and so we shall find it in the form of a huge steel box (redoubt) extending far enough ahead and astern to include within its walls the machinery moving the turrets, the ammunition hoists and the most important parts of the ship above the armored deck. It is expected that considerable portions of the bow and stern above the protective deck might and probably will be shot away in action, but unless our constructors are wrong in their calculations, this might be done and the battleship still be able to maintain a most formidable resistance. The destruction of the unarmored bow may impede the speed of the ship and cause her to steer badly, and water coming in here or at the stern may put the battleship on an uneven keel, perhaps to such an extent that she might be troubled to bring her guns to bear on an enemy. In such positions she would present an inviting target for the attack of the torpedo boat or the ram.

Primary and Secondary Battery.

The batteries of our battleship are known as primary and secondary. In the primary battery are the large guns from 8-inch to 13-inch with which she will attack the thick armor of her opponents over the vitals and the opposing heavy guns. The primary battery should be supplemented by smaller rapid-fire guns from 4-inch to 6-inch and with these she will attack the unarmored or thinly armed portions of the opposing ship and the portholes through which the heavy guns look out.

The secondary battery will be made up of smaller rapid-fire guns, such as Maxim, Nordenfeldt, Hotchkiss,

Driggs-Schroeder or Gatling, whose projectiles range in size from that of a rifle ball up to a 12-pounder and fire from 30 times for the latter to 800 or 1,000 times for the small machine guns. With these she will sweep away all men from the exposed positions on the hostile deck and defend herself when attacked by the torpedo boat.

Barbette and Turret.

These in the battleship must be far more powerful than in the cruiser.

The barbette is a steel tower intended to protect the heavy rollers on which the base of the turret rests, the machinery for turning it, the guns within the turret and all the machinery connected with them. The guns look out over the top of it and usually in a battleship it extends continuously down to the protective deck. Within this like a smaller tube within a larger one in a spy-glass is placed the turret, mounted on heavy rollers with suitable machinery for turning it and pierced with port-holes through which guns project.

The barbettes show very plainly in the pictures of the monitor "Monterey" and the battleship "Maine," and look like large hoops encircling the turrets at the base.

The Modern Warship.

Our warships are now propelled by engines of over 20,000 horse-power, and in addition have numerous auxiliary engines for heating, lighting, ventilating and working different parts of the ships. The "Columbia" has ninety-four engines and pumps. The boilers of the "Iowa" present more than an acre of heating surface. The "Indiana," if used as a ram at full speed, would strike with force sufficient to lift 100,000 tons one foot. One filling of the ammunition magazines of the "Kearsarge" cost $383,197.

The report of the chief of the bureau of equipment shows that last year the cruiser "New York" used her coal as follows: For moving the ship, 2,090 tons; for distilling water for her engines and crew, 831 tons; for running her pumps, 1,049 tons; for lighting the ship, 1,431 tons; heating, 453 tons; cooking, 88 tons; steam launches, 123 tons, and ventilating, 1,064 tons.

Apportionment of Weight.

In the construction of a battleship of 11,290 tons, 4,540 tons will be given up to the hull; 3,630 to armor, protective deck and cofferdam; 1,000 tons to her guns and ammunition; 1,170 tons to her machinery, stores, etc.; 625 tons for her coal; 325 tons allowed for her crew equipment and outfit, and the whole complete will cost $5,000,000.

The battleship of to-day represents a compromise of the ideas of numerous designers. Ever since the use of the explosive shell there has been a steady fight between the armor and the gun, first one ahead and then the other. In the beginning it was possible to cover the whole ship with armor, but to-day, when a 13-inch gun will penetrate 22 inches of steel at one mile, only the most vital parts of the ship can be covered, leaving the ends exposed. Some critics contend that with the bow or stern shot away so much water would be let in that the vessel would be almost unmanageable, or perhaps in the case of one like the "Indiana," whose center of gravity was high, would even capsize. Nevertheless, the battleship has the confidence of her designers.

Admiral Sampson, in North American Review, says of her: "She mounts heavy guns to pierce the armor of her enemies; she mounts numerous guns of lighter calibre to enable her to meet similar fire from all sorts of craft and to destroy the quick-moving torpedo boats, which would escape the slow-working heavy guns. She carries armor to protect herself against any but the heaviest projectiles, and, so far as possible, against even these. She carries torpedoes to destroy an enemy who may, in the manœuvres of battle, come within her reach. She carries such a supply of coal and ammunition as will enable her to perform her duty between the times when she can renew her supply. Being essentially a fighting machine, she does not require high speed to enable her to escape from an enemy. When war shall come between any of the great nations which depend in whole or in part upon their naval strength, it will be the battleship which will settle the issue."

The behavior of his ships at Santiago shows that his confidence was well placed.

Monitor.

The name of the first of a series of boats of peculiar construction built by Ericsson has come to designate a type. The characteristics of the monitor are its low freeboard, thick armor and armament of a few heavy guns. Their engines are comparatively light, and the "Monterey," the fastest in the United States service, has a record of only 13.6 knots under the most favorable circumstances.

Cause of Popularity.

The theatrical appearance of the first monitor, and its excellent service at a critical moment, seem to have given it a somewhat higher value in the eyes of most Americans than its abilities will justify. It is a most useful vessel within its sphere, but that sphere is limited. Secretary Long says in his report: "There is no advantage to be gained by building ships of this description. Such a vessel cannot attain to high speed. It can neither overtake nor escape from a battleship. Its comparative smallness of target, usually mentioned as one of its chief advantages, is apparent rather than real, for that feature of the battleship which changes the size of the target, although vulnerable, is not indispensable to the safety or fighting efficiency of the vessel. The chief defect to be found is the serious disadvantage under which guns are fought in any but the smoothest water."

Duties.

A boat of this class lies low in the water, is light of draft and not fitted for work in heavy seas. As harbor defense boats they can render excellent service, their light draft permitting them to move about in the water where an opposing, heavy draft battleship could not follow, and thus choose their own ground and distance at which they fight. If the monitor elected to fight the battleship at long range, as she perhaps would, the small target she presents and her heavy guns would be decidedly in her favor, as the battleship could get but little good out of its secondary battery of rapid-firers if fighting at more than 2,500 yards. The low speed of the monitor gives any other ship the option of accepting or declining battle with it. It can only fight when the "other fellow" is willing.

Construction.

The monitors of the United States range in length from 200 feet in the "Jason," "Nahant" and "Lehigh" class, to 259 feet 4 inches for the "Terror" class, and 289 feet for our largest one, the "Puritan." Beam, 46 feet, 55 feet 9 inches, and 60 feet 1½ inches; draft, 11 feet 6 inches, 14 feet 7 inches, and 18 feet 1 inch, respectively, for the classes named.

The bottom will be double, with numerous water-tight chambers coming up to within 3 feet of the waterline, where it forms a shelf on which an armor-belt of from 5 inches to 13 inches in thickness and 7 feet in width rests. A protective deck from 2 to 3 inches in thickness heads the armor-belt at the top.

The barbettes and turrets of the later monitors will be from 9 inches to 14 inches, and the conning tower 8 inches to 10 inches in thickness, of good Harveyized steel. Originally the monitors were planned to carry four heavy guns. The rise of the torpedo-boat has compelled them to strengthen the superstructure and mount some rapid-fire guns. Of course, guns in this position are as much exposed on the monitor as on any type of ship.

Turrets.

The tops of the turrets of monitors, $1\frac{1}{2}$ inch steel, expose a vulnerable point to a plunging fire. This would render them unsuited to attack land batteries at high elevation.

Within each turret are placed two heavy guns, with a peculiarly effective device for "training." Between the guns, and looking through slits, in a projection in the top of the turret, called "sighting-hood," stands the operator whose duty it is to aim the guns. In front of him, and looking through two small openings, are two crossline, telescopic sights. By turning a small hand wheel he moves these sights to the right or left until they bear on the target. Another wheel depresses or elevates them. These sights, by a refinement of mechanism, are made to correspond with the guns, and so when the telescopic sight in the sighting-hood points directly at the target the corresponding gun in the turret is properly aimed.

Electricity, steam, or hydraulic power supply the force required to move the guns and the machinery of the turret. In the early monitors the turret revolved upon a spindle, but in our later ones the spindle has been discarded for heavy rollers on the decks.

A SECTIONAL VIEW OF A MONITOR'S TURRET,

Showing hood over 12" gun, machinery for moving turret and hoisting ammunition.

Torpedo Boats.

The torpedo boat seems to have made its first successful appearance during our late Civil War. It was then a very crude affair. R. O. Crowley, electrician for the Confederate States, has told of some of the difficulties under which they labored, and their results. One of their most successful trials was the attempt to blow up the United States ship "Minnesota." With a small launch fitted with a long spar at her bow, to which was attached the torpedo arranged to explode upon contact, they steamed, in the darkness of the night, through the blockading fleet without their identity being discovered, although frequently challenged by lookouts. The "Minnesota" was found, the torpedo was lowered, the spar run out, and a dash made for her side. Although the torpedo was loaded only with gunpowder, the explosion was terrific, and resulted in such severe damage to the "Minnesota" that she was compelled to be docked. The torpedo boat escaped in safety.

Cushing.

It was in a similar boat, and with a spar torpedo, that Lieutenant Cushing, of the United States Navy, made his successful attack upon the ironclad "Albemarle."

"Cigar Boat."

One of the most heroic achievements of any navy was that of the "cigar boat," constructed at Mobile, Ala., and sent by rail to Charleston in the summer of 1863. It was made of boiler iron, was about 30 feet long, 4 feet wide, and 9 feet in depth. The interior was reached by two manholes, in the tops of which were glass bull's-eyes, through which the navigator looked when directing his craft. It was moved by a screw propeller, and the power furnished by a crank turned by the crew. Along the sides were wings which could be adjusted at an angle. When the front of the wings were inclined downward and the screw turned the boat would dive; upon their being reversed it would come to the surface. Ordinarily it floated with only the manholes a little above the water. It seems to have been the prototype of the "Holland Boat." A tube of mercury served to mark its depth in the water.

It was intended that this boat should pass under the vessel attacked, towing in its wake a torpedo which would be exploded by contact or electricity when the torpedo touched the vessel. There was not sufficient water in Charleston harbor to allow this, and the boat was rigged with a spar torpedo. Thrice she sunk in her trials with the loss of all on board, but although service in her seemed certain death, there never was any difficulty in securing a new crew for her. After thirty men had lost their lives on board her, Lieutenant Geo. E. Dixon of Alabama secured as a volunteer crew Captain J. F. Carlson of the army, Arnold Becker, C. Simpkins, Jas. A. Wicks, F. Collins, —— Ridgeway and directed a final attack against the United States ship "Housatonic," which was reported the next morning to have been sunk by a torpedo, and nothing was heard of an attacking boat. Long afterward, when the Government attempted to raise the "Housatonic," the little "cigar boat," with its gallant crew, was found not far from her victim.

The history of the spar torpedo in America may be summed up as follows: United States ship "New Ironsides" seriously injured off Charleston, October, 1863; sloop-of-war "Housatonic" destroyed off Charleston, February, 1864; monitor "Osage" destroyed by drifting torpedo, March, 1865; the Confederate ironclad "Albemarle" destroyed October 27, 1864. All of the torpedoes were charged with common black powder.

The brilliant achievements of the torpedo boat in the Civil War inclined the navies of Europe to look upon it with favor, and they soon began to make experiments. The weapon used at that time was, as we have seen, the spar torpedo, and this meant that it was necessary to come alongside and in contact with the enemy before the boat was discovered and disabled.

Small rapid-fire guns and modern searchlights were not then in use, and the boat in the hands of fearless men on a dark or foggy night was a dreaded and dangerous enemy.

Late in the '60's the "Whitehead" torpedo was introduced, and in the early '70's European nations took it up and began the construction of boats especially designed to carry it. The first were then about 57 feet long, $7\frac{1}{2}$ feet wide, with 90 horse-power engines, giving a speed of 16 knots. To-day they are from 100 feet to 200 feet long, 12 feet to 20 feet wide, and driven by 6,000 horse-power engines, giving them a speed of 30 knots and upward, and fitted with a "Whitehead" or some similar automobile torpedo supposed to have an effective range up to 800 yards.

There is no well marked line dividing the coast defense torpedo boat from the sea-going torpedo boat and the latter from the torpedo boat destroyer. The safety of the boat depends upon its small size and extreme speed. If the size is increased to give more speed and sea-going qualities, it defeats the very object for which it was originally intended; *i. e.*, a boat small enough to approach the enemy under cover of fog, smoke or darkness without being discovered and disabled before it is within effective range of its torpedo.

The old boats were fitted with three torpedo tubes, two on deck and one in the bow. The bow tube is now discontinued, as the boat under motion throws up a big bow wave that interferes with the accurate firing of the bow tube, and further, before the torpedo can gain headway, the boat, at a high rate of speed, is likely to run it down. The torpedo boat will also mount machine guns and light rapid-fire guns, and the torpedo boat destroyer, rather heavier rapid-fire guns, 6-pounders and 12 pounders, to enable them to destroy the torpedo boat.

Duties of the Torpedo Boat.

It is intended that a boat costing a few thousand dollars, and manned by a score of men, will attempt to destroy the expensive cruiser or warship costing millions. If discovered, her fate is almost certain; it is upon secrecy that her success depends. She relies upon her small size, her color as nearly resembling her surroundings as posssible, fog, smoke or darkness. The torpedo boat must also act as the protector of the fleet from hostile torpedo boats. To destroy these she must discover them, and to discover them it is necessary that the size and surface of the guarding boat should not be so plainly visible to the attacking boats that they will make her out in time to avoid her. The modern torpedo boat destroyer with its large size (400 tons) may, under ordinary circumstances, defeat its own purpose.

Rough Water.

The extreme speed of the torpedo boat is made in still water; with its small tonnage and light draft the speed materially decreases in rough water, while in a heavy sea-way they would fall an easy prey to a fast cruiser.

Sailors taken from their pleasant quarters in larger vessels find the change to the torpedo boat irksome, and many stories are afloat as to the danger of such service even in times of peace. It will be interesting to note that Massachusetts has annually 40,000 of her sailor population who earn a livelihood in fishing boats of an average of 50-tons displacement.

Torpedo Boat in Action.

No vessel has yet, when in motion on the open sea, been destroyed by the "Whitehead" torpedo.

If a torpedo boat headed directly for her enemy was discovered at 2,400 yards, it would be necessary for her to get within 500 yards or 600 yards before she could use her torpedo. Even at a high rate of speed she would thus be exposed to the fire of 6-pounders, 12-pounders and large rapid-fire guns for at least three minutes. A 12-pounder in that time would easily discharge from 20 to 30 aimed shots, one of which, well placed, would disable the approaching boat. The larger rapid-fire guns, six-inch, could discharge in that time 15 to 20 aimed shots, any one of which would, perhaps, be effective.

The Japanese, when tired after a battle, with ammunition low, dared not risk a night action with a fleet when Chinese torpedo boats were known to be in the vicinity. The Chinese boats at the battle of the Yalu did no effective work. In theory they should have dashed into the battle under cover of the smoke and wrought their enemies great damage. One tried and its engines went wrong. Another one fired three times at close quarters and missed each time.

Torpedoes can do little against battleships while their secondary battery is in good shape. Three attacked the "Olympia" at Manilla; one was quickly sunk, one retired, and the third was beached to prevent sinking.

The torpedo boat's time will come at the close of the battle, when the ships are partially disabled, the crews tired, the smoke hanging over the scene, and the rapid-fire battery dismounted or silenced, then after a ship is disabled, perhaps on uneven keel, she will fall an easy prey to the torpedo boat.

The moral effect of the torpedo boat will have a very real influence upon warfare. The constant strain upon the nerves in keeping a lookout will wear upon a fleet, and the danger that a floating fortress costing millions of dollars will be destroyed by the insignificant yet terrible little enemy will make nations careful about building larger and more expensive warships. The knowledge that a harbor is defended by such a fleet will tend to keep an attacking squadron at a distance at least a portion of the time. All in all, the very fear that torpedo boats incite will well repay their construction, if they render no further service. Even so high an authority and staunch an adherent of the battleship as Admiral Colomb, of England, is beginning to look with favor on boats of the "destroyer" class.

> "She's a floating boiler crammed with fire and steam,
> A dainty toy, with works just like a watch;
> A weaving, working basketful of tricks —
> A pent volcano and stoppered at top notch.
> She is Death and swift Destruction in a case
> (Not the Unseen, but the Awful — plain in sight).
> The Dread that must be halted when afar;
> She's a concentrated, fragile form of Might!
> She's a daring, vicious thing
> With a rending deadly sting —
> And she asks no odds nor quarter in the fight!"*

The Automobile Torpedo in Battle.

Previous to this quarter century the only torpedoes used in action were either of the towing or spar variety. The development of the electric searchlight and rapid-fire gun rendered these varieties obsolete, and inventive talent began to turn itself to a torpedo that could be used at longer range.

"Whitehead."

The "Whitehead" torpedo, now most generally used, appeared in crude form in 1868. It is a long, fish-shaped shell, with three compartments. The first chamber contains the explosive charge, the second chamber the compressed air cylinder furnishing the motive power, and the third chamber the machinery for turning the screw pro-

---

* James Barnes in "McClure's" for June, 1898.

peller at the stern. The torpedoes of to-day are from fourteen to eighteen inches in diameter, from eleven to eighteen feet long, carry from 120 to 220 pounds of gun-cotton, and can run about 800 yards, the greater part of the distance at a thirty-knot rate.

"Warhead."

The front chamber of the torpedo, called the "warhead," is detachable, and contains the wet gun-cotton for the charge and the machinery necessary to explode it. The warhead is kept in the ammunition magazine and attached to the torpedo the last thing before entering action. Wet gun-cotton is used because it is one of the safest of the high explosives. As one writer has expressed it, "Wet gun-cotton may be safely chopped up with an axe." It can only be exploded by the concussion of another explosive. The fulminate fuse igniting a small quantity of dry gun-cotton is usually used to ignite the charge. It is said that in the fight at Cardenas a projectile struck a torpedo of the boat "Winslow" and actually passed through the gun-cotton. Authorities claim the shell must strike the detonating cap to cause an explosion.

Discharging Torpedo.

The torpedo is thrown from the tube by a light charge of powder, and on its passage the machinery within it is set in motion and it at once begins to propel itself, which gives it the name "automobile." If fired directly ahead, care must be taken that the boat does not overrun it before the torpedo has gathered headway of its own. Much skill is required in the use of the torpedo. If fired at a target which is in motion, allowance must be made for the position of the target by the time the torpedo can reach it. If fired from the broadside of a torpedo boat, allowance must be made for the "acquired motion" of the boat. In practice, dummy torpedoes fired from submerged broadside tubes have sometimes been broken in two as they entered the water, or even become entangled in the screw propeller of the boat. Such an event would be highly disastrous in action. A warship of considerable size at fifteen knots would have surrounding it a body of water in motion of considerable strength. Some authorities say this would afford protection from the torpedo.

The modern torpedo is a very complicated piece of machinery, and costs the Government, complete, $3,500. It possesses a contrivance by which it can be floated at any required depth so that it will strike beneath the armor belt.

"Howell."

The "Howell" torpedo is the invention of an American officer, and differs from the "Whitehead" chiefly in having within it a large balance-wheel, in place of the compressed air motor, which, before launching, is spun up to a high speed, and by its momentum after it is launched continues to drive the screw propeller.

Ram.

"There are many who are in love with 'the small swift ram,' but it is doubtful how far such a ship is attainable, and how far she would be useful if the ideal could be obtained. Ability to ram depends upon speed and handiness in the assailant and the want of these qualities in the assailed. To obtain a high speed, not only upon the measured mile, but in a sea-way, the boilers must be heavy and the engines powerful. This necessarily involves a high displacement, as the hull must be strong to withstand the jar of the machinery and the violent concussion of ramming. If the ram is given guns and armor she becomes a battleship; if she is left without them she is liable to be destroyed by gun-fire long before she can use her sole weapon; and that weapon is a most uncertain and two-edged one."*

Early Use.

The ram was a well-known and effective weapon of ancient naval warfare. Even in the days when galleys were propelled by rows of slaves chained to the bench it was often used with decisive results. The ram of the Greek vessel is said to have won the day for them in that all-important naval battle with Xerxes' fleet at Salamis. Two thousand years afterward the allied Christian fleet used it with equal effect against their Turkish enemies at the battle of Lepanto.

With the development of sail power and the decline of the galley, new methods of warfare found but little use for the ram. The sea breeze could not always be commanded, and the low-powered, crushing, splintering projectile took its place. The application of steam again gave a motive power that could be controlled, and the ram once more came into prominence.

First Appearance in Modern Times.

March 8, 1862, a Federal fleet of wooden sailing vessels lay at anchor in Hampton Roads. About mid-day the lookouts reported the approach of a low, black, unsightly craft, the long-looked-for "Merrimac." Grim and ugly as death she steamed down the river directly toward the frigate "Congress" and the sloop-of-war "Cumberland." Although combined the two mounted 74 guns, the shot fell harmlessly on her sloping deck, although through one open port she received some damage, the muzzle being knocked off two guns and 19 men killed or wounded. But the fire from her guns crashed through the thin walls of the wooden ship with terrible effect. Selecting the "Cumberland," she steamed directly at her

---

* Wilson's "Ironclads in Action."

helpless victim and struck her fairly amidships, backed off and rained in a destructive fire of shot. The latter was needless; the "Cumberland's" fate was already decided, for a hole in her side was made big enough for a man to enter. Dramatic and terrible, the ram issued from the obscurity of the past and made its appearance in modern warfare.

After the action at Hampton Roads numerous rams were constructed by either side, and clever, light draft craft proved themselves of considerable value, especially in defending narrow river channels where the heavier ships had little room for manœuvres.

Battle of Lissa, 1876.

The ram was again used at Lissa in the battle between the Austrian and Italian fleets. The Italians had a large fleet of good vessels, but their admiral, Persano, had little ability and less courage. At last, in obedience to repeated demands made upon him by his government, he set out across the Adriatic to attack the little Austrian town of Lissa. He did this, although there was an Austrian "fleet in being" commanded by Admiral Tegetthoff. The Italian ships were far superior to the Austrian; individually the men were as brave, but their admiral, Persano, was unfit for the command, and Tegetthoff was an able and energetic officer of long experience. When the Austrian fleet appeared in sight that of Italy was split up into numerous little groups separated by miles. Persano attempted to get them into some kind of order, but as often as they would approach anything like a formation he would change his mind and signal for something different. At the last moment he left his flagship and went on board a ram, and during the action half his commanders had no knowledge of his whereabouts. The Austrian ships were painted black; the Italian, gray, and Tegetthoff gave the laconic signal "ram everything gray." In his flagship the "Ferdinand Maximilian" he struck the "Re d' Italian," and almost rammed her through. The Italian ship sank at once, her men cheering as they went down. Tegetthoff afterwards said: "If I were to live a thousand years I would never ram another ship. You see the vessel attacked at one moment, and the next 800 men sliding into the sea with a vessel following them."

Another attack by the Austrian "Kaiser," a wooden ship was not so successful. She received a broadside at close range and was set on fire, and suffered a great loss in men. Persano, on board the Italian ram, distinguished himself by refusing to use his vessel whenever an opportunity offered. Under the able leadership of Tegetthoff the Austrians won a substantial victory.

An English authority who has made an exhaustive study of the history of the ram, assures us that there is only one case on record in which serious damage has been inflicted by the ram on any ship under steam with sea-room.

If battles are to be fought at long range and smokeless powder used, the ram will be exposed for some minutes to a severe fire and when within torpedo range it is liable to attack from torpedoes as well as guns, as all the battleships are fitted with torpedo tubes.

"If the fleets charge one another end-on, there may be cases when the ram will be used, but there will be great danger then of end-to-end collisions should the commanders on each side be determined, and these will almost certainly result in the loss of both ships, unless, indeed, the bows of the ship on one side are so weak as to take the full force of the collision and to break it. More probably the less determined man will swerve at the last minute and expose his side, as did Buchanan at Mobile."*

---

* Wilson's "Ironclads in Action."

What a Naval Battle Is Like.

"The battleship has to carry about with her all sorts of odds and ends which are essential to her in peace but useless in war. When the ship clears for action the boats cannot be taken below and must remain above to be shot to splinters and cause fire. Equally dangerous and difficult to dispose of are wooden companion ladders, mess tables, benches and the various impedimenta usually found between decks. If of wood, these will add to the risk of fire, which is very great. With the ship's upper deck thoroughly cleared of wood, there will be no wreckage to float and save the drowning, nor will the boats be of much use for saving life after a battle.

"The ships will begin their action at about 2,500 or 3,000 yards. Upon the upper works of the ship will fall most of the damage inflicted during the preliminary cannonade. They will have been prepared for the strain in every conceivable way. Round the funnels sacks of coal will be placed, and near the quick-firers, mantlets to catch splinters. The conning-tower and the positions from which the ships will be fought will also, doubtless, receive attention. In this way the injury done may be reduced to a minimum, but it will still be extensive. The effect of even small shells charged with high explosives upon unarmored structures is very deadly. Great holes will be torn in the outer plating; splinters and fragments of side and shell sent flying through the confined space within; and any wood that may be about, which has not been thoroughly drenched with water, will be set on fire. The funnels and ventilators may be riddled till they come down, and inside them, on the splinter-gratings, which commonly cross them at the level of the armor-deck, fragments of iron and wood will collect and obstruct the draft. If the ventilators are blocked, and the flow of air to the stoke-hold checked, the stokers and engine-room men will be exposed to terrible hardships—gasping in a hot and vitiated atmosphere for the air which cannot reach them. The boiler-force will fail and the steam-pressure sink. It is true that nothing of this kind appears to have happened at the Yalu, but the fire maintained there was not so accurate as it would probably be with highly-skilled and cool Western gunners.

"At the close of the long range cannonade will come the close action. The range will be diminished to 600 yards or 700 yards, and the stronger side will steam in to assure its victory. This will be the most terrible period of the action. Up to that time, indeed, the damage done to the vitals of the battleships will not have been serious, but no doubt the internal economy of these vessels will have been impaired. The heavy quick-firers, judging from the Yalu, will not, at long range, inflict much injury on the water-line. It will be upon the upper works, superstructures, military masts, funnels, ventilators, chart-houses, bridges and stacks of boats and top-hamper, that the hail of projectiles whether fired direct or ricochetting from the water, will descend."[*]

Under cover of the smoke or taking advantage of deranged steering-gear or silenced rapid-fire batteries, the cruel ram and the deadly torpedo boat will approach to administer the finishing blow to a partially disabled antagonist. The nervous strain on the officers and crew at this period of the battle will be something terrible.

Definition of Terms.

Arc of fire — That part of a circle through which a gun can be moved and fired. It is least in a broadside and greatest in a turret.

Armor-clad — A ship carrying vertical armor, that is, a belt, and on gun positions.

Axial fire — Fire straight ahead or astern, parallel to the ship's keel. Guns in the French navy are arranged

---

[*] Wilson's "Ironclads In Action."

to give powerful fire of this character. Strong bow fire is necessary to meet torpedo attacks and when in pursuit of an enemy. Strong stern fire is necessary in a ship fleet enough to fight by drawing her enemies after her.

Barbette — An armored tower inside which the guns are revolved. The guns fire over the top of the armor, and not through portholes, as in turrets. On our best battleships the barbette descends from the turret to the protective deck.

Belt — The strip of vertical armor along the side of a ship, protecting the vitals from gun fire and the ram.

Boilers, water-tube and tubular — In the first the water is carried in small tubes around which the fire passes; in the second the fire passes through tubes around which the water is placed.

Broadside fire — Fire from the guns placed along the side of a ship or in turrets that can be turned to fire over the ship's side.

Bunkers — The bins in which the ship carries her coal. When full they also serve for protection.

Casemate — The armored position in which a gun is placed.

Coal endurance — The distance a ship can steam at moderate speed without recoaling.

Commerce destroyer — A ship especially fitted to prey on the enemy's commerce.

Compound engines — Having two cylinders, one larger than the other. Steam is used at high pressure in the small cylinder, at a lower pressure in the larger cylinder. Triple expansion engines have three cylinders; quadruple expansion engines four cylinders.

Cordite — A kind of smokeless powder used in English service.

Dry dock — A dock into which a ship can be floated, the entrance closed, and the water pumped out, that workmen may get at any part of the ship.

"Fleet in being"— A fleet free to move and threaten any point it chooses. It is like a strong body of cavalry on an enemy's flank, threatening his communications with a base of supplies.

Floating batteries — Guns mounted on platforms or in ships not designed for speed, but to be anchored in front of some exposed position. The French floating batteries at Kimborn in the Crimean war were the first armored ships used in modern warfare.

Forced draft — Air driven into the furnaces by a powerful fan. It is a severe strain on the boilers, as it throws a current of cold air directly on the tubes and is likely to cause them to leak. When forced draft is used the air-tight doors of the fire rooms must be closed, and the atmospheric pressure in the room is increased.

Freeboard — That part of the ship extending above the waterline. It must be high in a ship designed for service in all kinds of weather. Guns mounted on a high freeboard have an advantage in rough weather over others.

High explosives — Explosives more powerful than gunpowder, as dynamite, melinite, cordite. These are used as bursting charges for armor-piercing shells.

Homogeneous fleet — Ships closely resembling each other in armor, guns and speed. Such a fleet is strong, and possesses a marked advantage in action over one in which the individual ships differ greatly from each other.

"Jeune Ecole"— The believers in the doctrine of Admiral Eube, of France, that the torpedo-boat and the cruiser have taken the place of the battleship, and that speed is everything. They attach much importance to commerce-destroyers and bombardments.

Knot — In the ordinary acceptance of the term, means a nautical mile, equal to 6,086.7 feet. Knots may be **reduced** to their approximate equivalent in statute miles by multiplying by 1.15. Statute miles may be reduced to their approximate equivalent in knots by multiplying by .87.

Light draft — Floating in but little water.

The log-line — Ordinarily a small line attached to a kite-shaped piece of board, weighted at one end so as to stand upright in the water and remain stationary when thrown overboard from a vessel in motion. Knots are tied in the line at intervals of the 120th part of a nautical mile, and the number of these that runs through a man's fingers in half a minute shows the rate of speed of the vessel for an hour.

There are now many kinds of patent logs which give the rate of speed with more or less accuracy.

Melinite — An explosive made from picric acid, used as a bursting charge in shells. On exploding it generates suffocating gases.

Nickel steel — An alloy of steel and nickel which gives great hardness and power to break up projectiles fired against it.

Palliser shell — A steel shell with a chilled point.

Personnel — The body of persons making up the naval force; used frequently with reference to their character. In distinction from material, meaning munitions of war, baggage, provisions, etc.

Plunging fire — Fire from guns used in forts placed at a considerable elevation. Plunging fire is dangerous to the " protective deck."

Recessed ports — A port in which the sides are cut at angle, or a portion of the side cut away to give greater freedom of movement of the gun. '

Scouts — Light, fast ships, whose duties are to discover the enemy and report.

CHAPTER IX.
Spanish Navy.

In comparing the naval power of Spain with that of the United States at the beginning of the war, it was easy to see that each was strong where the other was weak. Spain had eight magnificent armored cruisers that no country, not even England, could equal; the United States had but two. Spain had one first-class battleship, the "Pelayo." The United States had four ships and perhaps five that could certainly give her battle with the prospect of winning. The eight cruisers of the Spanish navy possessed a marked advantage in belonging to one class, which gave them speed, coal endurance, offensive and defensive power about equal. A fleet is no faster than its slowest vessel, a line of battle no more powerful than its weakest ship, as a chain is no stronger than its weakest link. The ships of the United States were built at different dates, of widely varying types, and Admiral Sampson's fleet was wonderful for its lack of uniformity. The cruiser "New York," with a speed of twenty-one knots, towing a monitor along at about eight knots, presented a unique spectacle trying to overhaul a fleet of cruisers. The United States was also deficient in torpedo-boats and torpedo-boat destroyers, and Spain was strong in this respect. It is little wonder that some European critics, forgetting the fact that "the man behind the gun" is the chief factor in a naval contest, prophesied that the American navy would find in the Spaniards a hard nut to crack.

The individual bravery of the Spaniards left nothing to be desired, and in the recent actions they have proven that as far as courage is concerned they are worthy the traditions of any navy. The modern warship is a huge floating machine, and bravery alone will not suffice.

There is nothing worse than a Spanish engineer unless it be a Spanish gunner.

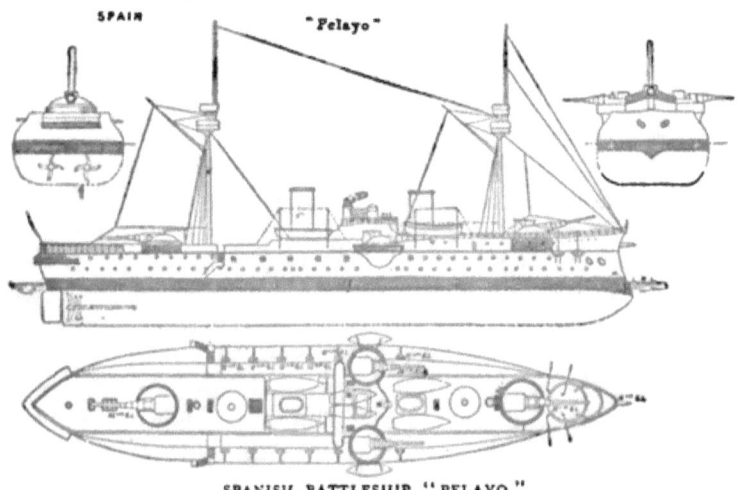

SPANISH BATTLESHIP "PELAYO."

Battleship "Pelayo."

This is the popular favorite of Spain, and the masses think her able to whip any ship in the world. She is an object of almost religious interest, and more engravings of her are found in Spain than of all other ships together.

The "Pelayo" was launched in 1887 and at that time represented the highest type of naval architecture. She is made of steel, displaces 9,900 tons, is 330 feet long, 66 feet wide and draws less than 25 feet of water. She has two screw propellers, moved by engines of 9,000 horsepower, and can make sixteen knots an hour.

From stem to stern she is protected by a belt of armor 7 1-2 feet wide 3 feet above and 4 1-2 feet below the water-line. This is 17.75 inches thick opposite the boilers and engines, decreasing to less than 12 inches at the ends. The protective deck, 4 inches thick, runs even with the top of the armor-belt.

THE ASCENDENCY OF AMERICA.

Prominent features shown in her pictures are two military masts, two barbette turrets, one fore and one aft; two sponsons, one on each side, and the bridge between the two smokestacks. She has a ram bow.

She mounts two 12.6-inch (32 centimeter) Hontoria guns, one forward and one aft, and two 11.2-inch (28 centimeter) guns in sponsons (armored bay windows), one on each side. She thus can fire directly ahead or astern one 12.6-inch gun and two 11.2-inch guns, or on broadside two 12.6-inch guns and one 11.2-inch gun. She is said to have, in addition, a new battery of nine 5.5-inch rapid-fire guns, six smaller rapid-fire guns and twelve machine guns. The energy of her gun-fire for one minute is 327,720 foot-tons.

Her quick-firing guns have no adequate armor protection and might easily be put out of service by a well placed shell and her barbettes do not extend down to the protective deck, so the space beneath them could be swept by shell fire, the supports cut away, and tumble guns and all into the hold of the ship. We think some of our gunners are clever enough to do this. A 13-inch shell well placed would do the business. About the time the "Pelayo" was completed it was said that she would wear English compound armor. If this is true, she is far less formidable than she appears on paper.

The "Vizcaya" Class.

Fine armored cruisers, made of steel, with 7,000 tons displacement, and drawing 21 feet 6 inches of water. They were built at Bilbao, Spain, and cost about $3,000,000 each. They carried 1,200 tons of coal, and should be able in theory to steam 12,000 miles at 10 knots speed without re-coaling, but this is probably too big an estimate. Each has an armor-belt 12 inches in thickness, gradually tapering toward the bow and stern, on top of which is a protective deck 3 inches thick, from which an armored tube rises to barbettes fore and aft 10½ inches thick, which contain her big guns.

The armament consists of 2 11.2-inch (28 centimeter) Hontoria guns and 10 5.5-inch (14 centimeter), 2 2.7-inch (7 centimeter), 8 2.2-inch (57 mm.), 4 1.4-inch (37 mm.) rapid-fire guns and 2 machine guns. The largest 12 guns would give an energy of 71,920 foot-tons for one

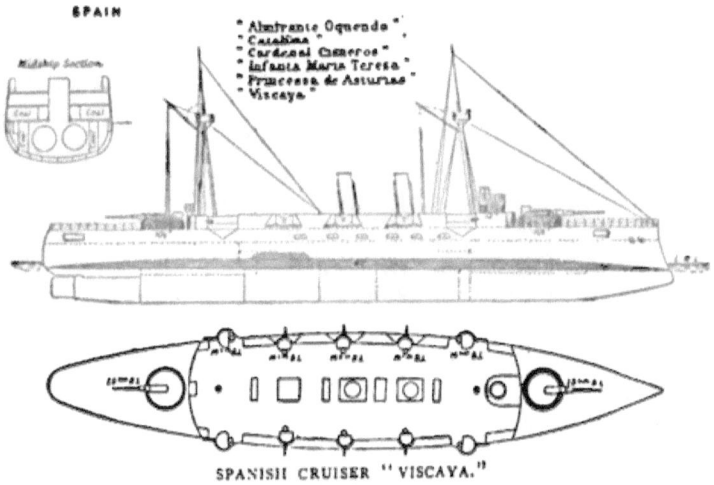

SPANISH CRUISER "VISCAYA."

discharge. One discharge from the "New York" gives an energy of but 52,572 foot-tons. The energy of gun fire of the Spanish vessel is 292,460 foot-tons for one minute. The "Almirante Oquendo" and the "Infanta Maria Teresa" were sister ships of the "Vizcaya," and with her sunk off Santiago July 3, 1898.

The "Cristobal Colon."

This was built by the Italian government and named "Guiseppe Garibaldi II." and was by them sold to Spain, who renamed her "Cristobal Colon." Though called an armored cruiser she was almost a battleship, for from stem to stern along the water line she had a belt of nickel-steel armor 6 inches thick and above this for 197 feet over the central portion of the ship, reaching to the base of the armor turret, the side armor was the same thickness. The armor on the side should have furnished excellent protection for the 10 6-inch rapid-fire guns which were mounted 5 on each side, and on the deck above these was another lighter battery of 6 4.7-inch rapid-fire guns protected by gun shields. She should have mounted 2 10-inch guns, but through poverty, neglect or corruption the heavy guns were never furnished. In addition to this she had 10 6-pounders and 10 1-pounders, 2 Maxims, and 5 torpedo tubes. Her displacement was 6,840 tons, length 328 feet, beam 59 feet 8 inches, draft 24 feet. She was driven by 2 vertical triple-expansion engines each attached to a propeller, giving her a speed of 20 knots. Her coal bunkers would carry 1,000 tons, and in addition she was built to use some liquid fuel.

The "Cristobal Colon" was beached in the action off Santiago July 3d and at present writing it is reported that she can be saved. She would be a most desirable addition to the American navy.

"Cardinal Cisneros" Class.

Spain has three cruisers belonging to this class. The "Cisneros" and "Princess de Asturias" were launched in 1896, and the "Cataluna" is not yet completed.

The "Cardinal Cisneros" has a hull of steel, 7,000 tons displacement, draft 21 feet 10 inches, armor-belt 11.8 inches thick, tapering to 6 and 8 inches at the ends. It runs from within 30 feet of the bow to within 50 feet of the stern. The ends are joined by transverse steel bulkheads 9.8 inches thick. The protective deck, 2 inches thick, extends even with the top of the belt and curves down below the level of the water at the bow and stern. There are cofferdams of cellulose behind the belt, and the vitals are further protected by from 6 to 9 feet of coal. The armor in the barbettes is 11.8 inches thick. The vessels are fitted with two sets of triple-expansion engines, giving a maximum speed of 20.3 knots. The coal capacity is 1,500 tons, which at a 10-knot rate, should allow them to steam 12,000 miles. They are armed with 2 11.2-inch guns, 10 5.5-inch rapid-fire guns and 2 2.7-inch, 4 2.2-inch and 4 1.4-inch smaller rapid-fire guns, and two machine guns. The energy of the gun-fire of the primary battery for one minute is 292,460 foot-tons. They are fitted with ram bows, and have two military masts with signal yards, fighting tops, 2 smoke-stacks, and 2 turrets, one fore and one aft, each mounting a heavy gun.

"Numancia."

The "Numancia" is an old broadside ship with iron hull, launched in 1863, and of 7,305 tons displacement.

Our information concerning her is meagre. Originally she had a side-plating 4.7 inches of wrought iron, and mounted muzzle-loading guns. With her old engines she was able to make 8 knots an hour, and with her muzzle-loading guns and wrought-iron armor she should not be very formidable. It was planned to reconstruct her, take off the wrought-iron armor and replace it by a steel belt 5.5 inches thick, protect her broadside guns by 5 inches of steel, and fit her with triple-expansion engines that would give her a speed of 18 knots. The striking feature would be one short smoke-stack, and two military masts, with fighting tops, in place of her full-rigged three masts. She is said to have 4 6.3-inch, 8 5.5-inch, 3 4.7-inch guns, all quick-fire. The energy of her gun-fire for one minute is 281,498 foot-tons.

"Vitoria."

The "Vitoria" is an old iron broadside training ship, launched at Blackwall, England, 1865. She is of 7,250 tons displacement, draft 25 feet 3 inches, speed 11 knots.

She has an armor belt 5.5 inches in thickness, and the guns and broadside are protected by 5-inch armor. She now mounts 6 6.3-inch, 6 5.5-inch, 6 4.7-inch guns, all quick-fire, and 12 machine guns. She is used as a training school for seamen. The energy of the gun-fire of her primary battery is 303,372 foot-tons per minute.

The striking features of the new model would be two military masts, each with fighting tops, two short smoke-stacks, and a bridge between the smoke-stacks and the mainmast. She ought not to be a match for any of our armored ships.

The "Emperador Carlos V."

This is the largest and the best of the Spanish cruisers and named after Spain's greatest Emperor. She is built of steel, has a displacement of 9,235 tons, 1,000 more than the "New York." She has 2 screw propellers moved by engines of 18,500 horse-power that in her trial for the fastest mile gave her a speed of 21.9 knots, an average of 20 knots for a longer time.

She was built at Cadiz, Spain, and launched in 1895, costing about $360,000. She is the only one of the Spanish vessels with Harveyized steel armor. Her belt is light, only 2 inches thick, but we understand that the broadside guns are also protected by 2 inches of steel armor. She has a very thick steel protective deck, $6\frac{1}{2}$ inches, a trifle heavier than that of the "New York."

Her armament consists of 2 11.2-inch Hontoria guns mounted in barbettes 10 inches thick, one forward and one aft and 8 5.5-inch, 4 3.9-inch, 2 2.7-inch, 4 2.2-inch rapid-fire guns, 6 machine guns and 6 torpedo tubes.

The energy of her gun-fire is 123,580 foot-tons per minute.

Her energy of gun-fire for one discharge would be 80,504 foot-tons, almost 60 per cent more than that of the "New York." She has a coal capacity of 1,200 tons; a crew of 535 officers and men; 2 military masts, each with one fighting top and signal yards; 3 tall smoke stacks and 2 bridges, one above the other just back of the forward turret. She is fitted with a ram bow.

Protected Cruisers.

Spain has a few protected cruisers, but they are no match for the magnificent American ships like the "Olympia," "Cincinnati," "Boston," and "Baltimore," as was proven at Manila. The "Isla de Cuba" and "Isla de Luzon" were built in England, and cost $223,500 each. The "Marques de la Ensenada" was built on identically the same lines in the government yards of Spain, and cost $1,439,973, a striking example of Spanish administration.

NAME.	Displace't. tons.	Armored Deck. Inches.	Armament.	Speed. Knots.
Alfonso XIII	5,000	4½	4 7.8-in. (Hontoria), 6 4.7-in., 6 2.2-in. Q. F., 6 1.4-in., 3 M.	20
Isla de Cuba*	1,030	2⅜	4 4.7-in. (Hontoria), 4 6-pr. Q. F., 2 3-pr., 2 M.	16
Isla de Luzon*	1,030	2½	4 4.7-in. (Hontoria), 4 6-pr. Q. F., 2 3-pr., 2 M.	16
Lepanto	4,826	4¾	4 7.8-in. (Hontoria), 6 4.7-in. Q. F., 6 6-pr., 4 3-pr., 5 M.	20

* Destroyed at Manila.

NAME.	Displace't. tons.	Armored Deck. Inches.	Armament.	Speed. Knots.
Marques de la Ensenada.	1,030	2½	4 4.7-in. (Hontoria), 5 Q. F., 4 M.	15
Rio de la Plata........	1,800	1	2 5.5-in. Q. F., 4 3.9-in., 4 2.2-in., 6 M.	20

Unprotected Cruisers.

NAME.	Tons, displace't.	Armament.	Speed. Knots.
Alfonso XII..........	3,090	6 6.2-in (Hontoria), 2 2.7-in., 6 6-prs., Q. F., 4 3-prs., 5 M.	17.5
Aragon..............	3,342	6 6.2-in. (Hontoria), 2 3.3-in., (Krupp), 4 2.9-in., 2 M.	14
Castilla.*...........	3,342	4 5.9-in. (Krupp), 4 4.7-in., 2 3.3-in., 4 2.9-in., 8 Q. F. 2 M.	14
Conde de Venadito....	1,130	4 4.7-in (Hontoria), 2 2.7-in., 2 Q. F., 5 M.	14
Don Antonio de Ulloa*.	1,130	4 4.7-in. (Hontoria), 2 2.7-in., 2 Q. F., 5 M.	14
Don Juan de Austria*...	1,130	4 4.7-in. (Hontoria), 3 2.2-in., Q. F., 2 1.5-in., 5 M.	14
Infanta Isabel..	1,130	4 4.7-in. (Hontoria), 2 2.7-in., 3 Q. F., 4 M.	14
Isabel II............	1,130	4 4.7-in. (Hontoria), 2 7.7-in., 4 Q. F., 3 M.	14
Navarra	3,342	4 5.9-in., 2 4.7-in., 2 3.4-in., 4 2.9-in., 4 M.	14

* Destroyed at Manila.

UNPROTECTED CRUISERS.—*Continued.*

NAME.	Tons displace't.	Armament.	SPEED. Knots
Nueva Espana	630	2 4.7-in. (Hontoria). 4 2.2-in., Q. F.	18
Quiros	315	2 2.2-in. Q. F., 2 M.	11.5
Reina Christina *	3,520	6 6.2-in. (Hontoria), 2 2.7-in., 3 2.2-in. Q. F., 2 1.5-in., 6 3-prs., 2 M.	17.5
Reina Regente	5,000		20
Reina Mercedes	3,090	6 6.2-in. (Hontoria), 2 2.7-in., 3 2.2-in. Q. F., 2 1.5-in., 6 1.4-in., 2 M.	17.5
Velasco *	1,152	3 5.9-in. 4-ton (Armstrong). 2 2.7-in. (Hontoria), 2 M.	14.3

* Destroyed at Manilla.

Torpedo-boat Destroyers.

At the breaking out of the war Spain had a very formidable fleet of torpedo-boat destroyers. They were large enough to keep at sea with a fighting fleet — a small torpedo boat cannot do this — and given enough speed and gun-power to overtake and destroy the smaller torpedo boats; hence the name torpedo-boat destroyer.

The present war by no means settles the merits of the torpedo-boat destroyer, for the Spaniards have not used theirs as the designers had intended. Their large size unfits them for attack in the daytime, and whenever they have rashly undertaken this they have met with disaster.

NAME	Length.	Displacement.	Trial Speed.	Armament.	Coal Capacity.
	Feet.	Tons.	Knots.		Tons.
Furor	220	380	28	2 12-pr., 2 6-pr., 2 1-pr.	100
Terror	220	380	28	2 12-pr., 2 6-pr., 2 1-pr	100
Audaz	225	400	30	2 14-pr., 2 6-pr., 2 1 pr.	90
Osado	225	400	30	2 14-pr., 2 6-pr., 2 1-pr.	90
Pluton	225	400	30	2 14-pr., 2 6-pr., 2 1-pr.	90
Proserpina	225	400	30	2 14-pr., 2 6-pr., 2 1-pr.	90

Torpedo Boats.

Spain has a strong fleet of torpedo boats. The "Ariete," launched in 1887, made a speed record of 26.1 knots on her trial. That for several years stood as an international record and gave the Spanish boats a high reputation.

The following are first-class torpedo boats: Acevedo, Ariete, Azor, Barcelo, Bustamente, Ejercito, Habana, Halcon, Julian Ordofiez, Orion, Rayo, Retamosa, Rigel, Seza. Six additional boats of this class are building.

Second-class: Aire, Castor, Pollux, Peral. Three additional boats of this class are building.

CHAPTER X.
American Navy.

Admiral George Dewey.

He was born in Montpelier, Vt., December 26, 1837, and is the third son of Julius Yemens Dewey, M. D., a prominent physician of Montpelier, who founded and was for many years president of the National Life Insurance Company of that city. Young Dewey, in his boyhood, seems to have engaged in about as many fights as General Sherman, and to have thus early in life acquired the habit of coming out as victor. His early school-life was spent in the Washington County Grammar School, of Montpelier. The scholars there had the reputation of being hard to manage and were engaged in frequent conflicts with their teachers, in which young Dewey seems to have figured prominently.

He entered the naval academy at Annapolis, was made acting midshipman September 23, 1854, and lieutenant, 1861. He was ordered to the steamer "Mississippi" in the West Gulf squadron and served under Farragut. During the Civil War he displayed marked coolness and heroism, and was a great favorite with his commanders and fellow-officers. It is interesting to note that in the battle of Manila, Captain Coghlan of the "Raleigh," Captain Dyer of the "Baltimore," and Captain Gridley of the "Olympia," Dewey's flagship, serving under him, had also served with him an apprenticeship under Farragut.

Made a commodore and placed in charge of the Asiatic squadron, he worked long and hard to put it in shape for the coming struggle with Spain which he saw was impending. The result shows how thorough was his preparation. The day before the formal declaration of war was made, Secretary Long cabled Dewey to Hong Kong as follows:

"War has commenced between the United States and Spain. Proceed at once to the Philippine Islands. Commence operations at once, particularly against the Spanish fleet. You must capture vessels or destroy them. Use utmost endeavors."

May 1st he could report the Spanish fleet as annihilated. In a few days after receiving news of his great victory, he was sent the following despatch:

"WASHINGTON, *May* 7.

"*Dewey, Manila:* President, in the name of the American people, thanks you and your officers and men for your splendid achievement and overwhelming victory. In recognition he has appointed you Acting Admiral and will recommend a vote of thanks to you by Congress.   LONG."

Commodore Schley (sly).

The face of Winfield Scott Schley is almost as familiar to our readers as that of Admiral Dewey. He is a descendant of a well known Maryland family and was born at Frederick, Maryland, October 9, 1839. He entered the naval academy at Annapolis and was made acting midshipman in 1856. He served with Farragut in the Mississippi river and about Port Hudson, took part in several skirmishes and assisted in cutting out from under heavy fire two supply schooners of the Confederates. He was made Lieutenant July 16, 1862, only two years after leaving the naval academy. Later he served in the Pacific squadron as the executive officer of the "Wateree," suppressed an insurrection among the Chinese coolies in the Chincha Islands. During a revolution in San Salvador he landed to protect the custom house and the United States Consulate. In 1869 he was appointed to the "Benicia" and served with her in the Asiatic station until 1872, taking part in the attack upon the forts upon the Salee river in Corea, where Lieutenant Hugh McKee was killed. In 1874 he was made a Commander.

When the necessity of relief for the Greely expedition became apparent in 1884 he was placed in command of it, and June 22d, rescued Lieutenant Greely and six men at Cape Sabine. He found them almost at the point of death; a few hours more and he would have been too late. In recognition of his services in this respect President Arthur appointed him Chief of the Bureau of Equipment where he served until 1888 when he was reappointed to the same office by President Cleveland. He was made Captain March 3, 1888. Upon leaving the bureau he was given the "Baltimore," and in that vessel carried back to Stockholm, Sweden, the remains of the distinguished John Ericsson, famous for his building of the "Monitor." The "Baltimore" was assigned to duty on the Pacific squadron and was under his command when some of his crew were assaulted and killed by a mob at Valparaiso, Chile, 1891.

He is a very popular officer in the service and has received two gold medals from his native State, Maryland, and a gold watch for his services in the expedition which saved Lieutenant Greely.

His distinguished services during the present war have made his name and face familiar to our readers.

Admiral Sampson.

William T. Sampson was born in Palmyra, N. Y. February 8, 1840. His career is a striking example of what industry, intelligence and courage can secure. Others of our prominent naval officers have belonged to rich and influential families, whose influence sometimes opportunely secured for them a chance to make known their abilities. Admiral Sampson had none of these advantages. His father was a farmer in moderate circumstances and could not allow his son to devote all of his time even to the local schools, and he was frequently compelled to leave school to assist at home on the farm in the work there during the busy season. Handicapped as he was, nevertheless young Sampson soon distanced the rest of the boys at the Union School at

Palmyra. A local Congressman, attracted by his intelligence and bright manner, secured for him an appointment at the naval academy, which he entered in 1857, and from which he was graduated at the head of his class three years later.

Serving off Charleston in 1865, he was ordered by the admiral to enter the harbor and remove or destroy all submarine mines and torpedoes by which the city was protected from invasion. The service required was a difficult and dangerous one, and the work was conducted under a heavy fire from the enemy's sharpshooters. A number of his men being killed about him, Lieutenant Sampson ordered them under cover as much as possible, while he himself remained a target for their rifles, and calmly superintended the work. While swinging in the current the "Patapsco" struck a submarine mine, which exploded and sent her to the bottom with seventy of her crew. Lieutenant Sampson was thrown about 100 feet by the force of the explosion, but was rescued with twenty-five of his men. His commanding officer, in the official report of the disaster, speaks in high terms of his lieutenant's coolness and bravery.

He was appointed Superintendent of the Naval Academy in 1886 and held this position until 1890. In 1892 he became Inspector of Ordnance and in 1893 was made Chief of the Bureau of Ordnance. While in that position he had charge of the manufacture of the heavy guns and tested the turrets and ordnance machinery connected with many of our battleships now under his command.

It is a striking compliment to Captain Sampson that he was placed at the head of the "Maine" Court of Inquiry, the President recognizing that a thorough knowledge of a ship from the bottom of her keel to the tip of her masts and a level head was of more value in that position than an ability to coin unique phrases.

When it became apparent that hostilities with Spain were about to break out the President appointed Acting Rear-Admiral Sampson to the command of the fleet. He transferred his flag to the cruiser "New York," kept the fleet in perfect readiness, had Havana blockaded the afternoon of the same day the President issued the proclamation giving notice of intention to blockade that port.

The new navy owes a heavy debt to Admiral Sampson. He devised the superimposed turrets which are the distinctive feature of the battleships "Kearsarge" and "Kentucky." The great naval gun factory at Washington was constructed while he was Chief of the Bureau of Ordnance. In the navy he is regarded as a high authority on torpedo work, and his lectures at the War College produced a profound impression all over the world.

In personal appearance Admiral Sampson is of slight build, blue eyes, shoulders a trifle rounded, with considerable gray in his hair and beard. He is a man of few words, but personally very well liked. He has the reputation of being cool, level-headed, full of resources, and a capital man to have about in an emergency. This son of what Lincoln loved to term the "plain people" has proved his right to a recognized position among our leaders.

Captain Alfred Thayer Mahan.

He was born September 27, 1840, and was appointed to Annapolis Naval Academy from New York in 1856. He was made lieutenant in 1861 and served as such during the Civil War, rising by successive steps to that of captain in 1885. He was president of the Naval War College from 1886 to 1889 and again from 1890 to 1893.

Captain Mahan is the first and as yet the only writer to show conclusively the important part that naval power has played in the fortunes of nations and its general influence upon the history of the world. His book, "The Influence of Sea Power Upon History," which appeared in 1890, won him international recognition.

"The strategic conditions of the Mediterranean will be reproduced in the Caribbean Sea, and in the international struggle for the control of the new highway of commerce (Panama Canal) the United States will have the advantage of geographical position." He points out that the carrying trade of the United States is at present insignificant, only because the opening of the West since the Civil War had made maritime undertakings less profitable than the development of the internal resources of the country.*

A few years ago Captain Mahan retired from the navy, devoted himself to his literary work, and has produced "The Influence of Sea Power Upon History," "Life of Nelson," "Life of Admiral Farragut," "Influence of Sea Power Upon the French Revolution and Empire," and "The Interest of America in Sea Power Present and Future."

At the outbreak of the Spanish-American war he was in Italy, but came home at the request of the Washington administration and has been acting as a member of the War Board and adviser to the Secretary of the Navy. No modern writer on naval affairs is more widely quoted than Captain Mahan, and by English writers his works are credited with having had a deep influence in the development of what we are now calling the "new national policy" of the United States.

---
* Warner's "World's Best Literature," vol. xvi., page 9580.

Rate of Pay for Sea Service.

	Per year.		Per year
Rear-Admirals	$6,000	Assistant Surgeons, Assistant Paymasters and Assistant Engineers	1,700–1,900
Commodores	5,000		
Captains	4,500		
Commanders	3,500	Chaplains	2,500
Lieutenant-Commanders	2,800–3,000	Boatswains, Gunners, Carpenters and Sailmakers	1,200
Lieutenants	2,400–2,600		
Lieutenants (junior grade)	1,800–2,000		Per month.
Ensigns	1,200–1,400	Chief Masters-at-Arms	$65.00
Naval Cadets (at Academy $500)	950	Chief Boatswains' Mates	50.00
		Chief Gunners' Mates	50.00
Mates	1,200	Chief Quartermasters	50.00
Medical and Pay Directors and Medical and Pay Inspectors and Chief Engineers having the same rank at sea	4,400	Masters-at-Arms	40.00
		Boatswains' Mates	40.00
		Gunners' Mates	40.00
		Quartermasters	40.00
		Schoolmasters	40.00
		Machinists	55.00
Fleet Surgeons, Fleet Paymasters and Fleet Engineers	4,400	Blacksmiths	50.00
		Seamen Gunners	26.00
		Seamen	19–24
Surgeons, Paymasters and Chief Engineers	2,800–4,200	Apprentices	15–21
		Firemen	30–35
Passed Assistant Surgeons and Passed Assistant Paymasters	2,000–2,200	Musicians	30–32
		Landsmen	16.00
Passed Assistant Engineers	2,000		

The salary attached to many of the officers is gradually increased for long periods of service. A chief engineer at starting has $2,800; after twenty years in the service, $4,200.

Prize Money for Our Navy.

The commanding officer of the fleet or squadron receives one-twentieth of all prize money awarded to any vessel or vessels under his immediate control.

Fleet Captain: The fleet captain is entitled to one one-hundredth part of the award made to any vessel or vessels of the fleet or squadron for which he serves except in the case where the capture is made by the vessel in which he is serving, and in that case he shares in proportion to his pay with the other officers and men on board the vessel.

Commander of a Vessel: The commander of a single vessel is given one-tenth of the money awarded to his vessel if it is acting at the time of the capture under the command of the commanding officer of a fleet, squadron or division, and three-twentieths of it if it was acting independently.

Officers and Crew: After there has been deducted from the prize money the sums to which the commanding officers are entitled, the remainder shall be awarded to the officers and crew of the vessel in proportion to the pay each draws.

Who Share: All vessels of the navy that are within signaling distance of the vessel or vessels making the capture, and in such circumstances as to render efficient aid if required, share in the prize.

When the District Court of the United States shall determine that a prize was of inferior force to the captor, one-half the proceeds of the sale shall go to the captor and one-half to the United States, but if the prize was of equal or superior force to the vessel making the capture, the entire net proceeds of the sale shall go to the captor.

Section 4635 of the Revised Statutes authorizes the payment of a bounty of $100 for each man on an enemy's ship of war that is destroyed in action.

Prize Courts.

Before a prize can be sold and prize money awarded to the captors the legality of the capture must be confirmed by a court having jurisdiction in the matter.

The prize courts of this country are United States District and Circuit Courts with an appeal from the Circuit Court up to the Supreme Court of the United States. These courts decide the questions of belligerency, neutrality, capture, contraband, and from their decision are derived the title to prizes. All sales of captured prizes are illegal when made within neutral ports.

Energy of Gun-Fire.

Two English writers, Lord Brassey and Admiral Colomb, each independently in 1896 introduced a new standard for measuring gun-power of vessels; that is, "energy of gun-fire per minute." The power of the gun is measured by the force its projectile could exert. This force is termed energy and is measured by the number of tons it could lift one foot, hence called foot-tons. The 13-inch gun has a muzzle energy of 33,627 foot-tons, that is, the force with which the projectile leaves the gun would be sufficient to lift that many tons one foot. In computing the energy of gun-fire for the vessels of the United States navy we have assumed that each vessel would enter action with her guns loaded and fire them at the following rate of speed: 13-inch, one round in 3 minutes; 12-inch, one round in 2.8 minutes; 10-inch, one round in 2 minutes; 8-inch, one round in 1.5 minutes; 6-inch, slow-fire, one round a minute; 6-inch rapid-fire, six rounds a minute; 5-inch rapid-fire, ten rounds a minute; 4.7-inch, rapid-fire, twelve rounds a minute; 4-inch rapid-fire, fifteen rounds a minute. This speed is far higher than could be maintained in actual combat, but has been attained at drill. Energy of gun-fire would not measure accurately the fighting efficiency of a vessel, but a gun that can be fired only once a minute must be at a disadvantage when opposed to one that can be fired six times as fast.

· The private gunmakers of England are turning out

some remarkable guns and selling them to whoever will buy them. As an example of this the Blanco Encalada, a Chilian cruiser, at target-practice fired four shots from an 8-inch gun in sixty-two seconds, *and took the ammunition from the magazine.* Another Chilian cruiser, the Almirante O'Higgins, belongs to the same class as the New York and Brooklyn. A little larger than the New York and not so large as the Brooklyn, she mounts in her primary battery four 8-inch, ten 6-inch, and four 4.7-inch guns, all rapid-fire. Her energy of gun-fire for one minute should be 606,000, while that of the New York for the same time is only 208,688. A few examples like this should convince our authorities of the advisability of getting a modern armament on board our vessels.

At the close of the Civil War the United States had the most powerful navy in the world, but no effort was made to keep it up and it was not long before this country had not a modern gun afloat in its navy nor a single modern warship for the performance of the most ordinary duty abroad. We had no plant that could turn out a ton of steel armor. Gun forgings for our cannon were bought abroad. The "Texas," launched at the United States Navy Yard at Norfolk, Va., was even built from plans purchased in England.

In 1883, the protected cruisers "Atlanta," "Boston" and "Chicago," and the dispatch boat "Dolphin," were authorized. They were built by John Roach & Company of Chester, Penn., and launched the following year. This was the beginning of the "new navy."

In 1885 Congress authorized the building of the protected cruiser "Charleston." The plans were purchased abroad and the contract went to the Union Iron Works, San Francisco Cal. The vessel was launched in 1888, and commissioned in 1889. The construction of the cruiser "Newark" was authorized the same year and contract given Wm. Cramp & Sons, Philadelphia, Penn.

She was launched in 1890 together with the torpedo-boat "Petrel."

An appropriation of $3,178,046 was made to complete the "Amphitrite," "Miantonomoh," "Puritan," and "Terror," the keels of which had been laid a decade before.

In 1886 were authorized the "Maine" and "Texas," two second-class battleships, the cruiser "Baltimore" and the dynamite cruiser "Vesuvius." In 1890 three first-class battleships, "Indiana," "Massachusetts" and "Oregon." The "Indiana" was the first to be launched (Feb. 28, 1893) and the first to be commissioned five years from date of the act authorizing her construction. Since that time our naval progress has been fairly rapid, and each ship when completed has usually represented the best of its type afloat. Within the past fifteen years $400,000,000 has been appropriated for the navy, about 50 per cent. of it within the last five years.

Importance of Sea Power: Our navy has been a rather neglected child and never a very popular one in some parts of the country, but the excellent service it has lately given us should reconcile all opposition. The destruction of the Spanish fleets at Santiago and Manila has dealt crushing blows to Spanish power. It is the superior condition of our navy that has so quickly enabled us to carry the war into Spain's territory, and its well demonstrated effectiveness will make Europe likely to hesitate before interferring with us.

It is interesting to note that when Japan began her recent war with China she had only 160,000 tons of steam merchant vessels afloat. It is four years since, and her merchant tonnage now aggregates more than 400,000. The recent partition of China is a striking example of what it costs a nation to be unprepared for war, and especially to be weak in sea power. None of the nations, with the exception of Russia, who are wringing concessions from that ancient country could make their force felt other than through their naval power.

Commerce destroyers and harbor defense monitors alone are not sufficient. Captain Mahan has shown that although American privateers did immense damage to English commerce during the war of 1812, yet the commerce of England increased with great rapidity, because by means of her battleships she kept control of the sea and blockaded our ports.

For many years the policy of the United States has been to maintain a strictly defensive navy, apparently forgetting that this would give an opponent the option of attacking and secure him from attack whenever he ceased to press the offensive. It is an axiom of war that the best defense is an aggresive offensive movement. If our first line of defense is confined to our coasts, we must simply man the defenses and sit there until in his own good time the opponent chooses to attack. If our first line of defense is a fleet of modern sea-going battleships, we have the advantage of making the attack near the opponent's coast if we so choose, and derive all the advantage of beginning, at our option, the warfare thousands of miles from our own defenseless cities.

Kinds of Battleships.

The battleships of the United States are divided into two classes, the coast-line defense battleship and the sea-going battleship. A coast-line defense battleship lies lower in the water, the sides are not so high and the heavy guns are not carried so far above the water line. In moderately still water this would be an advantage, as it would not present so large a target for the enemy's guns, but as the water roughens the advantage decreases and becomes a weakness.

The "Indiana," the "Massachusetts" and the "Oregon," three sister ships, are our coast-line defense battleships. The "Iowa" is at present the only sea-going battleship in commission, but to this list will soon be added the "Kentucky," "Kearsarge," "Alabama," "Wisconsin" and "Illinois."

The "Oregon."

She was made at the Union Iron Works at San Francisco, Cal., and her exceptionally fine performance in her long voyage attracted such attention that her builder, I. N. Scott, was at once invited by the Czar of Russia to come to St. Petersburg and make contracts for building Russian war vessels. As an illustration of how long it takes us to build a good battleship, the "Oregon" was authorized by the act of June 30, 1890; the contract was signed with the builder November 19 following; the keel was laid November 19, 1891; she was launched October 26, 1893; date of completion, according to contract, November 19, 1893, and was first commissioned July 15, 1896, rather more than six years from the time Congress passed the act authorizing her construction. The "Oregon" class are the heaviest gunned battleships in the world — that is, they mount more heavy guns than any other, but many others excel them in energy of gun-fire per minute.

The "Oregon" is 348 feet long, 69 feet 3 inches wide and draws, when fully loaded, 27 feet 1 3-4 inches of water. She then displaces 10,288 tons. Her motive power is furnished by twin-screw vertical triple-expansion engines — that is, the vessel has two screw propellers, and the steam from her boilers is used three times: first when fresh from the boiler on the high pressure cylinder, then, as it cools somewhat, in the intermediate cylinder; last, as it becomes cooler, in the low pressure cylinder. At her trial she made an average speed of 16.79 knots for four hours.

She made her remarkable voyage from San Francisco,

Cal., to Jupiter Inlet, Fla., 13,000 miles, at an average speed of more than 13 knots an hour for the whole distance. She made 375 miles in one day, an average of nearly 16 knots an hour. The fortitude of her firemen is shown when we remember that during the whole of this voyage the temperature in the engine-room never fell below 125° and sometimes reached 150.°

In the pursuit of the "Cristobal Colon" off Santiago, when her men in the fire-room were falling from exhaustion, the engineer asked Captain Clark to fire a gun, because if the men could hear the music of the guns and feel that they were in the thick of the action their indomitable pluck would enable them to return to their work.

Her primary battery consists of 4 13-inch guns mounted in pairs in turrets fore and aft, 8 8-inch guns mounted in pairs in four turrets, two on each side, and 4 6-inch guns, two on each side.

Her secondary battery of rapid-fire guns consists of 20 6-pounders, 6 1-pounders, 4 Gatlings and 2 field guns.

The armor belt of the "Oregon" is 190 feet long, 7½ feet wide and 18 inches thick. At each end there is a barbette running from the protective deck to the 13-inch guns, 35 feet in diameter, 17 inches thick and 12 feet high. The turrets of the 13-inch guns are 15 inches thick and the bases are protected by the barbettes. The turrets of the 8-inch guns are 8 inches thick but have no protection at the base. A 6-inch shell well placed would put them out of service. Above the armor belt up to the gun deck the sides are protected by 5-inch armor. The conning tower has 10-inch armor. The 6-inch guns are protected by 6-inch armored casemates.

The "Iowa."

Differs chiefly from the "Oregon" class in being a little larger, having a higher freeboard, mounting 12-inch guns in place of 13-inch, and 6 4-inch rapid-fire guns in place of 4 6-inch slow-fire guns. The armor of the "Iowa" is not so thick as that of the "Oregon" but it has been treated by the reforging process which is supposed to increase materially its efficiency. She is a fine, seagoing battleship, and could use her upper guns in a gale when those of the "Oregon" would be unserviceable.

"Kentucky" and "Kearsarge."

The striking feature of these vessels is the placing of an 8-inch turret above the 13-inch turret. By this arrangement the ship saves the weight of 2 turrets and 4 8-inch guns, and is able to bring as many guns to bear on each broadside as the "Oregon." The disadvantages are that if the 13-inch turrets were disabled it would put the 8-inch turrets out of action also. They mount 14 5-inch rapid-fire guns and should be superior to the ships of the "Indiana" class.

According to law battleships are named after States, and in order to perpetuate the name "Kearsarge" a special act of Congress was necessary. She was launched March 24, 1898, and Mrs. Herbert Winslow, wife of Lieutenant Winslow whose father commanded the old "Kearsarge" in her famous battle with the "Alabama," broke the time-honored bottle of wine over the bow of the new ship and said "I christen thee ⸰ Kearsarge.'"

The Kentucky was christened with a bottle of water taken from a spring where Abraham Lincoln as a boy used to drink. They should be ready for commission January of 1899.

"Alabama," "Wisconsin" and "Illinois."

These seagoing battleships will be complete and ready for commission about October, 1899. They will differ from ships now in commission in having 13-inch guns that can be fired almost twice as fast, and fourteen 6-inch rapid-fire guns in place of 8-inch and 6-inch slow-fire guns of the "Indiana" class.

NEW BATTLESHIPS. — By act of May 4, 1897, three new battleships were authorized, to be known as numbers ten, eleven and twelve, and named "Maine," "Missouri" and "Ohio." These ships are to be 386 feet long, 72 feet wide, draw $23\frac{1}{2}$ feet of water, with a displacement of 11,500 tons, fitted with ram bows and two military masts with fighting tops mounting three machine guns in each.

There will be a belt of armor extending from the bow as far astern as the after turret. This will be $16\frac{1}{2}$ inches thick and $7\frac{1}{2}$ feet wide over the middle portion and taper to 4 inches thickness at the bow. Connecting the ends of the belt will be a transverse bulkhead at least 12 inches thick with another forward of the boiler space, the same thickness. The turrets will be protected by barbettes 15 inches in thickness in the front and 10 inches in the rear. There will be side armor from the armor belt up to the main deck, and extending from barbette to barbette, $5\frac{1}{2}$ inches thick. The turrets will be 14 inches thick. A protective deck 5 inches thick on the slopes and $2\frac{3}{4}$ inches thick on the flat will extend the whole length of each vessel, and about the water line will be a belt of cellulose.

The primary battery will consist of four 13-inch guns mounted in two barbette turrets on the midship line, one forward and one aft, ten 6-inch rapid-fire guns on broadside of the main deck and four 6-inch rapid-fire guns on the upper deck within the superstructure. The 6-inch guns will be protected by $5\frac{1}{2}$-inch armor, and between the guns there will be a splinter bulkhead (partition), $1\frac{1}{2}$ inches thick.

The secondary battery will consist of at least twenty-four small rapid-fire and machine guns. The smaller guns will be protected by gun shields, and each vessel will carry two submerged torpedo tubes.

BATTLESHIPS.

NAME AND DATE OF LAUNCH.	BATTERIES.		ARMOR.					Speed, knots; displacem't, tons.	Gun fire for one minute.
	Main.	Secondary.	Belt.	Barb.	Turrets.	Slopes.	Flat.		
			Inch.	Inch.	Inch.	Inch.	Inch.		Foot-tons.
Alabama . . . . . May 18, 1898.	4 13″ B. L. R. 14 6″ R. F. guns.	16 6-pdr. R. F. 4 1-pdr. R. F. 1 Colt. 2 field guns.	Top 16½ Bottom 9½. Water line 13¾.	15 10	17 15	For'd 3″. Aft. 4″.	2¾.	16 11,525	403,644
Illinois.	Same as	Alabama.							
Indiana. . . . . . . Feb. 28, 1893.	4 13″ B. L. R. 8 8″ B. L. R. 4 6″ B. L. R.	20 6-pdr. R. F. 6 1-pdr. R. F. 4 Gatlings.	18	17 8 6	15 6		2¾.	15.547 10,288	209,688
Iowa . . . . March 28, 1896.	4 12″ B. L. R. 8 8″ B. L. R. 6 4″ R. F. guns.	26 6-pdr. R. F. 4 1-pdr. R. F. 4 Colts. 2 field guns.	14	15 8 & 6	15 8 7		2¾.	17.087 11,340	250,378
Kearsarge . . . . March 24, 1898.	4 13″ B. L. R. 4 8″ B. L. R. 14 5″ R. F. guns.	20 6-pdr. R. F. 6 1 pdr. R. F. 4 Colts. 2 field guns.	Top 16½ Bottom 9½. Water line 13¾.	15 12	17 15 11 9	For'd 3″. Aft. 5″.	2¾.	16 11,525	423,312
Kentucky. . . .	Same as	Kearsarge							
Massachusetts. June 10, 1893.	4 13″ B. L. R. 8 8″ B. L. R. 4 6″ B. L. R.	20 6-pdr. R. F. 4 1-pdr. R. F. 4 Gatlings. 2 field guns.	18	17 8 6	15 6		2¾.	16.21 10,288	209,688
Oregon . . . . . October 26, 1893.	4 13″ B. L. R. 8 8″ B. L. R. 4 6″ B. L. R.	20 6-pdr. R. F. 4 1-pdr. R. F. 4 Gatlings. 2 field guns.	18	17 8 6	15 6			16.79 10,288	209,688
Wisconsin	4 13″ B. L. R. 14 6″ R.F. guns	16 6-pdr. R. F. 4 1-pdr. R. F. 1 Colt. 2 field guns.	Top 16½. Bottom 9½. Water line 13¾.	15 10	17 15	For'd. 3″. Aft. 4″.	2¾.	16 11,525	403,644

Our Modern Monitors.

The United States has six modern, double turreted monitors, of low freeboard, coast-defense type. They are of iron hull, excepting the "Monterey," which is of steel. The "Amphitrite," "Monadnock," "Monterey," and "Puritan," each have two steel barbette turrets; the "Miantonomah" and the "Terror" have turrets without the barbettes; and those of the "Miantonomah" are of compound instead of all steel armor. They each have one military mast.

NAME AND DATE OF LAUNCH.	BATTERIES.		ARMOR IN INCHES.			Speed, knots; displacement, tons.	Gun fire per minute.
	Main.	Secondary.	Sides.	Turrets.	Barb.		Foot-tons.
Amphitrite.... June 7, 1883.	4 10" B. L. R. 2 4" R. F. guns.	2 6-pdr. R. F. 2 3-pdr. R. F. 2 37mm H. R. C. 2 1-pdr. R. F. G.	9 5	7½	11½	10.5 3,990	88,590
Miantonomah.. December 5, 1876.	4 10" B. L. R.	2 6-pdr. R. F. G. 2 3-pdr. R. F. G. 2 1-pdr. R. F. G.	7	11½		10.5 3,990	61,140
Monadnock.... September 19, 1883.	4 10" B. L. R. 2 4" R. F. guns.	2 6-pdr. R. F. 2 3-pdr. R. F. 2 37mm H. R. C. 2 1-pdr. R. F. G.	9 5	7½	11½	12 3,990	88,590
Monterey..... April 28, 1891.	2 12" B. L. R. 2 10" B. L. R.	6 6-pdr. R. F. 4 1-pdr. R. F. 2 Gatlings.	13 8 6	For'd 8" Aft 7½"	For'd 13" Aft 11½"	13.6 4,084	82,540
Puritan...... December 6, 1882.	4 12" B. L. R. 6 4" R. F. guns.	6 6-pdr. R. F. 2 37mm H. R. C. 2 1-pdr. R. F.	14 10 6	8	14	12.4 6,060	186,290
Terror....... March 24, 1883.	4 10" B. L. R.	2 6-pdr. R. F. 2 3-pdr. R. F. 2 37mm H. R. C. 2 1-pdr. R. F. 2 Gatlings.	7	11½		10.5 3,990	61,140

Armored Cruisers.

The United States has built but two armored cruisers, the "New York" and the "Brooklyn," and the war with Spain has shown us how useful these were and how desirable others would be. Lieutenant Eberle of the United States navy, in the "Naval Institute" for March, says: "We should have more armored cruisers, cruisers that can fight under all conditions of weather, to accompany our battleships for defensive purposes during the severe weather. When a vessel of the 'Oregon' type is in a moderate gale, rolling from fifteen to twenty-five degrees, with her main deck awash, an armored cruiser of the 'Brooklyn' class could come along and 'knock seven bells' out of her."

Cruisers are Named After Cities.—"New York."

The "New York" was the first of these vessels built. She was authorized by the act of Congress, Sept. 7, 1888, and the contract let to Wm. Cramp & Sons of Philadelphia, Pa. She was launched in 1891 and commissioned August 1, 1893. The cost of her hull and machinery was $2,985,000; armament about $1,000,000; whole cost $4,038,408.07. She was the finest and most powerful armored cruiser in the world, but in five years marked advances in naval architecture have been made and she no longer occupies that proud position. She is 380 feet 6 1-2 inches long; 64 feet 10 inches wide; and draws, fully loaded, 26 feet 8 inches of water, giving her 8,200 tons displacement. Her engines of 17,401 I. H. P. move twin screw propellers which gave her a trial record of 21 knots an hour. She can steam 13,500 miles at a 10-knot speed without re-coaling. She is covered by a protective deck 6 inches thick on the slopes and 3 inches on the flat, and carries on her side a belt of armor over the machinery space, 4 inches in thickness. The turrets are 5 1-2 inches thick, and their bases, turning machinery, etc., is protected by barbettes. Her broadside guns are protected by 4 inches of armor and from each barbette run down to the magazine armored tubes through which the ammunition is hoisted to her heavy guns.

Her armament consists of six 8-inch slow-fire rifles, two in the forward turret, two in the aft, and one each in the broadside turrets. She mounts on each broadside six 4-inch rapid-fire guns. Her secondary battery of rapid-fire guns consists of eight 6-pdr. and two 1-pdr., four Gatlings and two field guns. She has two tubes for firing Whitehead torpedoes.

Her high freeboard gives her light and air, and fine quarters for the officers and crew, and places her heavy guns 25 feet above the water line. The ship has four engines, each screw propeller being driven by two. Off Santiago the "Cristobal Colon" had about seven miles the start of the "New York," which was slowly steaming in the opposite direction with her forward engines uncoupled when the "Colon" appeared, but in spite of all the disadvantages the "New York" caught her after a run of about forty-five miles, and did not use her forward engines either.

The energy of fire for one minute of the primary batteries of the "New York" is 209,688 foot-tons. It is to be regretted that so good a ship as the "New York" is fitted with so poor an armament; 8-inch rapid-fire guns are now made that have far more energy and can be fired five times as fast as those of the "New York."

"Brooklyn."

The "Brooklyn" was authorized by act of Congress in 1892, and contract awarded the Cramps who had been so successful in building the "New York." The vessel was launched in 1895, and entered into commission December, 1896. She has greater displacement, coal endurance and gun power than the "New York." Her admirers claim that she has more speed, for the "Brooklyn" at her trial averaged 21.91 knots for four hours and earned a premium of $350,000 for her builders. But on that trial the "Brooklyn" only displaced 8,150 tons, and when fully manned and equipped she displaces 9,215 tons. She is 400 feet 6 inches long, 64 feet 8 1-4 inches wide, and draws, fully loaded, 26 feet 2 inches of water. She is moved by vertical triple expansion engines of 18,769 indicated horse-power, driving twin screw propellers. She has a protective deck the same as the "New York," 6 inches on the slopes and 3 inches on the flat. Her turrets are 5½ inches in thickness, protected by barbettes 8 inches thick in front and 4 inches in the rear. The boilers are all below the protective deck, placed in three water-tight compartments. The hull is made of mild steel, and is subdivided into 242 water-tight compartments. For the greater part of its length the bottom is double and 3 1-2 feet thick. The armor belt is 192 feet long, 8 feet wide and 3 inches thick, and extends along the sides opposite the engine and boiler spaces. All the armor is of Harveyized nickel steel. The ship has two military masts, each with two fighting tops, a ram bow, four torpedo tubes, three very high smoke stacks, which are almost equivalent to giving her a forced draft.

The armament consists of eight 8-inch slow-fire guns, mounted in pairs in four turrets, one forward, one aft and one on each side. There are twelve 5-inch rapid-fire guns mounted in sponsons on each side. Her secondary battery consists of twelve 6-pdr., four 1-pdr. guns, four Colt automatics, four machine guns and two field guns. The energy of gun fire of the primary battery for one minute is 284,168 foot tons. Her splendid service off Santiago has made her name a familiar one. In the battle in which Cervera's fleet was destroyed, the "Brooklyn" was struck twenty times by shell and many times by pieces of bursting shell and the smaller shot of machine guns.

The "Columbia."

The "Columbia" and "Minneapolis" were far and away the finest and speediest protected cruisers in the world at the time they were completed, and the "Columbia" holds the international long-distance record for cruisers, as the "Oregon" does for battleships. That she might be given the test of an ocean voyage she was ordered to run from Southampton, England to New York at full speed. She left Southampton Friday July 6, 1895, and reached Sandy Hook the following Friday, having steamed the entire distance 3,090 knots in 6 days, 23 hours and 49 minutes, at an average speed of 18.41 knots an hour. The whole trip was made under natural draft. It was intended to make one day's run under forced draft, but her complement of men was not sufficient to enable her to get the coal from her farther bunkers to her furnaces fast enough.

The "Columbia" has a displacement of 7,375 tons, a speed of 22.8 knots and an armament of one 8-inch, two 6-inch slow-fire and eight 4-inch rapid-fire guns in her primary battery. Her secondary battery of rapid-fire guns consists of twelve 6-pdr., four 1-pdr., two Colts and one field gun. Her gun power is not formidable, but she was built for speed rather than fighting.

The "Minneapolis."

The sister ship of the "Columbia" closely resembling her in most respects. She has two very large smokestacks in place of the four smaller ones of the "Columbia," carries more coal, has more powerful engines and a little higher speed, having the record of 23.07 knots. Her armament is the same as that of the "Columbia."

The "Olympia."

Dewey's famous flagship is our most powerful protected cruiser. She has a speed of 21.7 knots and a powerful armament of four 8-inch slow-fire guns in pairs in two turrets of Harveyized steel 3½ inches thick, whose bases are protected by barbettes of 4-inch nickel-steel, an unusual protection for the armament of so light a cruiser, ten 5-inch rapid-fire broadside guns mounted in sponsons 4 inches thick. The arrangement is such that she can fire five of them directly ahead or astern and use five of them in broadside. Her secondary battery consists of fourteen 6-pdr., seven 1-pdr., four Gatlings and one field gun.

The following table will show the strength of the United States in protected cruisers, many of them have been refitted and the "Newark," "Charleston" and "Chicago" have been rebuilt.

Ram "Katahdin."

The "Katahdin" is the only ship of its kind in any navy in the world. She was authorized in 1889, and went into commission in 1896. She is 250 feet and 9 inches long, 43 feet and 5 inches wide, and draws 16 feet of water, and has a speed of 16.11 knots. The two cuts shown of her give a good idea of her peculiar shape that enables her to turn easily in the water. Her turtle-back deck is of 6-inch armor on the sides, tapering to two inches on top. The conning tower rising above this is heavily armored and when ready for action, water is let into some of her apartments until the edges of the boat are beneath the water line. Below she is protected by an armored belt five feet wide, ranging from six to three inches thick. In these days when the high power gun seems to have lately demonstrated its efficiency, the value of the ram remains to be proven, especially as this one has a speed less than that of the battleships.

PROTECTED CRUISERS.

NAME AND DATE OF LAUNCH.	BATTERIES.		ARMOR.		Speed, knots; Displacement, tons.	Cost.	Gun fire per minute.
	Main.	Secondary.	Slopes.	Flat.			
			Inches.	*Inches.*			
Atlanta October 9, 1884.	6 6" R. F. guns. 2 8" B. L. R.	2 6-pdr. R. F. 2 3-pdr. R. F. 2 1-pdr. R. F. 2 Colts. 1 field gun.	1½	1½	15.60 3,000	$ 617,000	131,366 foot-tons.
Baltimore October 6, 1888.	4 8" B. L. R. 6 6" B. L. R.	4 6-pdr. R. F. 2 3-pdr. R. F. 2 1-pdr. R. F. 4 37 H. R. C. 2 Colts. 1 field gun.	4	2½	20.096 4,413	1,325,000	48,682 foot-tons.
Boston December 4, 1884.	6 6" B. L. R. 2 8" B. L. R.	2 6-pdr. R. F. 2 3-pdr. R. F. 2 1-pdr. R. F. 2 47 H. R. C. 2 37 H. R. C. 2 Gatlings.	1½	1½	15.60 3,000	619,000	32,660 foot-tons.
Charleston July 19, 1888.	2 8" B. L. R. 6 6" B. L. R.	4 6-pdr. R. F. 2 3-pdr. R. F. 2 1-pdr. R. F. 4 37 H. R. C. 2 Colts. 1 field gun.	3	2	18.20 3,730	1,017,500	32,660 foot-tons.
Chicago December 5, 1885.	4 8" B. L. R. 14 5" R. F. guns.	2 6-pdr. R. F. 2 1-pdr. R. F. 2 Colts. 1 field gun.	1½	1½	18 4,500	889,000	288,804 foot-tons.
Cincinnati November 10, 1892.	10 5" R. F. guns. 1 6" B. L. R.	8 6-pdr. R. F. 2 1-pdr. R. F. 2 Colts. 1 field gun.	2½	1	19 3,213	1,100,000	186,173 foot-tons.

Protected Cruisers—Continued.

NAME AND DATE OF LAUNCH.	BATTERIES. Main	BATTERIES. Secondary	ARMOR. Slopes	ARMOR. Flat.	Speed, knots; Displacement, tons.	Cost.	Gun fire per minute.
Columbia...... July 26, 1892.	1 8″ B. L. R. 2 6″ B. L. R. 12 4″ R. F. guns.	12 6-pdr. R. F. 4 1-pdr. R. F. 4 Colts. 1 field gun.	4	2	22.8 7,375	2,725,000	123,357 foot-tons.
Minneapolis... August 12, 1893.	1 8″ B. L. R. 2 6″ B. L. R. 8 4″ R. F. guns.	12 6-pdr. R. F. 4 1-pdr. R. F. 2 Colts. 1 field gun.	4	2½	23.073 7,375	2,690,000	123,357 foot-tons.
Newark...... March 19, 1890.	12 6″ R. F. guns.	8 6-pdr. R. F. 4 1-pdr. R. F. 4 Colts. 1 field gun.	3	2	19 4,098	1,248,000	230,688 foot-tons.
Olympia...... November 5, 1892.	10 5″ R. F. guns. 4 8″ B. L. R. Armor 3½ and 4½ inches.	14 6-pdr. R. F. 7 6-pdr. R. F. 6 Gatlings. 1 field gun.	4¾	2	21.686 5,870	1,796,000	325,444 foot-tons.
Philadelphia.. September 7, 1889.	12 6″ B. L. R.	4 6-pdr. R. F. 4 3-pdr. R. F. 2 1-pdr. R. F. 3 37mm H. R. C. 4 Gatlings. 1 field gun.	4	2½	19.678 4,324	1,350,000	33,276 foot-tons.
Raleigh...... March 31, 1892.	10 5″ R. F. guns. 1 6″ B. L. R.	8 6-pdr. R. F. 4 1-pdr. R. F. 2 Gatlings. 1 field gun.	2½	1	19 3,213	1,100,000	186,173 foot-tons.
San Francisco. October 26, 1889.	12 6″ B. L. R.	4 6-pdr. R. F. 4 3-pdr. R. F. 2 1-pdr. R. F. 3 37mm H. R. C. 4 Gatlings. 1 field gun.	3	2	19.525 4,098	1,428,000	33,276 foot-tons.

THE ASCENDENCY OF AMERICA. 379

U. S. RAM KATAHDIN.

Showing how her keel structure allows her to turn quickly.

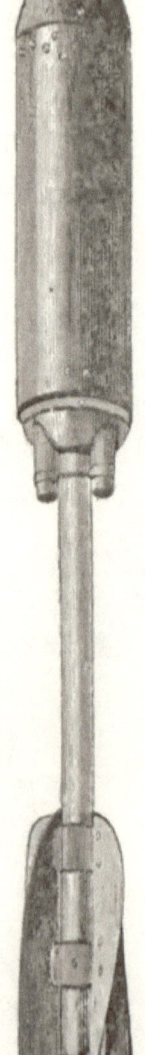

COMPLETE PROJECTILE OF DYNAMITE CRUISER "VESUVIUS."

The screw-like tail gives a rotary motion to the projectile, as "rifling" does to a bullet, and keeps it from turning end over end. Extreme length of projectile, about 8 feet; diameter, about 14¾ inches; explosive.

Charge, 50 to 250 pounds of guncotton.

Dynamite Gun Boat "Vesuvius."

The United States possesses in this vessel the only one of its type found in any navy. She was built by William Cramp & Sons of Philadelphia, Pa., and cost $350,000, exclusive of her armament. This consist of three 15-inch dynamite guns, with a secondary battery of three 3-pound rapid-fire guns. She has a displacement of 929 tons and a speed record on her trial of 21.42 knots. The peculiar feature of the "Vesuvius" is the three dynamite tubes, 54 feet long, built into the boat and passing from below the water line up through her deck, at an angle of about 18°. The screw-shape vane gives a rotary motion to the projectile when fired and keeps it from turning end over end. Four sizes of the projectiles are made, the largest about 15 inches in diameter, and carrying about 250 pounds of gun cotton. The "Vesuvius" is really a floating gun carriage. The guns are aimed by turning the boat until the tubes point in the proper direction. The elevation is given by the amount of compressed air admitted into the gun. Great things have been expected of her, but as yet she is almost an unknown quantity. The work done at Santiago seems to have been to frighten rather than to harm people. In experiments made by the ordnance department last year 307 pounds of wet gun cotton was hung against the face of a thick steel plate and a chicken tied 43 feet away. The heat of the explosion only burned the face of the plate, and the chicken was scorched, but not killed.

Unprotected Cruisers.

The United States has three unprotected cruisers, the "Detroit," "Marblehead" and "Montgomery," each having a displacement of 2,089 tons. The "Marblehead" will be remembered for her effective work in support of the marines landed at Guantanamo Bay, Cuba. They each have an armament of 10 5-inch rapid-fire guns, with a secondary battery of 6 6-pounders, 2 1-pounders, 2 Colt's and one field gun. They have no armor protection except gun shields.

Unarmored Steel Gunboats.

"Bancroft," "Bennington," "Castine," "Concord,' "Helena," "Machias," "Nashville," "Petrel," "Wilmington" and "Yorktown." The "Machias," the largest, has a displacement of 1,777 tons; the "Bancroft," the smallest, 839 tons. "Petrel," 892 tons, was the little boat sent into the shoal water to finish off the Spanish fleet at Manila. The "Castine," "Helena," "Machias," "Nashville" and "Wilmington" each mount 8 4-inch rapid-fire guns in their main battery; the "Bennington," "Concord" and "Yorktown" each mounts 6 6-inch slow-fire guns; the "Petrel" 4 6-inch slow-fire, and the "Bancroft" 4 4-inch rapid-fire. They all have some machine guns.

Composite Gunboats.

"Annapolis," "Marietta," "Newport," "Princeton," "Vicksburg" and "Wheeling." These are all little boats of 1,000 tons displacement, and each has an armament of 6 4-inch rapid-fire guns, with a secondary battery 4 6-pounders, 2 1-pounders, one Colt and one field gun. The "Marietta" will be remembered for her exceptionally long cruise from Alaska to San Francisco, thence around the Horn to Florida with the battleship "Oregon."

Torpedo-boats and Torpedo-boat Destroyers.

These are named after distinguished naval officers not living. Of these there are built the following torpedo-boats: "Cushing," "Ericsson," "Foote," "Stilleto," "Porter."

There are now being built, or authorized to be built:

TORPEDO-BOATS.		TORPEDO-BOAT DESTROYERS.	
"Rogers,"	"Barney,"	"Bainbridge,"	"Macdonough,"
"Winslow,"	"Biddle,"	"Barry,"	"Paul Jones,"
"Dahlgren,"	"Blakely,"	"Chauncey,"	"Perry."
"T. A. M. Craven,"	"DeLong,"	"Dale,"	"Preble."
"Davis,"	"Nicholson,"	"Decatur,"	"Stewart,"
"Fox,"	"O'Brien,"	"Hopkins,"	"Truxtun,"
"Morris,"	"Shubrick,"	"Hull,"	"Whipple,"
"Talbot,"	"Stockton,"	"Lawrence,"	"Worden."
"Gwin,"	"Thornton,"		
"Mackenzie,"	"Tingey,"		
"Bagley,"	"Wilkes."		

Secretary Long in his report for 1897 summarized the naval strength of the United States as follows:

First-class battleships	9	Special class	6
Second-class battleships	2	Steel torpedo-boats	22
Armored cruisers	2	Wood torpedo-boats	1
Armored rams	1	Iron cruising vessels	5
Double-turreted monitors	6	Wooden cruising vessels	11
Single-turreted monitors	13	Sailing vessels	6
Protected cruisers	13	Tugs	14
Unprotected cruisers	3	Wooden steam vessels unfit for sea service	8
Gun-boats	10		
Composite gun-boats	6	Wooden sailing vessels unfit for sea service	6

Of these, 109 were available for service. According to the report of the Navy Department, July 1st, 1898, we had 301 vessels, of which 236 were available, showing that in six months we had built or purchased 126 vessels and had lost only one, the "Maine." Some of these were tugs, colliers, receiving ships, etc. Of the 236, 38 were auxiliary cruisers and converted yachts.

CHAPTER XI.
Armor, Ordnance and Defense.

Something resembling armor was used in ancient days, but it was chiefly to strengthen the sides of the vessel to withstand the shock of the ram. Coming down to modern times, the Stevens family, who were such distinguished engineers, demonstrated that four inches of wrought iron plate would keep out spherical shot fired from the smooth-bore cannon of that day. Prior to 1812 explosive shells had been fired only from mortars, but Colonel Bomford of the United States army devised a long-chambered gun for firing shell directly at the target. This was called a columbiad. Little progress was made in the development of the idea here, but General Paixhan, a celebrated artillerist of France, took up the idea and in 1822 perfected it. At the battle of Sinope nine Russian ships armed with smooth-bore shell guns opposed eleven Turkish ships armed with the ordinary cannon of the day. The battle lasted about an hour and only one Turkish ship escaped. French inventors were quick to realize the importance of this lesson, Napoleon III. ordering the construction of his iron-plated floating batteries, used with such great effect at Kimburn about two years later; and the great French naval engineer, Depuy De Lome, designed armored frigates.

Wrought iron plates had defeated the common shell and the solid round shot, and now began a battle-royal between the gunner and the armorer. The spherical shot gave place to an elongated form with a sharp point. This penetrated the plate and the gun scored its first victory. The armorer, seeing he must defeat the projectile by breaking it up, welded a face of steel over the wrought-iron backing and evolved "compound armor." Then the "Palliser" shot was cast, the point "chilled," making it very hard, and this penetrated and broke up the steel face of the armor-plate. The armorer replied with a solid steel plate and the defeat of the gun was predicted, but it was not for long. A steel projectile was soon used and the gun scored another victory. Then came the nickel alloy, which rendered the armor tougher and less likely to break upon attack, but the gunner replied by adding chromium to the steel he used, and produced a projectile equal to the nickel armor.

Harveyized Armor.

The American Harvey improved upon nickel steel by placing the armor-plate in the chamber of a furnace, covering the face with charcoal and heating the whole until the charcoal gave off some of its carbon, which was taken up by the face of the armor-plate. The plate was then "tempered," and Harveyized armor made a sensation in military circles.

William Corey, of Pittsburgh, Pa., in 1895, patented a method for compressing the plate after it had passed through all the former processes. According to his theory, super-carbonizing tends to crystallize steel. By his method the plate is reheated to a temperature of about 2,000° and subjected to enormous pressure, which restores its former tenacity and actually reduces the cubic contents of the plate about 5%.

In response to these methods, the artillerist, by a unique device, added 15% to the efficiency of his projectile. He covered the hard tempered steel point with a cap of soft steel, increased its velocity, and achieved a wonderful result. A 6-inch shell passed through a 10-inch reforged Harveyized plate, twelve inches of oak timbers, three boiler-plates of 7.16-inch wrought iron, and buried itself eight feet in the sand practically uninjured. A recent trial at the Indian Head proving grounds, Virginia, of a 6-inch plate made by the Carnegie company, according to German methods, showed a marked advance in the armor. At present Americans make better thin plate than found elsewhere, but the French and German methods have produced better heavy plate. The Bethlehem Iron Company and the Carnegie Company have secured rights to use European methods.

At present the gun has much the better of the argument, and its resources are not exhausted. A service charge in the United States navy produces a pressure within the gun of about fifteen tons per square inch. Wire-wound guns have sustained a pressure per square inch of thirty-two tons, and slow-burning powder has given a velocity of over 3,000 feet a second, and the gunner has these in reserve.

Velocity in Foot-seconds.

This term means the number of feet a projectile flies in a second. The rate of speed at the muzzle of a gun is called muzzle velocity. "High-power guns" in the United States are those whose projectiles have a muzzle velocity of 2,000 or more feet a second. Sound travels 1,100 feet a second, and a bullet from the best modern rifles moves more than twice as fast.

The three chief reasons why a high velocity is desirable are:

1. When shooting at an object in motion, that the bullet may shoot the mark before the object has time to move far.

2. Penetration and energy are greater with a high velocity, being approximately in proportion to the square of the velocity. A shot with a velocity of 2,000 feet a second would penetrate four times as far as a shot with a velocity of 1,000 feet a second.

3. The path of the projectile is not a straight line, but a curve, and at long range part of its course is so far from a straight line as to be above the target at which it is fired. *Danger space* is the horizontal distance through

which the projectile passes when it is neither too far above nor too far below to strike the target. The higher the velocity the straighter the path of the ball. A shell thrown from a mortar at an angle of 55° or 60° has a danger space as wide as the deck of the vessel at which it is aimed ; a shell from a " high power gun " aimed directly at the target has a much wider danger space.

Gun Making.

The invention of gunpowder is popularly ascribed to two monks, Roger Bacon, who wrote of it in 1267 and Bertholdus Schwartz about 1320, but there is ample evidence to show that gunpowder or something very much like it was used by the Chinese in the propulsion of rockets 1,000 years before, and the exact formula for gunpowder was known to the Arab chemists as early as the close of the 8th century. The Moors early introduced fire-arms into western Europe and are said to have used artillery against Saragossa (A. D. 1118) and it seems certain that a little later they defended Niebla by machinery which threw darts and stones by the means of fire. Artillery is said to have been used by Henry III. of England against the Duke of Gloucester in 1267, by the Spaniards against Cordova in 1280 and it is shown by the expense accounts of Edward III. that cannon were used in his wars.

Until recently, nearly all guns were made from cast iron. Sir William Armstrong said that for his first experiments he was unable to obtain steel large enough to make a gun with calibre one inch in diameter. It was the need of some material stronger than iron for use in projectiles and guns that stimulated Bessemer in his effort to make cheap steel. His discovery revolutionized gun making.

A " Built-up " Gun.

The principle parts of the gun are, the tube, a hollow steel forging extending the full length of the bore, the jacket, covering about two-fifths of the tube; the jacket-hoops shrunken over the jacket; and the chase-hoops shrunken over that part of the tube in front of the jacket.

The gun is subjected to two stresses, one transverse, the other longitudinal. The tube takes up the greater part of the transverse, and the jacket the longitudinal stress.

Let us suppose a half dozen hoops, placed one within another and fitting loosely. An expansive force exerted within the inner hoop will burst it before much stress is felt upon the next hoop and the stress being delivered from one to another successively, hardly more force is required to burst all the hoops than to burst any one. Suppose another arrangement of the hoops by which the first hoop is clasped by the second and the second clasped tighter by the third, and so on to the outer one. The expansive force then exerted within the innermost hoop must be sufficient to burst all of them combined. The built-up gun is based on that principle.

The steel in a gun must be of the best quality. In battle the gun will be hit by projectiles; in firing the rifling will be subjected to enormous stress, and the gases formed by the exploding powder have a destructive effect upon the steel. The United States uses steel made by the "Siemens Open Hearth Process," subjected to the Whitworth process of fluid compression. When the steel is melted it is poured into a strong cylinder and subjected to hydraulic pressure, which squeezes out the gas or air bubbles within the casting and makes the metal much denser and devoid of flaws. Severe tests of the metal are made, and it must show an elastic limit of from 46,000 to 50,000 pounds to the square inch without a permanent change in form. In its test for tensile strength it must stretch at least fifteen per cent before giving way under a stress of from 86,000 to 93,000 pounds to the square inch. The "tube" is cast solid, then bored and a heavy steel **shaft** (mandrel) passed through on which the tube is subjected to hydraulic pressure **or** hammer forging to enlarge and elongate **it**. It is **then** roughly finished, **tempered** in oil and **sent** to **the** gun factory **at** Washington. Upon arriving at the shop the tube is **put into** an enormous lathe and turned to exactly **the required** diameter, then placed upright in a pit adjoining a **furnace** wherein the jacket is being heated. The jacket has been carefully bored out and its **inner diameter is** slightly smaller than the outer diameter of the tube. It is placed within a chamber, where it is heated by air blown through a white hot **furnace** burning crude oil. It is subjected to this for twenty-nine hours, until the temperature is raised to about 600° Fahrenheit. It is carefully measured to see that it **is** expanded enough to go over the tube, seized by **a** crane, carried to the pit where the tube is and lowered **over it** at about the rate of a foot a minute until it clasps the rear part of the tube and extends back of it far enough **to** form the **screw** box where the breech mechanism **is** contained. **When** in the desired position the interior of the gun is cooled by streams **of** water. When thoroughly cool it is placed in the lathe, the other part carefully turned to a new diameter and the other hoops shrunk on. Each process is expensive and requires the greatest care.

Breech Mechanism.

The breech **of** the **gun is** closed **by a steel** plug, threaded and screwed **in.** In the innerpart of the jacket that projects over the **rear of** the tube (screwbox), **is cut a** heavy screw thread. **It** is then divided **into 12** parts and alternate divisions cut away, so that half **the** screw-box **is** made **up** of threaded surface **and** half of channels where the thread has been cut away. The breech-plug **is cut in the** same manner, and when **in position** can be pushed directly into the **gun,** the

THIRTEEN INCH GUN AT PROVING GROUNDS.

S, sleeve; C, cylinder; P, piston; B P, breech plug; H H', hinges of the tray; Tr, tray; Sc, screw turning the breech plug. Weight, 60½ tons; Range, 12 miles; Projectile weighs 1100 lbs., and penetrates 22 inches of steel at the distance of one mile. It costs nearly $700 each time the gun is fired.

threaded portion of the breech-plug fitting the channel in the jacket, and the threaded portion of the jacket fitting the corresponding channel in the breech-plug. The breech-plug is then given a slight turn and the threaded portion of the plug moves into the corresponding threaded portion of the screw-box, and the breech is securely closed. In the cut of the 6-inch rapid-fire gun the breech is open, the screw-box and the threaded portion of the plug are each shown, but in this case every other sixth part of the circumference has been cut away, instead of every other twelfth as in the 13-inch gun.

By means of a crank-like handle turning bevel gearing, the breech-plug is turned one-sixth or one-twelfth as required, the threads no longer interlock and the plug is moved directly back until it rests on the tray, the whole then swinging to one side, exposing the powder chamber and giving a chance to load the gun. Compare the cuts of the 13-inch and 6-inch guns.

Recoil.

The gun moves backward with the same energy the projectile moves forward and if not controlled this force would tear the ship to pieces or drive the gun through the deck.

The cannon of the 4th of July occasions with which the boys are familiar have projections called trunnions on which the guns rest, but no trunnion ever forged could withstand the recoil from a large cannon and even if the trunnions held, it would only be to tear the deck out of the ship. The recoil of a 16-inch gun is more than 64,000 tons, equivalent to lifting 64 loads of hay as high as the Eiffel Tower and yet this enormous force is controlled without allowing the gun to move more than three times the diameter of its bore. This is done by means of pistons working in " recoil cylinders" (see cut 13-inch gun). The thirteen-inch has four recoil cylinders fastened to the sleeve, with piston-rods fastened to the rear of the gun. The piston head is attached to the piston-rod and is in the front part of the cylinder when the gun is fired. The recoil cylinders are stationary. When the gun is fired it slides back in the sleeve and draws the piston-rod and head back through the cylinder. The cylinders are filled with water for the heavy guns and a mixture of water and glycerine for the lighter ones. Grooves are cut in the inner surface of the recoil cylinder and as the piston-head starts back the water passes the grooves, but in the back part of the cylinder the grooves grow shallower until they disappear, the resistance to the piston-head becoming greater and greater until the gun is brought to a stop with a recoil of only 39 inches. The water in front of the piston-head escapes through a valve and the hydraulic engine forces water into the cylinder in the rear of the piston-head which drives it to the front of the recoil cylinder and returns the gun to its former position "in battery."

The total length of the gun is 40 feet; weight, 60 1-2 tons; the greatest diameter of the gun body, 49 inches; the length of the rifled bore, 30.87 feet, rifling 52 grooves .05 of an inch deep. The projectile for the gun will weigh 1,100 pounds, is made of forged steel; its length about three times its diameter, fired by a charge of 550 pounds of brown powder. This will give a pressure in the powder chamber of 15 tons to the square inch, move the projectile with a velocity of 2,100 foot-seconds, give a muzzle energy of 33,627 foot-tons and penetrate 26 2-3 inches of steel at the muzzle. This gun fires a round in three minutes; the new one will have twice that speed.

The largest gun made in the United States is the 16-inch rifle, which when mounted will constitute a part of the harbor defense of New York City. This is one of the largest and most powerful cannon in the world. The gun when complete will weigh about 140 tons. Its extreme length will be nearly 50 feet, the shell will weigh 2,370 pounds; 1,060 pounds of brown powder will give the projectile a velocity at the muzzle of 2,000 feet a second and an energy of 64,084 foot-tons. Elevated at an angle of 45°, the extreme range of the gun should be 13.6 miles. It will be used only for harbor defense. The friends of the gun claim that no ship on earth can stand the terrible crushing effect of one of its projectiles at close range, and the opponents of the gun say that it is extremely unlikely that a ship in motion could be hit by it.

Twelve-Inch Mortars.

Modern mortars differ only from breech-loading rifles in length. They pass through the same processes of construction, load at the breech and are rifled. They fire explosive shells at a high angle. The shell is expected to describe a huge curve and descend upon the practically unprotected deck of the attacking ship. The thick armor of a ship is carried on the sides to withstand direct fire; it is possible to give but little protection against vertical or "plunging" fire. The 12-inch mortars defending the harbor of New York (see cut) are placed in pits beneath the surface of the ground. Their location is unknown to the general public, and there is nothing visible at a distance to indicate their presence. The field defended is laid off into a series of imaginary squares, and the gunner in the pit trains the mortar to bear upon any particular square as directed. It is not necessary that the gunner see the enemy; his movements can be directed from a distance by telephone. The mortar throws a shell 12 inches in diameter, weighing 1,000 pounds and charged with 100 pounds of explosive. They fire at an angle of 35° to 65° and have an effective range of five or six miles. This half ton of steel falling from the clouds would easily penetrate the protective deck of any ship afloat, and even if it didn't explode in the magazine or machinery compartments, would pass on through the bottom of the ship.

Disappearing Gun Carriages.

Heavy guns used for harbor defense are now mounted on disappearing gun carriages. The Buffington-Crosier carriage is probably as good as any, if not the best in the world. The gun is held on four long arms moved by hydraulic or pneumatic machinery. It is loaded beneath the level of the parapet over which it is raised, remains but an instant to be fired and then disappears from sight. Disappearing gun carriages, mines and heavy breech-loading mortars have increased materially the resources of the defense.

Extreme Range,

Several years ago a German 9.45-inch Krupp gun with an elevation of $45°$ attained a range of 12.42 miles. It is estimated that the projectile rose 4.6 miles above a straight line drawn from the firing point to the target; or, in other words, the gun might be fired over any range of mountains in America and hit the target on the other side. The celebrated "Queen's Jubilee" shot, fired in England, 1888, was made with a wire-wound 9.2-inch gun; the 380 pound projectile was given a muzzle velocity of 2,360 feet per second, and the gun with an elevation of $45°$ had a range of 12.4 miles. Guns on shipboard cannot be given an extreme elevation. The size of the turret ports will not allow it and the gun in its recoil would strike the deck. Guns in a turret can only be given an elevation of about $17°$ and have an effective range of perhaps six miles. The extreme range on land is believed to be $7\frac{1}{2}$ miles for the 6-inch gun; 9 miles for the 8-inch gun; 11 miles for the 10-inch gun; $11\frac{1}{2}$ miles for the 12-inch gun; $13\frac{1}{2}$ miles for the 16-inch gun.

Rapid-fire Guns.

In the old style gun the crew must get out of the way of the recoil, the gun must be sponged after each shot to put out any lingering sparks of fire before placing the powder charge, the breech mechanism was clumsy and slow, and after all these operations had been performed the gun must be aimed. Now, ammunition for rapid-fire guns is put up in metallic cases like revolver cartridge; the sponge is not required, the barrel of the gun alone recoils, the sights have been removed from the barrel and placed on the carriage and the gunner simply keeps his sights on the target, pays no attention to the loading of the gun, and squeezes an electric bulb when the gun is ready to be fired. The great weight of breech mechanism, powder and projectile, precludes making rapid-firers of the extremely heavy guns. The United States is behind other nations in this respect. On the Chilian cruiser " Blanco Encalada " four rounds were fired in 62 seconds from an 8-inch gun and the ammunition taken from the magazine below the protective deck. In the English navy a crew at drill fired an Elswick 8-inch gun three rounds in 28 seconds. On board the " Royal Sovereign " a 13.5-inch gun was fired seven rounds in 12 minutes, making six hits on a target at a range of 1,600 to 2,200 yards, while the ship was steaming at eight-knot speed. A similar gun on the " Empress of India " fired four rounds in six minutes. The following table shows what the best guns in the United States navy can do. One or more varieties of some of the guns are made and we have selected the best. The table is compiled from the 1898 edition of Radford's " Naval Gunnery."

DIAMETER OF BORE.	Rounds per Minute.	Muzzle Velocity.	Muzzle Energy.	Weight of Shell.	Weight of Powder.	Penetration in Steel. Inches.
4-inch gun........	15	2,000 foot-sec.	915 foot-tons.	33 lbs.	14 lbs.	7.18
5-inch gun........	12	2,230 foot-sec.	1,754 foot-tons.	50 lbs.	28 lbs.	9.
6-inch gun........	6	2,150 foot-sec.	3,204 foot-tons.	100 lbs.	47 lbs.	11.38
8-inch gun........	1	2,150 foot-sec.	8,011 foot-tons.	250 lbs.	115 lbs.	16.10
10-inch gun.......	1 in 2 min.	2,100 foot-sec.	15,285 foot-tons.	500 lbs.	240 lbs.	20.1
12-inch gun.......	1 in 2.8 min.	2,100 foot-sec.	25,985 foot-tons.	850 lbs.	425 lbs.	24.16
13-inch gun.......	1 in 3 min.	2,100 foot-sec.	33,627 foot-tons.	1100 lbs.	550 lbs.	26.66

Secondary Battery.

Smaller rapid-fire guns make up the secondary battery. Of these the Maxim, the Driggs-Schroeder and the Hotchkiss are the ones used in the United States. When these 6-pound guns were tested prior to purchase by the Government, the Hotchkiss fired 28 rounds in one minute, 83 rounds in three minutes; the Maxim, 20 rounds in one minute and 65 rounds in three minutes; the Driggs-Schroeder, 34 rounds in one minute and 83 rounds in three minutes. The honors are supposed to be about even between the Hotchkiss and the Driggs-Schroeder. The latter gun is made by the celebrated firm of Cramp Brothers of Philadelphia. The accuracy of the guns is remarkable. Ten rounds were fired at a target 26 feet by 40 feet, at a distance of a mile, all hitting the target, and the most of them pretty close to the center of impact.

Machine Guns.

These guns have a caliber and range about equal to that of a modern rifle. The Gatling, so called from its inventor, Dr. Richard Gatling of the United States, consists of ten barrels (sometimes five), made to turn something like the cylinder of a revolver, each barrel being fired as it comes opposite a given point. The gun is operated by turning a crank, has a range up to 1,000 yards or more, and in the hands of a cool and competent operator is one of the most deadly weapons of modern warfare.

In a test before a naval board 63,000 cartridges were fired without stopping to wipe out the barrels, and at the end of the test the gun was in good condition. Having ten barrels and firing one at a time the Gatling does not heat as do the single barrel guns. Its bore is 30-100 of an inch, bullet weighs 220 grains, has a muzzle velocity of 2,000 feet, and can penetrate 48 inches of pine. A

Gatling of .236 caliber using a smokeless cartridge has lately been perfected.

The Colt automatic is a new machine gun recently become familiar to us. It has a thick barrel and does not heat as rapidly from firing and so has no water-jacket. All that is necessary is to keep the finger pressed on the trigger and the gun aimed, and it continues to fire at the rate of 400 shots per minute until all the cartridges are exhausted. The cartridges are carried in a belt and fed into the gun by the recoil, each recoil of the barrel ejecting a shell and jerking a cartridge into place. The bullet weighs 112 grains of .236 caliber, moves with a muzzle velocity of 2,500 feet a second, and will penetrate 60 inches of pine boards. The gun alone weighs 40 pounds; with all its mountings complete, 94 pounds.

The cut herewith gives an excellent representation of the Maxim automatic gun. It is operated the same as the Colt, simply by pressing the trigger. In this case we see the barrel enveloped by a water-jacket to keep cool the parts heated by the friction of firing. Maxim has also made a fully automatic 9-pounder gun that fires 60 shots in a minute.

Projectiles.

The projectiles used for breech-loading guns are common armor-firing shell and shrapnel. Common shell is hollow, of cast or drawn steel, containing a bursting charge of powder exploded by a fuse either on impact or at the end of a certain length of time after leaving the gun. In length a shell is usually $3\frac{1}{2}$ times the caliber. Common shell are used against masonry, earthworks and unarmored sides of vessels, and are effective by reason of the explosion, which sets fire to inflammable material. In common shell a fuse is placed either in the nose or at the base. An armor-piercing shell made of forged steel with an especially hardened point formerly contained a small bursting charge ignited by heat generated by the penetration of the shell through the armor. Armor-piercing shell are made of forged, oil-tempered steel, treated by special processes, and containing special alloys to allow excessive hardness of point in tempering. Such shells are forged solid, turned to the required dimensions, bored out for the bursting charge, tempered and hardened. The base is closed by screwing into it a heavy steel plug. The point of the armor-piercing shell is covered with a lubricant, and over this is placed a cap of soft steel. The cap dishes the hard face of the armor to its elastic limit, and the projectile then passes through the cap, aided by the lubricant, and attacks the plate when it has left only the local resistance. Shrapnel shell is made of cast iron or of steel with much thinner walls, and is filled with small leaden balls packed in sulphur, with a small bursting charge of powder. Shrapnel is used against boats and exposed bodies of men. It is intended to explode before reaching the target, and the bursting charge placed in the base of the shell scatters the balls and drives them forward. The sulphur merely holds the balls in place. The compression band is a strip of soft copper fitted around the projectile near its base. The explosion of the charge forces the projectile past the compression slope, the copper is squeezed into the rifling grooves, prevents the escape of the gas and gives the whirling motion to the projectile, probably about 72 revolutions a second.

Smokeless Powder.

Black powder when exploded leaves 50% of solid residue, which appears in the form of smoke. A smokeless powder is one that on explosion generates nothing but gaseous matter. The volume of gas evolved from the same weight is much greater in smokeless powder than in black or brown powder, and the force exerted on the projectile is greater. Smokeless powder is usually made from gun cotton, nitro-glycerine, or some of its compounds. In appearance it is hard, lighter than the ordinary powder, pale yellow in color, and usually put up in the form of sticks about ⅜ of an inch in diameter, having a hole through the center. It also appears in flat strips. The English kind is called "cordite."

Small Arms.

The rifle used by the navy is the Lee–Metford, calibre .236; weight of bullet, 112 grains; powder, 33 grains; giving the bullet a muzzle velocity of 2,600 feet a second, and an extreme range of two miles. Up to 300 yards the Lee has greater penetration and a flatter trajectory than either the Krag or the Springfield. Used as a magazine gun it gives a greater rapidity of fire than either of the others. The bullet has a hard lead core covered with a copper jacket. The Krag–Jorgensen was invented by Col. Krag, chief of ordnance of Norway. The United States pays him a royalty of $1.00 on each gun. This is a magazine gun of .30 calibre; weight of bullet, 220 grains; powder, 40 grains; extreme range, 4,000 yards; muzzle velocity; 2,000 feet. The bullet is a steel shell, filled with lead to give it weight. Beyond 1,000 yards it is a more accurate gun than either the Springfield or the Lee. The Lee and the Krag gun each fire five shots and use smokeless powder. The Springfield is a single shot breach-loading gun, using black powder; calibre, .45; extreme range, 3,500 yards; velocity; 1,300 feet; with a leaden bullet. The wounds made by the small calibre guns at short range are frightful. As the bullet loses its velocity the wound becomes a small, clean puncture.

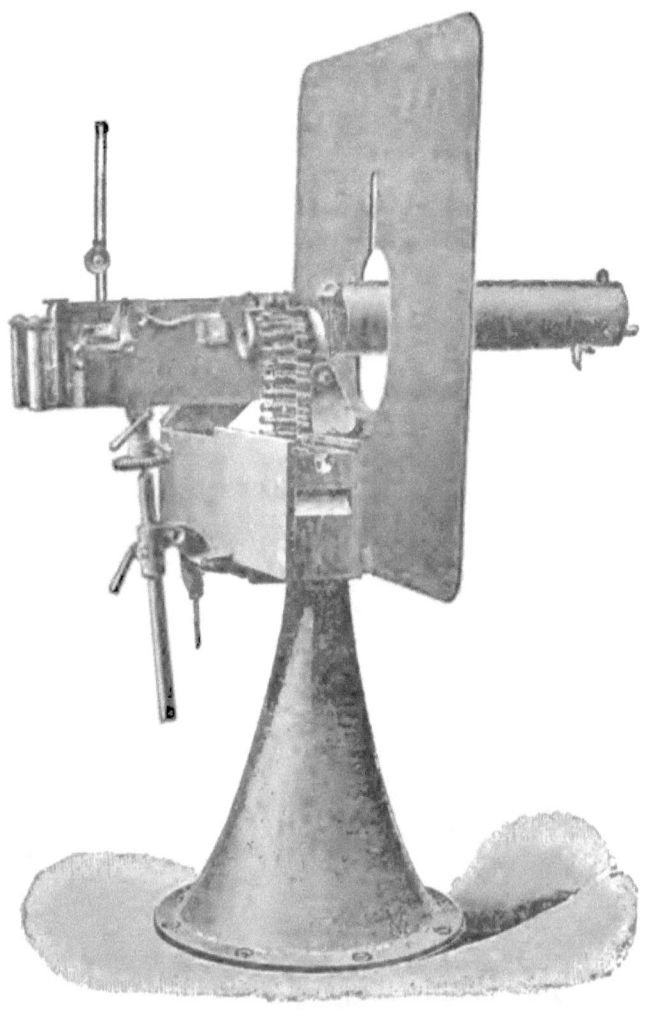

MAXIM AUTOMATIC NAVAL GUN.

Caliber, 0.303-inch; 700 shots per minute can be fired; 500 rounds of ammunition weigh but 44 pounds. This cut shows the belt carrying the cartridges and the tip of the muzzle of the gun surrounded by the "water jacket."

CHAPTER XII.

The Army and its Leaders.

The report of the Secretary of War for the year ending June 30, 1897, shows the strength of the regular army of the United States at that time to have been 27,532 officers and men. It has never been the policy of the United States to maintain a large standing army, as do many of the nations of Europe. On a peace footing Germany's standing army numbers 585,440, Russia's 863,672, France's 644,564, Italy's 231,355, Austria-Hungary's 358,697, Turkey's 700,620, Spain's 128,183, Japan's 284,741, and Great Britain's 222,870. While it is not considered necessary that the regular army of the United States should be increased to anything like these figures, the present war and its evident results make it manifest that the size of our regular army, which has heretofore been too small, will hereafter be entirely inadequate, and that the time has been reached in our national growth when the army should be definitely increased to a size proportionate with our vast population and increased responsibilities. Since the last report of the Secretary of War there have been added to the service two regiments of artillery, so that the army as now organized consists of ten regiments of cavalry, seven regiments of artillery, twenty-five regiments of infantry, an engineering battalion, and a signal corps, so that the army as now organized contains over 29,000 officers and men on a peace footing.

On account of the present war the regular army has been organized on a war footing in conformity with a bill passed by Congress April 23, 1898, and with all arms of the service recruited up to their full strength in conformity with the provisions of this bill the twenty-five infantry regiments contain 32,885, the artillery 16,886, cavalry 12,447 officers and men, and with the increase in the engineering and signal corps the grand total of officers and men on the present war footing is 64,985. At the end of the war the army will be reduced to a peace basis by transfer in the same arm of the service, absorption, promotion or honorable discharge, under such regulations as the Secretary of war may establish. There will result no permanent increase of the regular army beyond that provided by the law in force prior to the present war, except an increase of twenty-five majors in the infantry arm.

Beside the regular army we rely for protection upon the National Guard and the volunteers. The National Guard is composed exclusively of state troops under the command of the governors of the respective States, and is largely the result of the policy of this country of maintaining a small standing army. The latest reports received at the office of the Adjutant-General, show the total number in the National Guard of the various States and Territories to have been 115,627 in 1896, and the number now is somewhat greater. Congress makes an appropriation each year for the support of the National Guard in the various States, and the States also accord help and build armories in order that the troops may be well drilled. By this means they furnish a high order of volunteers in time of war.

The volunteers, which form a branch of the service only to be found in war, are such as offer their services upon the call of the President. In the recent call for volunteers it was the President's wish that the National Guard or State militia should be used as far as their number would permit, because they were organized, equipped and drilled. The National Guard responded promptly, and most of the regiments were mustered into the service. On April 23d the President issued a proclamation calling for 125,000 volunteers. After the battle of Manilla and the bombardment of San Juan de Porto Rico, a second call was made by the President for 75,000 additional volunteers. The officers of the National Guard, below the rank of Brigadier-General, were in nearly every case retained. The higher officers were appointed by the President and were taken from West Point graduates, the State militia, or civil life. Some of the regiments of volunteers were of a special character, such as Roosevelt's "Rough Riders" and the "Astor Battery."

The following are the sub-divisions of the army on a war footing as provided by the new army bill passed April 23, 1898:

A *company* is an infantry organization consisting of 106 enlisted men, one second lieutenant, one first lieutenant and commanded by a captain. A *troop* is the corresponding cavalry organization and consists of 100 enlisted men, one second lieutenant, one first lieutenant and a captain. A *battery* is the corresponding artillery organization and consists of 173 enlisted men in the light artillery, 200 men in the heavy artillery, one second lieutenant, one first lieutenant, and commanded by a captain. The President is empowered to add an extra second lieutenant to each battery of artillery.

A *battalion* consists of four companies, troops or batteries and is commanded by a major.

A *regiment*, which is the administrative unit, is composed of twelve companies, troops, or batteries, one lieutenant-colonel, and is commanded by a colonel.

A *brigade* consists of three or more regiments commanded by a brigadier-general and sometimes by a colonel.

A *division* consists of three brigades, and there may be an independent brigade of cavalry or artillery, and is commanded by a major-general or a brigadier-general.

A *corps* is the largest tactical unit of a large army, fully organized with separate staff, infantry, cavalry, and artillery regiments, as well as auxiliary services, so that it is really a small army complete in itself and is usually composed of three divisions. It is commanded by a major-general.

An *army* is divided into two or more corps and is commanded by a major-general.

Logically the army should be commanded by a general, each corps by a lieutenant-general, a division by a major-general, and each brigade by a brigadier-general. This would necessitate, however, a large increase in the salary of officers, and the Congress of the United States has not seen fit to put it into operation.

The commander-in-chief of the army is, of course, *ex officio*, the President of the United States. The Secretary of War is the Hon. Russell A. Alger, and the Assistant Secretary of War the Hon. George D. Meiklejohn. The following are the departmental officers with the rank of brigadier-general: Adjutant-General, Samuel Breck; Inspector-General, Jos. J. Breckenridge; Quartermaster-General, G. H. Weeks; Commissary-General, Wm. H. Bell; Surgeon-General, Geo. M. Sternberg; Paymaster-General, Thaddeus H. Stanton; Chief of Engineers, John M. Wilson; Chief of Ordnance, Daniel W. Flagler; Judge Advocate General, G. N. Lieber; Chief Signal Officer, A. W. Greeley; and with the rank of colonel, Chief Record and Pension Officer, F. C. Ainsworth.

The pay of the officers in active service is as follows: Lieutenant-General, $11,000; major-general, $7,500; brigadier-general, $5,500; colonel, $3,500; lieutenant-colonel, $3,000; major, $2,500; captain (mounted), $2,000; captain (on foot), $1,800; regimental adjutant, $1,800; regimental-quartermaster, $1,800; first lieutenant (mounted), $1,600; first lieutenant (on foot), $1,500; second lieutenant (mounted), $1.500; second lieutenant (on foot), $1,400. These amounts are increased ten per cent. after five years' service, twenty per cent. after ten years' service, thirty per cent. after fifteen years' service, and forty per cent. after twenty years' service; but the maximum pay of a colonel is limited to $4,500 and of a lieutenant-colonel to $4,000. The pay of a private in any arm of the service is $13 per month for the first and second years, $14 for the third year, $15 for the fourth year, $16 for the fifth year. After five years' continuous service he receives $2 per month extra. During this war twenty per cent. is added to the pay of all enlisted men, but not to that of the officers.

Military Schools.

The United States has but one military academy, which is located at West Point, N. Y., and military instruction under the direction of lieutenants of the regular army, detached for that service, is given in about one hundred colleges throughout the United States. The West Point cadets come from the various States and Territories of the Union, each Congressional district and Territory being entitled to one cadet in the academy, the nomination being made by the representative. This nomination is usually made after a competitive examination, but may be given directly. There are also ten other appointments which are usually conferred upon the sons of officers of the army and navy by the President of the United States. Therefore, the number of students is limited to 371. Foreign governments may, however, have cadets educated at the academy by authorization of Congress. The course of instruction requires four years and is largely mathematical and professional. The appointees must be between the ages of 17 and 22 years, of sound health, and free from any infirmity which may render them unfit for military service. The discipline is very strict, even more so than in the army. During his stay at West Point, each cadet receives $540 per year, and after graduation he is commissioned a second lieutenant in the United States army. On account of the rigid requirements a large proportion of the cadets fall by the wayside each year. The number in attendance September 1, 1897, was 338. The school can accommodate a much larger number, and it has been proposed to add two cadets from each State, one to be appointed by each United States senator.

The number of students who received military instruction at the 100 colleges throughout the country was 15,608 in 1896.

Nelson A. Miles,

Major-General in command of the army, was born at Westminster, Mass., August 8, 1839. His ancestors settled in Massachusetts colony in 1643. He was reared on a farm and in early manhood engaged in mercantile pursuits in Boston. Early in 1861 he raised a company of volunteers and offered his services to his country. He was given the commission of a captain, but being considered too young for the responsibilities of that command he joined the Army o. the Potomac as first lieutenant in the 22d Massachusetts volunteers. In 1862 he was commissioned by Gov. Morgan of New York as lieutenant-colonel and colonel of the 61st New York volunteers. At the earnest request of Gens. Meade and Grant he was made a brigadier-general of volunteers by President Lincoln. He was perhaps engaged in more hard-fought battles than any general officer of our army, including 35 distinct battles and over 100 serious affairs in which artillery, cavalry and infantry were engaged. He commanded regiments, brigades and divisions, and at one time, February, 1865, was in command of the second army corps, which numbered at that time over 25,000 men, and which is believed to be the largest command ever handled by an officer in this country at 25 years of age. In the latter part of the war his command was the first division, second army corps, the largest of all the divisions.

General Miles was wounded at the battles of Fair Oaks, Fredericksburg and Chancellorsville, and received four brevets for gallantry and distinguished service. At the close of the war he commanded the district of North Carolina during the work of reconstruction, and on the reorganization of the army he was appointed colonel of infantry. He was made a brigadier-general, U. S. A., in 1880 and a major-general in 1890. He has successfully conducted Indian campaigns in all parts of our great West, and has on several occasions prevented Indian wars by judicious and humane settlement of the difficulties without the use of military power.

Major-General John R. Brooke was born in Pennsylvania July 21, 1838, and was a farmer boy of 23 when he responded to the first call of President Lincoln for troops in 1861. He participated with credit in nearly all of the battles of the Army of the Potomac, rising from captain to brigadier-general of volunteers, receiving two brevets for distinguished services. Since the war he has been on duty in the West, in command of the department of the Platte and of the department of the Missouri. "When he fights he wins" is the reputation he has acquired among those who have served under him.

Major-General Wm. R. Shafter came from what Lincoln called the "plain people." He entered the 17th Michigan Infantry as first lieutenant in 1861 at the age of 25. He served with distinction through the war and was twice brevetted for gallant and meritorious service. Since the war he has served with distinction in the Indian campaigns as colonel of the 24th Infantry, and as brigadier-general in command of the department of the Pacific. General Shafter weighs over 300 pounds, is gruff, sturdy and warm-hearted. He has been criticised for his conduct of the campaign against Santiago, but his best reply to this criticism is found in the completeness of his victory. He has won such honors as came to Grant, and escaped the humiliations of less energetic and venturesome leaders.

Major-General Wesley Merritt was born in New York city in 1836, graduated from West Point in 1860, and during the Civil War rapidly rose to the rank of major-general of volunteers. He received six brevets for gallant and meritorious service. In 1866 he was appointed colonel of the 9th Cavalry, and later for several years managed the Military Academy at West Point. Since then he has worked himself up from grade to grade in the Indian campaigns, and many military men, especially West Pointers, regard him as the greatest genius of the army.

Major-General Joseph Wheeler graduated at West Point in 1859 and entered the Confederate army at the breaking out of the civil war. He was rapidly promoted, serving as lieutenant of artillery, colonel of infantry, brigadier-general, major-general, and lieutenant-general of cavalry. In 1864 he received the brevet of general of the Confederate army. After the war he became a lawyer and planter in Alabama and for the past dozen years has been a representative in Congress.

As a cavalry officer Gen. Wheeler ranked with Sheridan. Audacious, fearless, aggressive, energetic, and an excellent strategist, his campaigns throughout the civil war were marked by dash and valor. He captured Gen. Prentiss' division at Shiloh, covered the retreat from Shiloh to Corinth and Perrysville, winning the highest commendation from Confederate generals; turned Rosencrans' flank at Murfreesboro and distinguished himself at Chickamauga, Missionary Ridge and in the struggle from Chattanooga to Atlanta. He was wounded three times and had sixteen horses shot under him. An indefatigable student and worker, and as a legislator handles public questions in a masterly way.

Major-General Fitzhugh Lee was born in Virginia in 1835, graduated from West Point in 1856, and was returned there as instructor of cavalry in 1860, where he continued until the beginning of the civil war. He entered the Confederate army as first lieutenant of cavalry and rapidly rose to major-general. Was severely wounded at Winchester after three horses had been shot under him. After the war he retired to his farm in Stafford county, Va., for several years, and was elected governor of Virginia in 1885 for a term of four years. In 1896 he was appointed by President Cleveland to be consul-general at Havana, where he remained until the breaking out of the present war.

Major-General James H. Wilson graduated from West Point in 1860, just in time to win his major-general's double star within three years of his graduation. He was one of the greatest cavalry leaders produced by the Union side during the Civil War. He is most famous for his dashing cavalry raid into Alabama and Louisiana in 1865. The consummate skill and brilliant success with which he handled 12,000 troopers in this campaign proved the wisdom of General Grant in selecting him for this important command. At this time General Wilson was about twenty-seven years of age, and the men who swung into their saddles at the sound of his bugle to follow his battle-flag were mostly youngsters from twenty to twenty-five years of age, though all seasoned veterans of three or more years' service. General Wilson retired from the army in December, 1870, and has since been engaged successfully in railroad management in the United States and China.

Colonel Theodore Roosevelt was born in New York City, October 27, 1858, his father's people having lived in that city for eight generations. He is quick, intense, nervous, incessant, and an actor in, not a spectator of, the drama of the times. Sickly as a boy, his first active work was in making himself a physically able fellow. He graduated from Harvard in 1880. He believes "that in a free republic like ours, it is a man's duty to know how to bear arms and to be willing to do so when the occasion arises," and he evidenced his belief by joining the Eighth Regiment of the New York State Nat'l Guard in 1884, rising to be captain of one of its companies. In 1884 he started his cattle ranch in the Bad Lands of Dakota, where he spent several summers. In the New York State Convention of 1884 he first became conspicuous and was sent to the National Convention at Chicago. He was sent to the New York Legislature for three successive terms in 1883, 1884 and 1885. After General Harrison's election as President, he appointed Roosevelt as Civil Service Commissioner, and that post he held until he became a police commissioner in 1895. From this position he was appointed Assistant Secretary of the Navy under the present Administration, and at the breaking out of the present war resigned to go to the front as lieutenant-colonel of Roosevelt's "Rough Riders."

CHAPTER XIII.

The Future of America.

It will help us to form an intelligent estimate of the possibilities before us and the probable future of our nation if we will briefly consider its early difficulties and the progess it has made. For generations the United States has held steadfastly to the policy outlined by Washington in his farewell address:

> "If we remain one people, under an efficient government, the period is not far off when we may defy material injury from external annoyance. * * * Why forego the advantages of so peculiar a situation? Why quit our own to stand on foreign ground? Why, by interweaving our destiny with that of any part of Europe, entangle our peace and prosperity in the toils of European ambition, rivalship, interest, humor, or caprice? It is our true policy to steer clear of permanent alliances with any portion of the foreign world, so far, I mean, as we are now at liberty to do it; for let me not be understood as capable of patronizing infidelity to existing engagements."

We can better understand what called forth these wise utterances if we know something of the condition of the country at that time. The United States were practically but a small fringe of settlements on the Atlantic seaboard; to be driven from the coast was to endure all the privations of the forest, and that coast was at the mercy of any of the naval powers of the day. Their northwestern and southern boundaries were vague and indefinite; of them they knew little and cared less. Their western boundary was the Mississippi river, and this was supposed to rise somewhere in British America. Their census had shown that there were 3,929,241 inhabitants, rather more than half as many as are now found within the single State of New York, and of these one-fifth were in Virginia, one-ninth in Pennsylvania, and almost one-half south of the southern boundary of that State. The six largest cities of the country together numbered fewer inhabitants than Kansas City, Mo., can now boast. The total area of the United States was then 865,000 square miles and three-fourths of it was inhabited only by savages. England held fortified posts in our territory on the plea that the United States, in violation of treaty, had not repealed laws forbidding the recovery of debts due from their citizens to her subjects. Spain would make no treaty allowing free navigation of the Mississippi; domestic affairs were unhappy; the United States were allied by treaty to France; France declared war against Great Britian; Washington issued a proclamation of neutrality and his opponents at once cried "coward;" claimed that he had violated the Constitution; had usurped the power of Congress, because to proclaim neutrality was to forbid war; to forbid war implied the right to declare war, and Congress alone could do that. The Constitution was not working smoothly. A "Whiskey Insurrection" occurred in Pennsylvania; demagogues demanded that all property should be divided and held in common — since all had been engaged in defending it from English confiscation all were equally entitled to share in it. This motive was at the bottom of Shays' rebellion. If successful it would have annihilated all property and canceled all debts. The most bitter partisan feeling prevailed. The Secretary of State privately employed a scurrilous writer to attack the President in whose cabinet he served. This was the situation when Washington warned his fellow-countrymen to "beware of entangling alliances." There was, therefore, a real danger that a defeated faction might seek to avenge itself by calling in a stronger power. The recent magnificent exhibition of the united nation, of its unselfishness, its enormous resources and great area, make it difficult for us to look back and appreciate our former feebleness and comparative insignificance.

Territory Acquired.

Napoleon had obtained Louisana from Spain, but could not hold it against attack from Great Britain, and in 1803 Jefferson bought for 60,000,000 francs the territory from which we have since carved sixteen States, the United States agreeing to pay its own citizens spoliation claims due them from France. The control of the Mississippi and the development of the West were now assured, yet that magnificent domain was not secured without violent partisan opposition, and only Hamilton of all the Federal leaders could show the "high mind" and play the statesman. Jefferson, in the immortal Declaration of Independence, had said, "Governments are instituted among men deriving their just powers from the consent of the governed," yet he purchased a foreign colony without reference to its inhabitants, and not only without their consent but against their will. In 1819 Spain ceded the Floridas to us, the United States agreeing to pay its own citizens' claims for outrages sustained at the hands of Spain and to accept the Colorado river in Texas as a boundary in place of the Rio Grande. In 1845 Texas was annexed, which involved us in war with Mexico. This action was so far from meeting with unanimous approval, that an Ohio senator said he hoped the Mexicans would welcome our troops "with bloody hands to unhospitable graves." Nevertheless a half a million square miles were added to the public domain, and in 1853 the Gadsen purchase secured for $10,000,000 additional territory in the southern part of New Mexico, Arizona, and California. The northwestern boundaries of the Louisiana purchase were never accurately defined, and but for Marcus Whitman's heroic ride of 4,000 miles in the dead of winter across trackless prairies and pathless forests the territory that comprises Idaho, Oregon, and Washington would have been a part of British Columbia. In this case, as usual, the acquirement of territory met with great opposition from the conservative, the short-sighted, and the hysterical, who averred that it was worthless, remote, and indefensible. We think no one will venture to say that time has not justified the wisdom of the acquisition. Then in 1867 came Seward's purchase of Alaska for $7,200,000. Many estimable people could not see the wisdom of this, but the territory has since more than paid for itself in fisheries, furs and gold. In 1891 the little island of Navassa, in the West Indies, was acquired, and July 7, 1898, Hawaii became a part of the United States, three-fourths of a century after we had announced our intention of adding it to our public domain; and at the next meeting of Congress there will probably be added to our dominions the territory acquired in our war with Spain.

Colonial Extension.

The Phœnicians, Greeks, and especially the Romans, brought their colonies to a high state of perfection, and under Rome there were various grades of citizenship in her colonies — from the lowest up to the highest enjoyed by a citizen of the republic. Among the advantages of a colony is that it widens fields of enterprise and provides closed markets, in which the mother country can buy cheap and sell dear. It gives a larger choice of the means of livelihood. It appeals to the agriculturist because it offers him land. It furnishes a safety-valve for the outlet of the discontented population, and every new colony may be looked upon as a new market for home goods; a speculation that may be worth some expense to maintain. A glance at the map of the world shows how extensive this system has become. The colonies and dependencies of Great Britain cover one-sixth the whole surface of the globe, and embrace about the same proportion of its population. Germany, beginning the policy in 1884, has acquired over one million square miles and ten millions of population. France to-day has in dependencies a territory greater than the United States with a population of over fifty million souls, and the greater part of this has been secured since 1880. The Netherlands, with a home population less than that of Pennsylvania and an area slightly greater than that of Maryland, hold dependencies in the East Indies and West Indies aggregating 783,000 square miles, with a population of over 35,000,000. Evidently that little country is not alarmed about its needing a powerful navy to defend the distant domain. The idea of a colony frightens the average American, and yet under the name of "territory" the United States has practiced an extensive plan of colonization. She has given land outright to actual settlers and has sold it to others on the most favorable terms. She has governed the territories by her own laws until such time as she saw fit to grant them the rights of statehood. If the policy of colonization is a judicious one, there is little doubt about its constitutionality, for the United States Supreme Court has decided that Congress has absolute power when it comes to law-making for the territory. "It is, perhaps, natural for the mother country to regard the colony as an outlet for her own surplus population, and the tie between them is manifest in the case of commerce. Great Britain has maintained her trade more steadily in her own colonies than she has with all the rest of the world."

"Judging the Future by the Past."

McMasters, in his "Four Centuries of Progress," says:

"We have reached the Gulf, we have crossed the Mississippi, we have built up two-and-twenty Commonwealths on the plains beyond, we have made our Constitution sure and given Europe such an object lesson in 'government of the people, by the people, for the people,' as will not be in vain. Whatever abridges distance, whatever annihilates time, whatever alleviates human pain, has nowhere been so fostered as in these United States. Could we but stretch forth our hands and take out of the life of the world to-day every machine, every article of real necessity, every convenience, every comfort due to the ingenuity of our countrymen, we should bring back a condition of affairs which to us would be almost intolerable.

"As we have grown more intelligent, so we have grown more liberal, more tolerant, more humane. When this century opened there was not a blind asylum, nor a deaf-and-dumb asylum, nor a lunatic asylum, nor a house of refuge in all our land. We have cut down the number of crimes punished with death from fifteen to two. We have ceased to use the branding iron and the treadmill; we have abolished imprisonment for debt; we have exterminated slavery. We have covered our country with free schools and free libraries, and set up institutions for the protection not only of children but of dumb brutes. In the face of all these facts it is wicked to talk of degeneration and decay."

It is a century since Washington uttered his words of warning. In that time the public domain of the country has been more than quadrupled; the population has increased from less than four millions to more than seventy millions; its wealth and resources can hardly be computed. Instead of a feeble, struggling nation, at the mercy of any power, we are so strong that an Austrian Minister of State has openly threatened a coalition of Europe against us lest our free institutions become too dangerous to their systems of government. Have we become a "world power?" Does our action in the Venezuelan matter and the intervention in Cuban affairs answer the question?

CHAPTER XIV.

The Spanish-American War.

A Century of American Forbearance.

During our Revolutionary war, Spain, France and the United States were allies, and the treaty of peace signed in 1783 was between England on the one side and the allies on the other. Hardly was the ink on the treaty dry before Spain made extravagant claims concerning the boundaries of Florida, and even denied our right to territory between the Allegheny mountains and the Mississippi river. In 1795 Spain claimed that the land between the Allegheny and the Mississippi belonged to the Indians, and that she had purchased Chickasaw Bluffs of them. She denied our right to free navigation of the Mississippi, stopped goods in transit, levied exorbitant duties, sometimes 50% to 75% *ad valorem*. She intrigued with influential settlers of Kentucky and Tennessee until it seemed uncertain whether the settlers would become allies of Spain, set up an independent government or involve the United States in war. Numerous outrages, violations of treaty rights and indignities were practiced, and her territory was a harbor for the runaway slave, the escaped criminal and the bandit. Spain pleaded that she could not preserve order within her own territory.

Not to mention the cases of the "Black Warrior" and "Virginius," which we have touched upon, there were more than half a dozen American ships fired upon, overhauled and captured near Cuba from 1877 to 1880. The "Allianca" and "Competitor" cases are fresh in our minds. In 1877 the "Masonic," an American ship bound for Japan, was forced by stress of weather to put into Manila, where the cargo had to be taken out that repairs might be made. Spanish officers claimed the manifest was not correct and not only violated the treaty, but every rule of hospitality, by confiscating the ship and cargo. The case was arbitrated, and Italy awarded us $56,000 damages about six years after the offense was committed. The Cuban estates of naturalized Americans have frequently been confiscated; Americans have mysteriously died in prison without being brought to trial for any alleged offense; our treaty rights have been flagrantly violated, and Spain's conduct has been aggravating in the extreme.

Although there have been times in our history when the Americans seemed determined to possess Cuba, there have been other times when our support has saved it for Spain. Jefferson, in 1795, said, "We had with sincere and particular disposition courted and cultivated the friendship of Spain;" and in 1823, when France showed a disposition to acquire the island, Clay, as Secretary of State, said, "The United States for themselves desire no change in the political condition of Cuba." Van Buren, in 1840, probably saved the island from England for Spain when he said, "In case of any attempt from whatever quarter to wrest from her this portion of her territory, she may securely depend upon the military and naval resources of the United States to aid in preserving or recovering it." Professor Hart, in Harper's for June, 1898, says:

"So far from the Cuban policy of the United States having been one of aggression, few nations have shown more good temper toward a troublesome neighbor, more patience with diplomatic delays or more self-restraint over a coveted possession. The Cuban controversy has not been sought by the United States. It arises out of the geographical and political conditions of America."

President McKinley's message of April 11, 1898, gives a masterly review of Cuban affairs, and possessing, as he did, information not accessible to the public, nothing can better outline the situation for us.

The Present Revolution. — "The present revolution is but the successor of other similar insurrections which have occurred in Cuba against the dominion of Spain, extending over a period of nearly half a century, each of which, during its progress, has subjected the United States to great effort and expense in enforcing its neutrality laws, caused enormous losses to American trade and commerce, caused irritation, annoyance and disturbance among our citizens, and, by the exercise of cruel, barbarous and uncivilized practices of warfare, shocked the sensibilities and offended the human sympathies of our people."

Weyler's Policy of Reconcentration.

"The agricultural population, to the estimated number of 300,000 or more, was herded within the towns and their immediate vicinage, deprived of the means of support, rendered destitute of shelter, left poorly clad and exposed to the most unsanitary conditions. As the scarcity of food increased with the devastation of the depopulated areas of production, destitution and want became misery and starvation. Month by month the death rate increased in an alarming ratio. No practical relief was afforded to the destitute. The overburdened towns, already suffering from general dearth, could give no aid. By March, 1897, according to conservative estimates from official Spanish sources, the mortality among the reconcentrados, from starvation and the diseases thereto incident, exceeded 50 per cent. of their total number."

The horrible condition of affairs and the increasing destitution having been brought home to the minds of the American people by the speech of Senator Proctor, who had visited Cuba, the public conscience was touched, and in response to an appeal from the President, more than $200,000 was raised by voluntary subscriptions and sent to Cuba for the relief of the reconcentrados, and the civilized world was so impressed that the Spanish government deemed it politic to *authorize* the appropriation of $600,000 for the same purpose, and ordered the American contribution to be admitted into Cuba free of duty.

The De Lome Incident.

Early in February Senor De Lome, the Spanish minister at Washington, had written to Senor Canalejas, then at Havana and a Spanish official of high rank, a letter concerning the situation, certain passages of which were insulting to the President of the United States. The letter made plain that neither De Lome nor Canalejas believed in the sincerity of the "autonomy" proposals, but looked upon them as a blind for diverting the attention of the United States. Some Cuban sympathizer seems to have abstracted the letter from Canalejas and turned it over to the Cuban Junta in New York, who published it in full in the New York Journal. Upon its appearance, De Lome telegraphed his resignation to Madrid, which was immediately accepted, and when our minister, General Woodford, presented the request of the United States for De Lome's recall he was informed that De Lome was no longer a Spanish official.

Destruction of the "Maine."

President Cleveland was exceedingly careful not to wound the sensitive feelings of Spain, and while the Cuban insurrection was in progress American battleships did not visit Cuban ports, neither were the usual South Atlantic fleet maneuvers held. After the granting of so-called autonomy to Cuba and the appointment of officers, the administration saw no reason why the government ships should not resume their friendly naval visits at Cuban ports, especially as there had been rioting in Havana and it was thought the American consulate and the interests of the United States would be furthered by the presence of the battleship, and in accordance with former custom the "Maine," a second-class battleship, visited that port, reaching there about 11 o'clock January 25, 1898. Everything was quiet; no demonstrations were made and the customary formal visits between the officers were exchanged. The coming of the "Maine" angered the Spanish press and the volunteers, though outwardly the usual courtesy was shown by the highest officials. Suddenly, February 15th, at 9:40 P. M., without the slightest warning, a terrific explosion occurred on the port side under the quarters of the crew, and " 258 brave sailors and marines and two officers of our navy, reposing in the fancied security of a friendly harbor, were hurled to death, grief and want brought to their homes, and sorrow to the nation."

Captain Sigsbee of the "Maine" at once cabled the

Navy Department of the disaster and said, "public opinion should be suspended until further reports." The government at Washington at once appointed a Board of Inquiry, consisting of Captain Wm. T. Sampson, of the "Iowa," Captain F. E. Chadwick, of the "New York," Lieutenant-Commander W. P. Potter, of the "New York," and Adolph Marix, Judge-Advocate of the court, to proceed to Havana as a Court of Inquiry. The wildest rumors were current and excitement at white heat, but following the example set by Captain Sigsbee, the nation with a self-control that excited favorable comment throughout the world, awaited the decision of the Court. The principal nations were quick to express their sympathy in this awful disaster. At this time the military resources of the United States were at a low ebb. There was not powder enough in the forts of New York to permit of gun practice for the artillery companies. The magazines of the navy were in not much better condition. It was at this stage that selfishness, partisanship and unworthy qualities passed into the background and a wave of patriotism, self-sacrifice and compassion swept over the country.

$50,000,000 for Defense.

The Naval Board of Inquiry at once began their work, and as week after week passed without any public expression from them, the tension became severe. While hoping for the best the administration was preparing for the worst. March 8th, the House of Representatives unanimously voted to place $50,000,000 at the unqualified disposal of President McKinley as an emergency fund for national defense, and the next day the Senate, by a unanimous vote, confirmed the appropriation.

Report of Board.

March 22, the Board of Inquiry made their formal report:

"The discipline and disposition of stores on board the ship was everything that could be desired. That there were two explosions of a distinctly different character with a short interval between them. The forward part of the ship was lifted to a marked degree at the time of the first explosion. The second explosion, in the opinion of the Court, was caused by the explosion of two or more of the forward magazines of the 'Maine.' A part of the outer wall of the ship 11 1-2 feet from the middle and 6 feet above the keel in its normal position, was forced up so as to be more than 4 feet above the surface of the water and therefore about 34 feet above what it would be if the ship had been sunk uninjured. The outside bottom plating was bent into a reversed V shape (see cut). At frame 18 the vertical keel is broken in two. This break is now about 6 feet above the surface of the water and about 30 feet above its normal position. In the opinion of the Court this effect could have been produced only by the explosion of a mine situated under the bottom of the ship and somewhat on the port side. The Court finds that the loss of the 'Maine' on the occasion named was not in any respect due to fault or negligence on the part of any of the officers or members of the crew of said vessel. In the opinion of the Court the 'Maine' was destroyed by the explosion of a submarine mine which caused the partial explosion of two or more of her forward magazines. The Court has been unable to obtain evidence fixing the responsibility for the destruction of the 'Maine' upon any person or persons."

Public Opinion.

The horrible tales of suffering sustained by the reconcentrados and the destruction of the "Maine" seemed likely to arouse public opinion to such a pitch that nothing but immediate war would satisfy it. The feeling in the United States was one of genuine sympathy and desire to assist the Cubans. The attitude of Europe was different. With the exception of England the great powers seemed to look upon the Cuban insurrection as something instigated and fostered by the United States for the express purpose of eventually giving this country an excuse to intervene and annex the island.

April 7, ambassadors of the six great powers called on the President and presented an address, and in the name of their governments made

"A pressing appeal to the feelings of humanity and moderation of the President and of the American people in their existing differences with Spain. They earnestly hope that further negotiations will lead to an agreement which, while securing the maintenance of peace, will afford all necessary guarantees for the re-establishment of order in Cuba. The powers do not doubt that the humanitarian and disinterested character of this representation will be fully recognized and appreciated by the American nation."

Although it was an unusual action for the President to grant an audience to more than one ambassador at a time and excited considerable criticism, his sturdy reply sufficiently indicated his position:

> "The Government of the United States appreciates the humanitarian and disinterested character of the communication now made on behalf of the powers named, and, for its part, is confident that equal appreciation will be shown for its own earnest and unselfish endeavors to fulfill a duty to humanity by ending a situation the indefinite prolongation of which has become insufferable."

The President's Message.

April 11th President McKinley sent his famous message to Congress, with consular correspondence. It was strong and conservative. It recited the horrors of Spanish methods and declared that the war must stop. His handling of the question of recognition met with a good deal of criticism, but subsequent events have only proven the wisdom of his position.

> "Nor from the standpoint of expediency do I think it would be wise or prudent for this Government to recognize at the present time the independence of the so-called Cuban Republic. Such recognition is not necessary in order to enable the United States to intervene and pacify the island. To commit this country now to the recognition of any particular government in Cuba might subject us to embarrassing conditions of international obligation toward the organization so recognized. In case of intervention our conduct would be subject to the approval or disapproval of such government. We would be required to submit to its direction and to assume to it the mere relation of a friendly ally.
>
> "When it shall appear hereafter that there is within the island a government capable of performing the duties and discharging the function of a separate nation, and having, as a matter of fact, the proper forms and attributes of nationality, such government can be promptly and readily recognized, and the relations and interests of the United States with such nation adjusted."

Why We Should Intervene.

> "1. In the cause of humanity and to put an end to the barbarities, bloodshed, starvation and horrible miseries now existing there, and which the parties to the conflict are either unable or unwilling to stop or mitigate. It is no answer to say this is all in another country, belonging to another nation, and is therefore none of our business. It is specially our duty, for it is right at our door.
>
> "2. We owe it to our citizens in Cuba to afford them that protection and indemnity for life and property which no government there, can or will afford, and to that end to terminate the conditions that deprive them of legal protection.

"3. The right to intervene may be justified by the very serious injury to the commerce, trade and business of our people, and by the wanton destruction of property and devastation of the island.

"4. The present condition of affairs in Cuba is a constant menace to our peace, and entails upon this Government an enormous expense. With such a conflict waged for years in an island so near us and with which our people have such trade and business relations — when the lives and liberty of our citizens are in constant danger, and their property destroyed and themselves ruined — where our trading vessels are liable to seizure and are seized at our very door by warships of a foreign nation, the expeditions of filibustering that we are powerless to prevent altogether, and the irritating questions and entanglements thus arising — all these and others that I need not mention, with the resulting strained relations, are a constant menace to our peace, and compel us to keep on a semi-war-footing with a nation with which we are at peace."

On the 13th of April the House Committee of Foreign Affairs reported a resolution, which was adopted the same day by a vote of 322 to 19, directing the President to intervene at once in Cuban affairs, to use the army and navy to carry out the provisions of this act, and further directed him to establish in the island a free and independent government of the people. The House was prepared to support the President; the Senate was determined to grant formal recognition to the insurgents. Several conferences between the House and Senate were held, and finally, in the small hours of the morning of April 19th, the following resolutions were adopted:

1. "That the people of the Island of Cuba are, and of right ought to be, free and independent.

2. "That it is the duty of the United States to demand, and the Government of the United States does hereby demand, that the Government of Spain at once relinquish its authority and government in the island of Cuba and withdraw its land and naval forces from Cuba and Cuban waters.

3. "That the President of the United States be, and he hereby is, directed and empowered to use the entire land and naval forces of the United States, and to call into the actual service of the United States the militia of the several States to such an extent as may be necessary to carry these resolutions into effect.

4. "That the United States hereby disclaims any disposition or intention to exercise sovereignty, jurisdiction or control over said island, except for the pacification thereof, and asserts its determination when that is accomplished to leave the government and the control of the island to its people."

The President signed the resolution the next day and prepared and forwarded to the Spanish government an

THE ASCENDENCY OF AMERICA.   425

ultimatum giving them three days to accede to our demands. Upon receiving a copy of the President's ultimatum the Spanish minister at Washington asked for his passports, turned Spanish interests over to the French ambassador and left for Canada. Spain detained the ultimatum at the telegraph office until after she could call Minister Woodford, who was informed that the action of the president and Congress was regarded by Spain as a declaration of war, and on the morning of the 21st he was given his passports and escorted as far as the boundary line of France. England has held that the date of war began not with the formal declaration, but April 21st, the day Minister Woodford was handed his passports. The date is important and affects the validity of the capture of prizes.

Friday, April 22, the President issued a call for 125,000 volunteers and declared a blockade of the north coast of Cuba from Cardenas to Bahia Honda, inclusive, and the port of Cienfuegos on the south coast. Just previous to this Rear Admiral Sicard in command of the North Atlantic fleet at Key West had been retired and the command was given to Capt. William T. Sampson, who was made acting rear-admiral. The fleet consisted of the following vessels:

Battleships Iowa, Capt. Evans; Indiana, Capt. Taylor. Monitor Amphitrite, Capt. Barclay. Armored cruiser New York, Capt. Chadwick. Protected cruiser Cincinnati, Capt. Chester. Unprotected cruiser Detroit, Commander Dayton. Gunboats Wilmington, Commander Todd; Helena, Commander Swinburne; Nashville, Commander Maynard; Castine, Commander Perry; Machias, Commander Merry; Newport, Commander Tilley. Dynamite cruiser Vesuvius, Lieut.-Commander Pillsbury. Torpedo boats, Ericsson, Lieut. Usher; Foote, Lieut. Rogers; Winslow, Lieut. Bernadou; Hawk, Lieut. Hood; Hornet, Lieut. Helm; Maple, Lieut.-Commander Kellogg; Osceola, Lieut. Purcell; Scorpion, Lieut.-Commander Marix; Vixen, Lieut. Sharp; Wasp, Lieut. Ward; Wampatuck, Lieut. Jungen; Sioux, Ensign Charardi; Nezinscott, Mate Cleveland. Tug Leyden, Boatswain Angus, of the auxiliary fleet.

Before daylight Friday morning the fleet was in motion and at six o'clock the Spanish steamer Buena Ventura, the first prize, was captured by the Nashville, Patrick Mallia, gunner, having the honor of firing the first gun in the war. At one P. M. that day Havana was completely blockaded and soon numerous prizes of the American vessels began to make their appearance at Key West.

Operations Before Manila.

About the same time Commodore George Dewey, commanding the Asiatic squadron at Hong Kong, was ordered to find and destroy the Spanish fleet. He had under his command the Olympia (flagship), Baltimore, Boston, Concord, Raleigh, Petrel and the revenue cutter McCulloch. Commodore Dewey got under way without loss of time, left Mirs Bay April 27, and steered straight for the Philippines. Saturday, April 30th, he arrived off Subig Bay, some 30 miles north of Manila. The Boston, Baltimore and Concord reconnoitered the Bay looking for the Spanish fleet. Not finding them, the squadron headed for Manila Bay, taking care to arrive off the entrance after dark. The entrance is about six miles wide, and divided by Corregidor Island, where batteries were mounted, into two channels the larger and the smaller. Early Sunday morning before light, formed in line of battle, they started through the smaller channel. The "Olympia" was leading, followed by the "Baltimore," "Raleigh," "Petrel," "Concord," and the "Boston;" then the second line, made up of the revenue cutter "McCulloch" and the transports "Naushan" and "Zarifo." The entrance was guarded by fortifications mounting heavy guns and the channel was supposed to be defended by mines. The Spanish maps on which the navigators had relied proved to be worthless, but with their men at quarters and their guns trained in the direction of the batteries, they proceeded silently on the way, knowing every moment that they might be blown into eternity, and expecting that the guns of Corregidor

Island would certainly open on them, but there was only a silence so intense as to be awful in its strain. The "Olympia," the "Baltimore," the "Raleigh," the "Petrel" and the "Concord" had passed without discovery, when flames from the funnels of one of the ships attracted a sleepy sentinel. A bugle rang out, a rocket shot up, a flash, and a shot flew across the water. The "Boston" opened fire at the fort, which replied, but the fleet had passed the guard. They now slowly made a circuit of the bay, and when morning broke were off the city of Manila, but found no signs of the Spanish fleet there. Steaming slowly on, they soon came upon them drawn up in a small bay flanked by the heavy batteries of Cavite arsenal. About 5 o'clock the enemy opened fire. Dewey signaled his ships to close up, and turning to Captain Gridley of the "Olympia" said, "Any time when you are ready, Gridley." Gridley was ready and almost instantly the forward 8-inch guns spoke with a terrific crash. The smoke and splinters could be seen flying from the Spanish ship opposite, and a battle that is likely to change the destiny of this nation had begun.

"The squadron then proceeded to the attack, the flagship Olympia, under my personal direction, leading, followed at a distance by the Baltimore, Raleigh, Petrel, Concord and Boston in the order named, which formation was maintained through the action. The squadron opened fire at 5:41 A. M. While advancing to the attack two mines were exploded ahead of the flagship, too far to be effective. The squadron maintained a continuous and precise fire at ranges varying from 5,000 to 2,000 yards, countermarching in a line approximately parallel to that of the Spanish fleet. The enemy's fire was vigorous, but generally ineffective. Early in the enagagement two launches put out toward the Olympia with the apparent intention of using torpedoes. One was sunk and the other disabled by our fire and beached before they were able to fire their torpedoes.

"At 7 A. M. the Spanish flagship Reina Christina made a desperate attempt to leave the line and come out to engage at short range, but was received with such a galling fire, the entire battery of the Olympia being concentrated upon her, that she was barely able to return to shelter of the point. The fires started in her by our shell at the time were not extinguished until she sank. The three batteries at Manila had kept up a continuous fire from the beginning of the engagement, which fire was not returned by my squadron. The first of these batteries was situated on the south mole head at the entrance of the Pasig river, the second on the south portion of the walled city of Manila, and the third at Molate, about one-half mile further south.

At this point I sent a message to the Governor-General to the effect that if the batteries did not cease firing the city would be shelled. This had the effect of silencing them.

"At 7:45 A. M. I ceased firing and withdrew the squadron for breakfast. At 11:16 I returned to the attack. By this time the Spanish flagship and almost all the Spanish fleet were in flames. At 12:30 the squadron ceased firing, the batteries being silenced and the ships sunk, burned and deserted.

"At 12:40 the squadron returned and anchored off Manila, the Petrel being left behind to complete the destruction of the smaller gunboats, which were behind the points of Cavite. This duty was performed by Commander E. P. Wood in the most expeditious and complete manner possible.

"I am happy to report that the damage done to the squadron under my command was inconsiderable. There were none killed and only seven men in the squadron were slightly wounded. Several of the vessels were struck and even penetrated, but the damage was of the slightest, and the squadron is in as good condition now as before the battle.

"I beg to state to the Department that I doubt if any commander-in-chief was ever served by more loyal, efficient and gallant captains than those of the squadron under my command. Captain Frank Wildes, commanding the Boston, volunteered to remain in command of his vessel although his relief arrived before leaving Hong Kong. Assistant Surgeon Kindelberger, of the Olympia, and Gunner J. J. Evans, of the Boston, also volunteered to remain after orders detaching them had arrived. The conduct of my personal staff was excellent. Commander B. P. Lamberton, chief of staff, was a volunteer for that position, and gave me most efficient aid. Lieutenant Brumby, flag lieutenant, and Ensign E. P. Scott, aide, performed their duties as signal officers in a highly creditable manner. Caldwell, flag secretary, volunteered for and was assigned to a subdivision of the 5-inch battery. Mr. J. L. Stickney, formerly an officer in the United States Navy, and now correspondent for the New York 'Herald,' volunteered for duty as my aide, and rendered valuable service. I desire especially to mention the coolness of Lieutenant C. G. Calkins, the navigator of the Olympia, who came under my personal observation, being on the bridge with me throughout the entire action, and giving the ranges to the guns with accuracy that was proven by the excellence of the firing.

"On May 2, the day following the engagement, the squadron again went to Cavite, where it remains. On the 3d, the military forces evacuated the Cavite arsenal, which was taken possession of by a landing party. On the same day the Raleigh and Baltimore secured the surrender of the batteries on Corregidor Island, paroling the garrison and destroying the guns. On the morning of May 4 the transport Manila, which had been aground in Bakor Bay, was towed off and made a prize."*

The comparison of the losses in this battle is startling. Two officers and six men on board the "Baltimore" were slightly wounded, the only casualties on the side of the Americans. The Spaniards lost 101 killed and 280 wounded. There were destroyed two protected cruisers, five unprotected cruisers, a transport and a serv-

---

* Admiral Dewey's Official Report.

ing vessel, two vessels captured and other property captured and destroyed, all estimated to be worth about $6,000,000. The damage to the American fleet did not exceed $5,000.

The news of the victory electrified the world. Its effect in Europe was especially marked. A Spanish fleet defended by land batteries had been attacked and destroyed without loss of life to the assailants, an entrance to a harbor supposed to be almost inpregnable had been passed without loss and almost without discovery. The effect of the victory on the future of this country must certainly be a marked one. It has opened up to us the possibility of a "new national policy," and more than any other event seems to have aroused the American ambition for a wider sphere in international affairs.

Arrangements for the organization of a force of 20,000 men under the command of General Wesley Merritt were at once made and reinforcements hastened to the assistance of Admiral Dewey with the greatest possible dispatch. He had brought with him in the "McCulloch" from Hong Kong the rebel leader Aguinaldo, who at once proceeded to put himself in communication with the natives and organized the insurgents with himself at their head. He soon became so ambitious as to be a dangerous ally, declared himself "Dictator," and took to wearing a gold collar with a gold whistle. He was a strange mixture of shrewdness, diplomacy and childishness. He at times assisted the Americans and at other times refused them supplies. What he will do in the future remains to be seen.

The Germans had been looking with longing eyes at the Philippine Islands and seized the opportunity, under cover of protecting German interests, to send a strong force of war vessels to Manila, where they rendered themselves obnoxious by a very evident sympathy with the

Spanish cause and overbearing manners. Admiral Dewey exercised great tact, preserved control of the situation under the most trying circumstances, avoided any open rupture, and maintained the dignity of the United States. The firm stand taken by Admiral Dewey and the arrival of the first expedition of reinforcements under General Anderson, left the Germans no further excuse, and they withdrew.

An incident at Subig Bay threatened to attain international importance. The German cruiser "Irene" had refused to allow the insurgents to attack a Spanish position in Subig Bay. July 7th, Dewey sent the "Raleigh" and "Concord" to that point. As soon as the "Raleigh" opened fire on the fort the German cruiser discreetly withdrew. Fifteen hundred Spaniards surrendered without much resistance. The commander of the "Irene" said he had interfered in the cause of humanity, and offered to hand over to Dewey certain refugees, but his offer was declined.

The cruiser "Charleston," convoying three transports of the first relief expedition, reached Cavite June 30th. On the way they stopped at the island Guam, one of the Ladrones, took possession of it, left a company of the Fourteenth artillery in charge, and carried the governor, Spanish officers and 54 soldiers as prisoners of war to Manila. Admiral Dewey was reinforced by the double turreted monitors "Monadnock" and "Monterey" and the cruiser "Charleston." General Merritt upon his arrival extended his line before the city and was vigorously attacked July 31st, losing 13 dead and 47 wounded. The Spaniards were repulsed with great loss. It is likely that considerable trouble will be experienced in preserving order there until some settled form of government shall have been agreed upon.

THE ASCENDENCY OF AMERICA. 431

Matanzas.

The first engagement of the American navy with Spanish forts occurred April 27th, when three vessels of Admiral Sampson's fleet, the "New York," the monitor "Puritan" and the cruiser "Cincinnati," exchanged shots with the batteries at Matanzas. The ships fired about 300 shots at a range of from 3,500 to 7,000 yards. The damage to the enemy was probably insignificant. General Blanco reported it as one mule killed. None of our vessels were hit. Though the affair excited considerable comment at the time, it was important only in giving our men some target practice and demonstrating that the Spaniard is the poorest gunner on earth.

Reverse at Cardenas.

The most serious reverse sustained by the American navy was that at Cardenas, May 11th, when the unprotected cruiser "Wilmington," the gunboat "Machias," the revenue cutter "Hudson," and the torpedo boat "Winslow," made an attack on that port for the purpose of cutting out three small gunboats in the harbor. The draft of the "Wilmington" would not allow her to approach nearer than 2,000 yards, and as the gunboats could not be seen at that distance the "Winslow" was ordered to go in and find them. The torpedo boat had gone about 700 yards when she was fired upon by a gunboat and a shore battery. There was a sharp exchange of shots for about twenty minutes, when it became evident that the "Winslow" was disabled. Lieutenant Newcomb of the revenue cutter "Hudson," gallantly steamed in under fire, took the "Winslow" in tow, and brought her out in safety. The "Winslow" was disabled, one officer, Ensign Worth Bagley, and four men killed, and three men wounded, including Lieutenant

Bernardo, commander of the "Winslow." In this brave but ill-advised attempt we suffered a greater loss than in the naval victories at Manila and off Santiago combined.

Bombardment of San Juan.

May 12th, Admiral Sampson's squadron, consisting of the battleships "Iowa" and "Indiana," the armored cruiser "New York," the monitors "Terror" and "Amphitrite," and the cruisers "Detroit" and "Montgomery," with the torpedo boat "Porter," in search of the Cape Verde fleet, arrived off San Juan, Porto Rico. They entered the harbor, and not finding Cervera, engaged in some target practice with the fortifications and reported them silenced. The fleet suffered little damage.— the "New York" and the "Iowa" each being hit once, one man killed and six wounded. Though the action itself was a minor one, it was important in shaping the course of Cervera's fleet. He, hearing that Sampson was at San Juan, pushed on to Curacoa, an island about 75 miles from the Venezuela coast, belonging to the Netherlands. Cervera was unable to obtain any coal there, and being short of fuel, ran into Santiago, where Commodore Schley "bottled him up." Coal is not uniformly held to be contraband of war. Perhaps the Dutch inhabitants remembered the treatment their ancestors had received at the hands of the Duke of Alva.

The Santiago Campaign.

Admiral Cervera's fleet left the Cape Verde Islands April 25th, and for two weeks his movements were shrouded in mystery. The Atlantic cities feared attack, the blockade of Havana was likely to be raised, and the invasion of Cuba could not take place while such a powerful "fleet in being" was in existence. All offensive movements were paralyzed. May 13 news was received that Cervera's squadron had been sighted off

Martinique and on the 15th it was heard of at the island of Curacao. On the 13th Commodore Schley's "flying squadron" left Hampton Roads and steamed southward. Admiral Sampson's fleet left San Juan on the 15th, headed toward Cuba along the northern coast of San Domingo. The auxiliary scouts and the fleet cruisers "Columbia" and "Minneapolis" were searching for the Spanish fleet in mid-ocean. Information was received the 19th that Cervera had reached Santiago, and Commodore Schley was ordered from Cienfuegos, off which port he had arrived the 21st, to proceed at once to Santiago and blockade the narrow entrance to the harbor. He was able to report the 28th that he had seen and recognized the Spanish fleet in the bay of Santiago, and Lieutenant Blue was landed some distance from Santiago and alone made a perilous trip over the mountains to where he could see the harbor and recognize the fleet. All doubt was set at rest and the nation drew a breath of relief. The invasion of Cuba, which had been delayed, went forward vigorously. May 31st, Commodore Schley's squadron had the honor of engaging in a skirmish with the batteries about the entrance to the harbor with the "Cristobal Colon" in the background. Admiral Sampson joined Commodore Schley June 1st and assumed command of the fleet. A vigilant blockade was kept up. At three o'clock A. M. June 3d, Assistant Naval Constructor Richmond P. Hobson, with a crew of seven men, took the collier "Merrimac" into the narrow entrance of Santiago harbor under the fire of the guns from the Spanish forts and fleet, over the mines, and sunk her across the channel. No braver feat is recorded in the history of naval warfare. It was hoped the sunken ship would temporarily close the channel and prevent the exit of Cervera's fleet. Lieutenant Hobson and his men miraculously escaped serious injury, left the sunken ship on a raft, but were captured. Admiral Cervera sent an officer under a flag of truce to Admiral Sampson, telling him the men were all alive and offered to carry back to the prisoners messages and clothing. They remained as prisoners in Santiago until July 6th, when their exchange was effected by Gen. Shafter, Admiral Cervera saying at that time: "Daring like theirs makes the bitterest enemy proud that his fellow men can be such heroes."

The American fleet did not attempt to force the entrance.

The channel was too narrow, the batteries too strong and situated at too great a height, the attitude of jealous European powers too equivocal to permit the risk of the loss of a battleship. The action of the fleet was confined to occasional bombardments and a vigilant blockade that rendered escape for Cervera hopeless.

Landing at Guantanamo.

To secure a position for our ships to use when coaling Lieutenant-Colonel Huntington with about 600 marines' landed June 10th at Guantanamo. The landing was made under the protection of the guns of several vessels from Admiral Sampson's fleet. The country was covered with dense thickets of tropical growth, under cover of which Spanish soldiers and guerrillas kept up unceasing bushwhacking attacks. Unacquainted with the field and confined to the locality of the camp, our marines were at a serious disadvantage, although their efforts were ably seconded by the small body of Cuban insurgents who joined them. For two or three days the skirmishing was almost constant, but the little force of Americans held the ground secured and inflicted heavy loss on the enemy. Early Sunday morning the Spaniards made an attempt to rush the camp, but were driven back with severe loss. The "Texas" arrived and landed 40 marines with two Colt automatic guns and the "Marblehead" moved up and shelled the wooded hillside where the Spaniards were concealed. Again on the morning of the 13th the Spaniards tried to rush the camp, but with no better success. On the 14th, our forces somewhat strengthened, adopted an aggressive policy, sent out four columns and were soon actively engaged with the enemy. The Cuban insurgents rendered material service. The combined forces beat up the surrounding country, drove the enemy from the thickets, inflicted upon him a severe loss and captured one Spanish officer and seventeen privates. From this time the situation at Camp McCalla was greatly improved, intrenchments were thrown up, more Cuban reinforcements arrived, the war vessels gave their support, and the outer bay was securely held. The marines held their position, and the harbor has afforded a safe base of operations for Admiral Sampson's fleet.

The Destruction of Cervera's Fleet.

Admiral Cervera made a dash out of the harbor 9:35 A. M. Sunday, July 3. At this time the flagship "New York" was about seven miles from the entrance, Admiral Sampson having started to consult with General Shafter. The "Massachusetts" was coaling at Guantanamo and the others were in their usual blockading position, from two and one-half to four miles from the entrance, in the following order from eastward to westward: "Indiana," "Oregon," "Iowa," "Texas," and "Brooklyn." The auxiliaries "Gloucester" and "Vixen" lay close to the land and nearer the harbor entrance than the large vessels, the "Gloucester" to the eastward and the "Vixen" to the westward. The torpedo boat "Ericsson" was in company with the flagship.

The Spanish vessels came rapidly out of the harbor at a speed estimated at from eight to ten knots and in the following order: "Infanta Maria Teresa," (flagship), "Viscaya," "Cristobal Colon," and "Almirante Oquendo." * * * Following the "Oquendo" came the torpedo boat destroyer "Pluton" and after her the "Furor." The men of our ships were at Sunday quarters for "inspection;" the signal was made simultaneously from several vessels, "the enemy's ships escaping" and "general quarters" were sounded. The men cheered as they sprang to their guns and fire was opened probably within eight minutes by the vessels whose guns commanded the entrance. The "New York" turned about and steamed for the escaping fleet flying the signal "close in toward harbor entrance and attack vessels." * * * She was not at any time within the range of the heavy Spanish ships and her only part in the firing was to receive the individual fire from the forts in passing the harbor entrance and fire a few shots at one of the destroyers thought at the moment to be attempting to escape from the "Gloucester." The Spanish vessels upon clearing the harbor turned to the westward in column, increasing their speed to the full power of their engines. * * * The initial speed of the Spaniards carried them rapidly past the blockading vessels and the battle developed into a chase in which the "Brooklyn" and "Texas" had at the start the advantage of position. The "Brooklyn" maintained this lead. * * * Anticipating the appearance of the "Pluton" and the "Furor" the "Gloucester" was slowed, thereby gaining more rapidly a high pressure of steam, and when the destroyers came out, she steamed for them at full speed and was able to close at short range where her fire was accurate, deadly and of great volume. * * * Within twenty minutes from the time they emerged from Santiago harbor the careers of the "Pluton" and "Furor" were ended and two-thirds of their people killed. The "Furor" was beached and sunk in the surf; the "Pluton" sank in deep water a few minutes later. After rescuing the survivors of the destroyers, the "Gloucester" did excellent service in landing and securing the crew of the "Infanta Maria Teresa."

The Spanish cruisers* suffered heavily in passing our battleships, and the "Maria Teresa" and "Oquendo" were set on fire during the first fifteen minutes of the engagement; the former had her fire main cut by one of our first shots, a second set her on fire, and a third disabled one of her engines. Six and a half miles from Santiago harbor the "Maria Teresa" ran in on the beach, and a half mile farther on the "Oquendo" did the same. The Vizcaya was beached at Acerraderos, 15 miles from Santiago, at 11:15. She was burning fiercely, and her reserves of ammunition on deck were beginning to explode.

There remained now of the Spanish ships only the "Cristobal Colon," but she was their best and fastest vessel. * * * When the "Vizcaya" went ashore the "Colon" was about six miles ahead of the "Brooklyn" and "Oregon," but her spurt was finished and the American ships were now gaining upon her. Behind the "Brooklyn" and "Oregon" came the "Texas," "Vixen" and "New York." * * * At 11:50 the "Brooklyn" and "Oregon" opened fire and got her range, the "Oregon's" heavy shells striking beyond her, and at 1:20 she gave up without firing another shot, hauled down her colors and ran ashore at Rio Torquino, 48 miles from Santiago. * * * The "Iowa," assisted by the "Ericsson" and the "Hist," took

---

* Admiral Sampson's Official Report.

off the crew of the "Vizcaya," while the "Harvard" and "Gloucester" rescued those of the "Infanta Maria" and "Almirante Oquendo." This rescue of prisoners, including the wounded from the burning Spanish vessels, was the occasion of some of the most daring and gallant conduct of the day. The ships were burning fore and aft, their guns and reserve ammunition were exploding, and it was not known at what moment the fire would reach the main magazine. In addition to this a heavy surf was running just inside of the Spanish ships, but no risk deterred our officers and men until their work of humanity was completed. * * * The fire of the battleships was powerful and destructive, and the resistance of the Spanish squadron was in great part broken almost before they had gone beyond the range of their own forts. The fine speed of the "Oregon" enabled her to take a front position in the chase, and the "Cristobal Colon" did not give up until the "Oregon" had thrown a 13-inch shell beyond her.*

Although the destruction of the Spanish ships was so rapid and so thorough, very little damage was done the American squadron. The "Brooklyn" was hit more often than the others, but very slight damage was done, the greatest being to the "Iowa." The American loss was one man killed and one wounded, both on the "Brooklyn."

The Spanish plan of escape, so far as the ships were concerned was feasible, and had the Spanish fleet been in American hands, and *vice versa*, it would have undoubtedly been successful. The four Spanish cruisers were all of 20-knots speed, and the destroyers were supposed to be good for 28 to 30 knots. Against them were the "Iowa," 17.1 knots, "Oregon," 16.8 knots, "Texas," 17.8 knots, and the "Brooklyn," 21.9 knots. American gunnery won the day and won it in very short order. Santiago adds its eloquent testimony to the truth that to-day as of old, it is "the man behind the gun" that wins the fight. The moment Cervera's fleet was found its destruction became necessary.

Shafter's Army.

June 14th, Maj.-Gen. Shafter, commanding the 5th Army Corps of about 16,000 men, made up of all branches of the service, left Tampa for an attack on Santiago.

---

* Admiral Sampson's Official Report.

The force was composed wholly of regulars, except the 71st New York, the 2d Massachusetts and the 1st Volunteer Infantry (Rough Riders). They embarked on 35 transports with two water boats and with a strong convoy, headed by the battleship " Indiana," proceeded eastward along the north coast of Cuba around the eastern point, Cape Maysi, and arrived off Santiago June 20th. The expedition was remarkable in moving without an unpleasant occurrence, and was the largest of its kind since the Crimean war. Upon his arrival General Shafter with Admiral Sampson met Lieut.-Gen. Garcia, commanding about 4,000 Cubans, and made plans for a landing and attack on Santiago. On the 22d the fleet kept up a series of demonstrations along the coast for 20 miles, and so completely deceived the Spaniards that the army was landed in the face of a force nearly as great as its own without the loss of a single life. The harbors were shallow, the shores were rocky, the lighters usually thought necessary for such operations had sunk on their way to Cuba, yet in the face of all these difficulties the first landing was made the 22d at Daquiri, on the 23d another at Siboney. On the 24th the landing of troops continued, and an advance early in the morning reached La Guasina, four miles west of Siboney, where an action occurred. The 1st and 10th cavalry charged in front, the 1st Volunteer Cavalry charged in flank on the left and drove the enemy from his position, although we sustained a severe loss in killed and wounded. By nightfall a gain of more than a mile had been made. The troops in this action were under the command of Gen. Young. By June 25th our forces, Gen. Lawton's division in advance, occupied the high ridge of Savilla in full view of Santiago, distant about five miles. Gen. Wheeler's dismounted cavalry was some distance behind Lawton's division, Kent's division coming up in the rear of Wheeler's. By the 27th they had forced their way to points within three miles of Santiago. The light batteries came up and took position near Wheeler's division, about the center of the army as it then stood, the mounted squadron of the Second Infantry occupying a position near the battery.

Battle of El Caney: June 30th, Gen. Lawton, commanding the Second Division, made a reconnoissance of the village of El Caney. Gen. Shafter held a consultation and issued orders for an attack on the village July 1st with the object of passing through and turning the flank of the enemy.

The troops were pushed forward, moving at night by the light of the moon, and one battery of artillery reached a point commanding El Caney. About 7 A. M. the artillery opened fire at a range of 2,400 yards. They were out of range of the small arms and the enemy had no artillery. The engagement became general, and the fire was hot until 10 A. M., during which time all the lines were drawing closer to the enemy and a continuous fire of musketry being kept up. By afternoon they had closed in on the village. A stone fort or block-house situated on the highest point at the northern side commanded the fields, the fire of the artillery was concentrated on this, and between 1 and 2 o'clock an assault made by the infantry under Chaffee, Bates and Miles, carried the position. The small block-houses on the other side of the village kept up a fierce resistance, but were soon silenced by our infantry fire before the artillery could be brought to bear upon them. By night our troops occupied the main road leading into the city of Santiago.

Battle of San Juan. — July 1st found Wheeler's division bivouacked on the heights of El Pozo and Kent's division to his left near the road back of El Pozo. At 6:45 A. M. the first guns against El Caney were heard, and a little later Grimes' battery opened against San

Juan. By 9 o'clock Wheeler's division was in march toward Santiago. Continued skirmishing was kept up until the stream Aguadores was crossed, when the enemy opened volley fire against the dismounted cavalry who were going into position and crossing open ground. Kent's division followed Wheeler's, turning to the left and advancing under a severe fire. At one o'clock the whole force advanced, charged, and carried the enemy's first line of intrenchments. Here they halted and threw up a line of intrenchments facing the enemy, who were only 500 to 1,000 yards distant. The cavalry division occupied the captured crest, and regiments of Kent's division moved to the left. Gen. Bates, Independent Brigade after taking part in the battle of El Caney was moved back and went into position July 2d, at the extreme left of the lines.

Before Santiago.—During the whole of July 2d, heavy firing was kept up by both sides. Our troops were busy throwing up entrenchments to sustain their positions. Batteries of artillery going into action near San Juan, 600 yards from the enemy and firing black powder, were soon located and driven back with heavy losses. During this day there were many losses from hits made at extreme range, the bullets passing over the crest held by our first line and striking those in the rear. Spanish sharp shooters hidden in tree tops within our own lines inflicted severe loss and did not respect the wounded or hospital corps. The night of July 2d, the enemy made an attack upon our lines, but were driven back with very little loss to ourselves. It was evident that the city was doomed. On the morning of July 3rd, there was little firing on either sides, and the Spanish fleet left the harbor and were destroyed. The next ten days were taken up with negotiations for the surrender and a desultory firing.

The army and city capitulated on the 14th of July,

THE ASCENDENCY OF AMERICA. 441

Gen. Toral surrendering all the territory and forces in eastern Cuba, including about 12,000 soldiers who had never fired a gun against us, the United States agreeing to transport the Spanish soldiers to Spain, the officers to retain their side arms, and the officers and men their personal property. The Spanish commander was allowed to take the military archives belonging to his district. The Spanish volunteers and guerillas were allowed to remain upon giving their parole and surrendering their arms. The Spanish forces marched out with the honors of war and deposited their arms at a point mutually agreed upon. The number of troops surrendered amounted to more than 24,000. July 17, General Shafter reported to Washington as follows:

"I have the honor to announce that the American flag has been this instant, 12 o'clock noon, hoisted over the house of the Civil Government. An immense concourse of people was present, a squadron of cavalry and a regiment of infantry presenting arms and a band playing national airs. A light battery fired a salute of twenty-one guns."

Invasion of Porto Rico.

Soon after the fall of Santiago, Gen. Miles left with an army for Porto Rico. A landing was made July 25th on the south coast at Guanica, fifteen miles west of Ponce, and the port and town captured without loss, the inhabitants receiving them with open arms. Soon after Ponce, a city of 50,000 inhabitants, and the largest in Porto Rico, surrendered, the populace receiving the troops and saluting the flag with wild enthusiasm. The march inland was taken up in four columns, town after town falling into our hands after only light skirmishes, the Spanish soldiers surrendering or falling back and the inhabitants evincing the greatest pleasure at the appearance of the American troops. Peace negotiations closed the war without heavy fighting in Porto Rico.

Peace **Negotiations.**

The overtures of peace were made public August 2d. They stipulated that Spain should give up all claim to the island of Cuba, and cede to the United States, Porto Rico and an island in the Ladrones. Furthermore, the United States should occupy and hold Manila and surrounding territory pending the conclusion of a treaty of peace which should determine the final disposition of the Philippines. If these terms were accepted by Spain, commissioners of the United States would meet commissioners of Spain for the purpose of concluding a treaty of peace.

Sagasta summoned the heads of all parties to confer with him August 3d. The Ministry was in favor of peace, but uncertain of its power to make peace. Finally, on the evening of August 8th, Spain's answer was received and presented to the President through Monsieur Cambon, the French ambassador. In it she accepted our terms with the qualification that the protocol should contain certain concessions with regard to the withdrawal of the Spanish troops from Cuba, the disposition of the Cuban debt, and other subjects of controversy. On August 10th the protocol was drawn up, and in it no provision was made with regard to the exceptions given by Spain in her note. Monsieur Cambon agreed provisionally to the terms of the protocol in behalf of Spain, and cabled to Madrid for authority to attach his signature to the document as Spanish representative. The terms of the protocol were essentially the same as those forwarded to Spain ten days before, and the Spanish Ministry declared itself satisfied. By a brilliant diplomatic coup, President McKinley and Secretary Day had placed the Spanish Ministry in a position where they could no longer parley nor procrastinate.

In one hundred days Spain lost two fleets, an army and all her possessions in this hemisphere, and America stood forth a great " world power."

THE ASCENDENCY OF AMERICA. 443

Second Battle of Manila.

The same day the protocol was signed, President McKinley issued a proclamation announcing a general suspension of hostilities, and hurried off instructions to the various army and navy leaders at their different stations, but before the news reached Dewey at Manila a second battle had been fought. Almost a week before, Admiral Dewey and General Merritt had given the Spanish commander notice to remove all noncombatants.* A later demand for the surrender of the city having been refused, the fleet opened fire about 8:30 A. M., August 13, great care being observed to prevent any shot falling into the city proper. The enemy received the fire of the fleet without making any response.

Meanwhile the land forces were moving in two columns upon the Spanish works. A spirited action ensued, but the Spanish forces were unable to hold their position and retreated with heavy loss, leaving part of their line of defense in the possession of their opponents, who had suffered a loss of about 12 men killed and 40 wounded.

Spain foreseeing the disaster had, with characteristic diplomacy, technically "relieved" Captain General Augustin, for the express purpose of leaving no Spanish officer having jurisdiction over the whole group of islands, and the command of Manila had devolved upon General Jaudenes. This commander realizing the hopelessness of his position signified a willingness to come to terms.

The negotiations were carried on through the Belgian consul, who, with Flag Lieut. Brumby of the Olympia and Lieut. Col. Whittier of the army, went ashore from the flagship. Upon their return a white flag appeared on the Spanish fort, and General Merritt, with a military escort, went ashore to receive the surrender of the city. The Spanish flag that for more than 350 years had

---
* See Appendix.

floated over the Philippines as the symbol of sovereignty came down, and Lieut. Brumby had the honor of hoisting an American flag from the Olympia in its stead.

Captain General Augustin, by the connivance of the German Admiral, escaped on board the German warship "Kaiserin Augusta." The insurgents had remained spectators of the combat, and greatly to their disgust were not allowed to plunder the city.

Spain had hoped that the Peace Commission would find her still in possession of Manila when she would have claimed that the city could have held out indefinitely. A dispatch from Madrid announcing the peace negotiations was sent to the Spanish commander August 13, but the American flag, if allowance for difference in time is made, was then floating over the city, and even if the cable had been working between Manila and Hong Kong, the dispatch would have been too late.

The advantage of control of Manila thus passed to America.

Occupation of Porto Rico.

Porto Rico was invaded on the south, it appearing to be a part of General Miles' plan to drive all the enemy's forces before him and to leave open for them lines of retreat to San Juan on the north coast. There he expected to gather them in, leaving the whole island in the peaceable possession of the Americans, for four-fifths of the inhabitants evinced the greatest pleasure at the prospect of a change of government.

The campaign lasted nineteen days during which time there were five encounters rising to the dignity of skirmishes. Although the contour of the country offered many opportunities for defense, the Americans were uniformly and easily successful. Ensign Curtin of the "Dixie" landed at the port of Ponce, called the commander of the town proper to the *telephone* and demanded his surrender, which was yielded. About the only show of spirited defiance by a Spanish officer was the reply of Lieut. Col. Nuvillers to General Wilson's demand for his surrender, "Tell General Wilson to stay where he is if he wishes to avoid further bloodshed." The cessation of hostilities rendered an attack on Colonel Nuvillers unnecessary.

Porto Rico thus easily fell into the hands of the Americans. It had been a Spanish possession for more than 400 years, but a large majority of its inhabitants were overjoyed at their escape from the evils of Spanish administration.

Evacuation and Peace Commissions.

Agreeable to the terms of the protocol, each nation named within ten days members of the commissions, who were to meet within thirty days and arrange all the details of the evacuation of Cuba and Porto Rico.

President McKinley named as members of the Cuban commission, Maj.-Gen. James F. Wade, Rear Admiral William T. Sampson, and Maj.-Gen. M. C. Butler. Captain-General Blanco refused to serve on the commission, and Spain named his second in command, General Parrado, together with Captain Landera and the leader of the Cuban Autonomists, the Marquis Montoro.

The American members of the Porto Rican board were Maj.-Gen. John R. Brooke, second in command in Porto Rico; Rear Admiral Winfield S. Schley, and Brig.-Gen. William W. Gordon. The Spanish members were General Ortega, Captain Vallarino, and Senor Sanches Aquila.

By the terms of the protocol, the Peace Commission was composed of ten members, to meet in Paris before October 1, and America very properly headed her delegation with William R. Day, who had rendered such distinguished service as Secretary of State. Judge Day is popularly credited with being the author of the protocol of August 12. Judge Day's associates on the commission were Senator Cushman K. Davis, Senator William P. Frye, Whitelaw Reid of the *New York Tribune*, and Justice White of the Superior Court.

The Peace Commissioners.

The labors of the Peace Commission did not receive the unanimous approval of the United States Senate, before which body the treaty went for ratification, and for a time it seemed likely that an extra session of Congress would be called to ratify the treaty.

Taking advantage of the situation, the insurgents in the Philippines made themselves as obnoxious as possible. Their representative at Washington, Agoncillo, was never officially recognized by the Administration, but he put himself very much in evidence by his letters to the press and his calls upon members of the House and Senate. He may have been deceived by the opposition to the treaty into thinking that the United States could be worried into releasing the Philippines. He is popularly supposed to have sent a telegram to Aguinaldo urging him to make the night attack February 4, for the sake of its political effect in Washington, and his hurried departure from Washington for Montreal would indicate that he at least had knowledge of what was to come.

Late at night, Saturday, February 4, 1899, Aguinaldo's forces about Manila made a fierce attack upon the Americans under General Otis. Far from being surprised, the Americans were apparently well prepared and returned the attack with interest. The fight continued until daylight of the next day, when the navy, under Admiral Dewey, took a part with characteristic efficiency and the insurgents were defeated, their loss in killed, wounded, and prisoners amounting to 4,000, while that of the Americans was only four officers and fifty-three men killed and eight officers and 207 men wounded. The despised .45 caliber Springfield rifle, with which a large part of General Otis' men were armed, seemed to inflict more severe wounds than the Mausers of the insurgents.

Although the skirmishing continued for some time, interspersed with plots to burn the city and assassinate the officers and foreigners, yet Aguinaldo's power received such a severe blow by this defeat, that other cities began voluntarily to submit to the United States authority and send delegations to wait upon General Otis and Admiral Dewey.

Iloilo was captured by General Miller on **the 12th with** little effort, the insurgents setting fire to the city and withdrawing.

Treaty of Peace Ratified.

Contrary to Aguinaldo's expectations, the show of resistance in the Philippines did not produce the desired effect in the United States Senate and the treaty of peace with Spain was ratified February 6th. Party lines were not strictly drawn, Senators Hoar and Hale, republicans, voting against the treaty, while Senators Gray, Morgan, McEnery, McLaurin, and Jones (Silverite), democrats, voted for it.

But one branch of the Spanish Cortes voted to accept the treaty, and acting under the advice of her ministers the Queen dissolved the Cortes and signed the ratification March 18, 1899, without the consent of that body. According to the Spanish constitution the consent of the Cortes is necessary to the alienation of any Spanish territory. The Queen relies on the next Cortes to ratify her acts.

THE PROTOCOL.

The signing of the protocol took place in the Cabinet room of the White House, August 12, Monsieur Cambon, the French Ambassador, acting for Spain, and Secretary of State William R. Day for the United States. The ceremony took place in the presence of President McKinley and a few others. The document was prepared in duplicate, written in parallel columns in English and French, and each nation will preserve a copy in its archives. The ceremony was over at 4.23.

Provisions of the Protocol.

1. That Spain will relinquish all claim of sovereignty over and title to Cuba.
2. That Porto Rico and other Spanish islands of the West Indies and an island in the Ladrones, to be selected by the United States, shall be ceded to the latter.
3. That the United States will occupy and hold the city, bay, and harbor of Manila, pending the conclusion of a treaty of peace which shall determine the control, disposition, and government of the Philippines.
4. That Cuba, Porto Rico, and other Spanish islands in the West Indies shall be immediately evacuated, and that commissioners, to be appointed within ten days, shall, within thirty days from the signing of the protocol, meet at Havana and San Juan, respectively, to arrange and execute the details of the evacuation.
5. That the United States and Spain will each appoint not more than five commissioners to negotiate and conclude a treaty of peace. The commissioners are to meet at Paris not later than October 1.
6. On the signing of the protocol, hostilities will be suspended, and notice to that effect will be given as soon as possible by each government to the commanders of its military and naval forces.

The Treaty of Peace.

An armistice and the suspension of hostilities followed immediately the signing of the peace protocol. On August 26, President McKinley named the American Commissioners. The Commissioners left New York on September 17th and arrived in Paris ten days later. The first joint session of the commissions for the two governments was held on October 1. For over two months almost daily sessions were held, at which propositions and counter-propositions were exchanged, until finally the diplomatic contest was ended by the signing of the treaty by the Commissioners of both powers on December 10. On January 4, 1899, the treaty was transmitted to the Senate by the President. It was read in executive session and at once referred to the Committee on Foreign Relations. The committee reported the treaty favorably on January 11.

Text of the Treaty.

The United States of America and Her Majesty, the Queen Regent of Spain, in the name of her august son, Don Alfonso XIII., desiring to end the state of war now existing between the two countries, have for that purpose appointed as plenipotentiaries: —
The President of the United States: —
WILLIAM R. DAY, CUSHMAN K. DAVIS, WILLIAM P. FRYE, GEORGE GRAY, and WHITELAW REID, citizens of the United States;
And Her Majesty, the Queen Regent of Spain: —
DON EUGENIO MONTERO RIOS, President of the Senate; DON BUENAVENTURA DE ABARZUZA, Senator of the Kingdom and ex-Minister of the Crown; DON JOSE DE GARNICA, Deputy to the Cortes and Associate Justice of the Supreme Court; DON WENCESLAO RAMIREZ DE VILLA URRUTIA, Envoy Extraordinary and Minister Plenipotentiary at Brussels, and DON RAFAEL CERERO, General of Division.

Who, having assembled in Paris and having exchanged their full powers, which were found to be in due and proper form, have, after discussion of the matters before them, agreed upon the following articles: —

Article I. Spain relinquishes all claim of sovereignty over and title to Cuba.

And as the island is, upon its evacuation by Spain, to be occupied by the United States, the United States will, so long as such occupation shall last, assume and discharge the obligations that may under international law result from the fact of its occupation for the protection of life and property.

Article II. Spain cedes to the United States the island of Porto Rico and other islands now under Spanish sovereignty in the West Indies, and the Island of Guam, in the Marianas or Ladrones.

Article III. Spain cedes to the United States the archipelago known as the Philippine Islands, and comprehending the islands lying within the following lines: —

A line running from west to east along or near the twentieth parallel of north latitude, and through the middle of the navigable channel of Bachti, from the one hundred and eighteenth (118th) to the one hundred and twenty-seventh (127th) degree meridian of longitude east of Greenwich, thence along the one hundred and twenty-seventh (127th) degree meridian of longitude east of Greenwich to the parallel of four degrees and forty-five minutes (4.45) north latitude to its intersection with the meridian of longitude one hundred and nineteen degrees and thirty-five minutes (119.35) east of Greenwich, thence along the meridian of longitude one hundred and nineteen degrees and thirty-five minutes (119.35) east of Greenwich to the parallel of latitude seven degrees and forty minutes (7.40) north to its intersection with the one hundred and sixteenth (116th) degree meridian of longitude east of Greenwich, thence by a direct line to the intersection of the tenth (10th) degree parallel of north latitude with the one hundred and eighteenth (118th) degree meridian of longitude east of Greenwich, and thence along the one hundred and eighteenth (118th) degree meridian of longitude east of Greenwich to the point of beginning.

The United States will pay to Spain the sum of twenty million dollars ($20,000,000) within three months after the exchange of the ratification of the present treaty.

Article IV. The United States will, for ten years from the date of exchange of ratifications of the present treaty, admit Spanish ships and merchandise to the ports of the Philippine Islands on the same terms as ships and merchandise of the United States.

Article V. The United States will, upon the signature of the present treaty, send back to Spain, at its own cost, the Spanish soldiers taken as prisoners of war on the capture of Manila by the American forces. The arms of the soldiers in question will be restored to them.

Spain will, upon the exchange of the ratifications of the present treaty, proceed to evacuate the Philippines, as well as the island of Guam, on terms similar to those agreed upon by the Commissioners appointed to arrange for the evacuation of Porto Rico and other islands in the West Indies under the protocol of August 12, 1898, which is to continue in force till its provisions are completely executed.

The time within which the evacuation of the Philippine Islands and Guam shall be completed shall be fixed by the two governments. Stands of colors, uncaptured war vessels, small arms, guns of all calibers, with their carriages and accessories, powder, ammunition, live stock, and materials and supplies of all kinds belonging to the land and naval forces of Spain in the Philippines and Guam remain the property of Spain. Pieces of heavy ordnance, exclusive of field artillery, in the fortifications and coast defenses, shall remain in their emplacements for the term of six months, to be reckoned from the exchange of ratifications of the treaty; and **the United States may in the meantime purchase such material from Spain if a satisfactory agreement between the two governments on the subject** shall be reached.

Article VI. Spain will, upon the signature of the present treaty, release all prisoners of war and all persons detained or imprisoned for political offenses in connection with the insurrections in Cuba and the Philippines and the war with the United States.

Reciprocally the United States will release all persons made prisoners of war by the American forces, and will undertake to obtain the release of all Spanish prisoners in the hands of the insurgents in Cuba and the Philippines.

The government of the United States will at its own cost return to Spain, and the government of Spain will at its own cost return to the United States, Cuba, Porto Rico, and the Philippines, according to the situation of their respective homes, prisoners released or caused to be released by them respectively, under this article.

Article VII. The United States and Spain mutually relinquish all claims for indemnity, national and individual of every kind of either government, or of its citizens or subjects, against the other government, which may have arisen since the beginning of the late Insurrection in Cuba and prior to the exchange of ratifications of the present treaty, including all claims for indemnity for the cost of the war. The United States will adjudicate and settle the claim of its citizens against Spain, relinquished in this article.

Article VIII. In conformity with the provisions of Articles I., II., and III., of this treaty, Spain relinquishes in Cuba and cedes in Porto Rico and other islands in the West Indies, in the island of Guam, and in the Philippine Archipelago, all the buildings, wharves, barracks, forts, structures, public highways, and other immovable property which in conformity with law belong to the public domain and as such belong to the Crown of Spain.

And it is hereby declared that the relinquishment or cession, as the case may be, to which the preceding paragraph refers, cannot in any respect impair the property or rights which by law belong to the peaceful possession of property of all kinds of provinces, municipalities, public or private establishments, ecclesiastical or civic bodies, or any other associations having legal capacity to acquire and possess property in the aforesaid territories renounced or ceded, or of private individuals, of whatsoever nationality such individuals may be.

The aforesaid relinquishment or cession, as the case may be, includes all documents exclusively referring to the sovereignty relinquished or ceded that may exist in the archives of the Peninsula. Where any document in such archives only in part relates to said sovereignty a copy of such part will be furnished whenever it shall be requested. Like rules shall be reciprocally observed in favor of Spain in respect to documents in the archives of the islands above referred to.

In the aforesaid relinquishment or cession, as the case may be, are also included such rights as the Crown of Spain and its authorities possess in respect of the official archives and records, executive as well as judicial, in the islands above referred to, which relate to said islands or the rights and property of their inhabitants. Such archives and records shall be carefully preserved, and private persons shall, without distinction, have the right to require, in accordance with the law, authenticated copies of the contracts, wills, and other instruments forming part of notarial protocols or files, or which may be contained in the executive or judicial archives, be the latter in Spain or in the islands aforesaid.

Article IX. Spanish subjects, natives of the Peninsula, residing in the territory over which Spain by the present treaty relinquishes or cedes her sovereignty, may remain in such territory or may remove therefrom, retaining in either event all their rights of property, including the right to sell or dispose of such property or of its proceeds; and they shall also have the right to carry on their industry, commerce, and professions, being subject in respect thereof to such laws as are applicable to other foreigners. In case they remain in the territory they may preserve their allegiance to the Crown of Spain by making, before a court of record, within a year from the date of the exchange of ratifications of this treaty, a declaration of their decision to preserve such allegiance; in default of which declaration they shall be held to have renounced it, and to have adopted the nationality of the territory in which they may reside.

The civil rights and political status of the native inhabitants of the territory hereby ceded to the United States shall be determined by the Congress.

Article X. The inhabitants of the territories over which Spain relinquishes or cedes her sovereignty shall be secured in the free exercise of their religion.

Article XI. The Spaniards residing in the territories over which Spain by this treaty cedes or relinquishes her sovereignty shall be subject in matters civil as well as criminal, to the jurisdiction of the courts of the country wherein they reside, pursuant to the ordinary laws governing the same; and they shall have the right to appear before such courts and to pursue the same course as citizens of the country to which the courts belong.

Article XII. Judicial proceedings pending at the time of the exchange of ratifications of this treaty in the territories over which Spain relinquishes or cedes her sovereignty, shall be determined according to the following rules:—

First.—Judgments rendered either in civil suits between private individuals or in criminal matters, before the date mentioned, and with respect to which there is no recourse or right of reviews under the Spanish law, shall be deemed to be final, and shall be executed in due form by competent authority in the territory within which such judgments should be carried out.

Second.—Civil suits between private individuals which may on the date mentioned be undetermined shall be prosecuted to judgment before the court in which they may then be pending, or in the court that may be substituted therefor.

Third.—Criminal actions pending on the date mentioned before the Supreme Court of Spain against citizens of the territory which by this treaty ceases to be Spanish, shall continue under its jurisdiction until final judgment; but, such judgment having been rendered, the execution thereof shall be committed to the competent authority of the place in which the case arose.

Article XIII. The rights of property secured by copyright and patents acquired by Spaniards in the islands of Cuba and Porto Rico, the Philippines, and other ceded territories, at the time of the exchange of the ratification of this treaty, shall continue to be respected. Spanish scientific, literary, and artistic works not subversive of public order in the territories in question shall continue to be admitted free of duty into such territories for the period of ten years, to be reckoned from the date of the exchange of the ratifications of this treaty.

Article XIV. Spain shall have the power to establish consular officers in the ports and places of the territories the sovereignty over which has either been relinquished or ceded by the present treaty.

Article XV. The government of each country will, for the term of ten years, accord to the merchant vessels of the other country the same treatment in respect to all port charges, including entrance and clearance dues, light dues and tonnage duties, as it accords to its own merchant vessels not engaged in the coastwise trade.

This article may at any time be terminated on six months' notice given by either government to the other.

Article XVI. It is understood that any obligations assumed in this treaty by the United States with respect to Cuba are limited to the time of its occupancy thereof; but it will upon the termination of such occupancy advise any government established in the islands to assume the same obligations.

Article XVII. The present treaty shall be ratified by the President of the United States, by and with the advice and consent of the Senate thereof, and by Her Majesty, the Queen Regent of Spain; and the ratifications shall be exchanged at Washington within six months from the date hereof, or earlier if possible.

In faith whereof we, the respective plenipotentiaries, have signed this treaty and have hereunto affixed our seals.

Done in duplicate at Paris, the tenth day of December, in the year of our Lord One Thousand Eight Hundred and Ninety-eight.

INDEX.

	PAGE.
CUBA.	193–261
Present Conditions........................	193–212
Agricultural products.....................	197
Climate.................................	195
Coasts..................................	198
Compulsory education...................	212
Government.............................	210
Havana.................................	200
Isle of Pines............................	199
Mineral products........................	197
Matanzas...............................	201
Pinar del Rio...........................	200
Principal cities and towns...............	203–208
Provinces...............................	200
Puerto Principe.........................	202
Railroads...............................	208
Rivers..................................	195
Santiago de Cuba.......................	202
Soil....................................	197
Surface.................................	194
Wagon roads............................	208
History.................................	212–261
American Fillibusters....................	225
Black Eagle.............................	224
Black Warrior...........................	226
Bolivar.................................	224
British Capture Havana.................	219
British Influence.....................	220
Morro Captured......................	221
The Mine............................	221

CUBA — Continued.
- History.
  - Cuban Agents.. 236
  - **Cuban** Provisional Government................ 231
  - Cubans Recognized............................... 232
  - Cuban Successes 230
  - **Cuba's** Title 223
  - Discovery of.................................... 213
  - Death of Maceo................................. 253
  - Europe Concerned............................... 227
  - First Settlements............................... 216
  - Good Offices of United States................. 234
  - Havana "**Volunteers**"......................... 231
  - Hostilities **Begin**............................ 230
  - How Cuba's War Has Been Conducted......... 256
  - Influence of Spanish-American Colonies........ 224
  - Insurrection Planned............................ 249
  - Invasion of Velasquez 216
  - **Las** Casas..................................... 222
  - **Massacre** of Havana Students 246
  - Murder of Dr. Ruiz.............................. 254
  - **Negro** Plot.................................... 224
  - Negro Slavery 217
  - Ostend Manifesto............................... 228
  - Peace of Zangon 233
  - Perils to United States 235
  - Period of Conspiracies.......................... 225
  - San Domingo.................................... 223
- Spain's Irritating Course........................... 227
- Sufferings of Cuba.................................. 217–219
  - from Buccaneers 218
  - from Spanish Rule.............................. 218
- Sugar 222
- Summary.. 232
- **Ten Years'** War 229
- The "Allianca Affair ".............................. 250
- The "Competitor" Incident........................ 253

INDEX.

CUBA — Continued.
	PAGE.
The Quitman Expedition	227
The Cuba of the Future	261
The Reconcentrados Order	256–261
The Virginius Case	235–246
Blockade Runner	236
British Flag Refused	240
Cuban Agents	236
Cuban Flag	237
Diplomatic Action	241–246
Her Character Well Known	239
In Venezuelan Service	238
Protected by the "Kansas"	238
Successful Landing	238
Takes Military Stores Aboard	237
The Fatal Expedition	240
True Ownership Shown	239
United States Offers to Buy	225
Weyler	251
Why the Cubans Rebelled	247–249

INTERNATIONAL LAW 262–306
Armistice	293
Articles of Geneva Convention	304
Blockades	275–280
American Practice	277
A Declaration of Blockade	278
A Recognized Right	278
Pacific Blockades	279
Seward's Position	276
Capitulation	294
Changing Armament	300
Conference at Brussels	295
Crime	285
Declaration of Paris	274
Declaration of War	297
Defined	262
Deserters	286

INTERNATIONAL LAW — Continued.

	PAGE.
Duties of Neutrals	300
Flag of Truce	290
Giving of Quarter	286
Holy Alliance	263
Hospital Corps	286
Hospital Flag	291
How It Grew	263
Indemnity	301
Intervention	272
Law of War	281
Martial Law	280
Monroe Doctrine	266–272
Animus of Doctrine	271
A Policy, Not a Law	269
Enunciated	267
Its Principles	270
Jefferson's View	266
Madison's Opinion	267
Not Hostile to Monarchies	269
Origin of	266
Notice of Bombardment	282
Parole	292
Preservation of Order	283
Prisoners	287
Private Gain	285
Private Property	284
Private Property of Prisoners	285
Returning Non-combatants	282
Rights of a Neutral	301
Scouts and Spies	288
Spanish Declaration of War	298
Spoils of War	283
The Red Cross Society	303
Things Forbidden	282
Traitors	290
Treatment of Rebels	294

INDEX. 455

INTERNATIONAL LAW — Continued. PAGE.
   War... 297
   War Growing less Barbarous..................... 273

EVOLUTION OF THE MODERN NAVY........... 306–342
   American Ironclads................................ 309
   Apportionment of Weight......................... 322
   Armored Cruiser.................................. 315
   Armored Ships 308
   Barbette and Turret.............................. 321
   Battleships 318
   Class Requirements 311
   Commerce Destroyer.............................. 312
   Conning Tower................................... 317
   Cruisers' Duties.................................. 311
   Definition of Terms 339–342
   Development of the Ironclad..................... 306
   Displacement..................................... 310
   Double Bottom................................... 314
   First English Turret Ship........................ 309
   First Ironclad.................................... 307
   Forced Draft..................................... 307
   Fulton.. 306
   Gun Shields 313
   How War Ships Are Classed...................... 310
   Military Masts and Fighting Tops................ 317
   Monitor.. 310 & 323
      Cause of Popularity......................... 323
      Construction................................ 324
      Duties 324
      Turrets..................................... 325
   Primary and Secondary Battery................... 320
   Protective Deck 312
   Ram.. 334–337
      Battle of Lissa............................. 336
      Early Use................................... 335
      First Appearance in Modern Times........... 335

EVOLUTION OF THE MODERN NAVY—Continued.

	PAGE
Recessed Ports	316
Redoubt	320
Requirements	319
Revolving Turret	308
Sponsons	316
Stevens Family of Inventors	307
The Modern Warship	321
Torpedo Boats	327–334
"Cigar Boat"	327
Cushing	327
Discharging Torpedo	333
Duties of	330
"Howell"	334
Rough Water	330
The Automobile Torpedo in Battle	332
"Warhead"	333
"Whitehead"	332
Turret	313
Vitals	312
What a Naval Battle is Like	338

SPANISH NAVY ... 343–353

Battleship "Pelayo"	344
"Cardinal Cisneros"	347
"Numancia"	348
Protected Cruisers	350
The "Christobal Colon"	346
The "Emperador Carlos V"	349
The "Vizcaya" Class	345
Torpedo Boat Destroyers	352
Torpedo Boats	353
Unprotected Cruisers	351
"Vitoria"	349

AMERICAN NAVY. 354–382

Admiral George Dewey	354

AMERICAN NAVY — Continued.

	PAGE.
Admiral Sampson	356
" Alabama "	368
Armored Cruisers	372
" Brooklyn "	373
Captain Mahan	358
" Columbia "	375
Commodore Schley	355
Composite Gunboats	381
Dynamite Gunboat " Vesuvius "	380
Energy of Gunfire	362
" Illinois "	368
" Iowa "	367
" Kentucky "	368
" Kearsarge "	368
Kinds of Battleships	365
" Minneapolis "	375
Naming of Cruisers	372
Naval Strength of United States	382
New Battleships	369
" Olympia "	376
" Oregon "	366
Plans of Battleships	370–371
Plans of Cruisers	377–378
Prize Courts	361
Prize Money for the Navy	360
Ram " Katahdin "	376
Rate of Pay for Sea Service	360
Torpedo Boats	382
Torpedo Boat Destroyers	382
Unarmored Steel Gunboats	381
Unprotected Cruisers	380
" Wisconsin "	368

THE ARMY AND ITS LEADERS ... 401–410

Army	404
Battalion	403

THE ARMY AND ITS LEADERS — Continued.

	PAGE.
Brigade	403
Brooke, John R.	407
Commander-in-Chief.	404
Company	403
Corps.	403
Division	403
Lee, Fitzhugh.	409
Merritt, Wesley	408
Miles, Nelson A.	406
Military Schools.	405
National Guard	402
Pay of Officers.	404
Regiment.	403
Roosevelt, Theo.	409
Shafter, Wm. R.	407
Size of Army.	401
Volunteers.	402
Wheeler, Joseph.	408
Wilson, James H.	409

ARMOR, ORDNANCE AND DEFENSE............ 383–400

Arms, Small.	399
Battery, Secondary.	396
Breech Mechanism.	388
Extreme Range.	393
Gun, A "Built-up."	386
Gun, Machine.	396
Gun-Making.	386
Gun, Maxim Automatic.	397
Gun, Rapid Fire.	394
Gun Carriages, Disappearing.	393
Harveyized Armor.	384
Mortars, Twelve-Inch.	392
Powder, Smokeless.	398
Projectiles	397

INDEX. 459

ARMOR, ORDNANCE AND DEFENSE — Continued. PAGE.
   Recoil.. 390
   Velocity in Foot-Seconds........................... 385

THE FUTURE OF AMERICA.................. ... 411–416
   Colonial Extension................................. 414
   "Judging the Future by the Past.".................. 415
   Policy of Washington... 411
   Territory Acquired.......................... 412
      Alaska....................................... 414
      Florida 413
      Louisiana.................................... 413

SPAIN.
   Contemporary Spain...............................
      Army and Navy ....:....................... 50
      Character of the People...................... 53
      Cities...................................... 41
      Climate and Soil............................ 42
      Congress................................... 50
      Cortes..................................... 49
      Debt. 45
      Education.................................. 43
      Exports.................................... 45–46
      Finance.................................... 43
      Government................................ 49
      Military Schools............................ 52
      Ministry................................... 50
      Products................................... 46–49
         Agricultural........................... 46–48
         Non-Agricultural....................... 48–49
      Religion................................... 42–43
      Revenues.................................. 45
      Surface.................................... 42
      Taxes...................................... 45
   History 53
      Battle of Tours............................. 56

SPAIN — Continued.   PAGE.
    Cordova... 57
    Darwin's Theory Not **New**................... 58
    Early Colonization.................................
History.
    Globes in Schools................................ 58
    Invasion by Goths................................... 54
    Invasion by Moors................................... 55
    Iberia... 53
    Jewish Trade... 59
    Martel, Charles...................................... 56
    Navarre.. 60
    Pelayo... 59
    Saracens Invade France............................... 56
    Synopsis of Contemporary Events...................... 61
    Union **of** Kingdoms................................ 61

PERIOD OF DISCOVERY AND CONQUEST........ 66–100
    Abdication of Charles V.............................. 81
    Agriculture...................................... 88
    Antwerp.. 91
    Battle of Pavia...................................... 77
    Boleyn, Anne... 84
    Bosworth Field....................................... 70
    Cabot.. 71
    Cabral... 71
    Calais... 98
    Charles I.. 71
    Contemporary **Events**..................70, 83–85, 98–100
    Cortez... 83
    Council of Trent..................................... 76
    Cranmer.. 85
    De Soto.. 84
    Drake.. 99
    Edward IV.. 70
    Expulsion of the Jews................................ 69
    Expulsion of the Unbaptised Moors.................... 69

INDEX.   461

PERIOD OF DISCOVERY AND CONQUEST — Con.

	PAGE.
Ferdinand and Isabella	66
Flodden	71
Gonzalez de Cordova	71
Henry VIII	84
Huguenots	99
Inquisition	68
Invasion of England Planned	92–94
The Engagement	94–96
Knox	71
Las Casas	83
Lepanto	91
Loyola	73
Mary of England	85
Mary Stuart	99
Navarre	96–98
Order of Jesuits	73–76
Philip II	85–88
Pizarro	84
Raleigh	85
Revolt of the Netherlands	89–91
Shakespeare	98
Spanish Armada	99
St. Bartholomew	99
Trade and Industry	88
Treaty of Madrid	84
Voyage of Magellan	78–81
Zwingli	70

DECLINE OF SPANISH POWER ... 100–142

Alliance of England and France	113
Allied Invasion	119
Aix-la-Chapelle	127
American Revolution	129
Blenheim	120
Cession of Louisiana to France	136
Charles II	110

DECLINE OF SPANISH POWER — Continued.

	PAGE.
Charles III.	128
Charles IV.	133
Cromwell	103, 109
Difficulty of Conquering Spain	119
Family Compact	129
Ferdinand VI.	126
Gibraltar	117
James I.	108
"Jenkins' Ear"	122
La Salle	134
Moliere	107
Netherlands	101–103
Persecution of Spanish Moors	100
Philip III.	100
Philip IV.	106
Philip V.	114–117
Pyrenees	110
States General	104
Synopsis of Contemporary Events	103–106, 107–110, 112–114, 123–126, 127, 130–132, 138–142
Trafalgar	137

MODERN HISTORY ... 142–159

Abolition of Slavery	155
Alsace and Lorraine	158
American Civil War	157
Basque Provinces	150
Birth of Alphonso XIII	151
Bismarck	158
Carlists	150
Causes of Spain's Downfall	153
Chile	154, 158
Crimean War	156
Don Carlos	151
Ferdinand VII	142
Florida	145

INDEX. 463

MODERN HISTORY — Continued.
PAGE.
Holland... 154
Isabella II... 149
Lincoln, Abraham................................... 156–157
Maximilian... 157
Melendez... 146
Mexico.. 155
Napoleon... 154
Spanish in America................................. 148
Synopsis of Contemporary Events......... 154–159
Texas.. 156
War Between China and Japan................ 159
Wellington in Spain................................ 143

GROWTH AND LOSS OF SPAIN'S AMERICAN COLONIES 159
Argentine Republic 159
    Buenos Ayres Founded..................... 159
    Conquest of Natives........................ 159
    Independence 160
Chile 160
    Conquest of..................................... 160
    Invasion by Pizarro 160
    Independence 161
Colombian States................................... 166
    Invaded by Spaniards..................... 166–167
    Struggle for Independence............. 167–169
Mexico 170–181
    Early Inhabitants 170
    Invasion under Cortes.................... 171
    Montezuma the Emperor 172
    "The Melancholy Night"................ 175
    Republic Recognized...................... 178
    Texas and Mexico 179
    War with United States 180

GROWTH AND **LOSS OF SPAIN'S** AMERICAN COLONIES — Continued.

	PAGE.
Peru	161–166
Early Civilization	162–164
Invasion by Pizarro	161
The Inca's Ransom	165
The Royal Fifth	165
The Philippine Islands	181–187
Geography of	181
History	182
Manila	183
Population	183
Revenue	183
Spanish **Rule**	186
Porto Rico	187–190
Geography of	187
History	189
Why **Spain** Lost her Colonies	190–193
Colonial Administration	191–193
Cruelty to Natives	191
Ignores Commerce	190

THE SPANISH–AMERICAN WAR

THE SPANISH–AMERICAN WAR	417–443
A Century of American Forbearance	417
Appropriation of $50,000,000	421
Attitude of Europe	422
De Lome Incident	419
"Maine," Destruction of	420
Manila, Battle of	426
Merrimac, Sinking of	433
Peace Negotiations	442
Public Opinion	422
Report of Board of Inquiry	421
Santiago, Siege of	432
Weyler's Policy **of** Reconcentration	419
Appendix	443

www.ingramcontent.com/pod-product-compliance
Lightning Source LLC
Chambersburg PA
CBHW022113300426
44117CB00007B/689